THE WALLFLOWER

YAMATONADESHIKO SHICHIHENGE

16

Tomoko Hayakawa

Translated and adapted by
David Ury

Lettered by
Gabe Levine

Ballantine Books · New York

The Wallflower volume 16 is a work of fiction. Names, characters, places, and incidents are the products of the author's imagination or are used fictitiously. Any resemblance to actual events, locales, or persons, living or dead, is entirely coincidental.

A Del Rey Manga/Kodansha Trade Paperback Original

Published in the United States by Del Rey Books, an imprint of The Random House Publishing Group, a division of Random House, Inc., New York.

DEL REY is a registered trademark and the Del Rey colophon is a trademark of Random House, Inc.

Publication rights arranged through Kodansha Ltd.

First published in Japan in 2006 by Kodansha Ltd., Tokyo as *Yamatonadeshiko Shichihenge*

ISBN 978-0-345-50171-4

Printed in the United States of America

www.delreymanga.com

9 8 7 6 5 4 3 2 1

Translator/Adapter—David Ury
Lettering—North Market Street Graphics

Contents

A Note from the Author

Sunako finally left the house of her own free will. "Maybe she's finally ready to become a lady..." That's what I thought, but it turns out that not much really changed in Sunako's life... ♦♦ When will Sunako finally become a lady? I hope you'll keep reading, so you can find out.

Honorifics Explained

Throughout the Del Rey Manga books, you will find Japanese honorifics left intact in the translations. For those not familiar with how the Japanese use honorifics and, more important, how they differ from American honorifics, we present this brief overview.

Politeness has always been a critical facet of Japanese culture. Ever since the feudal era, when Japan was a highly stratified society, use of honorifics—which can be defined as polite speech that indicates relationship or status—has played an essential role in the Japanese language. When you address someone in Japanese, an honorific usually takes the form of a suffix attached to one's name (example: "Asuna-san"), is used as a title at the end of one's name, or appears in place of the name itself (example: "Negi-sensei," or simply "Sensei!").

Honorifics can be expressions of respect or endearment. In the context of manga and anime, honorifics give insight into the nature of the relationship between characters. Many English translations leave out these important honorifics and therefore distort the feel of the original Japanese. Because Japanese honorifics contain nuances that English honorifics lack, it is our policy at Del Rey not to translate them. Here, instead, is a guide to some of the honorifics you may encounter in Del Rey Manga.

-*san:*   This is the most common honorific and is equivalent to Mr., Miss, Ms., or Mrs. It is the all-purpose honorific and can be used in any situation where politeness is required.

-*sama:*   This is one level higher than "-san" and is used to confer great respect.

-*dono:*   This comes from the word "tono," which means "lord." It is an even higher level than "-sama" and confers utmost respect.

-kun: This suffix is used at the end of boys' names to express familiarity or endearment. It is also sometimes used by men among friends, or when addressing someone younger or of a lower station.

-chan: This is used to express endearment, mostly toward girls. It is also used for little boys, pets, and even among lovers. It gives a sense of childish cuteness.

Bozu: This is an informal way to refer to a boy, similar to the English terms "kid" and "squirt."

Sempai/
Senpai: This title suggests that the addressee is one's senior in a group or organization. It is most often used in a school setting, where underclassmen refer to their upperclassmen as "sempai." It can also be used in the workplace, such as when a newer employee addresses an employee who has seniority in the company.

Kohai: This is the opposite of "sempai" and is used toward underclassmen in school or newcomers in the workplace. It connotes that the addressee is of a lower station.

Sensei: Literally meaning "one who has come before," this title is used for teachers, doctors, or masters of any profession or art.

-[blank]: This is usually forgotten in these lists, but it is perhaps the most significant difference between Japanese and English. The lack of honorific, known as *yobisute*, means that the speaker has permission to address the person in a very intimate way. Usually, only family, spouses, or very close friends have this kind of permission. It can be gratifying when someone who has earned the intimacy starts to call one by one's name without an honorific. But when that intimacy hasn't been earned, it can be very insulting.

THE wallflower

YAMATONADESHIKO SHICHIHENGE

ヤマトナデシコ七変化♡

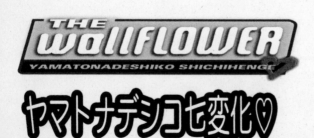

CONTENTS

WALLFLOWER'S BEAUTIFUL CAST OF CHARACTERS (?)

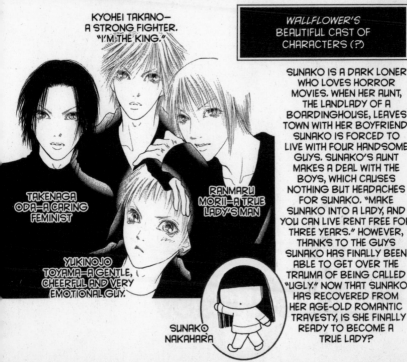

KYOHEI TAKANO—A STRONG FIGHTER. "I'M THE KING."
RANMARU MORII—A TRUE LADY'S MAN
TAKENAGA ODA—A CARING FEMINIST
YUKINOJO TOYAMA—A GENTLE, CHEERFUL AND VERY EMOTIONAL GUY.
SUNAKO NAKAHARA

SUNAKO IS A DARK LONER WHO LOVES HORROR MOVIES. WHEN HER AUNT, THE LANDLADY OF A BOARDINGHOUSE, LEAVES TOWN WITH HER BOYFRIEND, SUNAKO IS FORCED TO LIVE WITH FOUR HANDSOME GUYS. SUNAKO'S AUNT MAKES A DEAL WITH THE BOYS, WHICH CAUSES NOTHING BUT HEADACHES FOR SUNAKO. "MAKE SUNAKO INTO A LADY, AND YOU CAN LIVE RENT FREE FOR THREE YEARS." HOWEVER, THANKS TO THE GUYS SUNAKO HAS FINALLY BEEN ABLE TO GET OVER THE TRAUMA OF BEING CALLED "UGLY." NOW THAT SUNAKO HAS RECOVERED FROM HER AGE-OLD ROMANTIC TRAVESTY, IS SHE FINALLY READY TO BECOME A TRUE LADY?

Chapter 63
FISH OUT OF WATER

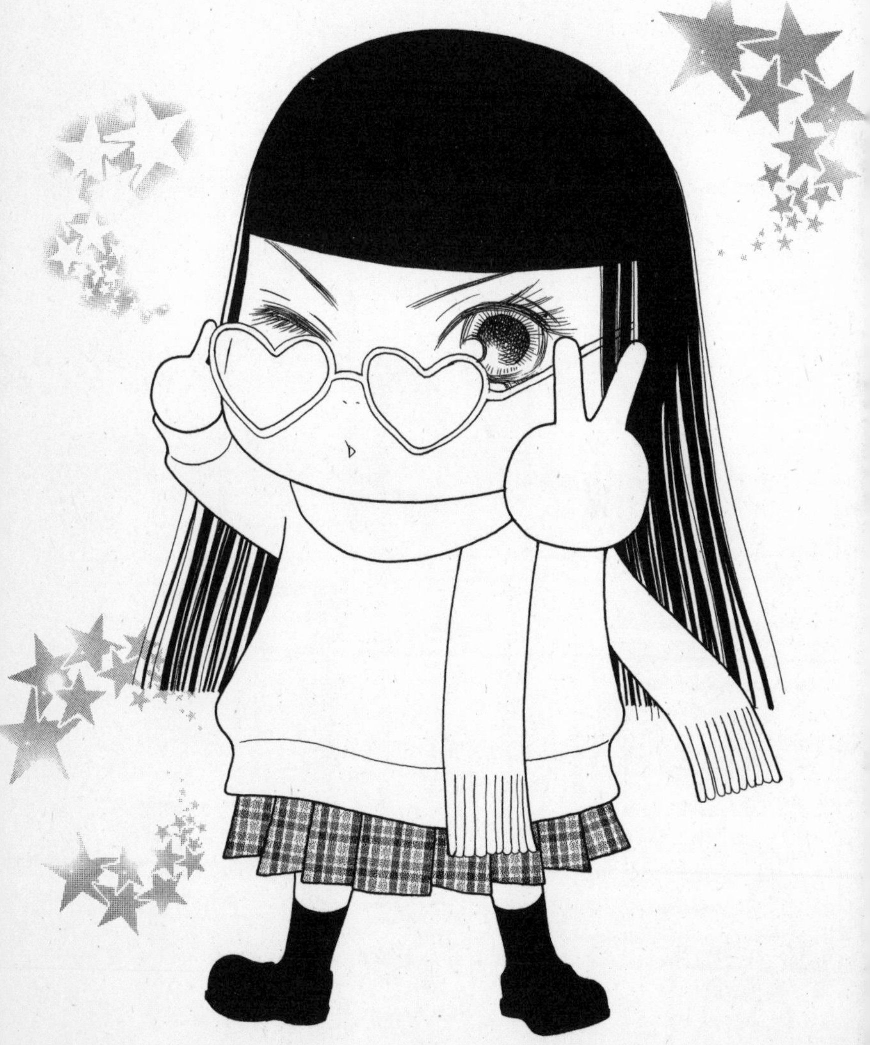

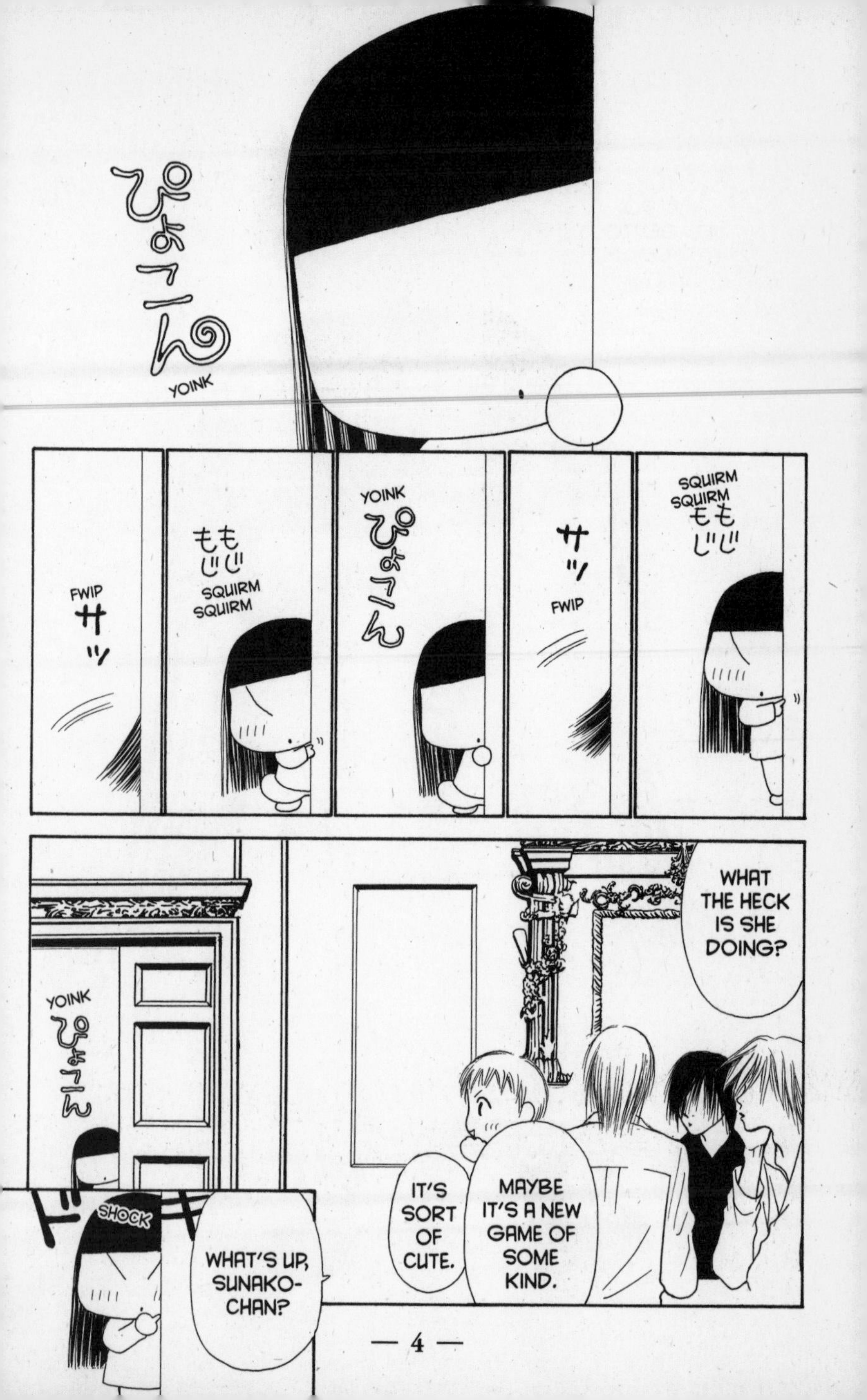
ぴょ〜ん
YOINK
SQUIRM SQUIRM
ももじじ
サッ
FWIP
YOINK
ぴょ〜ん
ももじじ
SQUIRM SQUIRM
FWIP
サッ
WHAT THE HECK IS SHE DOING?
MAYBE IT'S A NEW GAME OF SOME KIND.
IT'S SORT OF CUTE.
YOINK
ぴょ〜ん
ドキ
SHOCK
WHAT'S UP, SUNAKO-CHAN?

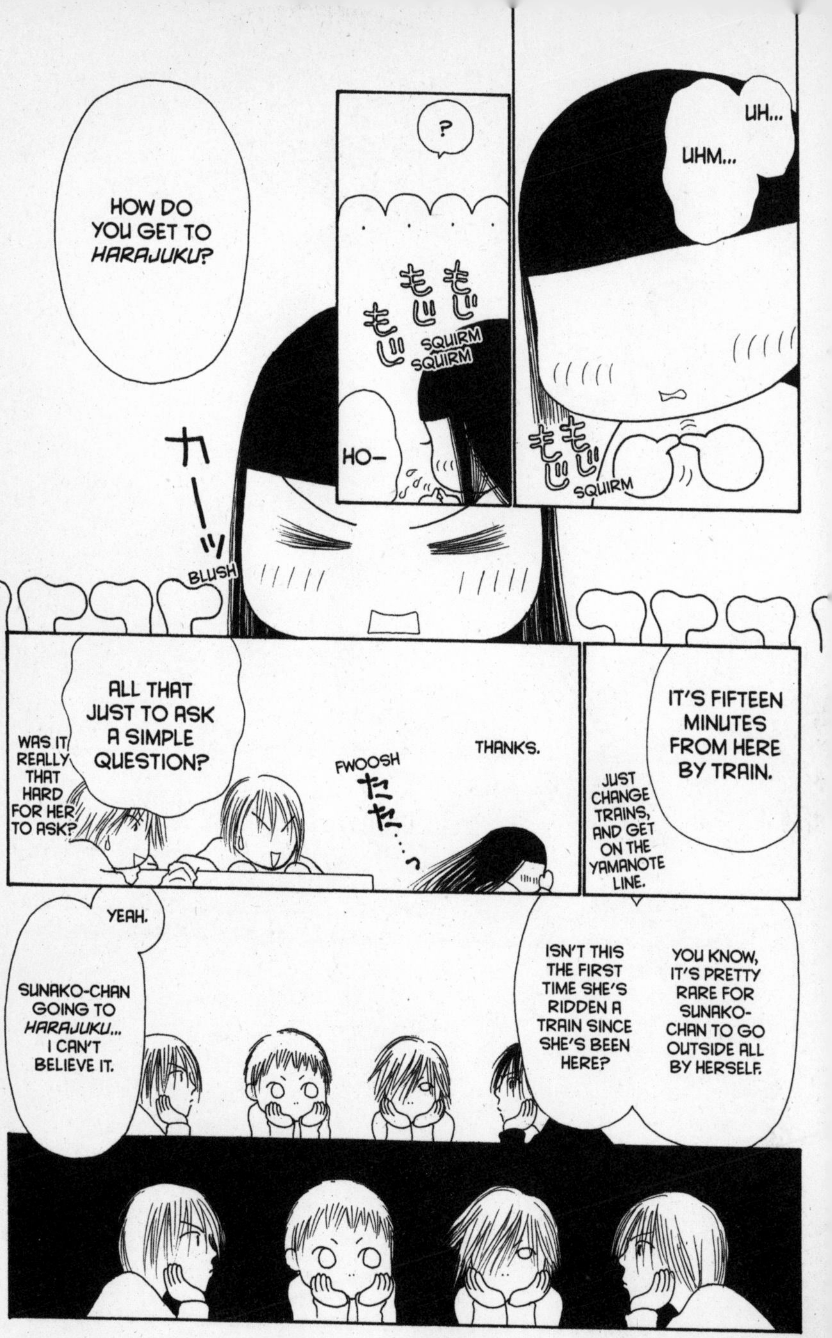
UH...
UHM...
もじもじ SQUIRM
?
. . .
もじもじもじもじ SQUIRM SQUIRM
HO—
HOW DO YOU GET TO *HARAJUKU*?
カーッ BLUSH
IT'S FIFTEEN MINUTES FROM HERE BY TRAIN.
JUST CHANGE TRAINS, AND GET ON THE YAMANOTE LINE.
THANKS.
たた… FWOOSH
ALL THAT JUST TO ASK A SIMPLE QUESTION?
WAS IT REALLY THAT HARD FOR HER TO ASK?
YOU KNOW, IT'S PRETTY RARE FOR SUNAKO-CHAN TO GO OUTSIDE ALL BY HERSELF.
ISN'T THIS THE FIRST TIME SHE'S RIDDEN A TRAIN SINCE SHE'S BEEN HERE?
YEAH.
SUNAKO-CHAN GOING TO *HARAJUKU*... I CAN'T BELIEVE IT.

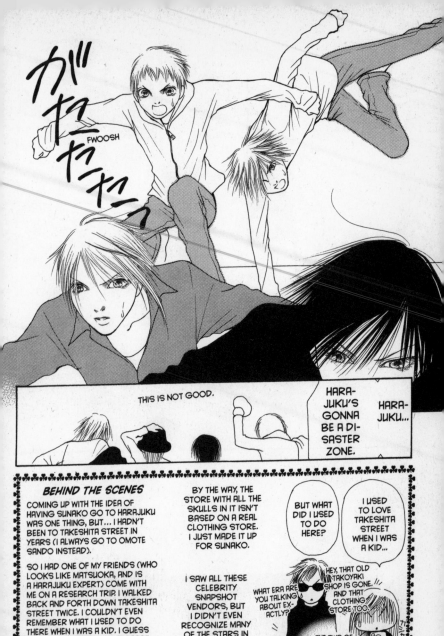

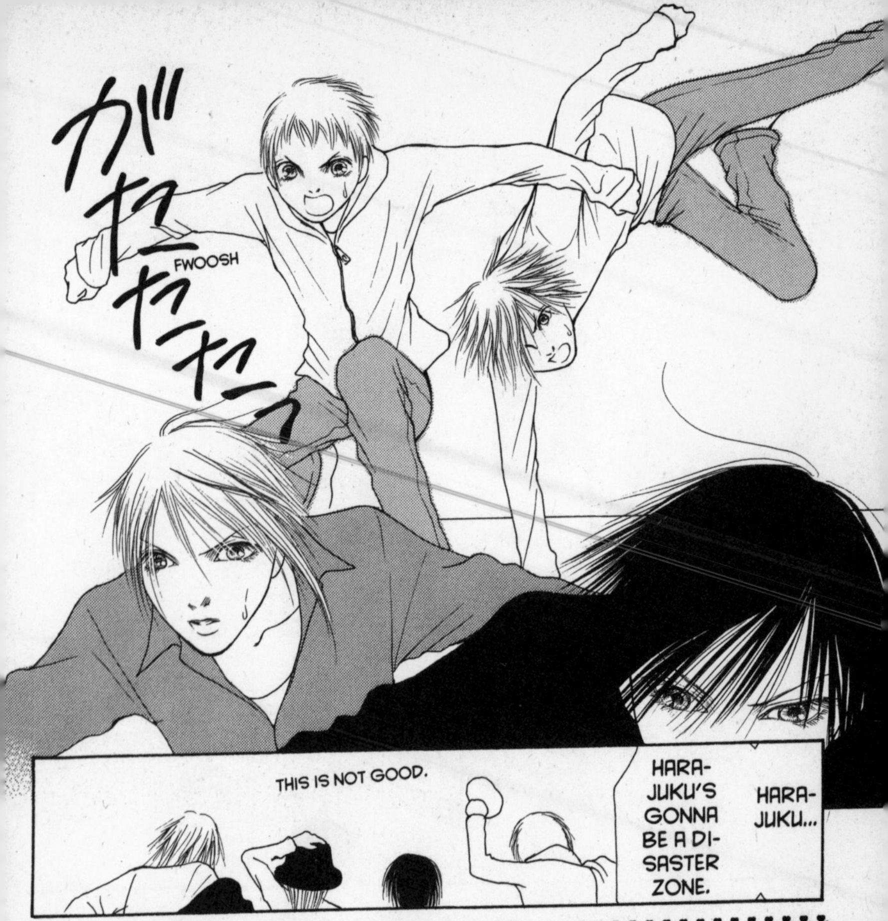
FWOOSH
HARA-JUKU...
HARA-JUKU'S GONNA BE A DI-SASTER ZONE.
THIS IS NOT GOOD.

BEHIND THE SCENES

COMING UP WITH THE IDEA OF HAVING SUNAKO GO TO HARAJUKU WAS ONE THING, BUT... I HADN'T BEEN TO TAKESHITA STREET IN YEARS (I ALWAYS GO TO OMOTE SANDO INSTEAD).

SO I HAD ONE OF MY FRIENDS (WHO LOOKS LIKE MATSUOKA, AND IS A HARAJUKU EXPERT) COME WITH ME ON A RESEARCH TRIP. I WALKED BACK AND FORTH DOWN TAKESHITA STREET TWICE. I COULDN'T EVEN REMEMBER WHAT I USED TO DO THERE WHEN I WAS A KID. I GUESS I'M ALL GROWN UP NOW. AT LEAST I'M OLD ENOUGH THAT I SHOULD BE A GROWN UP...

BY THE WAY, THE STORE WITH ALL THE SKULLS IN IT ISN'T BASED ON A REAL CLOTHING STORE. I JUST MADE IT UP FOR SUNAKO.

I SAW ALL THESE CELEBRITY SNAPSHOT VENDORS, BUT I DIDN'T EVEN RECOGNIZE MANY OF THE STARS IN THE PHOTOS.

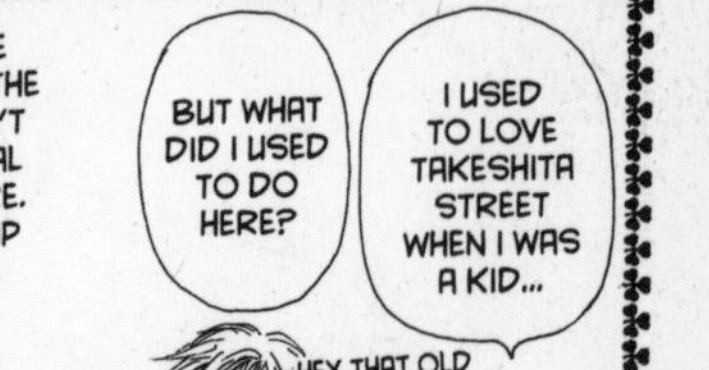
I USED TO LOVE TAKESHITA STREET WHEN I WAS A KID...
BUT WHAT DID I USED TO DO HERE?
HEY, THAT OLD TAKOYAKI SHOP IS GONE. AND THAT CLOTHING STORE TOO.
WHAT ERA ARE YOU TALKING ABOUT EX-ACTLY?
THE TWO OF THEM JUST KEPT ON WALKING.
CLICK
CLICK

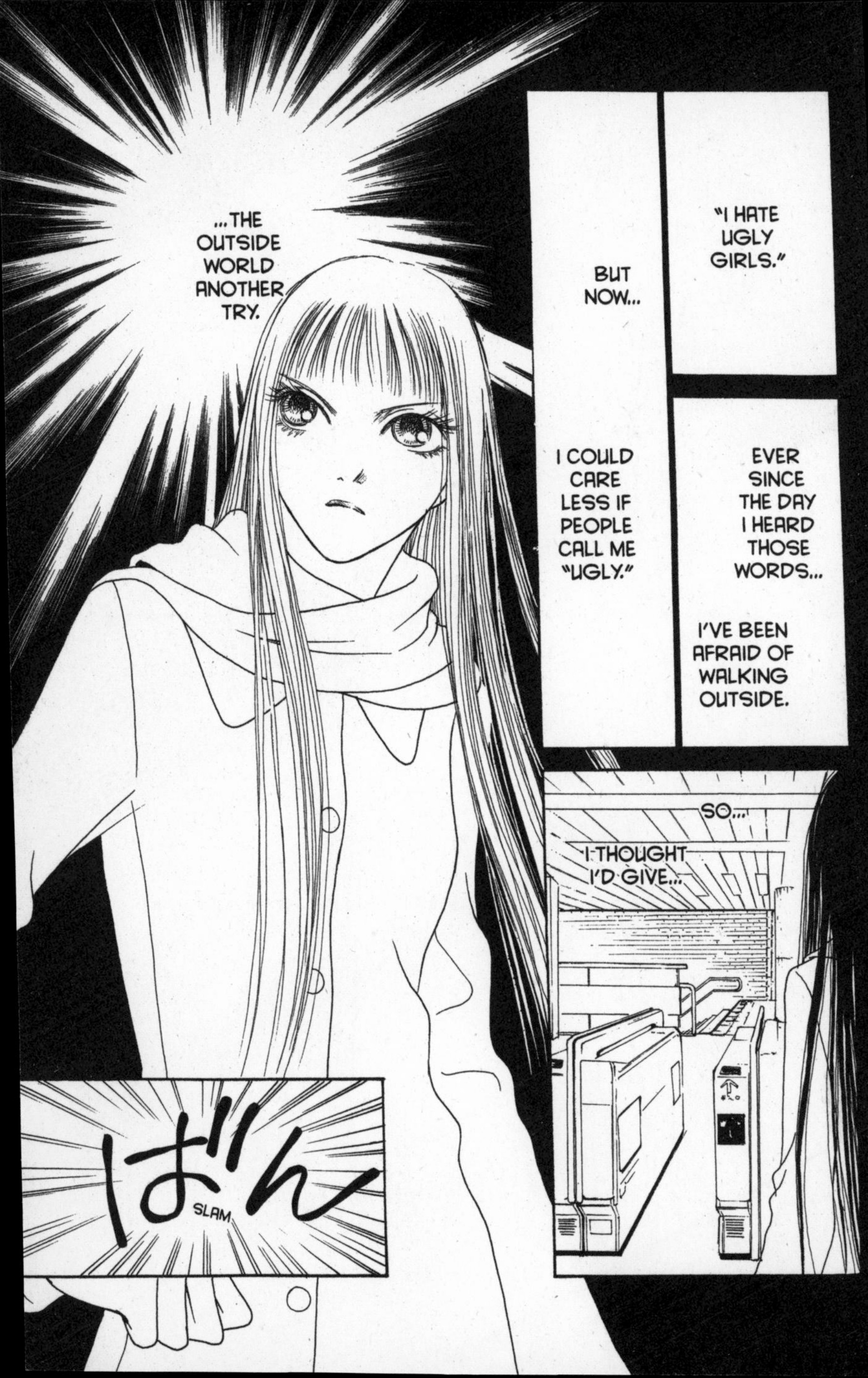
"I HATE UGLY GIRLS."
EVER SINCE THE DAY I HEARD THOSE WORDS...
I'VE BEEN AFRAID OF WALKING OUTSIDE.
BUT NOW...
I COULD CARE LESS IF PEOPLE CALL ME "UGLY."
SO...
I THOUGHT I'D GIVE...
...THE OUTSIDE WORLD ANOTHER TRY.
ばん
SLAM

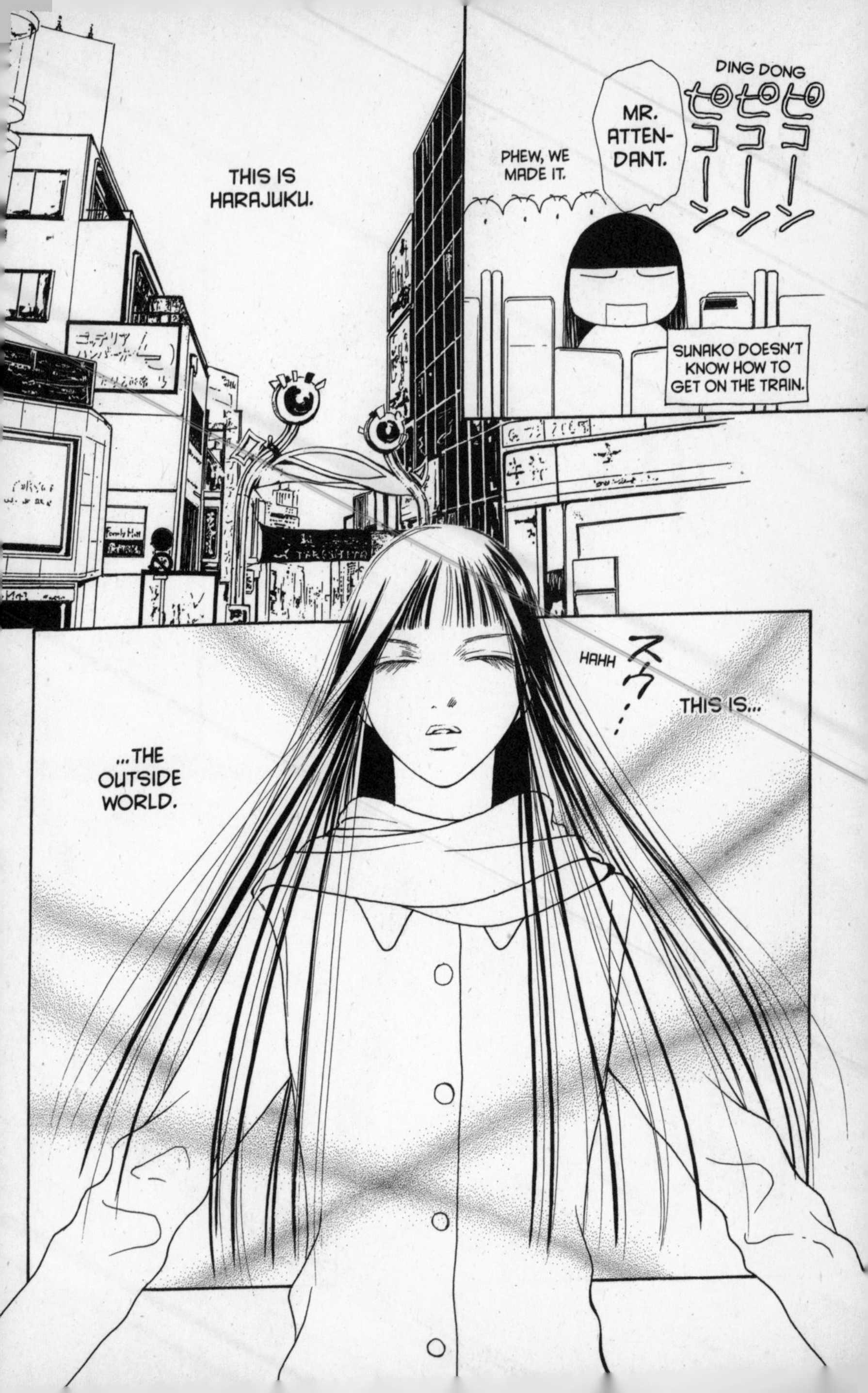
DING DONG
ピコーンピコーンピコーン
MR. ATTEN-DANT.
PHEW, WE MADE IT.
SUNAKO DOESN'T KNOW HOW TO GET ON THE TRAIN.
THIS IS HARAJUKU.
HAHH
スゥ…
THIS IS...
...THE OUTSIDE WORLD.

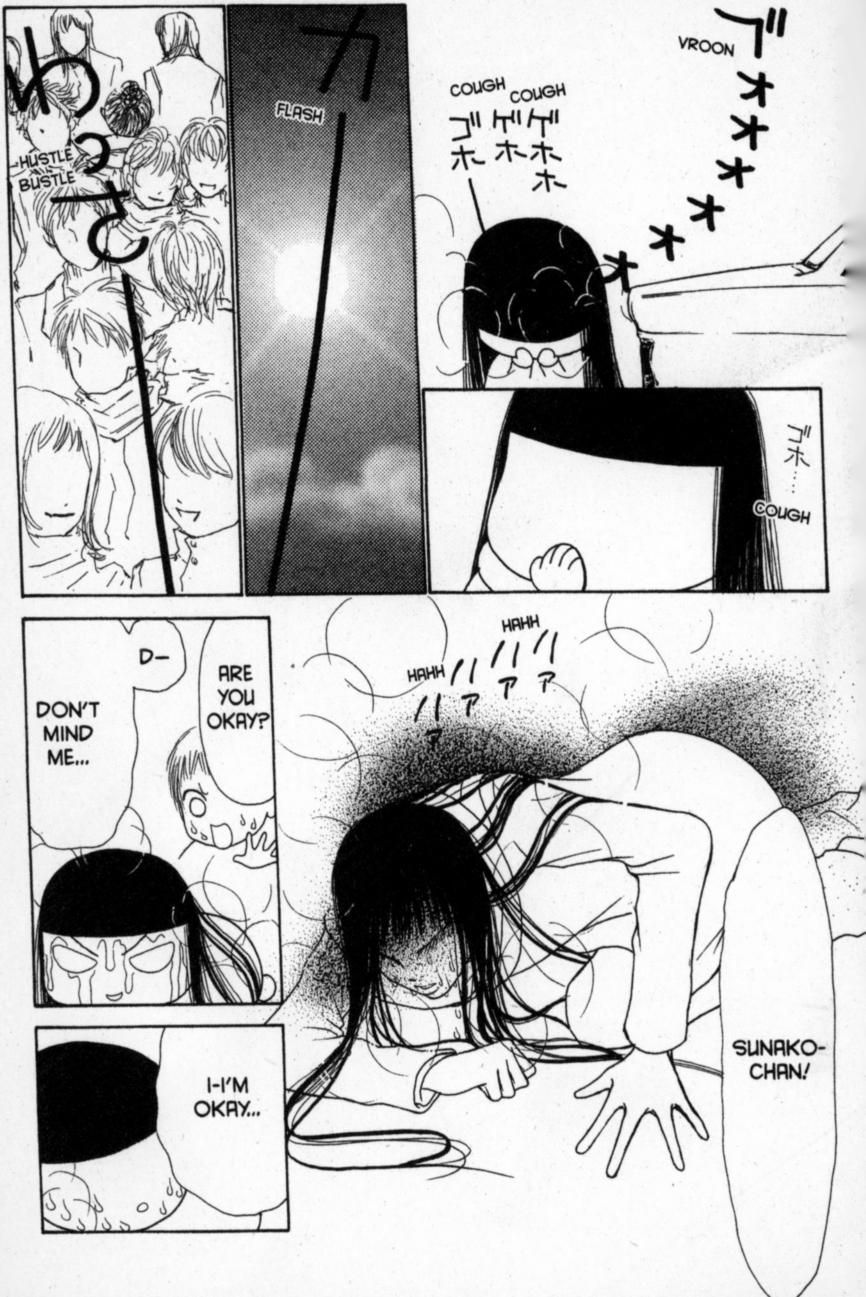

ゴオオオオオオ
VROON
ゲホホホ
ゲホー
ゴホ
COUGH COUGH
ゴホ…
COUGH
カ
FLASH
わっさ
HUSTLE BUSTLE
ハァハァハァ
HAHH HAHH
SUNAKO-CHAN!
ARE YOU OKAY?
D-
DON'T MIND ME...
I-I'M OKAY...

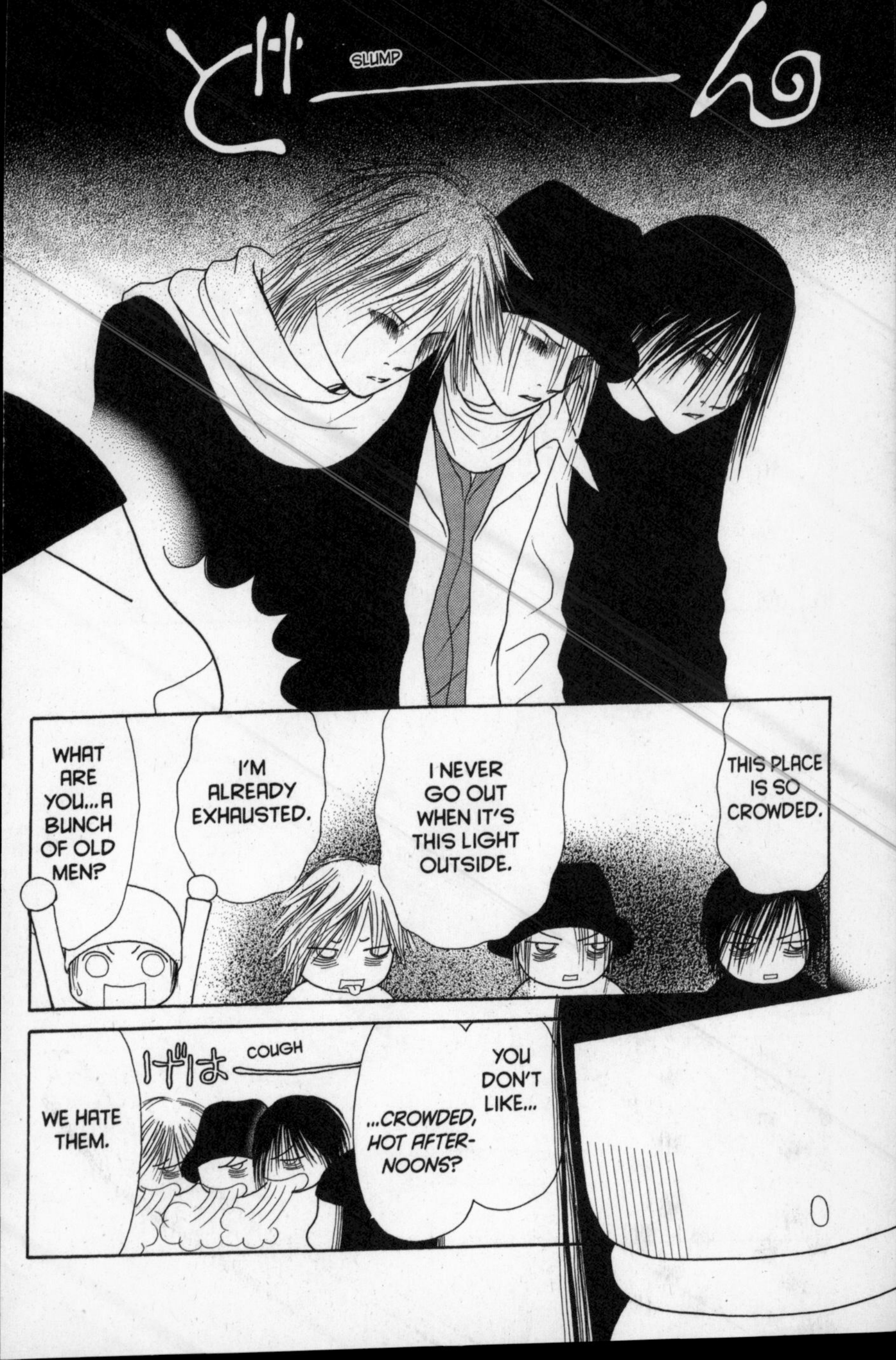
SLUMP
THIS PLACE IS SO CROWDED.
I NEVER GO OUT WHEN IT'S THIS LIGHT OUTSIDE.
I'M ALREADY EXHAUSTED.
WHAT ARE YOU...A BUNCH OF OLD MEN?
YOU DON'T LIKE...
...CROWDED, HOT AFTER-NOONS?
げはー
COUGH
WE HATE THEM.

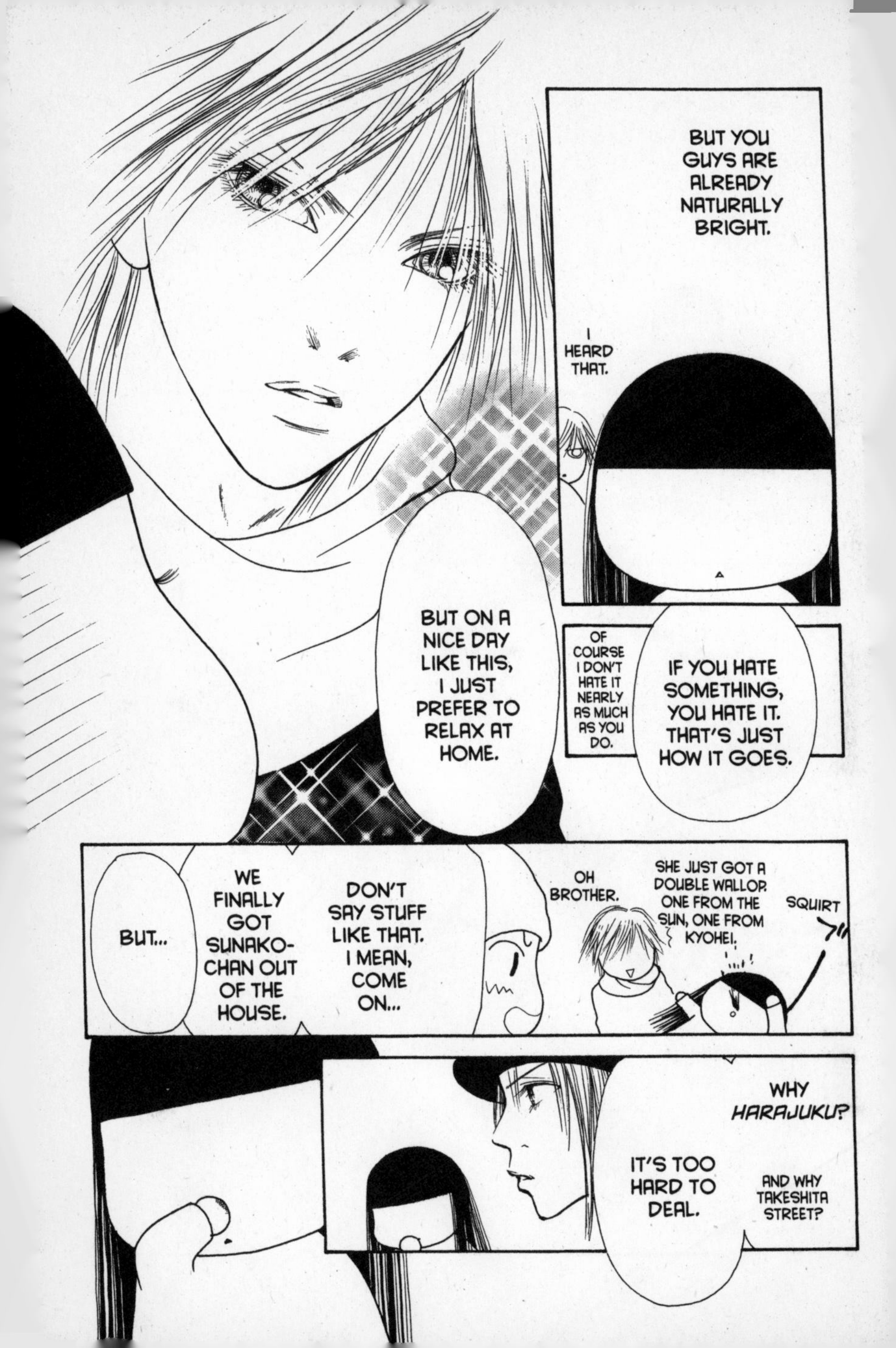
BUT YOU GUYS ARE ALREADY NATURALLY BRIGHT.
I HEARD THAT.
IF YOU HATE SOMETHING, YOU HATE IT. THAT'S JUST HOW IT GOES.
OF COURSE I DON'T HATE IT NEARLY AS MUCH AS YOU DO.
BUT ON A NICE DAY LIKE THIS, I JUST PREFER TO RELAX AT HOME.
SQUIRT
SHE JUST GOT A DOUBLE WALLOP. ONE FROM THE SUN, ONE FROM KYOHEI.
OH BROTHER.
DON'T SAY STUFF LIKE THAT. I MEAN, COME ON...
WE FINALLY GOT SUNAKO-CHAN OUT OF THE HOUSE.
BUT...
WHY HARAJUKU?
AND WHY TAKESHITA STREET?
IT'S TOO HARD TO DEAL.

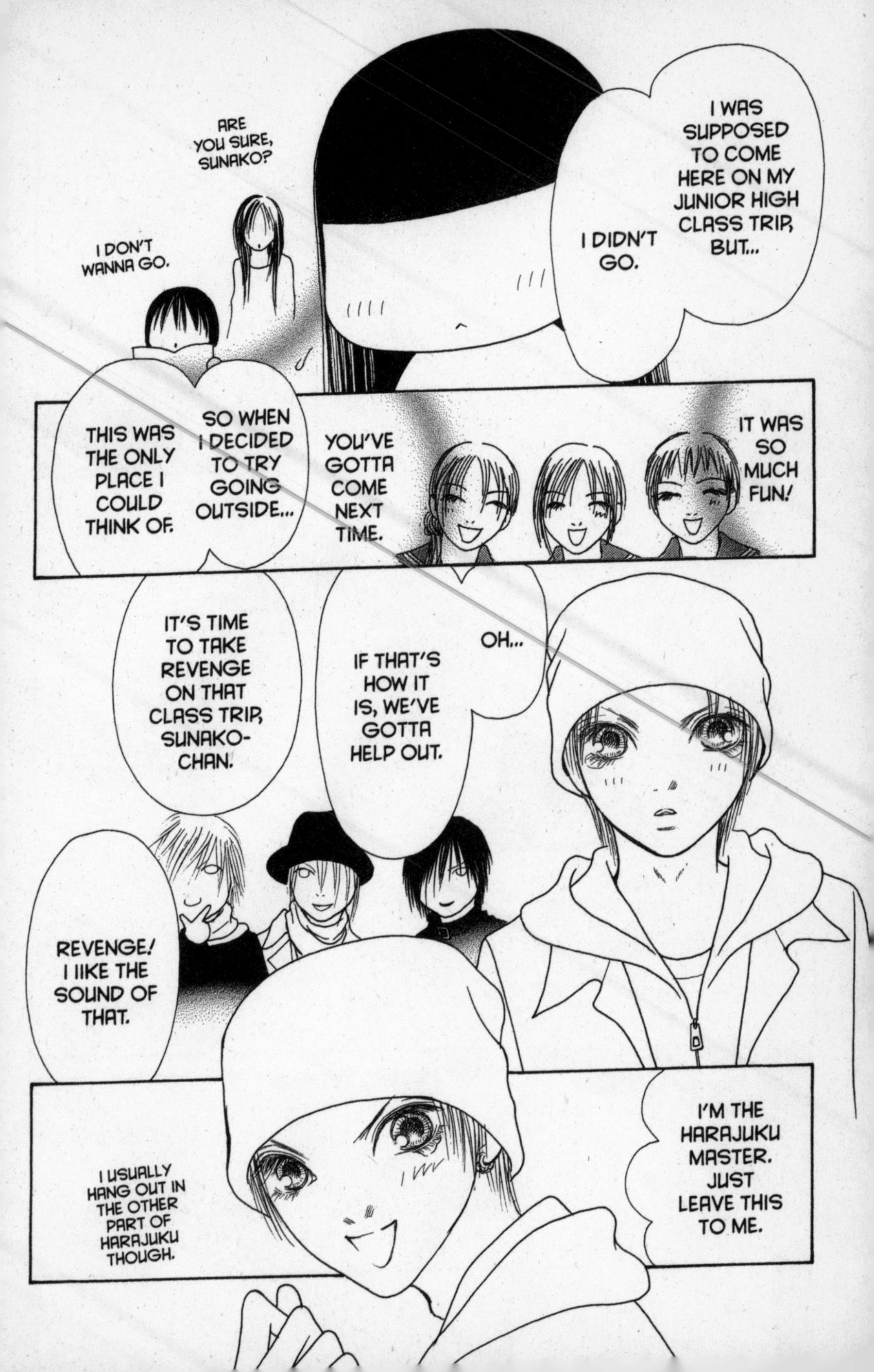
I WAS SUPPOSED TO COME HERE ON MY JUNIOR HIGH CLASS TRIP, BUT...
I DIDN'T GO.
ARE YOU SURE, SUNAKO?
I DON'T WANNA GO.
IT WAS SO MUCH FUN!
YOU'VE GOTTA COME NEXT TIME.
SO WHEN I DECIDED TO TRY GOING OUTSIDE...
THIS WAS THE ONLY PLACE I COULD THINK OF.
OH...
IF THAT'S HOW IT IS, WE'VE GOTTA HELP OUT.
IT'S TIME TO TAKE REVENGE ON THAT CLASS TRIP, SUNAKO-CHAN.
REVENGE! I IIKE THE SOUND OF THAT.
I'M THE HARAJUKU MASTER. JUST LEAVE THIS TO ME.
I USUALLY HANG OUT IN THE OTHER PART OF HARAJUKU THOUGH.

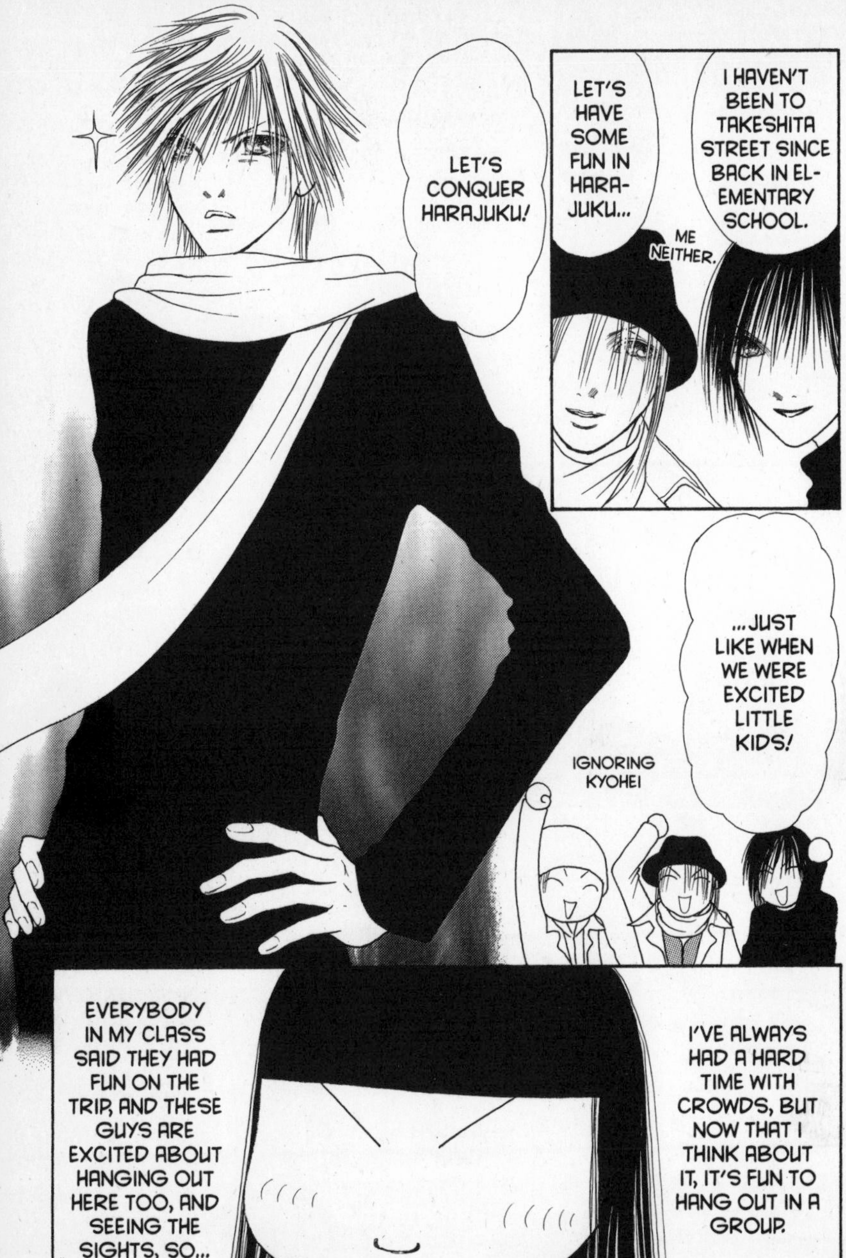
I HAVEN'T BEEN TO TAKESHITA STREET SINCE BACK IN ELEMENTARY SCHOOL.
ME NEITHER.
LET'S HAVE SOME FUN IN HARAJUKU...
...JUST LIKE WHEN WE WERE EXCITED LITTLE KIDS!
IGNORING KYOHEI
LET'S CONQUER HARAJUKU!
I'VE ALWAYS HAD A HARD TIME WITH CROWDS, BUT NOW THAT I THINK ABOUT IT, IT'S FUN TO HANG OUT IN A GROUP.
EVERYBODY IN MY CLASS SAID THEY HAD FUN ON THE TRIP, AND THESE GUYS ARE EXCITED ABOUT HANGING OUT HERE TOO, AND SEEING THE SIGHTS, SO...

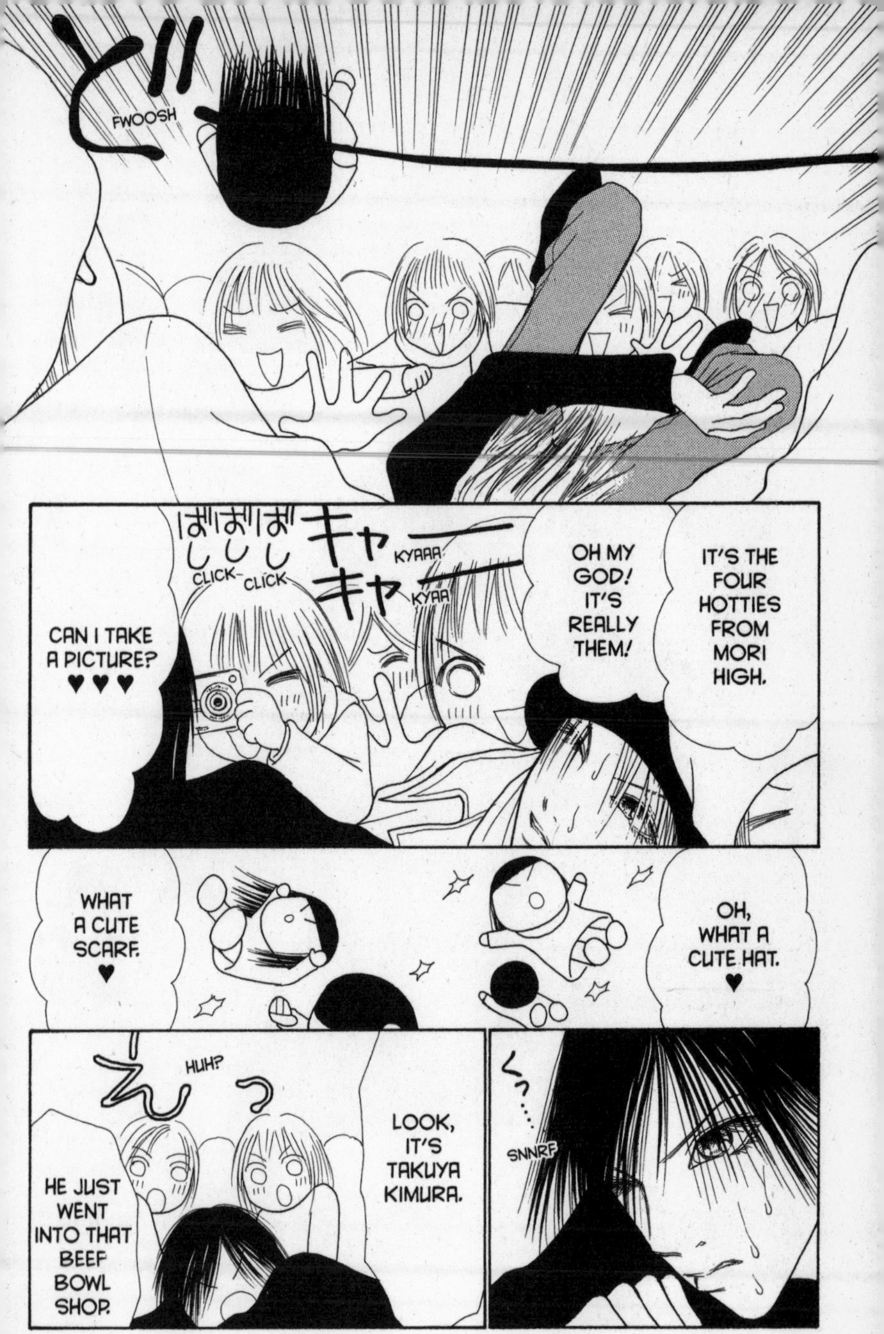
FWOOSH
IT'S THE FOUR HOTTIES FROM MORI HIGH.
OH MY GOD! IT'S REALLY THEM!
KYAAA
KYAA
CLICK
CLICK
CAN I TAKE A PICTURE? ♥♥♥
OH, WHAT A CUTE HAT. ♥
WHAT A CUTE SCARF. ♥
SNNRF
LOOK, IT'S TAKUYA KIMURA.
HUH?
HE JUST WENT INTO THAT BEEF BOWL SHOP.

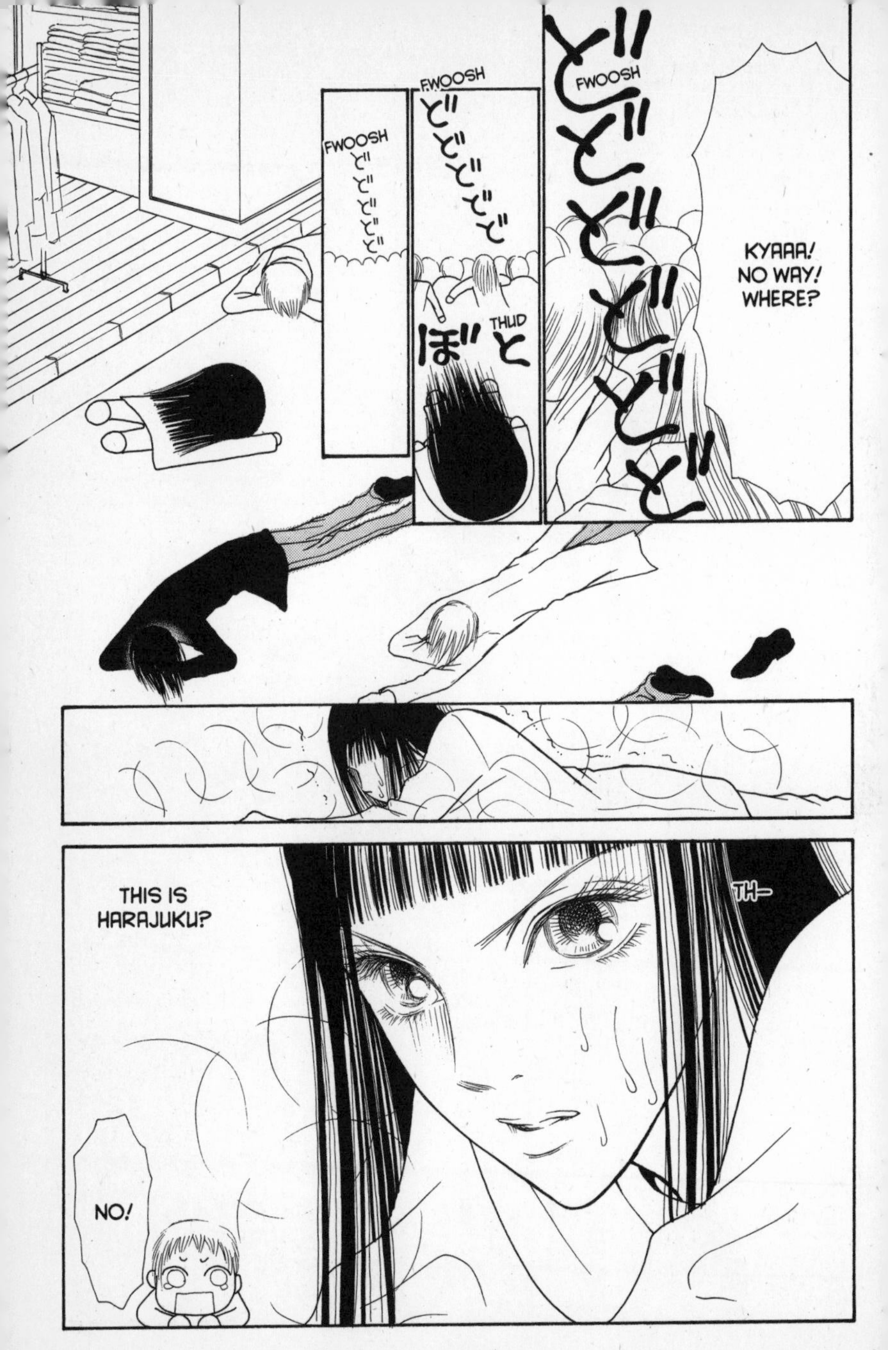
KYAAA! NO WAY! WHERE?
FWOOSH
FWOOSH
THUD
ぼと
FWOOSH
TH—
THIS IS HARAJUKU?
NO!

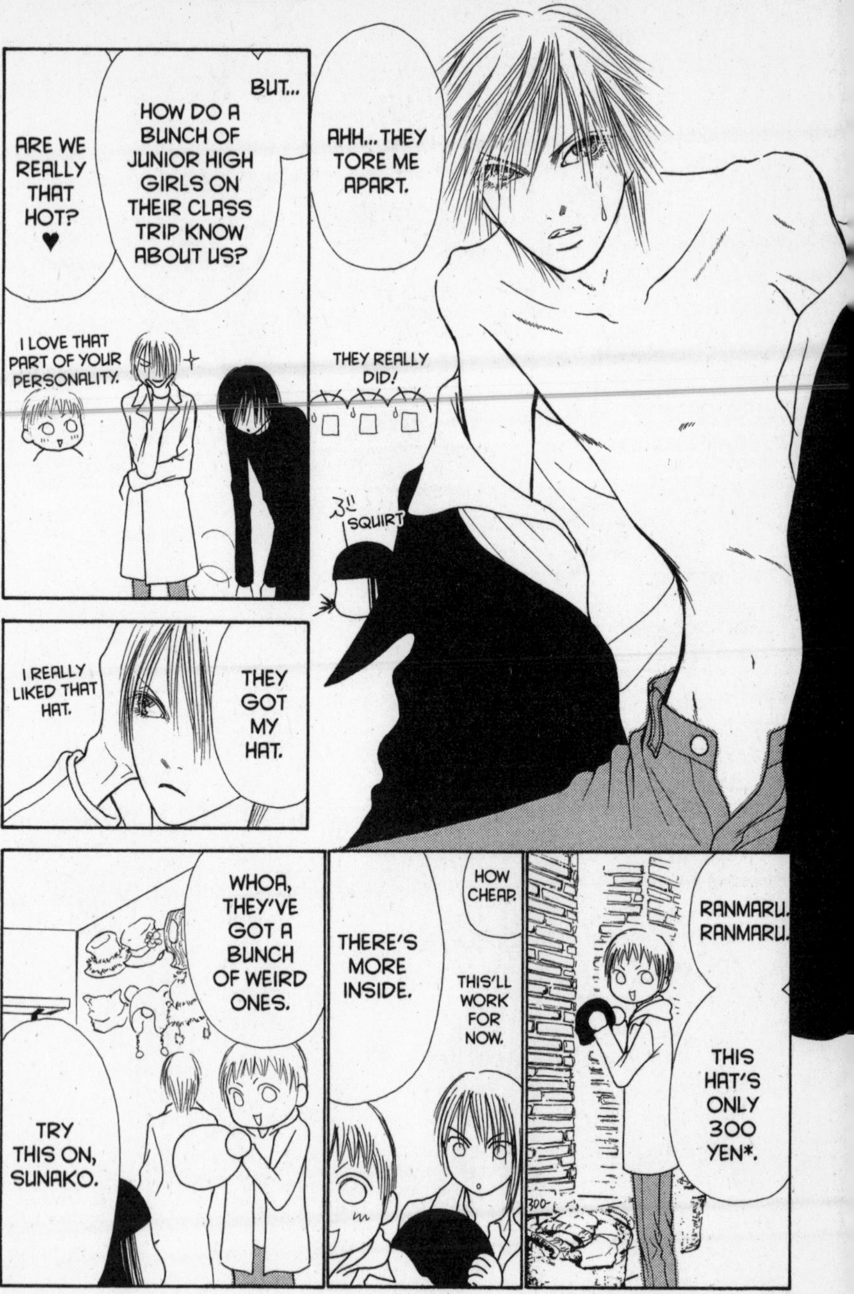
AHH... THEY TORE ME APART.
THEY REALLY DID!
SQUIRT
BUT... HOW DO A BUNCH OF JUNIOR HIGH GIRLS ON THEIR CLASS TRIP KNOW ABOUT US?
ARE WE REALLY THAT HOT? ♥
I LOVE THAT PART OF YOUR PERSONALITY.
THEY GOT MY HAT.
I REALLY LIKED THAT HAT.
RANMARU... RANMARU...
THIS HAT'S ONLY 300 YEN*.
HOW CHEAP.
THIS'LL WORK FOR NOW.
THERE'S MORE INSIDE.
WHOA, THEY'VE GOT A BUNCH OF WEIRD ONES.
TRY THIS ON, SUNAKO.

*$3

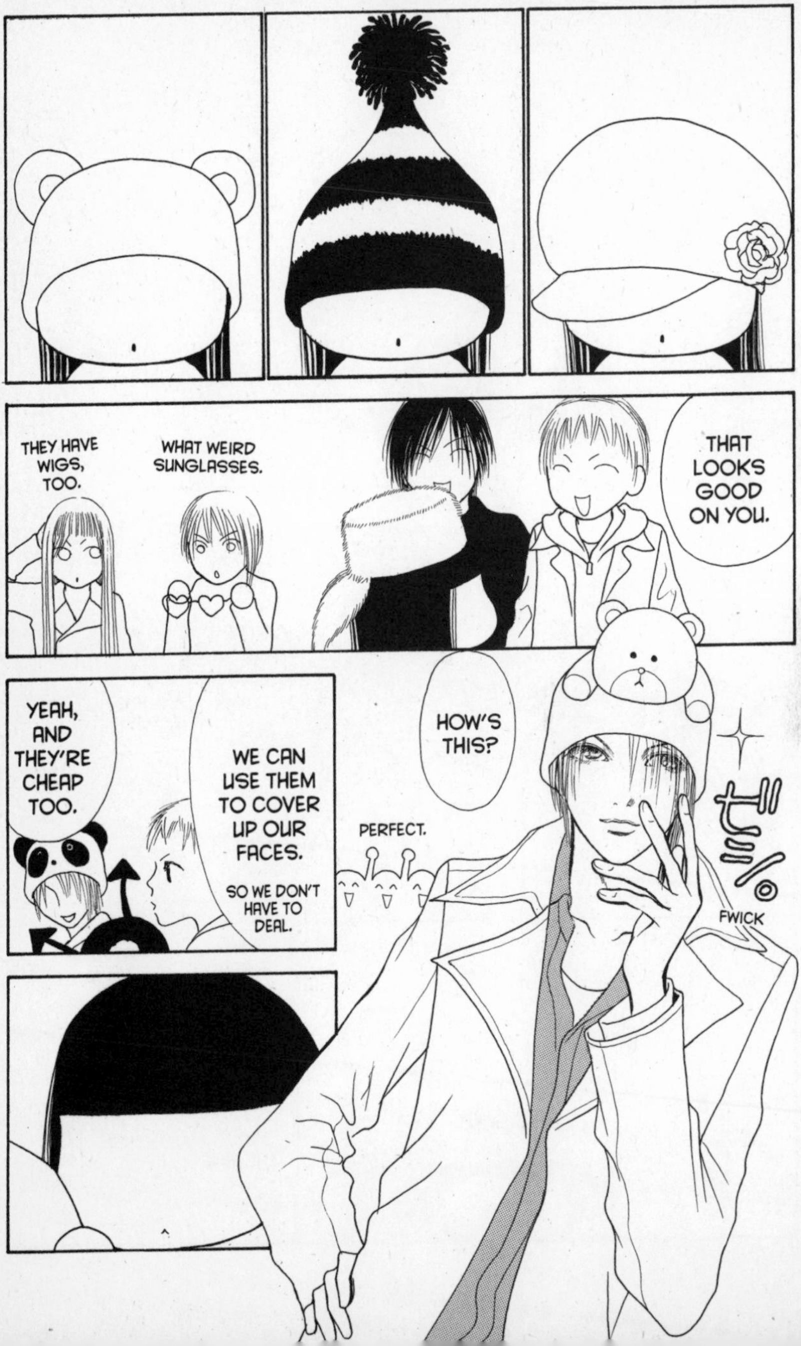
THAT LOOKS GOOD ON YOU.
WHAT WEIRD SUNGLASSES.
THEY HAVE WIGS, TOO.
HOW'S THIS?
FWICK
PERFECT.
WE CAN USE THEM TO COVER UP OUR FACES.
SO WE DON'T HAVE TO DEAL.
YEAH, AND THEY'RE CHEAP TOO.

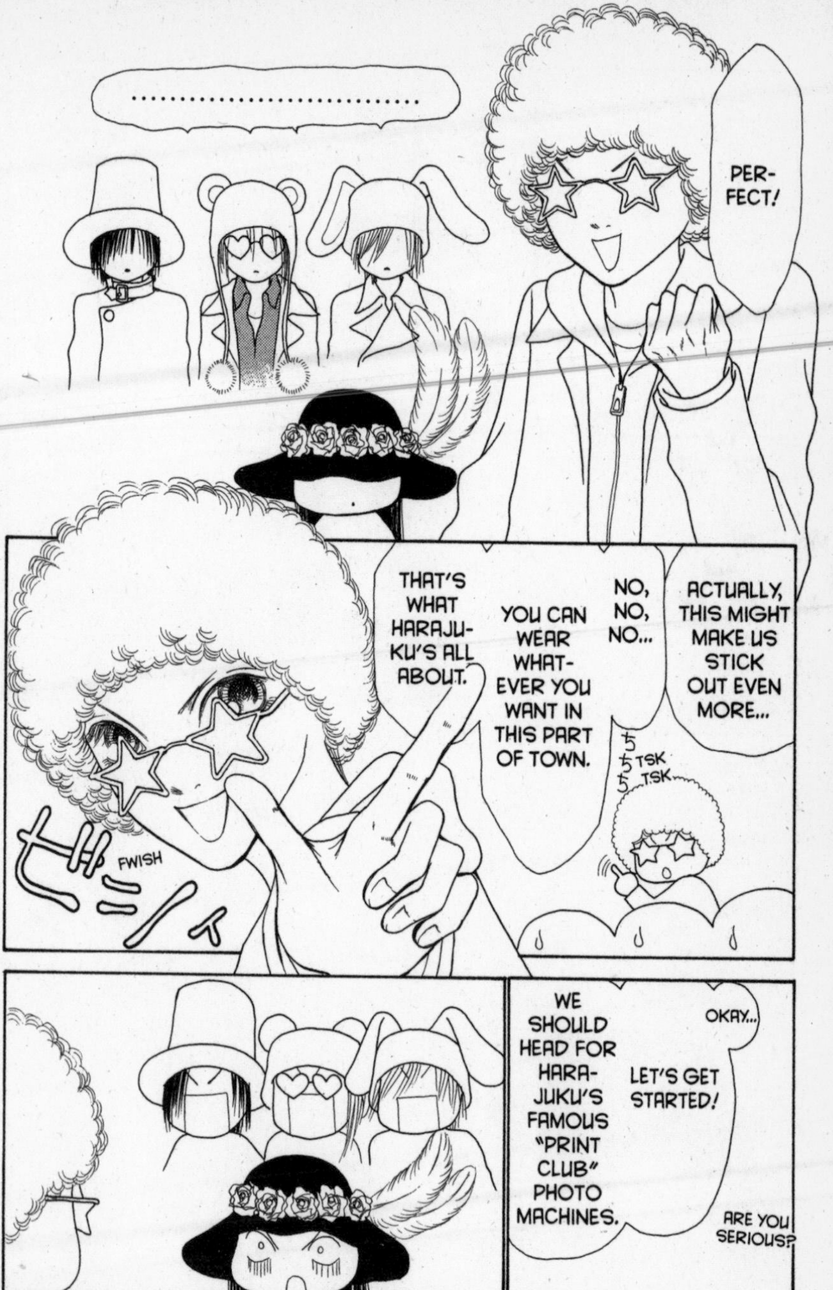
PER-FECT!
....
ACTUALLY, THIS MIGHT MAKE US STICK OUT EVEN MORE...
NO, NO, NO...
YOU CAN WEAR WHAT-EVER YOU WANT IN THIS PART OF TOWN.
THAT'S WHAT HARAJU-KU'S ALL ABOUT.
TSK TSK
FWISH
OKAY...
LET'S GET STARTED!
WE SHOULD HEAD FOR HARA-JUKU'S FAMOUS "PRINT CLUB" PHOTO MACHINES.
ARE YOU SERIOUS?

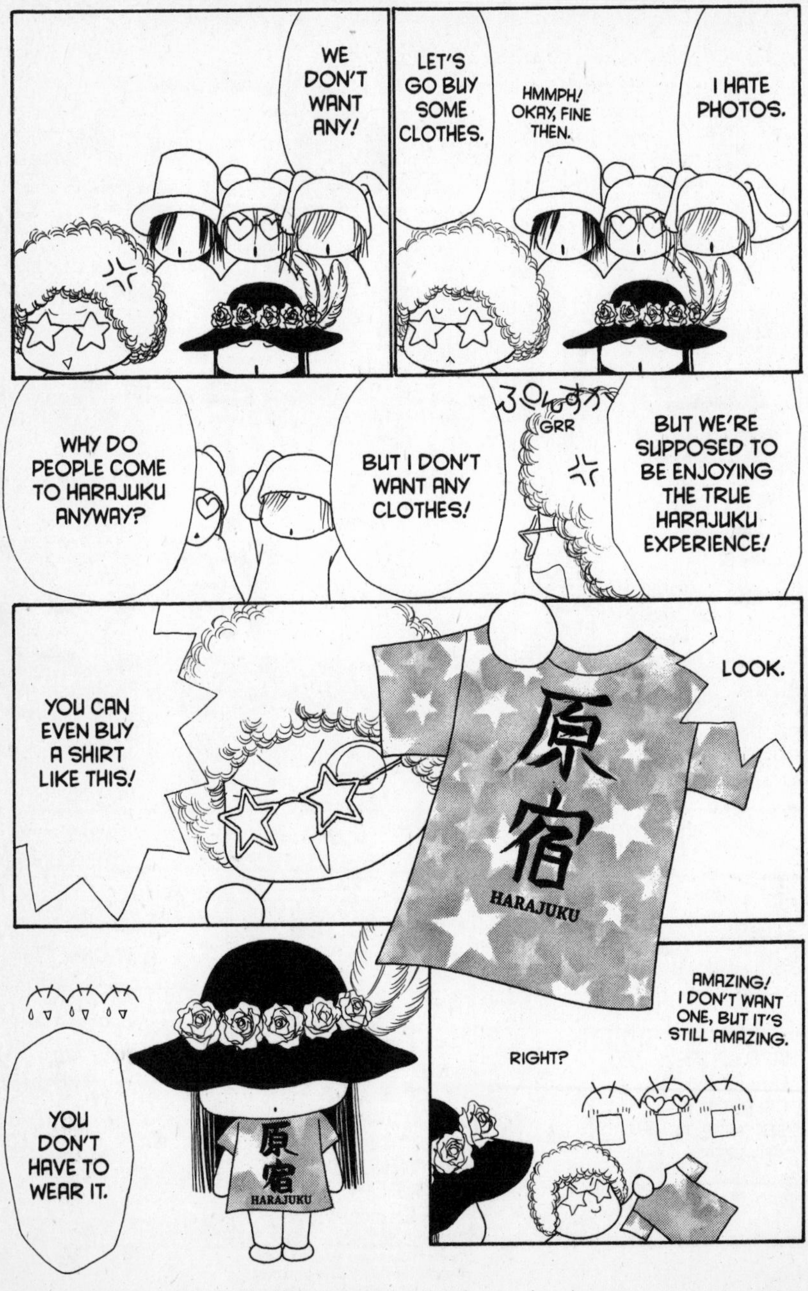
I HATE PHOTOS.
HMMPH! OKAY, FINE THEN.
LET'S GO BUY SOME CLOTHES.
WE DON'T WANT ANY!
BUT WE'RE SUPPOSED TO BE ENJOYING THE TRUE HARAJUKU EXPERIENCE!
ぷんすか
GRR
BUT I DON'T WANT ANY CLOTHES!
WHY DO PEOPLE COME TO HARAJUKU ANYWAY?
LOOK.
原宿
HARAJUKU
YOU CAN EVEN BUY A SHIRT LIKE THIS!
AMAZING! I DON'T WANT ONE, BUT IT'S STILL AMAZING.
RIGHT?
原宿
HARAJUKU
YOU DON'T HAVE TO WEAR IT.

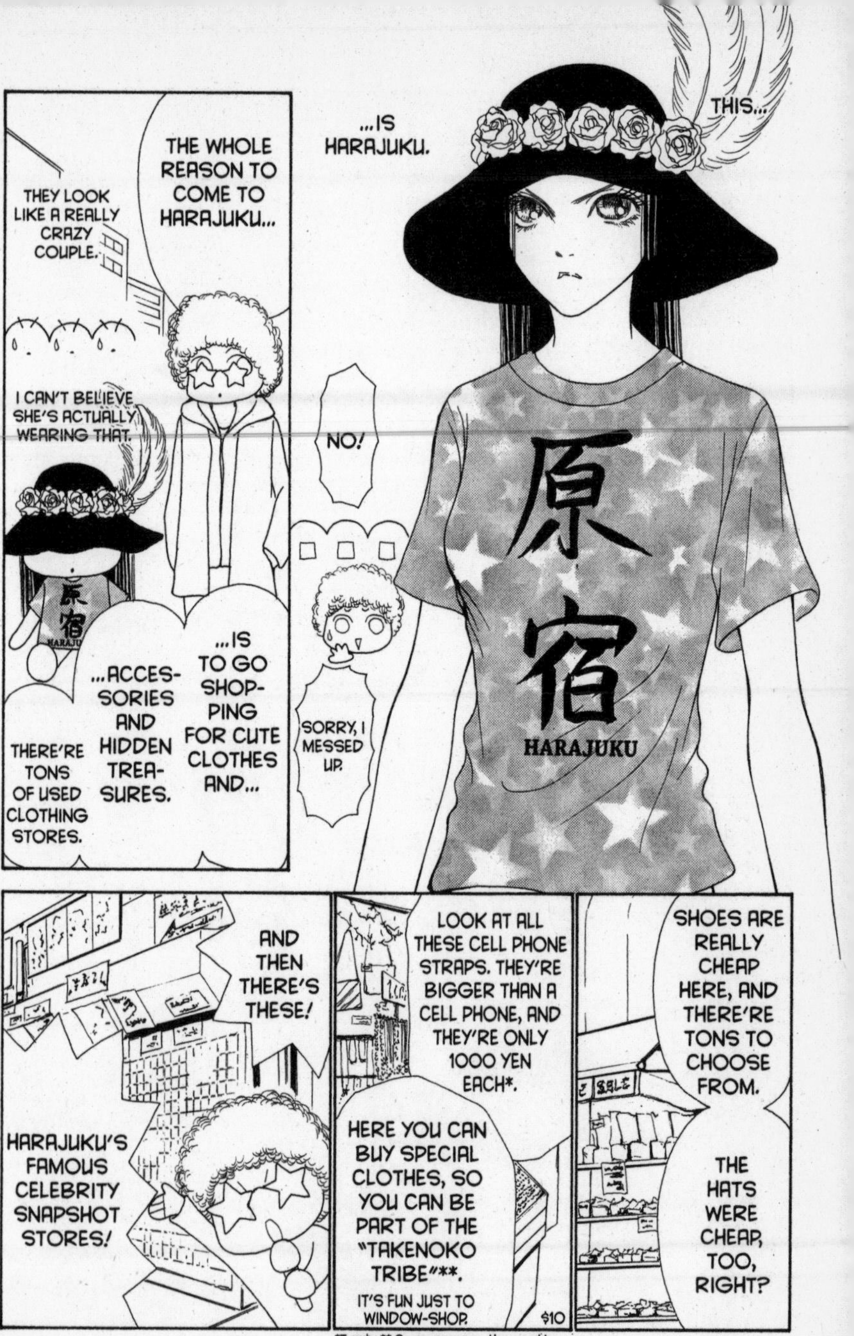
THIS...
...IS HARAJUKU.
原宿 HARAJUKU
NO!
SORRY, I MESSED UP.
THE WHOLE REASON TO COME TO HARAJUKU...
THEY LOOK LIKE A REALLY CRAZY COUPLE.
I CAN'T BELIEVE SHE'S ACTUALLY WEARING THAT.
...IS TO GO SHOPPING FOR CUTE CLOTHES AND...
...ACCESSORIES AND HIDDEN TREASURES.
THERE'RE TONS OF USED CLOTHING STORES.
SHOES ARE REALLY CHEAP HERE, AND THERE'RE TONS TO CHOOSE FROM.
THE HATS WERE CHEAP, TOO, RIGHT?
LOOK AT ALL THESE CELL PHONE STRAPS. THEY'RE BIGGER THAN A CELL PHONE, AND THEY'RE ONLY 1000 YEN EACH*.
HERE YOU CAN BUY SPECIAL CLOTHES, SO YOU CAN BE PART OF THE "TAKENOKO TRIBE"**.
IT'S FUN JUST TO WINDOW-SHOP.
$10
AND THEN THERE'S THESE!
HARAJUKU'S FAMOUS CELEBRITY SNAPSHOT STORES!

*Twenty ** Some years ago, they used to close down part of the street on Sundays. People would gather in groups to dance and play music. They were called the "Takenoko Tribe".

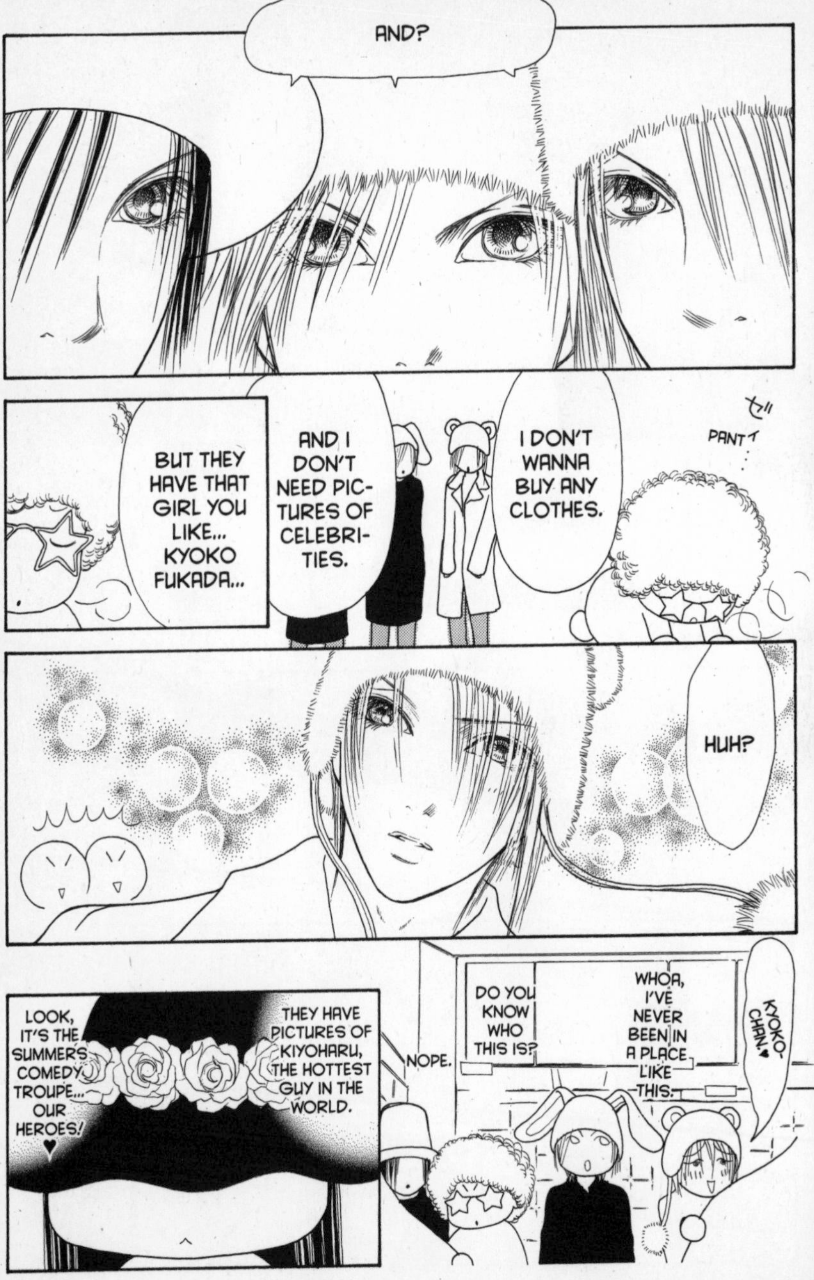
AND?
PANT
I DON'T WANNA BUY ANY CLOTHES.
AND I DON'T NEED PICTURES OF CELEBRITIES.
BUT THEY HAVE THAT GIRL YOU LIKE... KYOKO FUKADA...
HUH?
KYOKO-CHAN.♥
WHOA, I'VE NEVER BEEN IN A PLACE LIKE THIS.
DO YOU KNOW WHO THIS IS?
NOPE.
THEY HAVE PICTURES OF KIYOHARU, THE HOTTEST GUY IN THE WORLD.
LOOK, IT'S THE SUMMERS COMEDY TROUPE... OUR HEROES! ♥

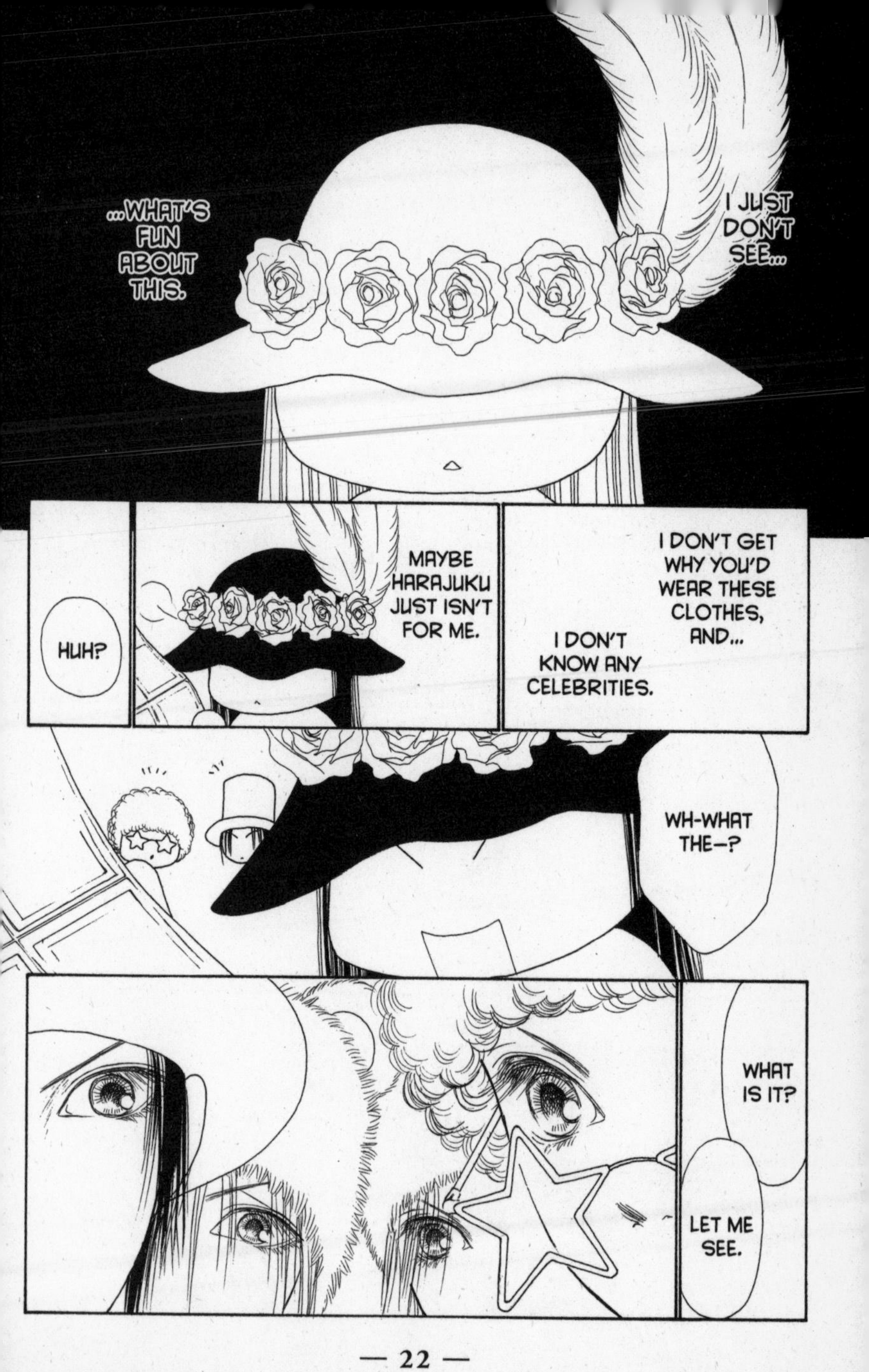
I JUST DON'T SEE...
...WHAT'S FUN ABOUT THIS.
I DON'T GET WHY YOU'D WEAR THESE CLOTHES, AND...
I DON'T KNOW ANY CELEBRITIES.
MAYBE HARAJUKU JUST ISN'T FOR ME.
HUH?
WH-WHAT THE—?
WHAT IS IT?
LET ME SEE.

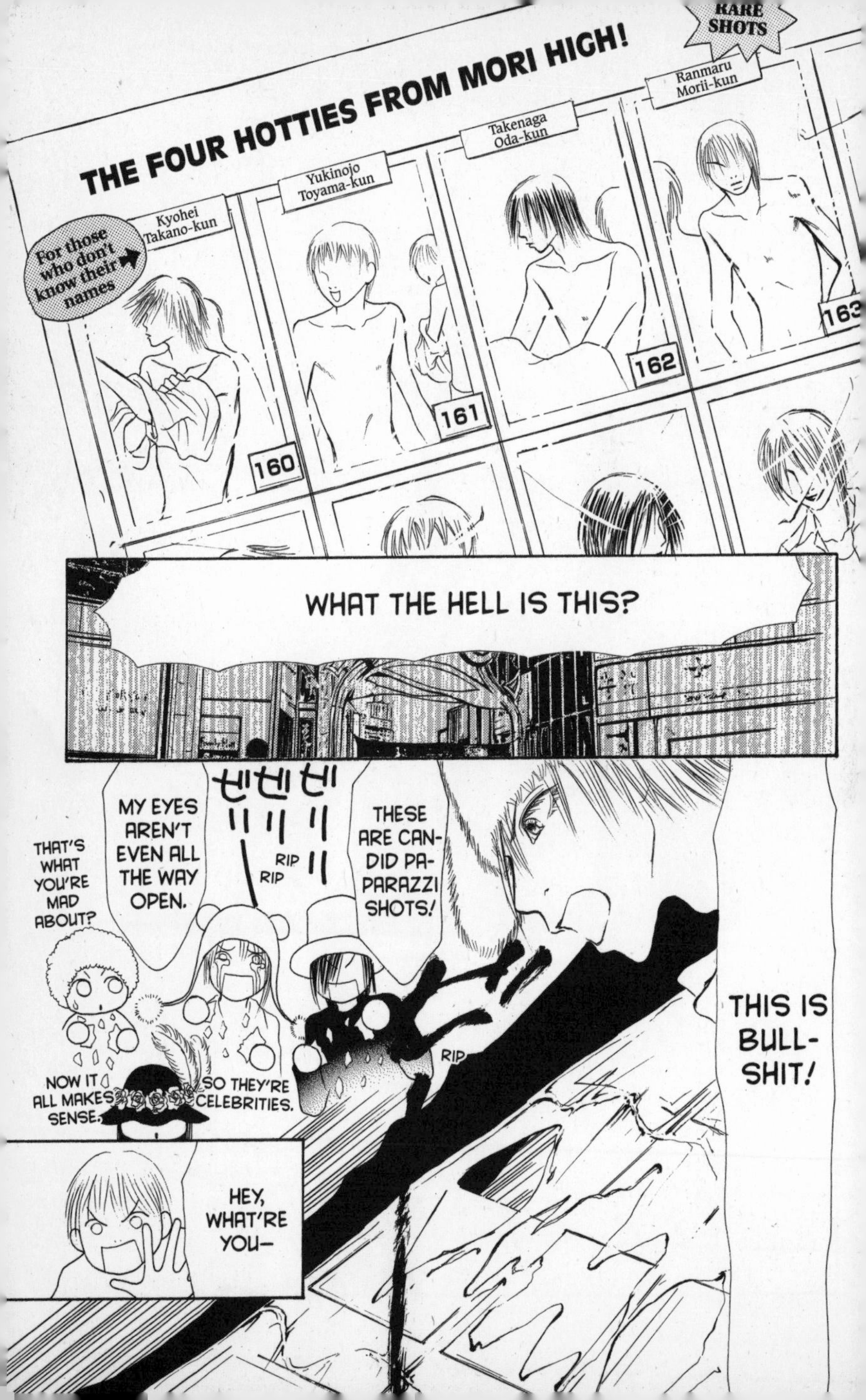
RARE SHOTS
THE FOUR HOTTIES FROM MORI HIGH!
For those who don't know their names
Kyohei Takano-kun
Yukinojo Toyama-kun
Takenaga Oda-kun
Ranmaru Morii-kun
160
161
162
163
WHAT THE HELL IS THIS?
THIS IS BULL-SHIT!
THESE ARE CAN-DID PA-PARAZZI SHOTS!
RIP RIP
MY EYES AREN'T EVEN ALL THE WAY OPEN.
THAT'S WHAT YOU'RE MAD ABOUT?
RIP
SO THEY'RE CELEBRITIES.
NOW IT ALL MAKES SENSE.
HEY, WHAT'RE YOU—

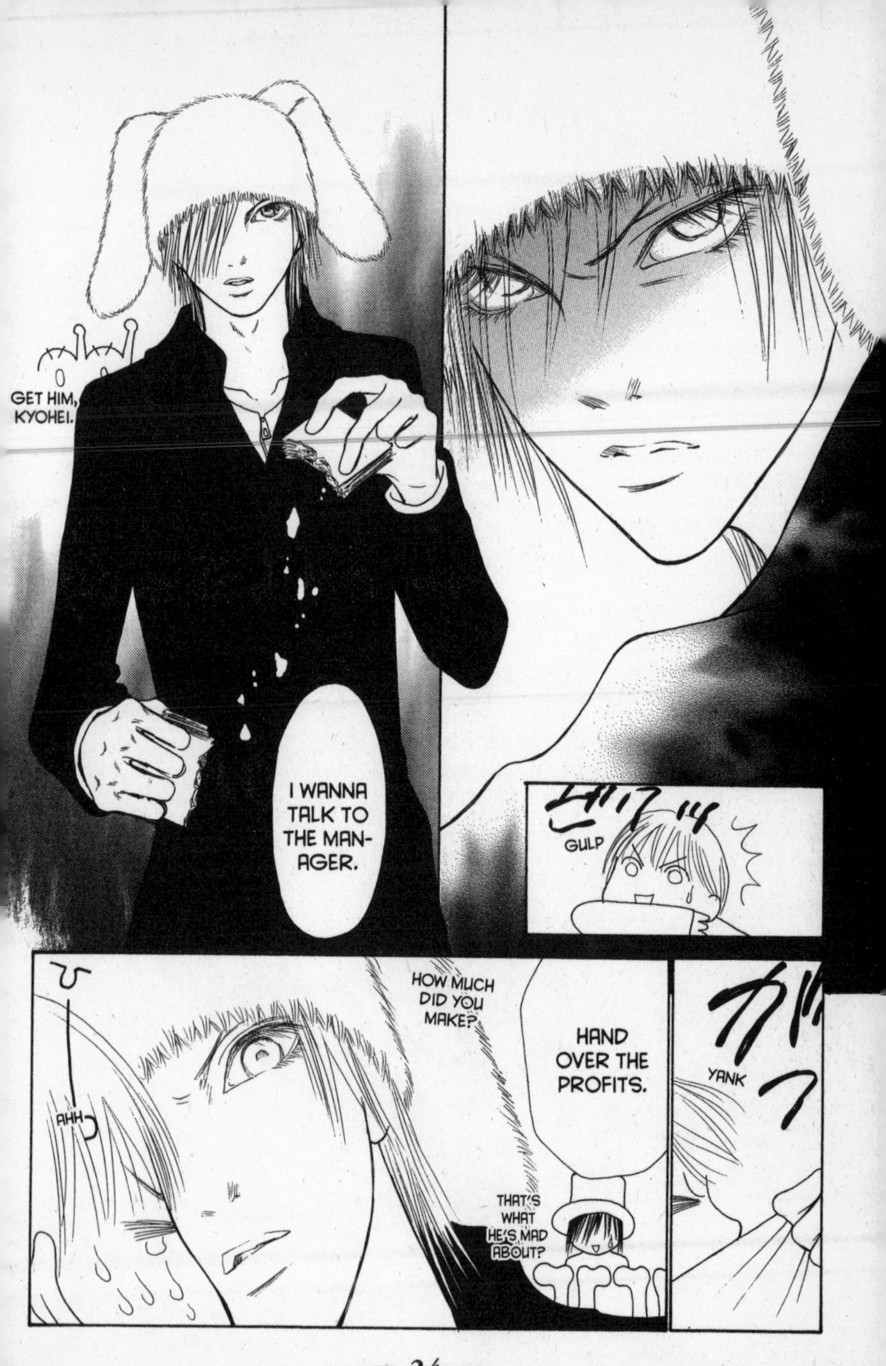
GULP
GET HIM, KYOHEI.
I WANNA TALK TO THE MAN-AGER.
YANK
HAND OVER THE PROFITS.
HOW MUCH DID YOU MAKE?
THAT'S WHAT HE'S MAD ABOUT?
AHH

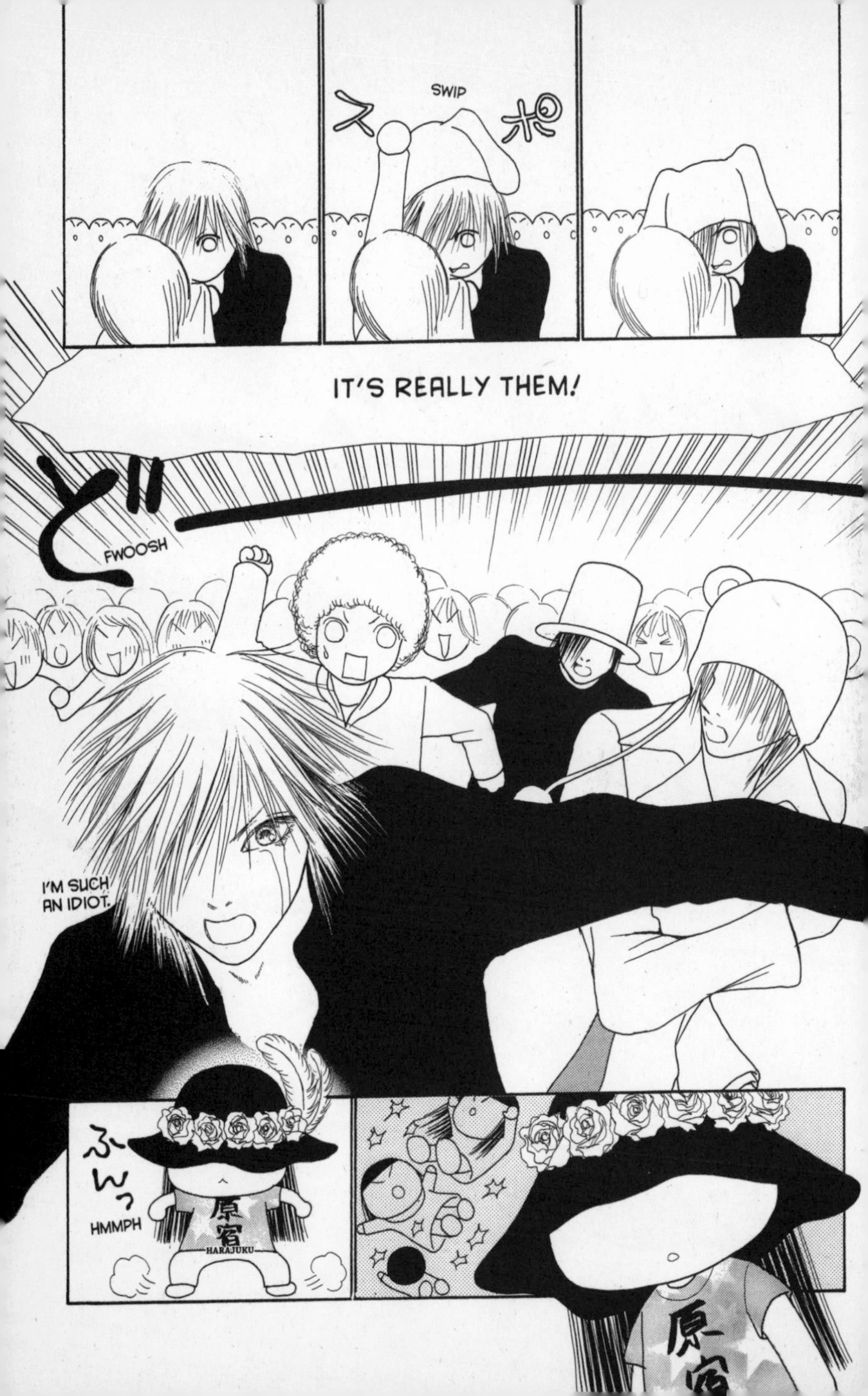
スポ
SWIP
IT'S REALLY THEM!
FWOOSH
I'M SUCH AN IDIOT.
原宿
ふんっ
HMMPH
原宿
HARAJUKU

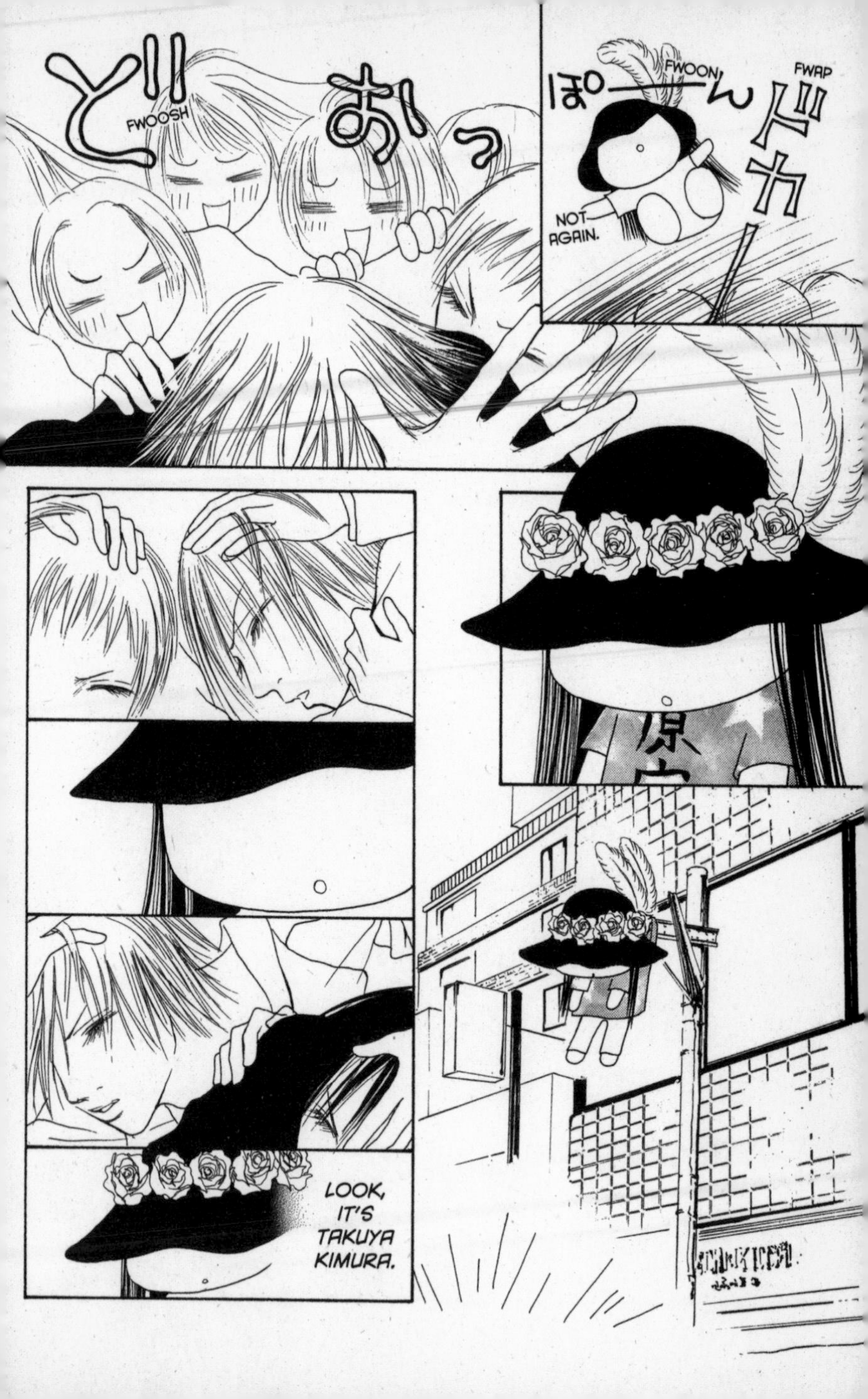
ぽーん
FWOON
ドカ
FWAP
NOT AGAIN.
FWOOSH
原
LOOK, IT'S TAKUYA KIMURA.

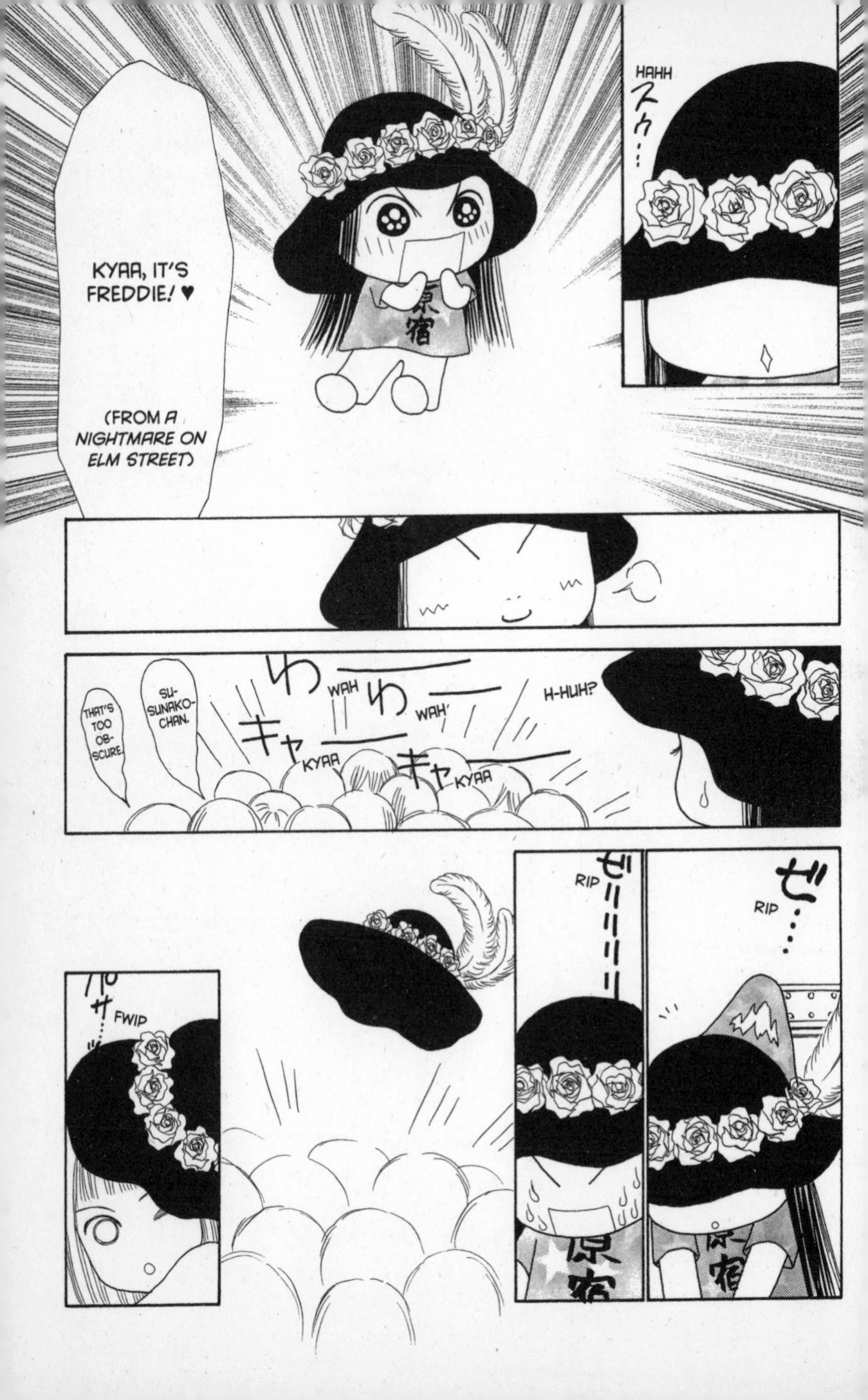
HAHH
スゥ…
KYAA, IT'S FREDDIE! ♥
(FROM A NIGHTMARE ON ELM STREET)
H-HUH?
わー WAH
わー WAH'
キャー KYAA
キャー KYAA
SU-SUNAKO-CHAN.
THAT'S TOO OB-SCURE.
ゼ… RIP
ゼリリリリ RIP
バサッ… FWIP

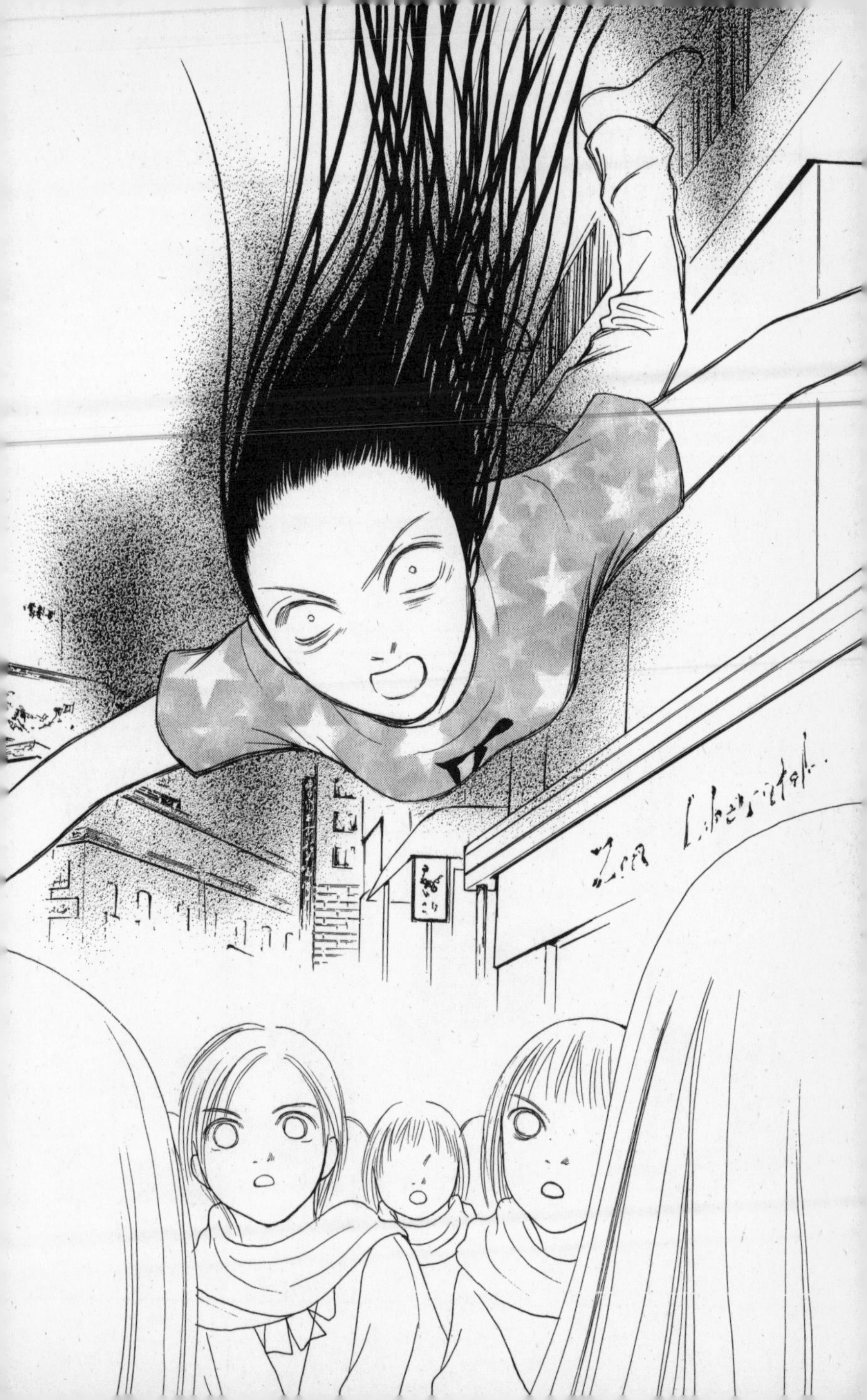

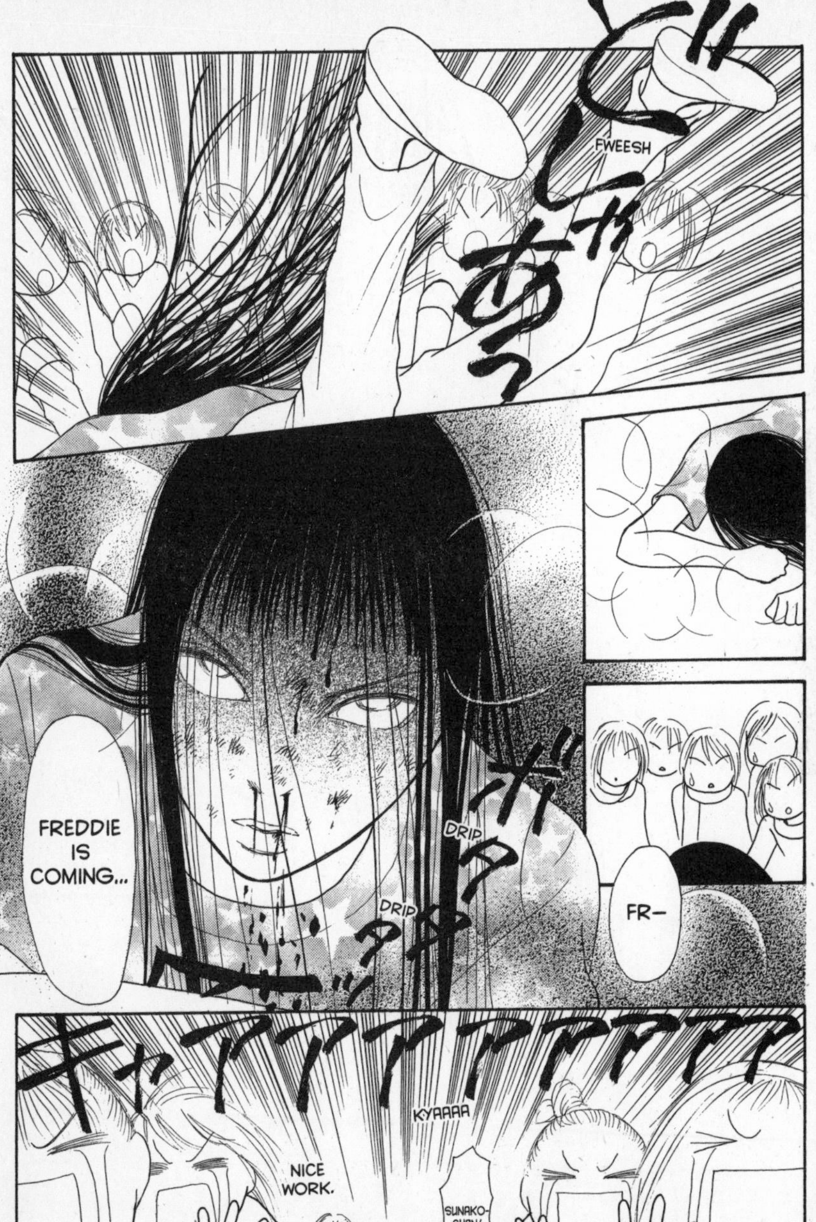
どしゃあっ
FWEESH
FR—
ボタタッ
DRIP
DRIP
FREDDIE IS COMING...
キャアアアアアアア
KYAAAA
SUNAKO-CHAN!
NICE WORK.

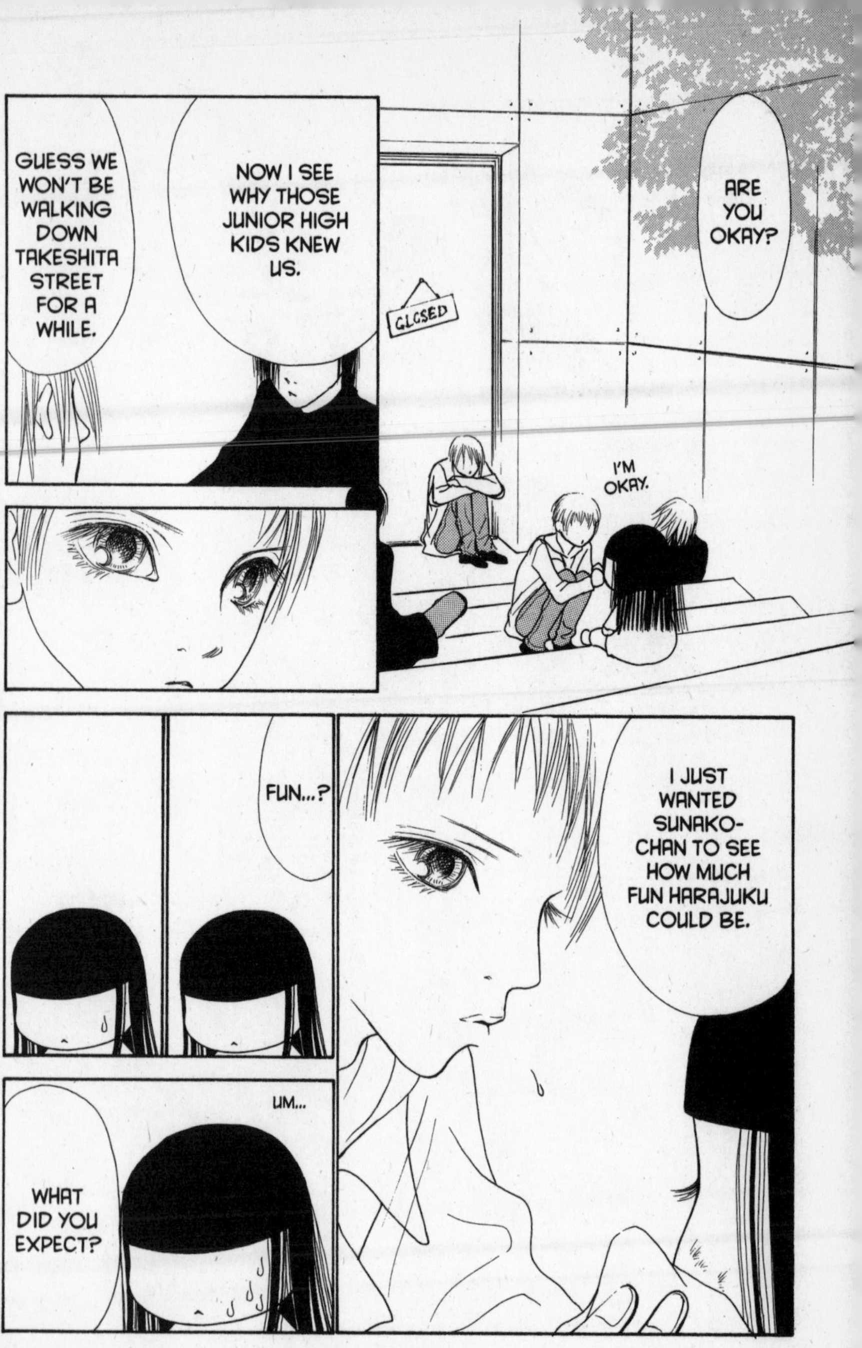
ARE YOU OKAY?
I'M OKAY.
NOW I SEE WHY THOSE JUNIOR HIGH KIDS KNEW US.
GUESS WE WON'T BE WALKING DOWN TAKESHITA STREET FOR A WHILE.
GLOSED
I JUST WANTED SUNAKO-CHAN TO SEE HOW MUCH FUN HARAJUKU COULD BE.
FUN...?
UM...
WHAT DID YOU EXPECT?

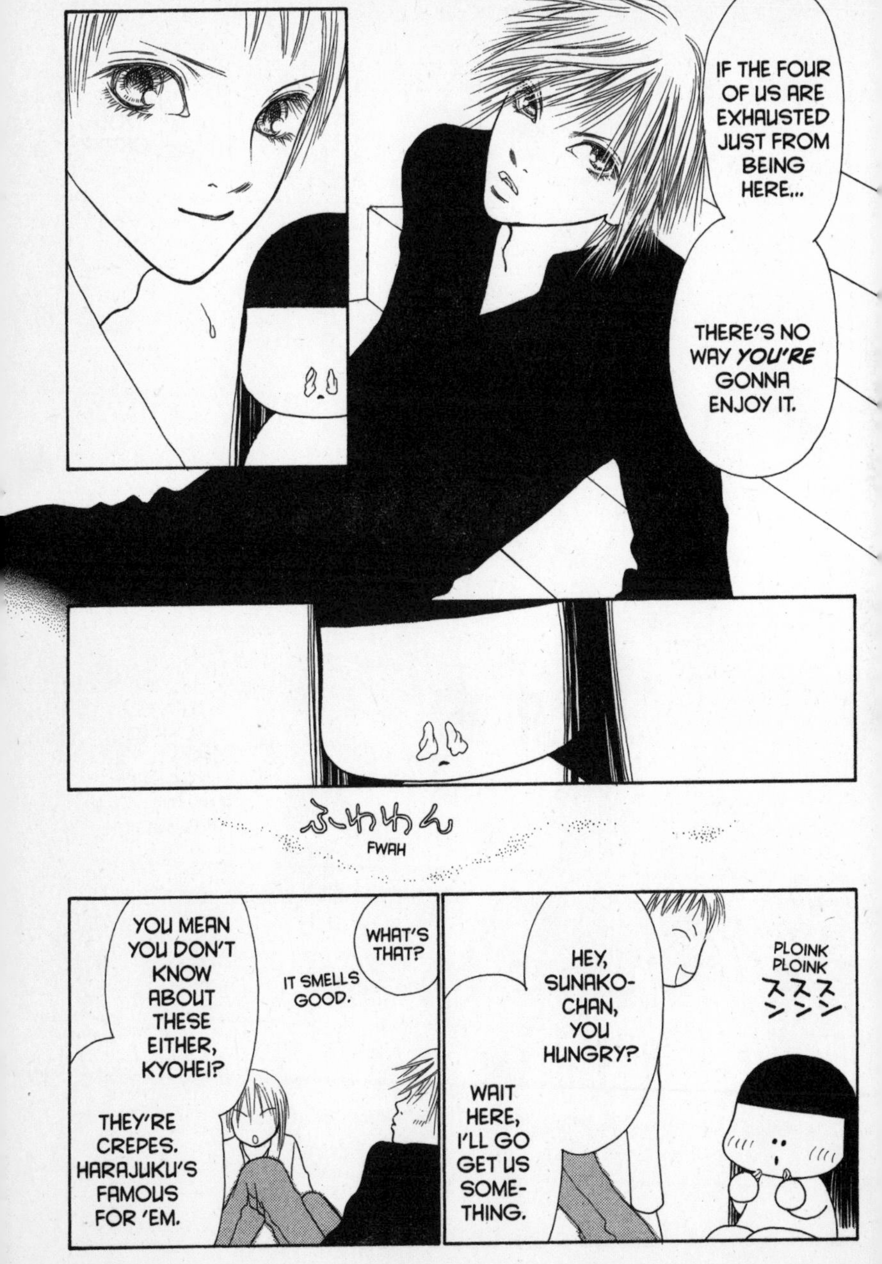
IF THE FOUR OF US ARE EXHAUSTED JUST FROM BEING HERE...
THERE'S NO WAY *YOU'RE* GONNA ENJOY IT.
ふわわん
FWAH
PLOINK PLOINK
スンスンスン
HEY, SUNAKO-CHAN, YOU HUNGRY?
WAIT HERE, I'LL GO GET US SOME-THING.
WHAT'S THAT?
IT SMELLS GOOD.
YOU MEAN YOU DON'T KNOW ABOUT THESE EITHER, KYOHEI?
THEY'RE CREPES. HARAJUKU'S FAMOUS FOR 'EM.

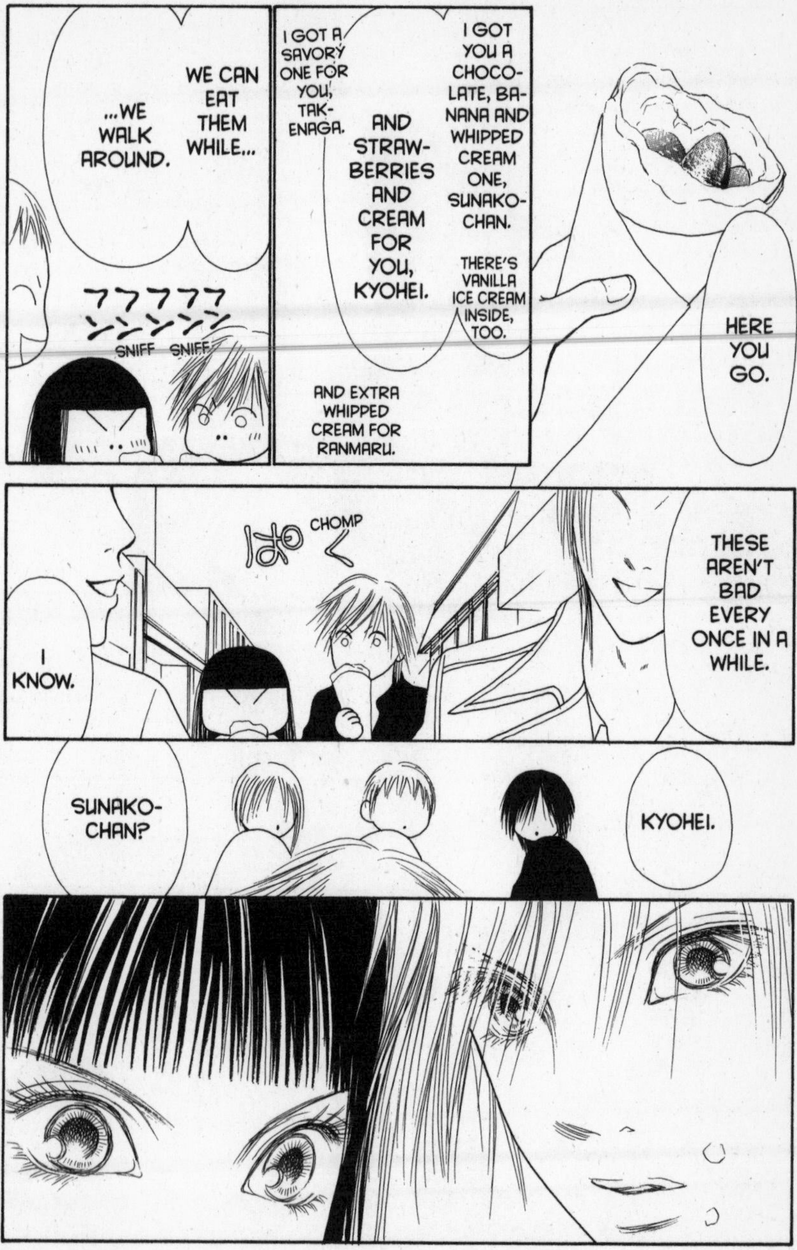
HERE YOU GO.
I GOT YOU A CHOCOLATE, BANANA AND WHIPPED CREAM ONE, SUNAKO-CHAN.
THERE'S VANILLA ICE CREAM INSIDE, TOO.
AND STRAWBERRIES AND CREAM FOR YOU, KYOHEI.
I GOT A SAVORY ONE FOR YOU, TAKENAGA.
AND EXTRA WHIPPED CREAM FOR RANMARU.
WE CAN EAT THEM WHILE...
...WE WALK AROUND.
SNIFF SNIFF
THESE AREN'T BAD EVERY ONCE IN A WHILE.
ぱく
CHOMP
I KNOW.
KYOHEI.
SUNAKO-CHAN?

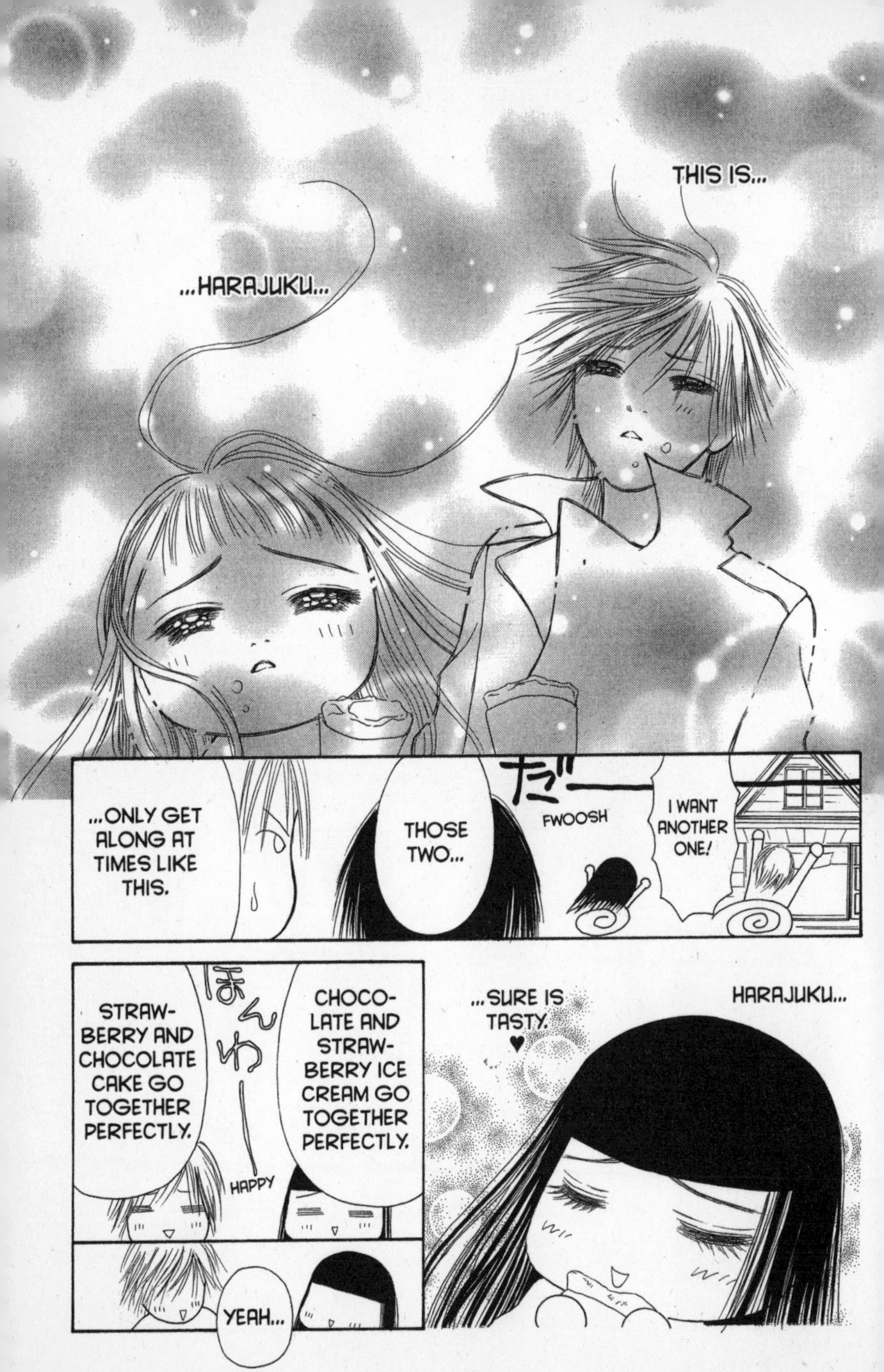
THIS IS...
...HARAJUKU...
I WANT ANOTHER ONE!
だ"ー
FWOOSH
THOSE TWO...
...ONLY GET ALONG AT TIMES LIKE THIS.
HARAJUKU...
...SURE IS TASTY. ♥
CHOCO-LATE AND STRAW-BERRY ICE CREAM GO TOGETHER PERFECTLY.
STRAW-BERRY AND CHOCOLATE CAKE GO TOGETHER PERFECTLY.
ほんわー
HAPPY
YEAH...

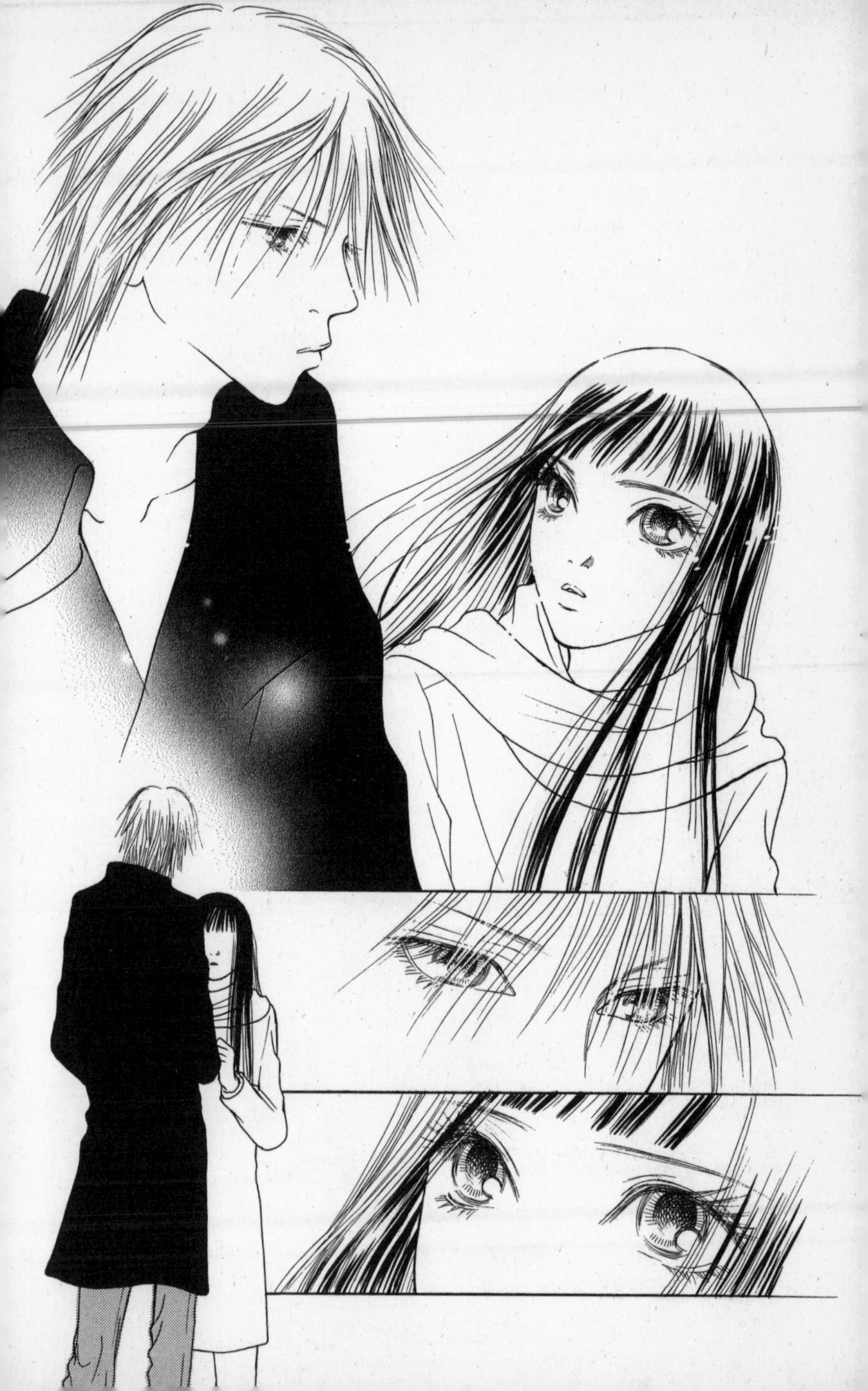

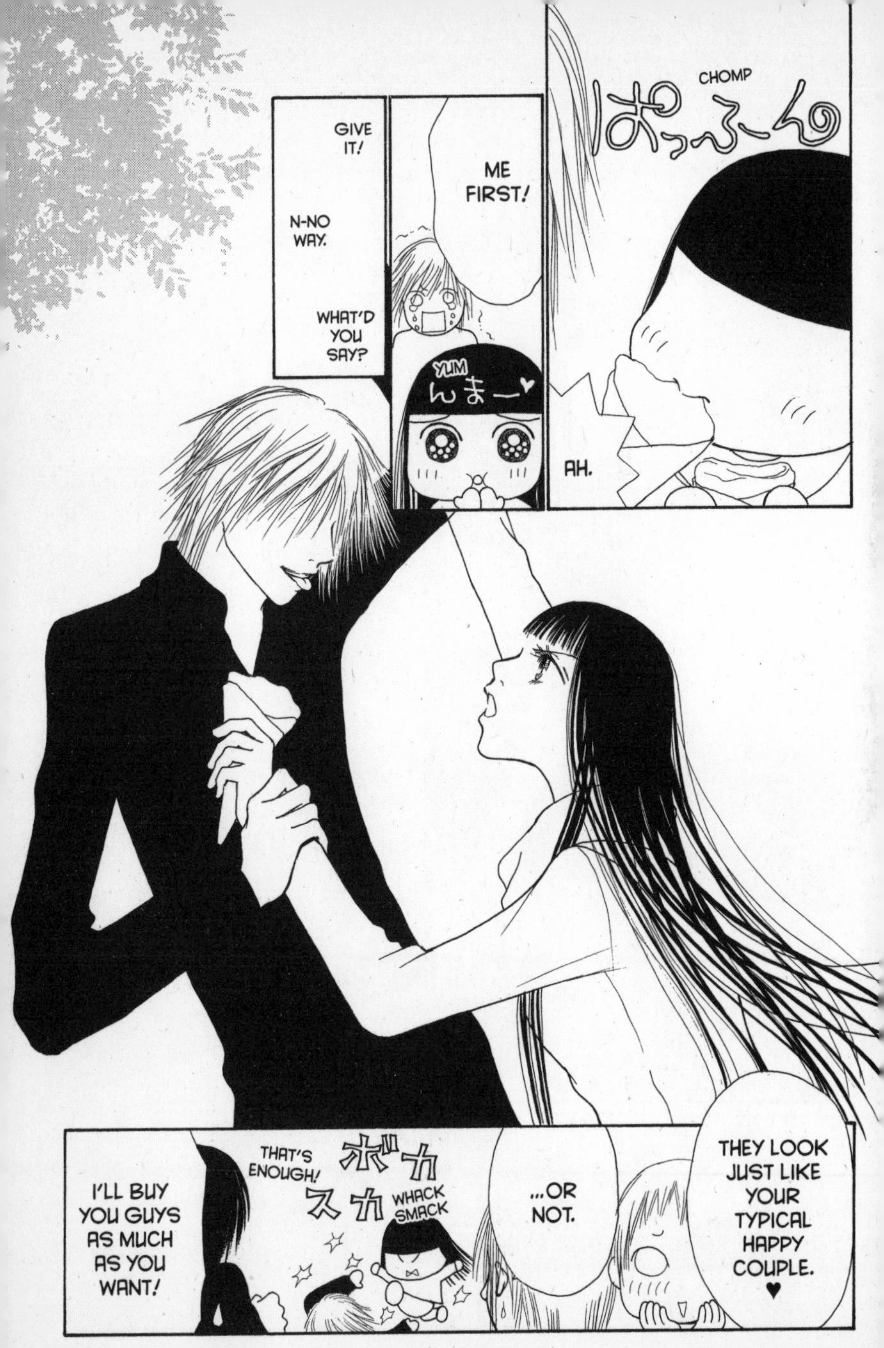
CHOMP
ぱっふ〜ん
AH.
ME FIRST!
YUM
んまー♥
GIVE IT!
N-NO WAY.
WHAT'D YOU SAY?
THEY LOOK JUST LIKE YOUR TYPICAL HAPPY COUPLE. ♥
...OR NOT.
THAT'S ENOUGH!
ボカ
スカ
WHACK SMACK
I'LL BUY YOU GUYS AS MUCH AS YOU WANT!

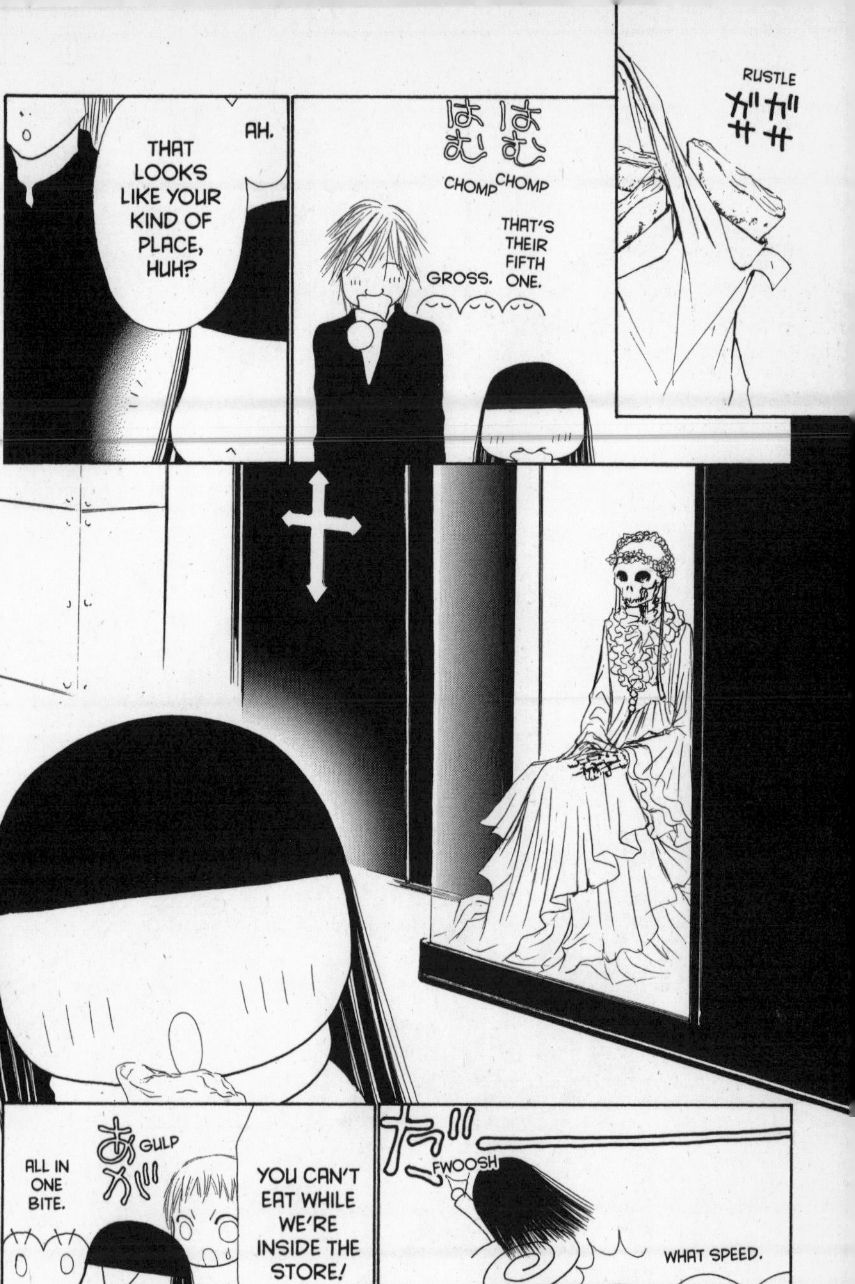
RUSTLE
ガサガサ
はむはむ
CHOMP CHOMP
THAT'S THEIR FIFTH ONE.
GROSS.
AH.
THAT LOOKS LIKE YOUR KIND OF PLACE, HUH?
たっ
FWOOSH
WHAT SPEED.
あが
GULP
YOU CAN'T EAT WHILE WE'RE INSIDE THE STORE!
ALL IN ONE BITE.

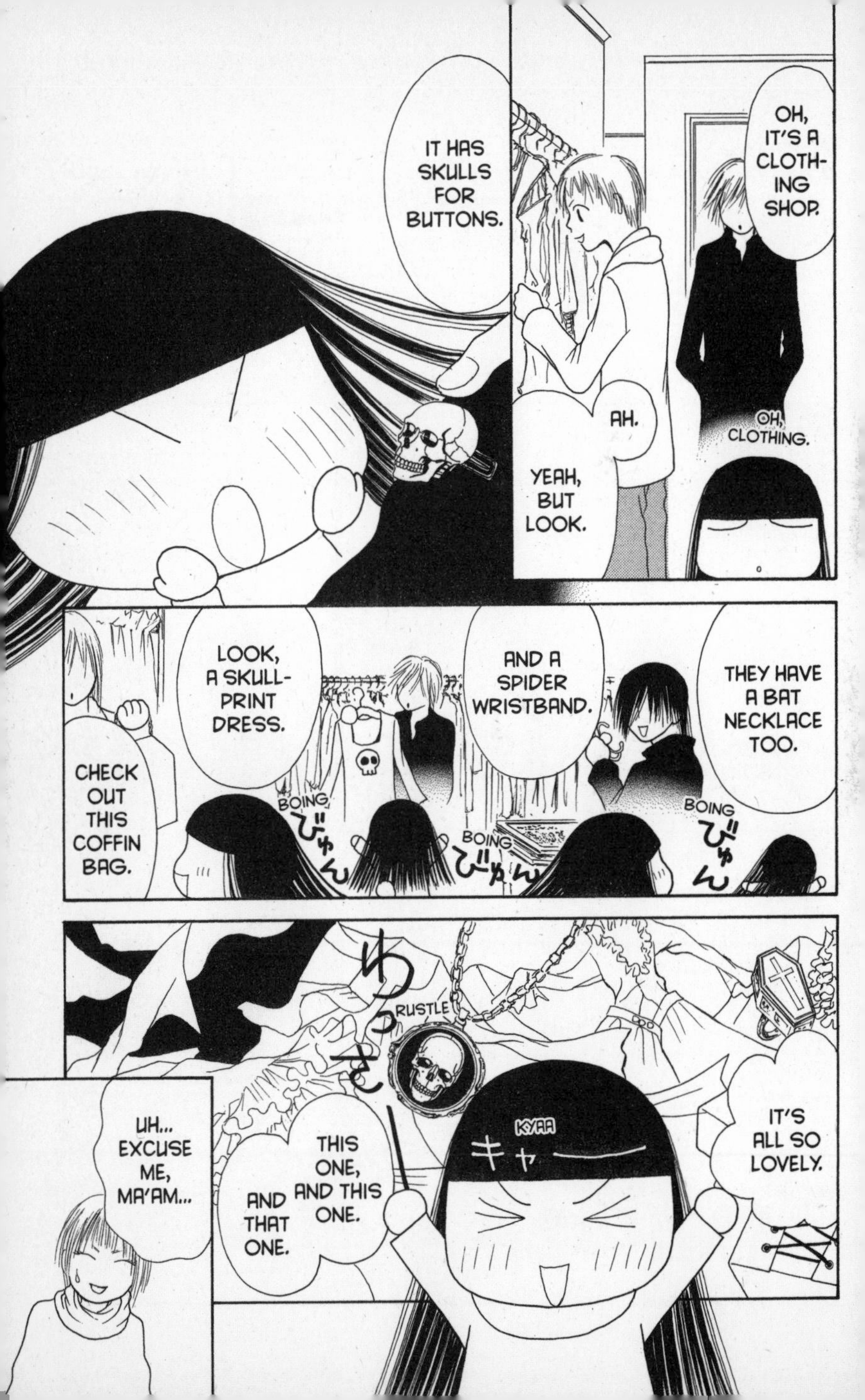
OH, IT'S A CLOTH-ING SHOP.
OH, CLOTHING.
AH.
YEAH, BUT LOOK.
IT HAS SKULLS FOR BUTTONS.
THEY HAVE A BAT NECKLACE TOO.
BOING びゅん
AND A SPIDER WRISTBAND.
BOING びゅん
LOOK, A SKULL-PRINT DRESS.
BOING びゅん
CHECK OUT THIS COFFIN BAG.
RUSTLE
IT'S ALL SO LOVELY.
KYAA キャー
THIS ONE, AND THIS ONE.
AND THAT ONE.
UH... EXCUSE ME, MA'AM...

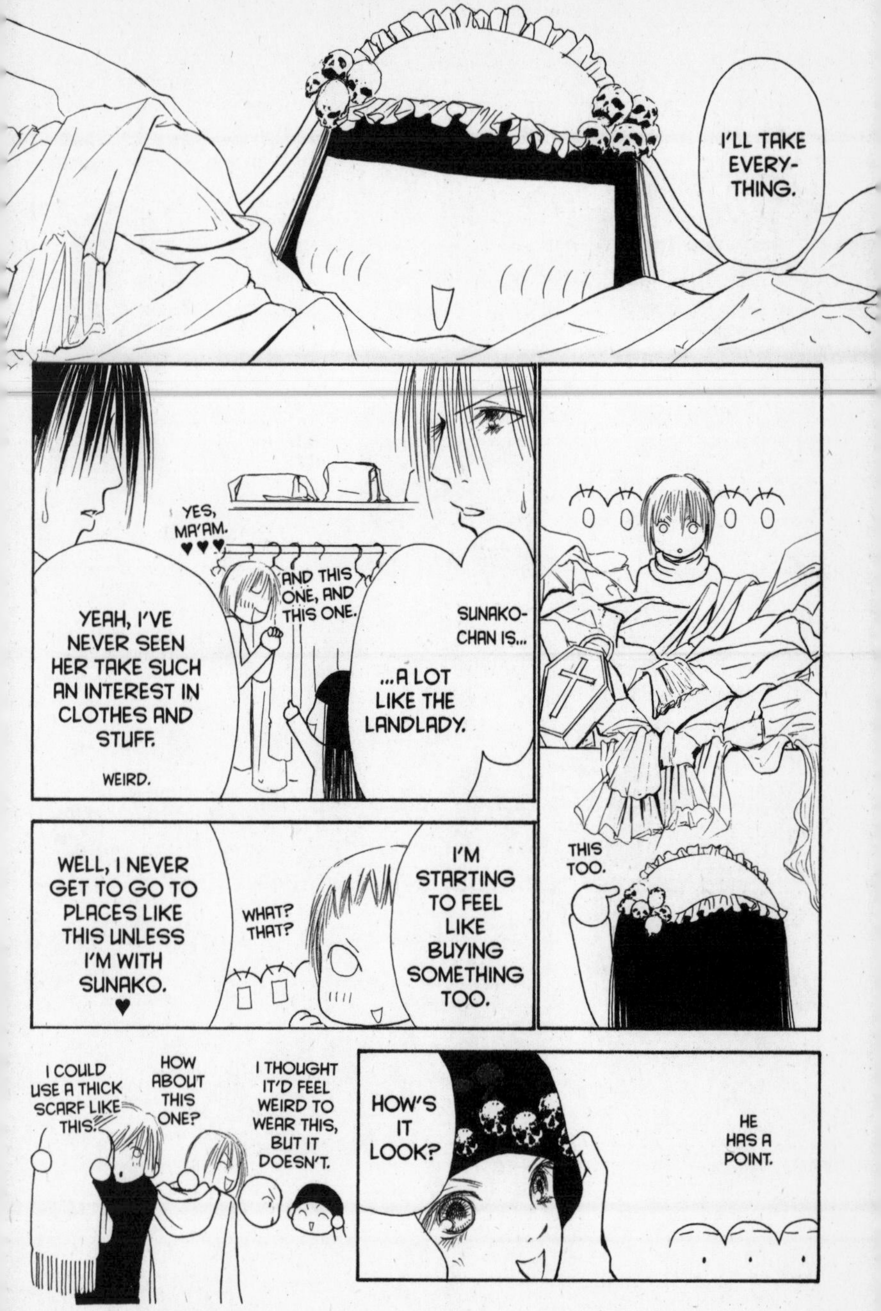
I'LL TAKE EVERY-THING.
THIS TOO.
SUNAKO-CHAN IS...
...A LOT LIKE THE LANDLADY.
AND THIS ONE, AND THIS ONE.
YES, MA'AM. ♥♥♥
YEAH, I'VE NEVER SEEN HER TAKE SUCH AN INTEREST IN CLOTHES AND STUFF.
WEIRD.
I'M STARTING TO FEEL LIKE BUYING SOMETHING TOO.
WHAT? THAT?
WELL, I NEVER GET TO GO TO PLACES LIKE THIS UNLESS I'M WITH SUNAKO. ♥
HE HAS A POINT.
HOW'S IT LOOK?
I THOUGHT IT'D FEEL WEIRD TO WEAR THIS, BUT IT DOESN'T.
HOW ABOUT THIS ONE?
I COULD USE A THICK SCARF LIKE THIS.

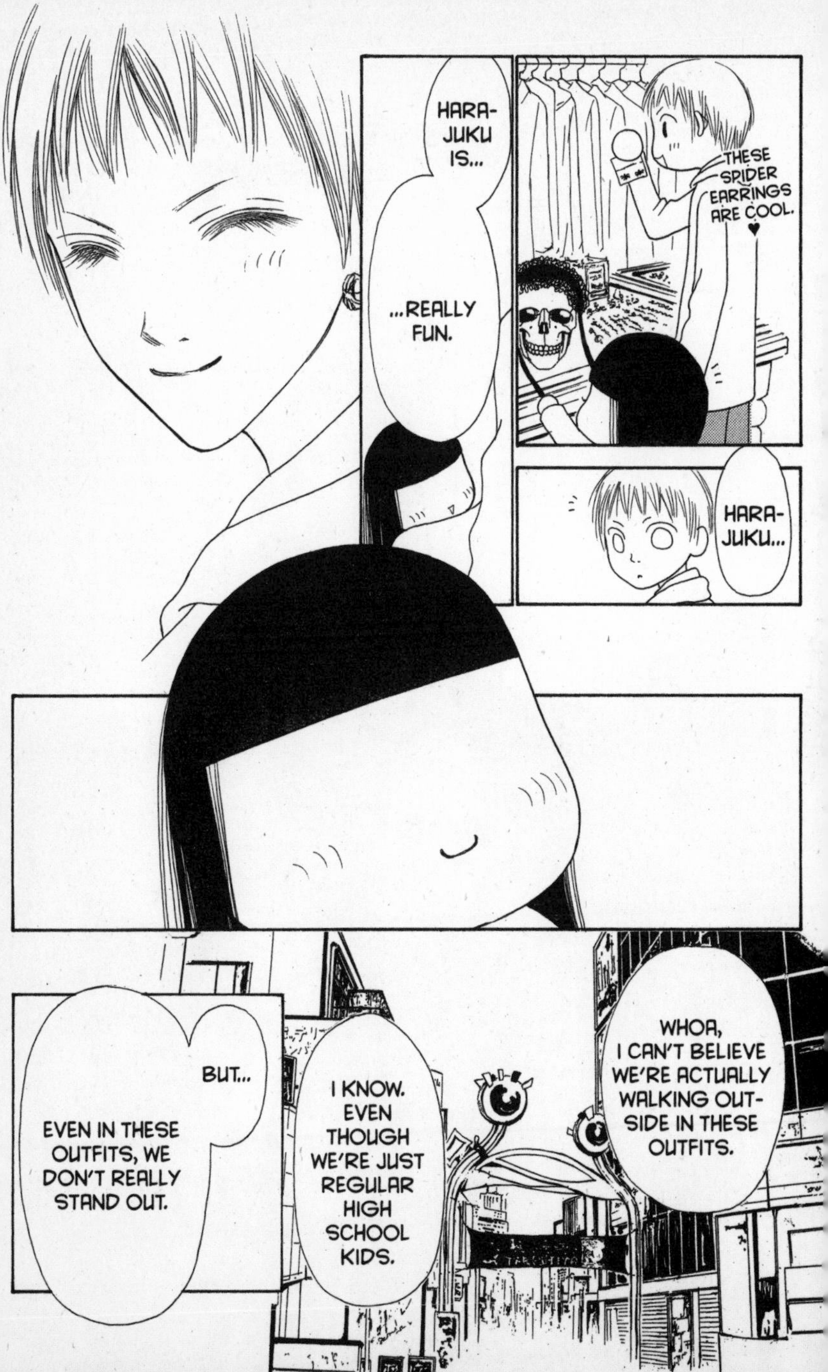
THESE SPIDER EARRINGS ARE COOL. ♥
HARAJUKU...
HARAJUKU IS...
...REALLY FUN.
WHOA, I CAN'T BELIEVE WE'RE ACTUALLY WALKING OUTSIDE IN THESE OUTFITS.
I KNOW. EVEN THOUGH WE'RE JUST REGULAR HIGH SCHOOL KIDS.
BUT...
EVEN IN THESE OUTFITS, WE DON'T REALLY STAND OUT.

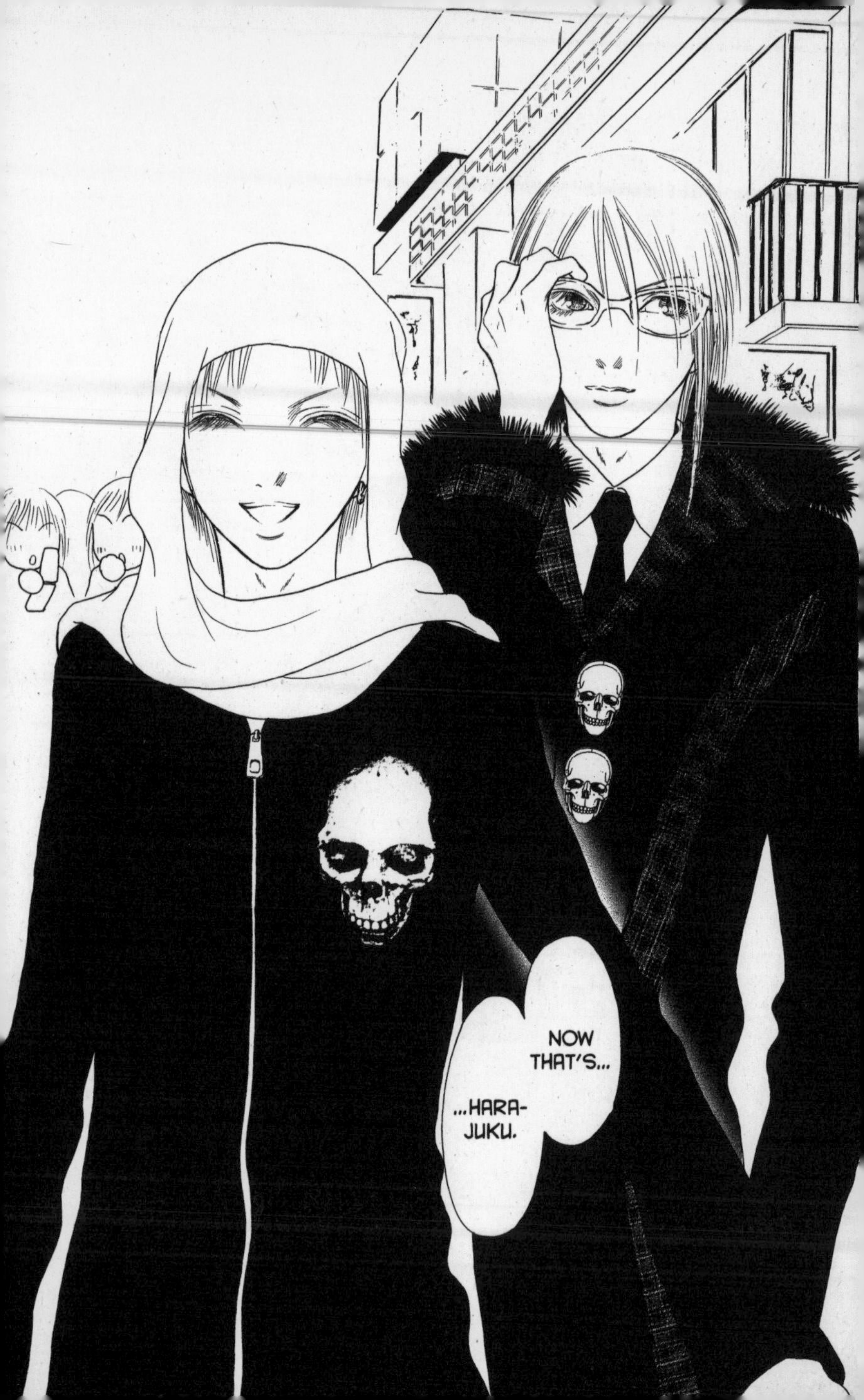
NOW THAT'S...
...HARA-JUKU.

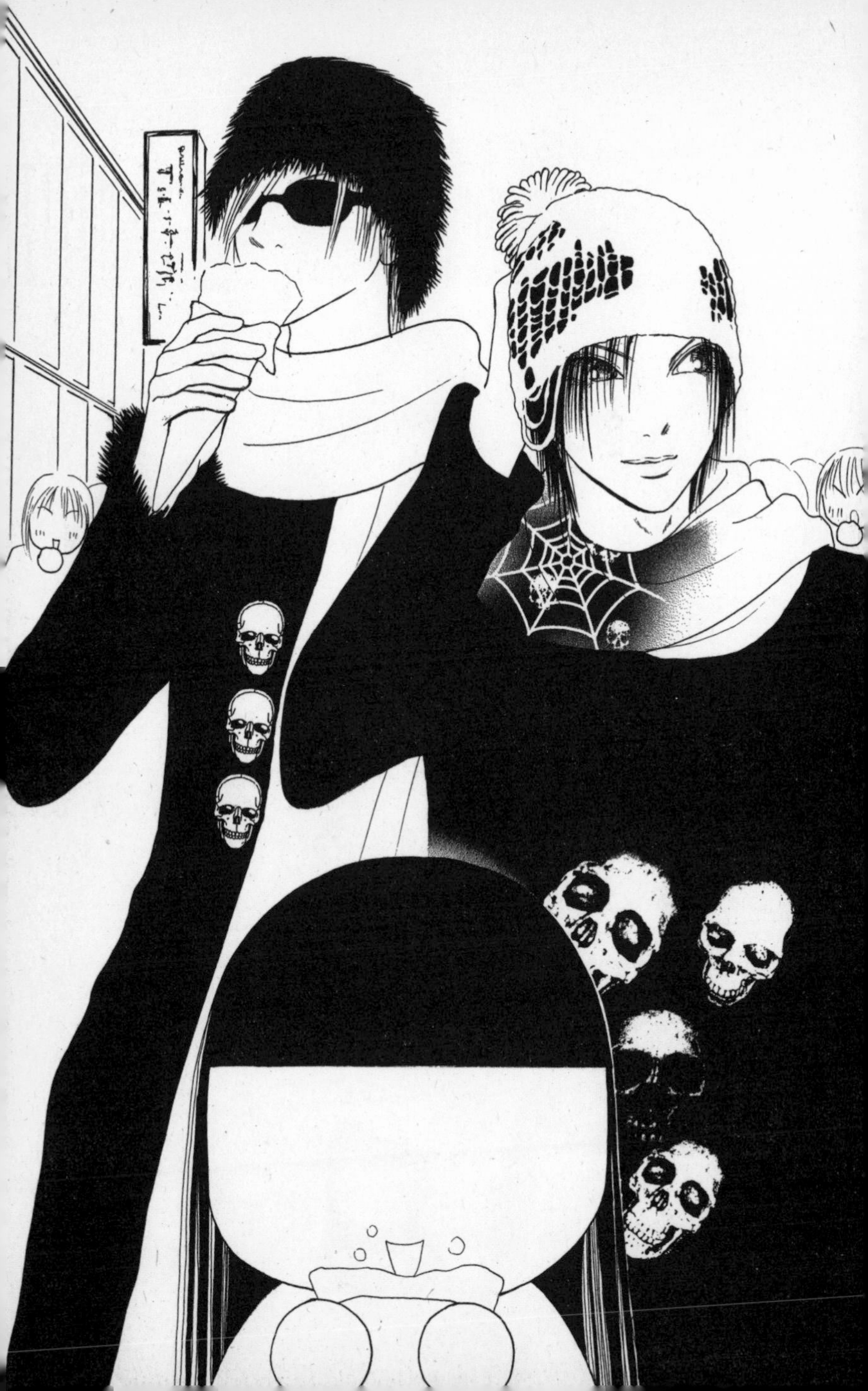

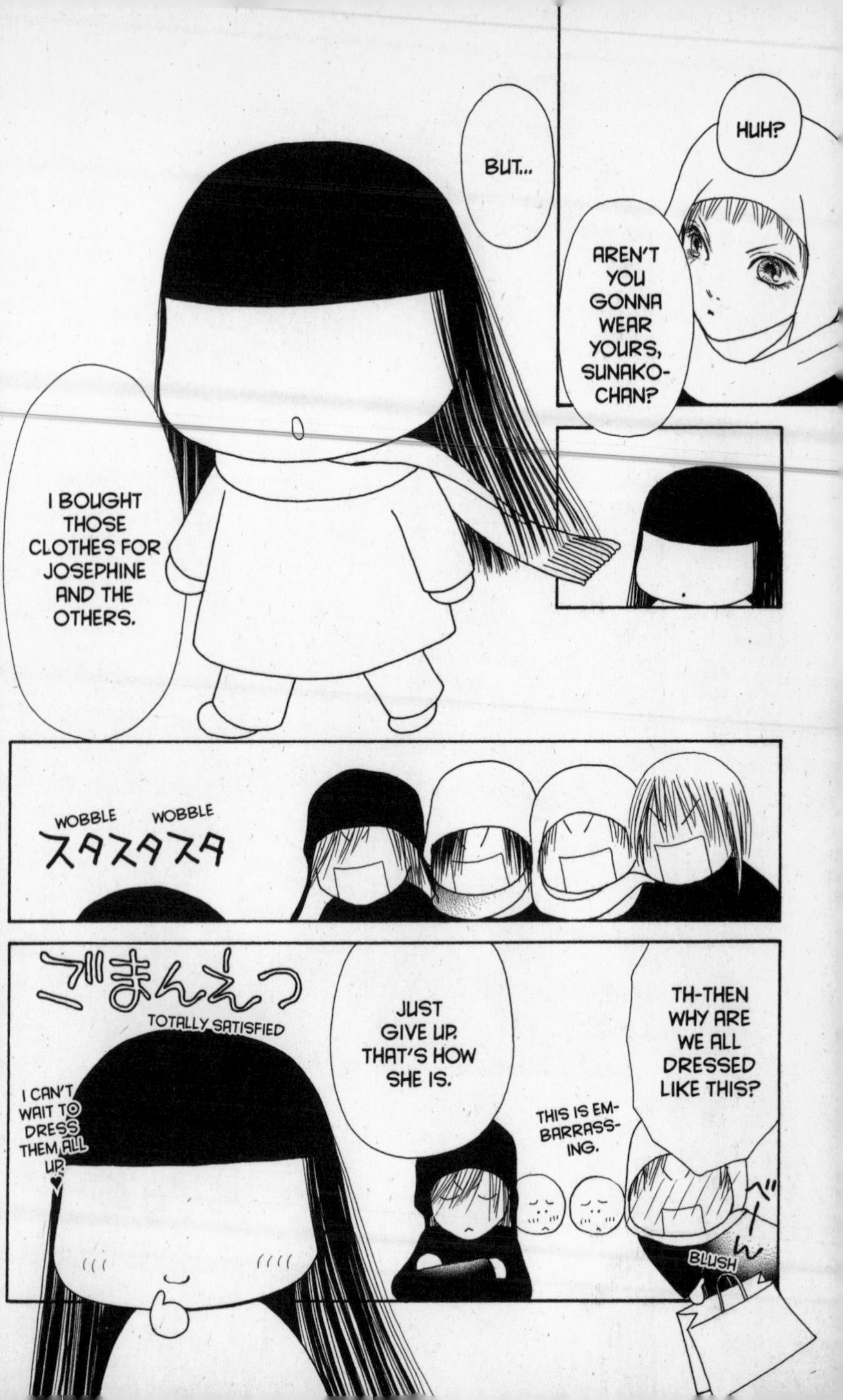
HUH?
AREN'T YOU GONNA WEAR YOURS, SUNAKO-CHAN?
BUT...
I BOUGHT THOSE CLOTHES FOR JOSEPHINE AND THE OTHERS.
スタスタスタ
WOBBLE WOBBLE
TH-THEN WHY ARE WE ALL DRESSED LIKE THIS?
べーん
BLUSH
THIS IS EMBARRASSING.
JUST GIVE UP. THAT'S HOW SHE IS.
ごまんえつ
TOTALLY SATISFIED
I CAN'T WAIT TO DRESS THEM ALL UP.♥

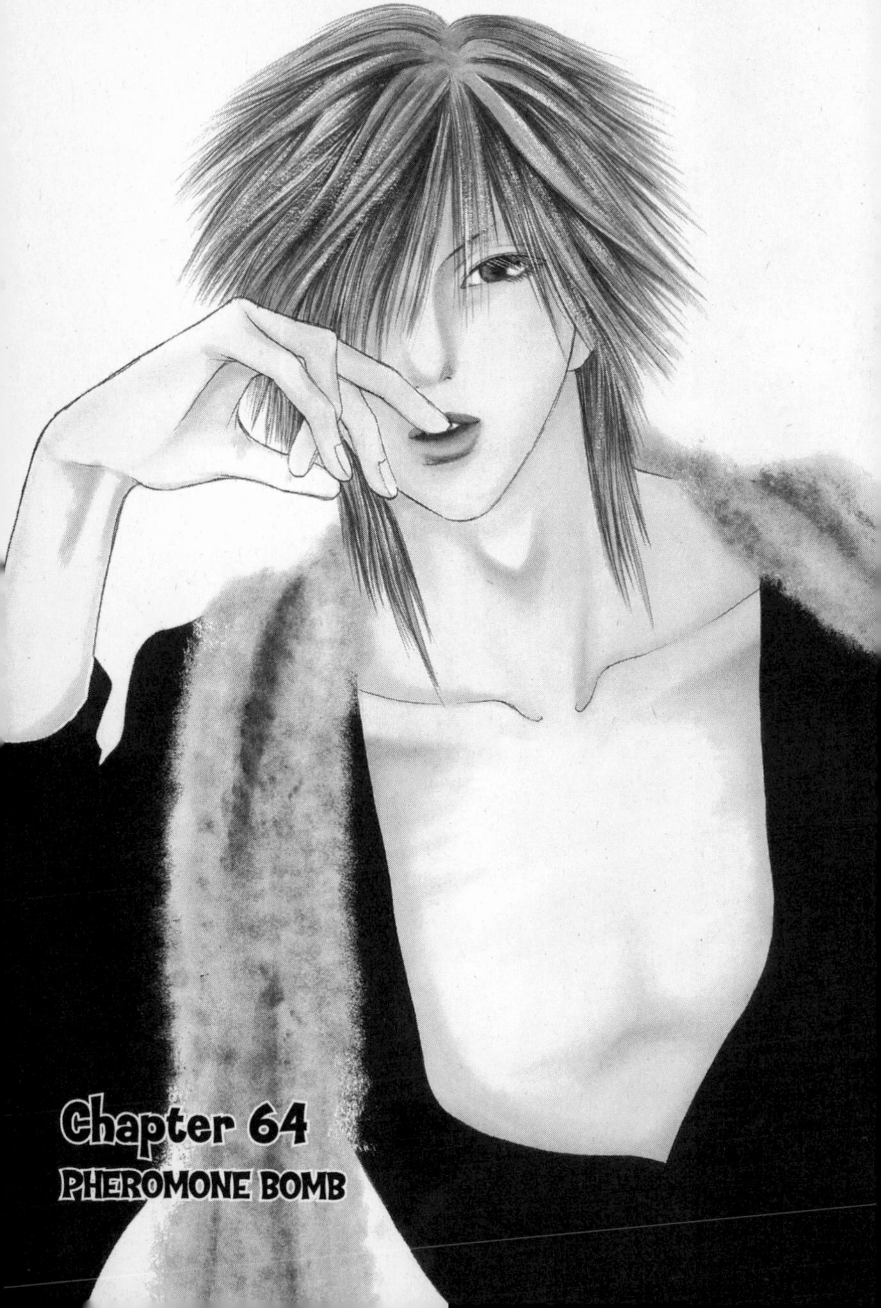

Chapter 64

PHEROMONE BOMB

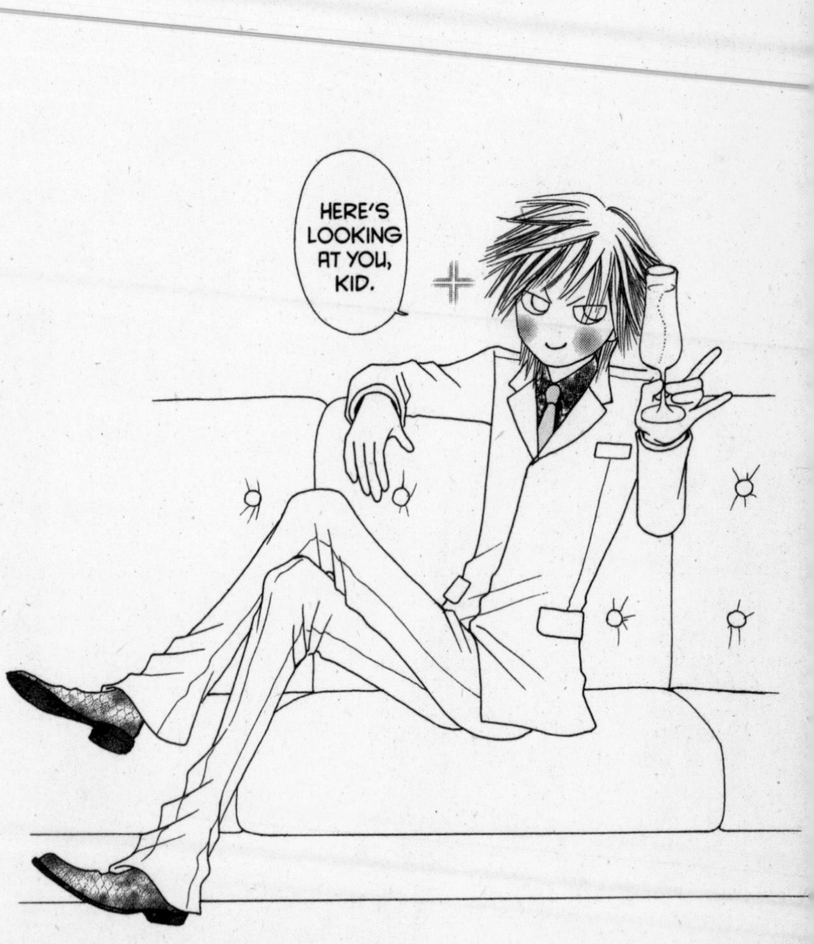
HERE'S LOOKING AT YOU, KID.

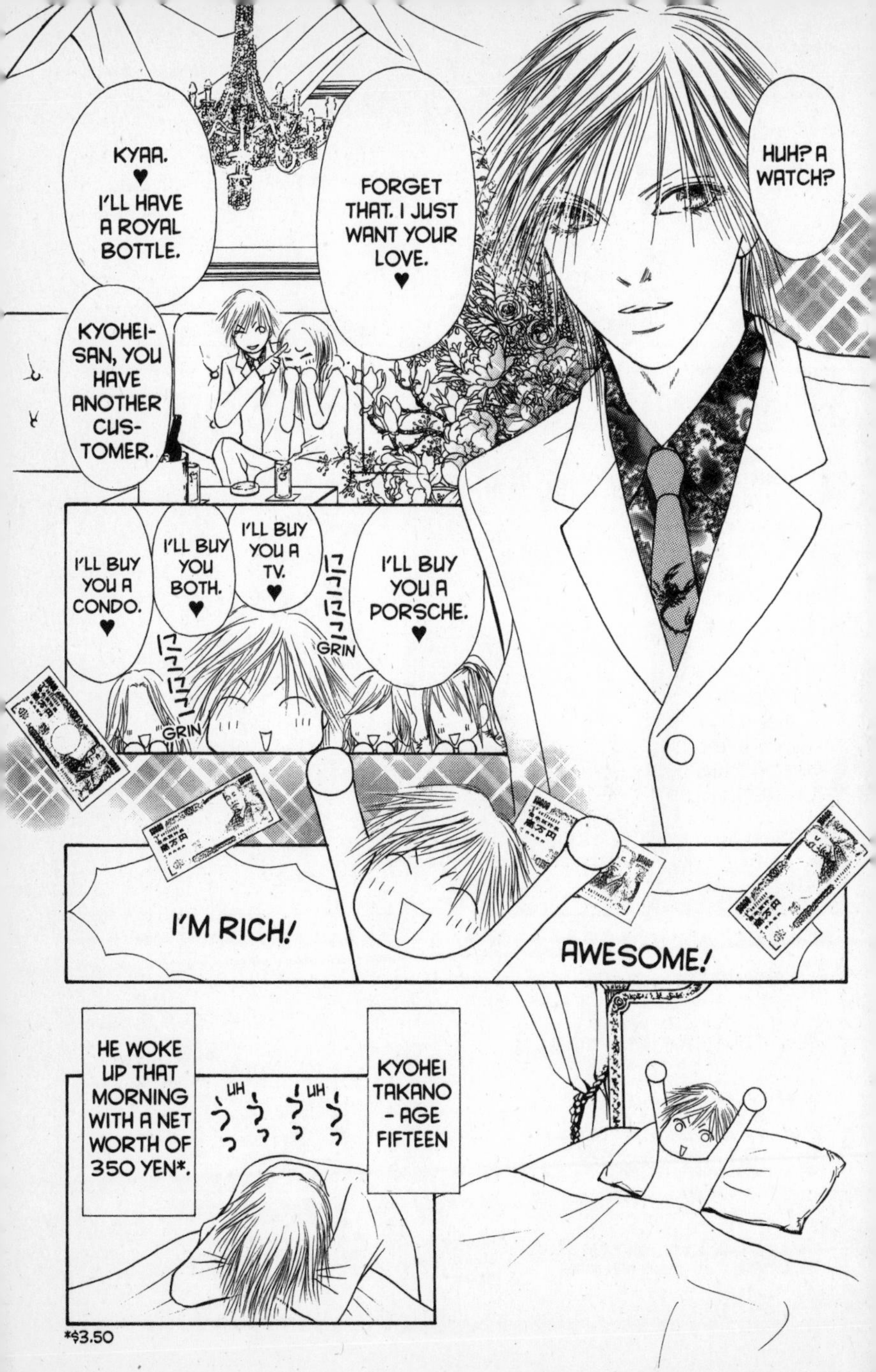
HUH? A WATCH?
FORGET THAT. I JUST WANT YOUR LOVE. ♥
KYAA. ♥ I'LL HAVE A ROYAL BOTTLE.
KYOHEI-SAN, YOU HAVE ANOTHER CUS-TOMER.
I'LL BUY YOU A PORSCHE. ♥
GRIN
I'LL BUY YOU A TV. ♥
I'LL BUY YOU BOTH. ♥
I'LL BUY YOU A CONDO. ♥
GRIN
AWESOME!
I'M RICH!
KYOHEI TAKANO - AGE FIFTEEN
UH
UH
HE WOKE UP THAT MORNING WITH A NET WORTH OF 350 YEN*.

*$3.50

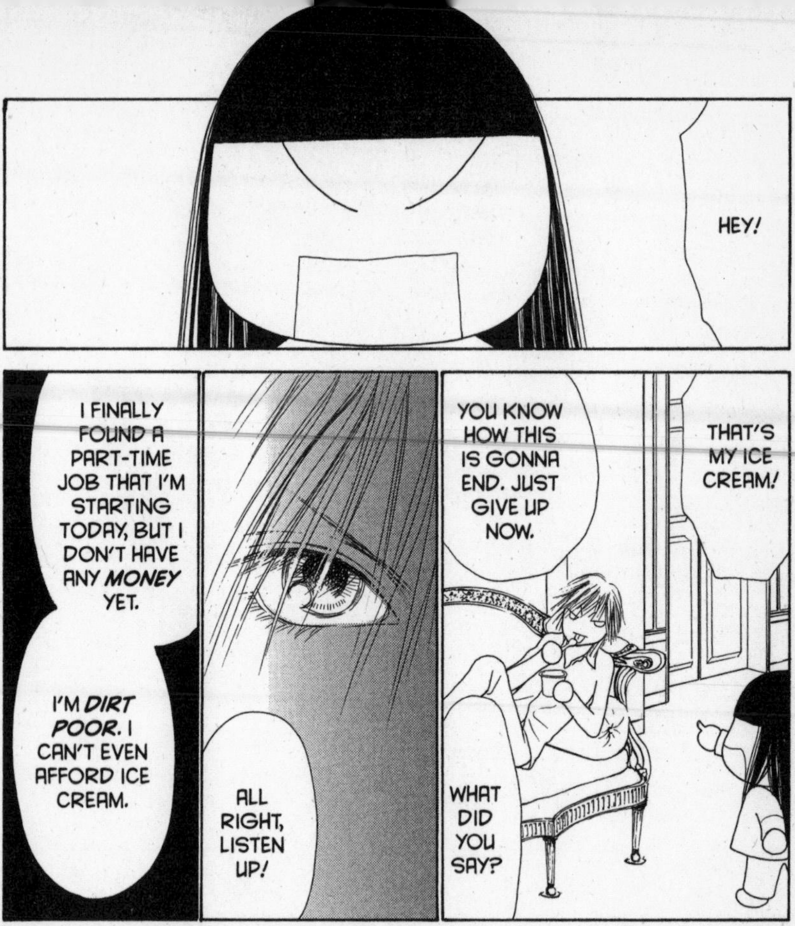
HEY!
THAT'S MY ICE CREAM!
YOU KNOW HOW THIS IS GONNA END. JUST GIVE UP NOW.
WHAT DID YOU SAY?
ALL RIGHT, LISTEN UP!
I FINALLY FOUND A PART-TIME JOB THAT I'M STARTING TODAY, BUT I DON'T HAVE ANY *MONEY* YET.
I'M *DIRT POOR*. I CAN'T EVEN AFFORD ICE CREAM.

BEHIND THE SCENES

THIS STORY IS FULL OF SPECIAL GUESTS. JUST BEFORE MY DEADLINE, KODANSHA HAD A NEW YEAR'S PARTY. SHOJO MANGA AUTHORS CAME FROM ALL OVER THE COUNTRY, BUT I DIDN'T GO. MY DEADLINE WAS FAST APPROACHING, AND I DIDN'T GET ANY SLEEP, BUT THANKS TO EVERYONE'S HELP, I HAD A GREAT TIME.♥

EVEN THOUGH THE PARTY WAS ONLY A FIVE- MINUTE TAXI RIDE FROM MY HOUSE.

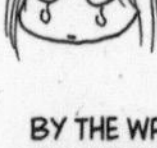

MIZUHO AIMOTO-SENSEI ♥♥♥, YUU YOSHII ♥, MACHIKO SAKURAI

THANKS GUYS! ♥♥♥

BY THE WAY, THE WORD *CHOOPAN* WAS A GANGSTER TERM FOR "HEAD BUTTING." IT WAS USED FROM THE LATTER HALF OF THE TWENTIES THROUGH THE EARLY FORTIES. IF YOU ASK AN OLD TOUGH GUY, HE MIGHT KNOW WHAT YOU'RE TALKING ABOUT.

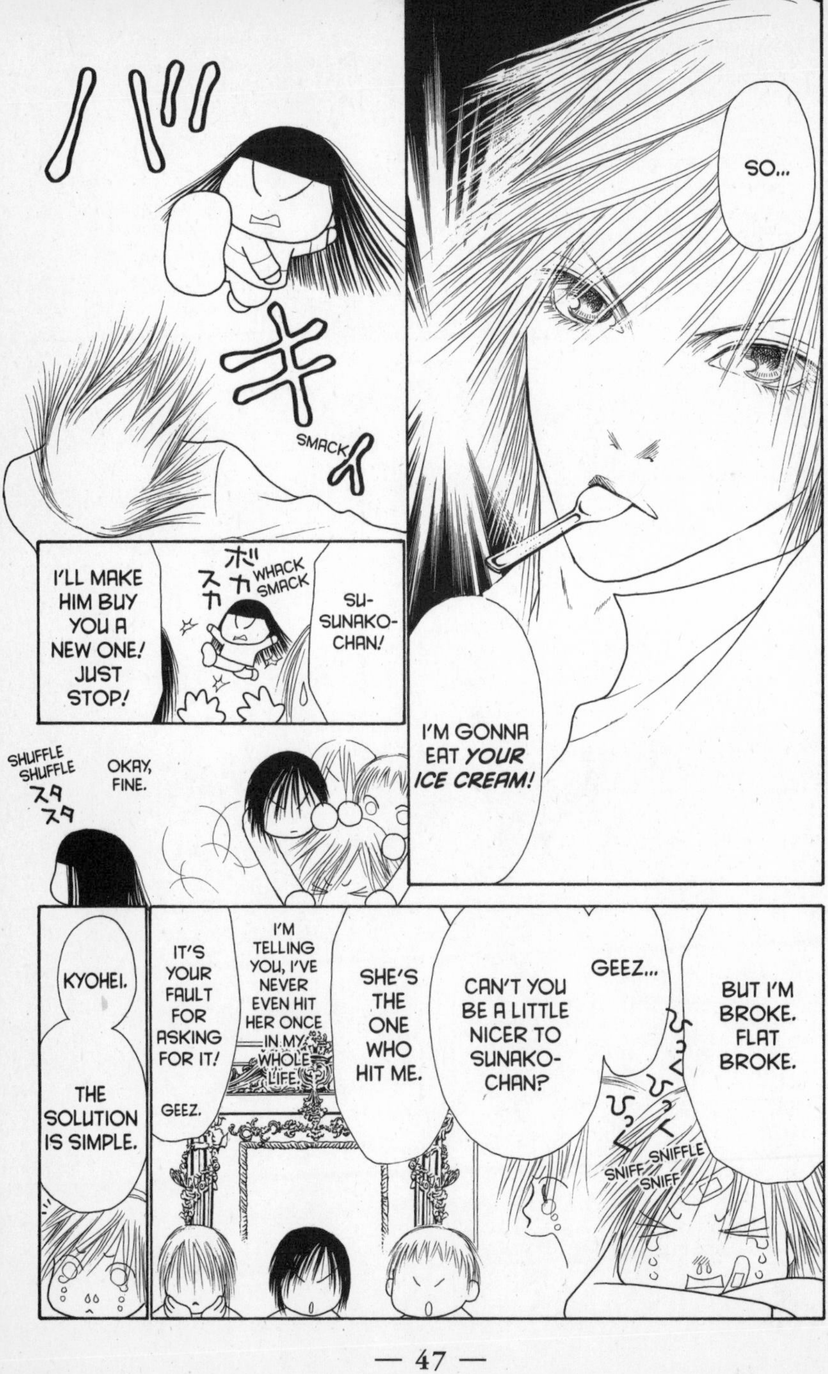
SO...
I'M GONNA EAT *YOUR ICE CREAM!*
バキ
SMACK イ
SU-SUNAKO-CHAN!
ボカ WHACK
スカ SMACK
I'LL MAKE HIM BUY YOU A NEW ONE! JUST STOP!
OKAY, FINE.
SHUFFLE SHUFFLE スタスタ
BUT I'M BROKE. FLAT BROKE.
GEEZ...
CAN'T YOU BE A LITTLE NICER TO SUNAKO-CHAN?
SNIFF SNIFFLE SNIFF
SHE'S THE ONE WHO HIT ME.
I'M TELLING YOU, I'VE NEVER EVEN HIT HER ONCE IN MY WHOLE LIFE.
IT'S YOUR FAULT FOR ASKING FOR IT!
GEEZ.
KYOHEI.
THE SOLUTION IS SIMPLE.

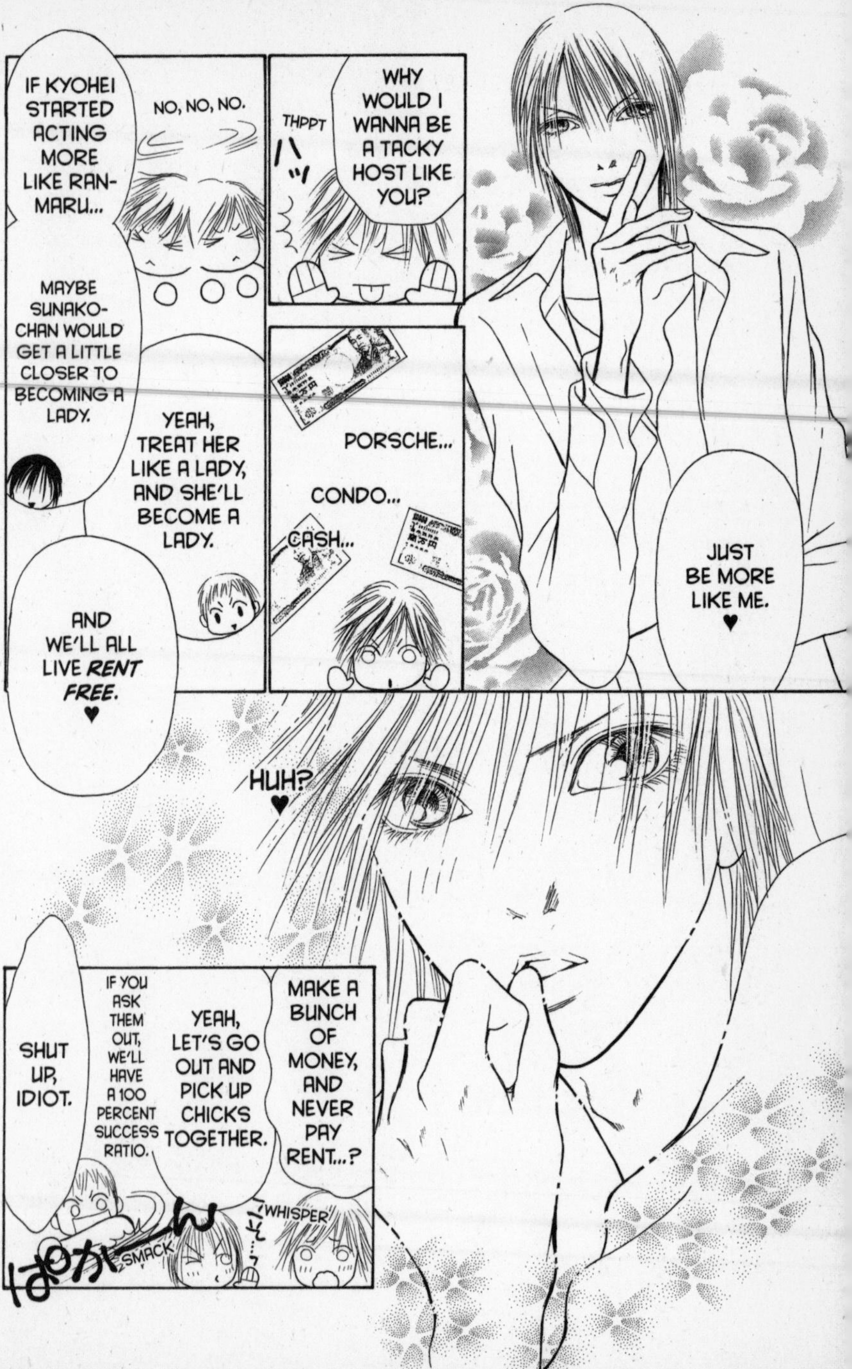
JUST BE MORE LIKE ME. ♥
THPPT
ハッ
WHY WOULD I WANNA BE A TACKY HOST LIKE YOU?
PORSCHE...
CONDO...
CASH...
IF KYOHEI STARTED ACTING MORE LIKE RAN-MARU...
NO, NO, NO.
MAYBE SUNAKO-CHAN WOULD GET A LITTLE CLOSER TO BECOMING A LADY.
YEAH, TREAT HER LIKE A LADY, AND SHE'LL BECOME A LADY.
AND WE'LL ALL LIVE *RENT FREE*. ♥
HUH? ♥
MAKE A BUNCH OF MONEY, AND NEVER PAY RENT...?
YEAH, LET'S GO OUT AND PICK UP CHICKS TOGETHER.
IF YOU ASK THEM OUT, WE'LL HAVE A 100 PERCENT SUCCESS RATIO.
SHUT UP, IDIOT.
WHISPER
SMACK

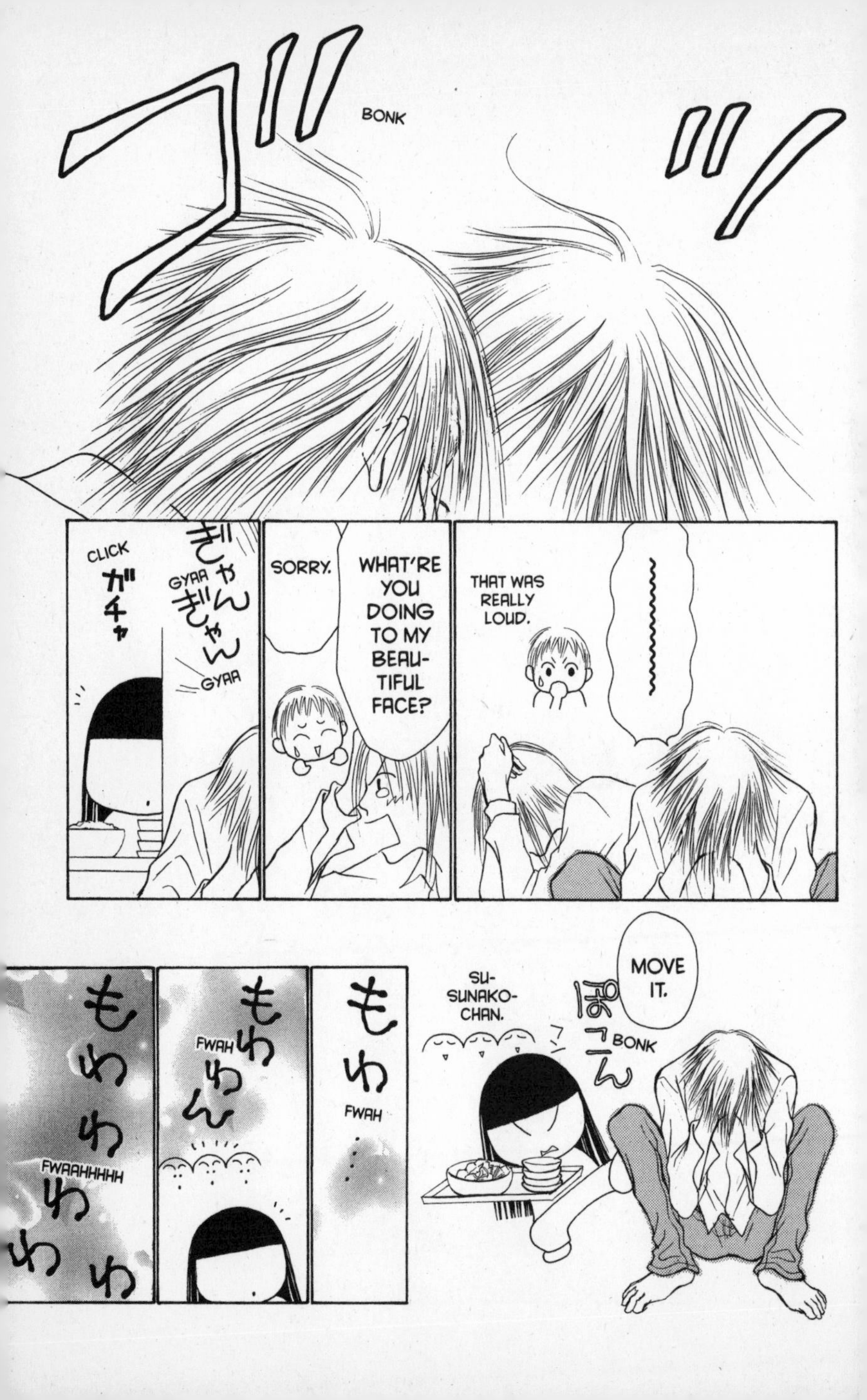
BONK
THAT WAS REALLY LOUD.
WHAT'RE YOU DOING TO MY BEAU-TIFUL FACE?
SORRY.
ぎゃんぎゃん
GYAA
GYAA
CLICK
ガチャ
MOVE IT.
ぽこん
BONK
SU-SUNAKO-CHAN.
もわ
FWAH
もわわん
FWAH
もわわわわわ
FWAAHHHHH

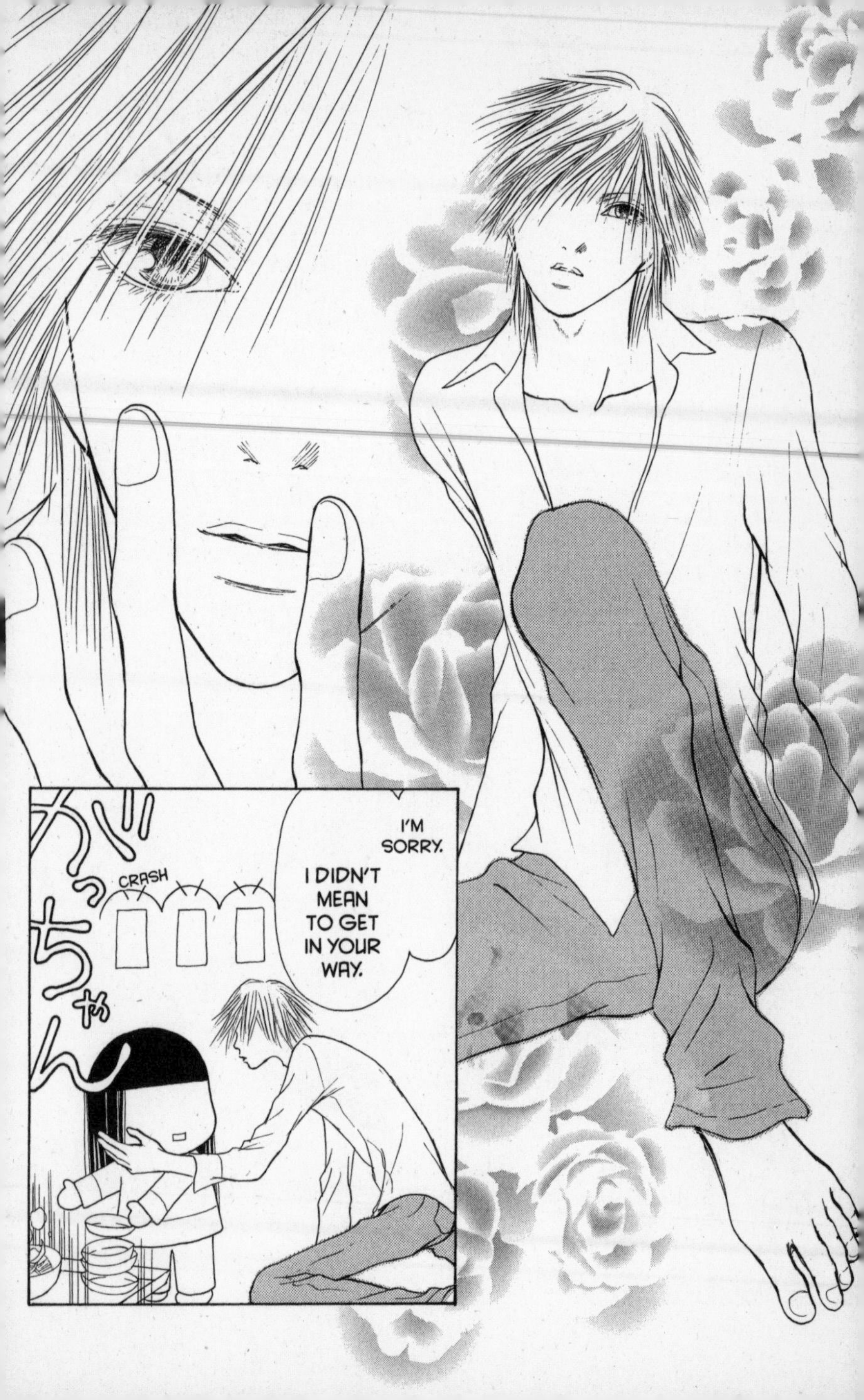
I'M SORRY.
I DIDN'T MEAN TO GET IN YOUR WAY.
CRASH

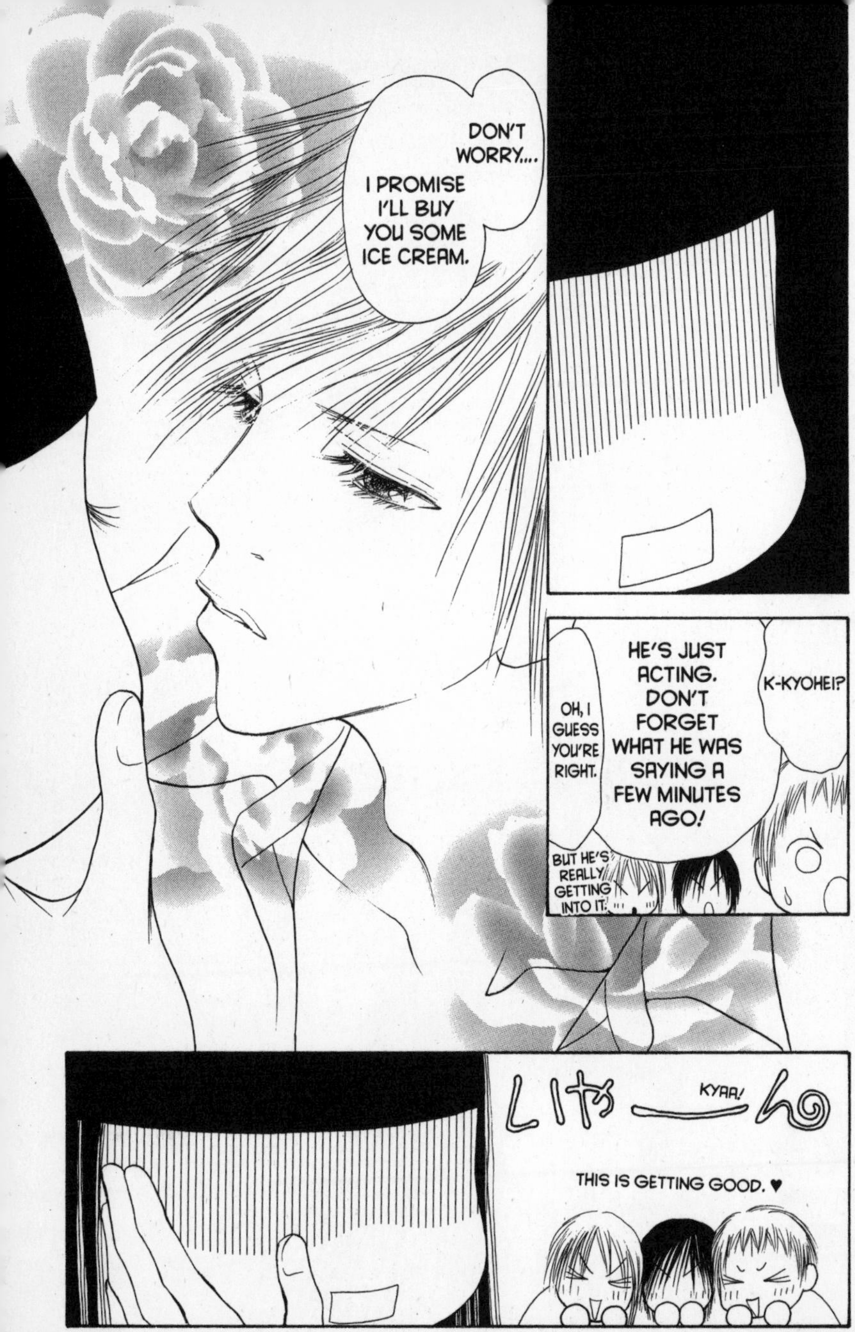
K-KYOHEI?
HE'S JUST ACTING. DON'T FORGET WHAT HE WAS SAYING A FEW MINUTES AGO!
OH, I GUESS YOU'RE RIGHT.
BUT HE'S REALLY GETTING INTO IT.
DON'T WORRY.... I PROMISE I'LL BUY YOU SOME ICE CREAM.
しやーん
KYAA!
THIS IS GETTING GOOD. ♥

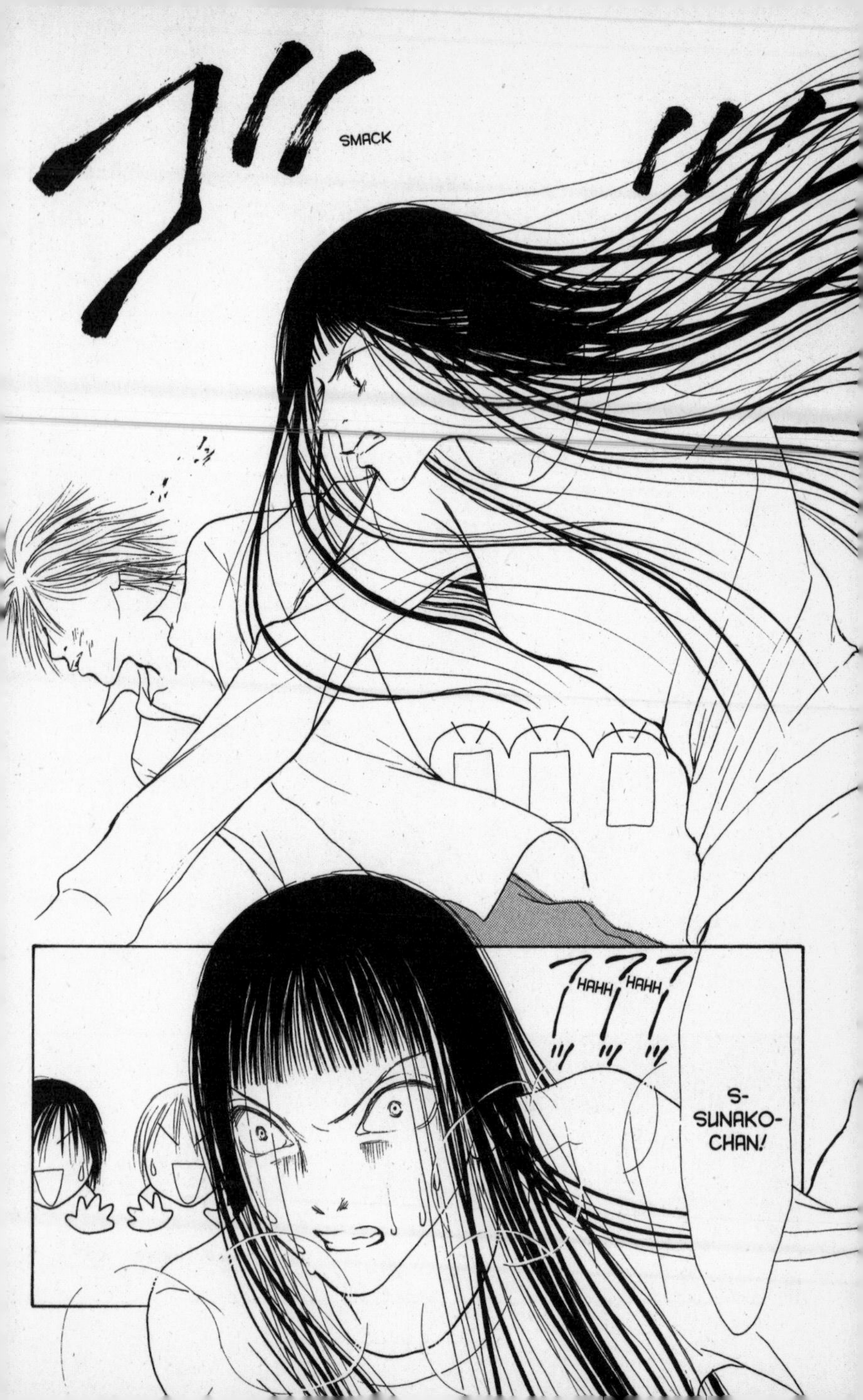
SMACK
HAHH HAHH
S-
SUNAKO-
CHAN!

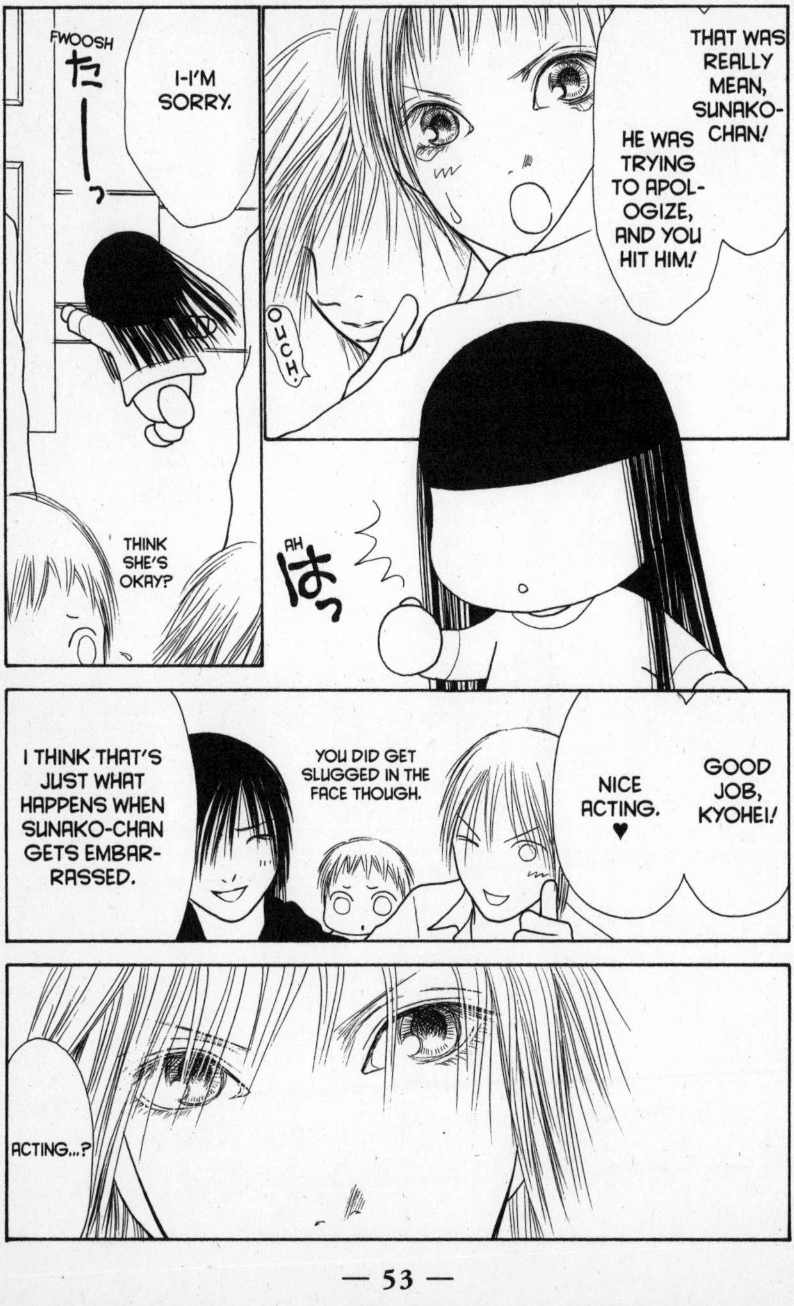
THAT WAS REALLY MEAN, SUNAKO-CHAN!
HE WAS TRYING TO APOLOGIZE, AND YOU HIT HIM!
OUCH.
AH
はっ
I-I'M SORRY.
FWOOSH
たーっ
THINK SHE'S OKAY?
GOOD JOB, KYOHEI!
NICE ACTING. ♥
YOU DID GET SLUGGED IN THE FACE THOUGH.
I THINK THAT'S JUST WHAT HAPPENS WHEN SUNAKO-CHAN GETS EMBARRASSED.
ACTING...?

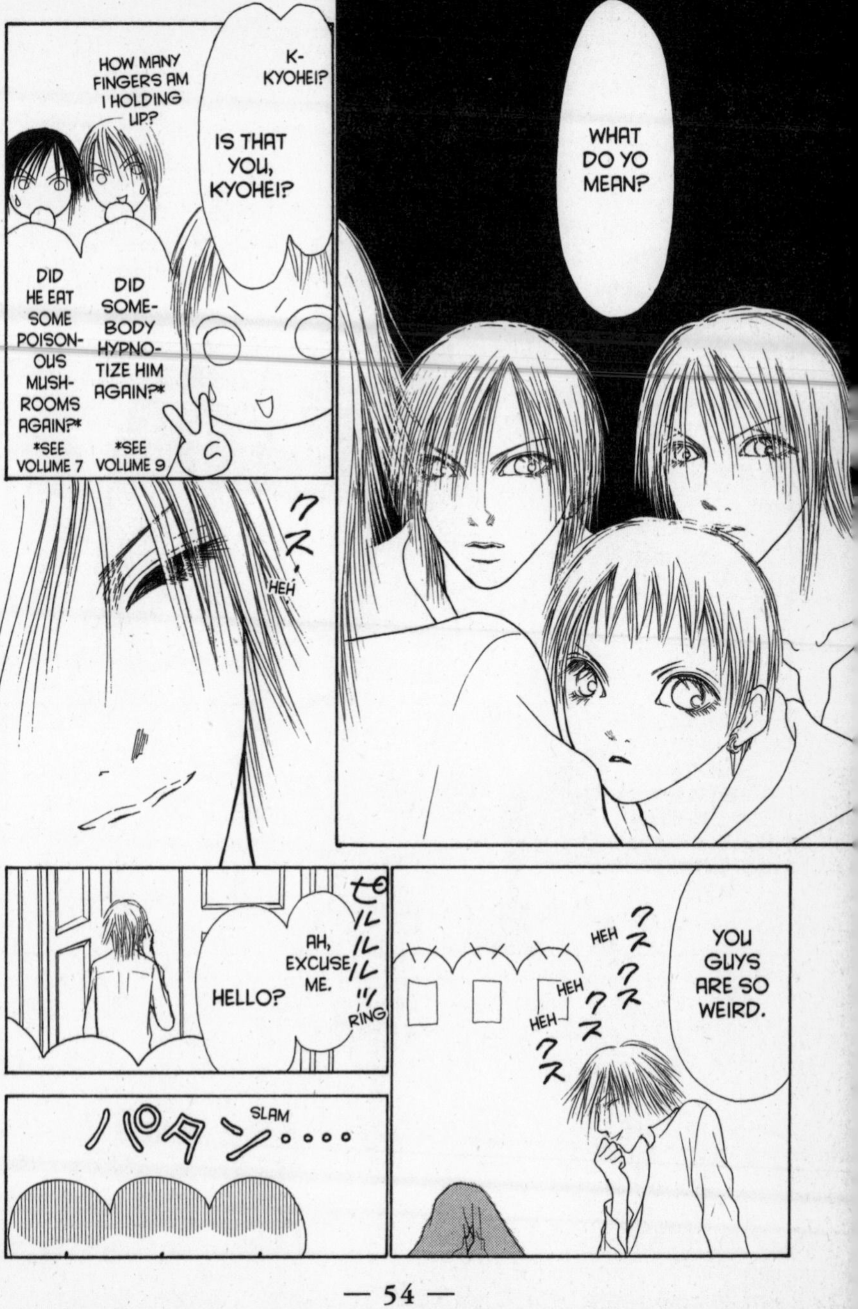
WHAT DO YO MEAN?
K-KYOHEI?
IS THAT YOU, KYOHEI?
HOW MANY FINGERS AM I HOLDING UP?
DID SOMEBODY HYPNOTIZE HIM AGAIN?*
*SEE VOLUME 9
DID HE EAT SOME POISONOUS MUSHROOMS AGAIN?*
*SEE VOLUME 7
クス
HEH
YOU GUYS ARE SO WEIRD.
クスクス
HEH
クス
HEH
クス
HEH
ピルルルッ
RING
AH, EXCUSE ME.
HELLO?
パタン....
SLAM

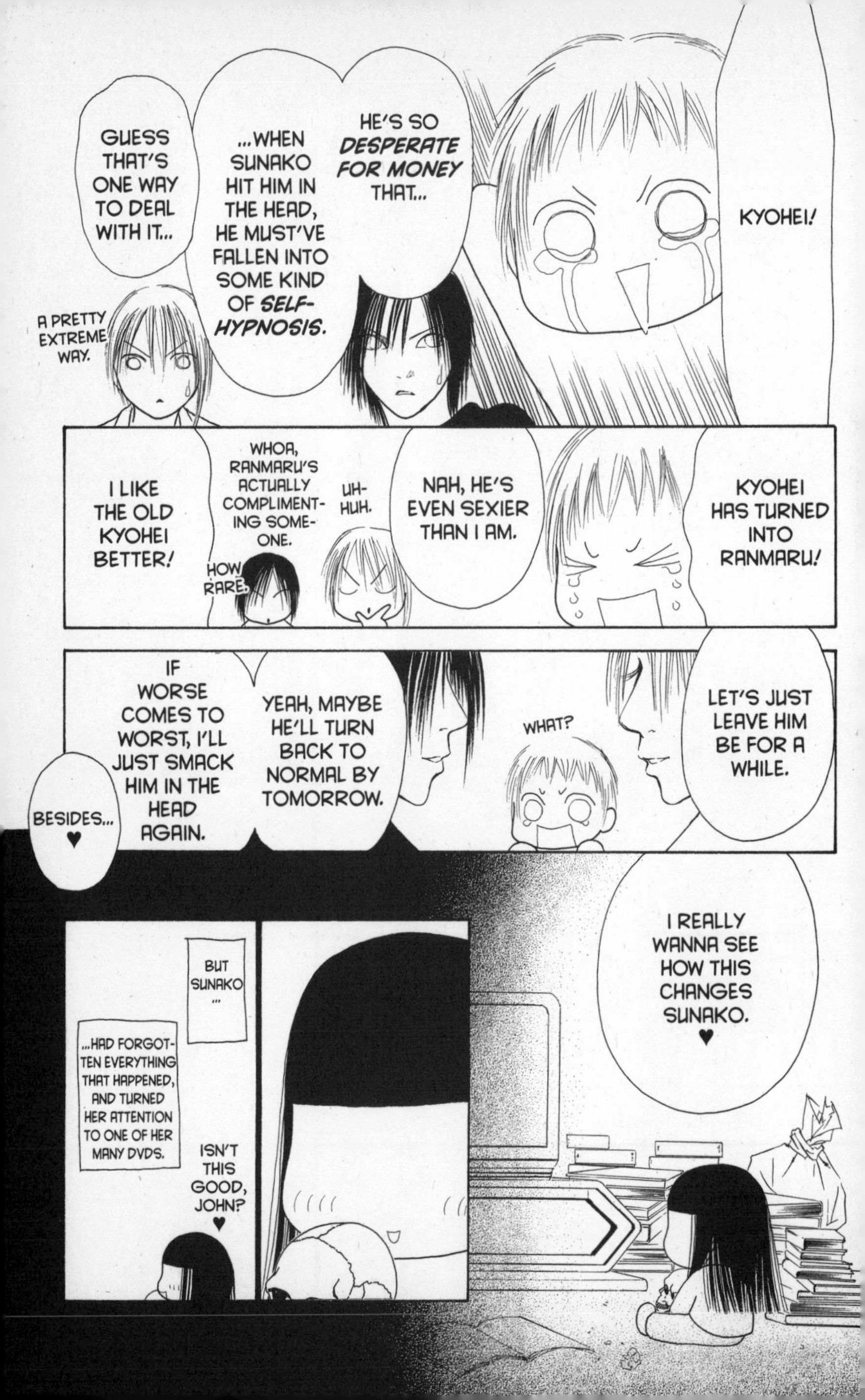
KYOHEI!
HE'S SO *DESPERATE FOR MONEY* THAT...
...WHEN SUNAKO HIT HIM IN THE HEAD, HE MUST'VE FALLEN INTO SOME KIND OF *SELF-HYPNOSIS*.
GUESS THAT'S ONE WAY TO DEAL WITH IT...
A PRETTY EXTREME WAY.
KYOHEI HAS TURNED INTO RANMARU!
NAH, HE'S EVEN SEXIER THAN I AM.
UH-HUH.
WHOA, RANMARU'S ACTUALLY COMPLIMENTING SOMEONE.
HOW RARE.
I LIKE THE OLD KYOHEI BETTER!
LET'S JUST LEAVE HIM BE FOR A WHILE.
WHAT?
YEAH, MAYBE HE'LL TURN BACK TO NORMAL BY TOMORROW.
IF WORSE COMES TO WORST, I'LL JUST SMACK HIM IN THE HEAD AGAIN.
BESIDES... ♥
I REALLY WANNA SEE HOW THIS CHANGES SUNAKO. ♥
BUT SUNAKO...
...HAD FORGOTTEN EVERYTHING THAT HAPPENED, AND TURNED HER ATTENTION TO ONE OF HER MANY DVDS.
ISN'T THIS GOOD, JOHN? ♥

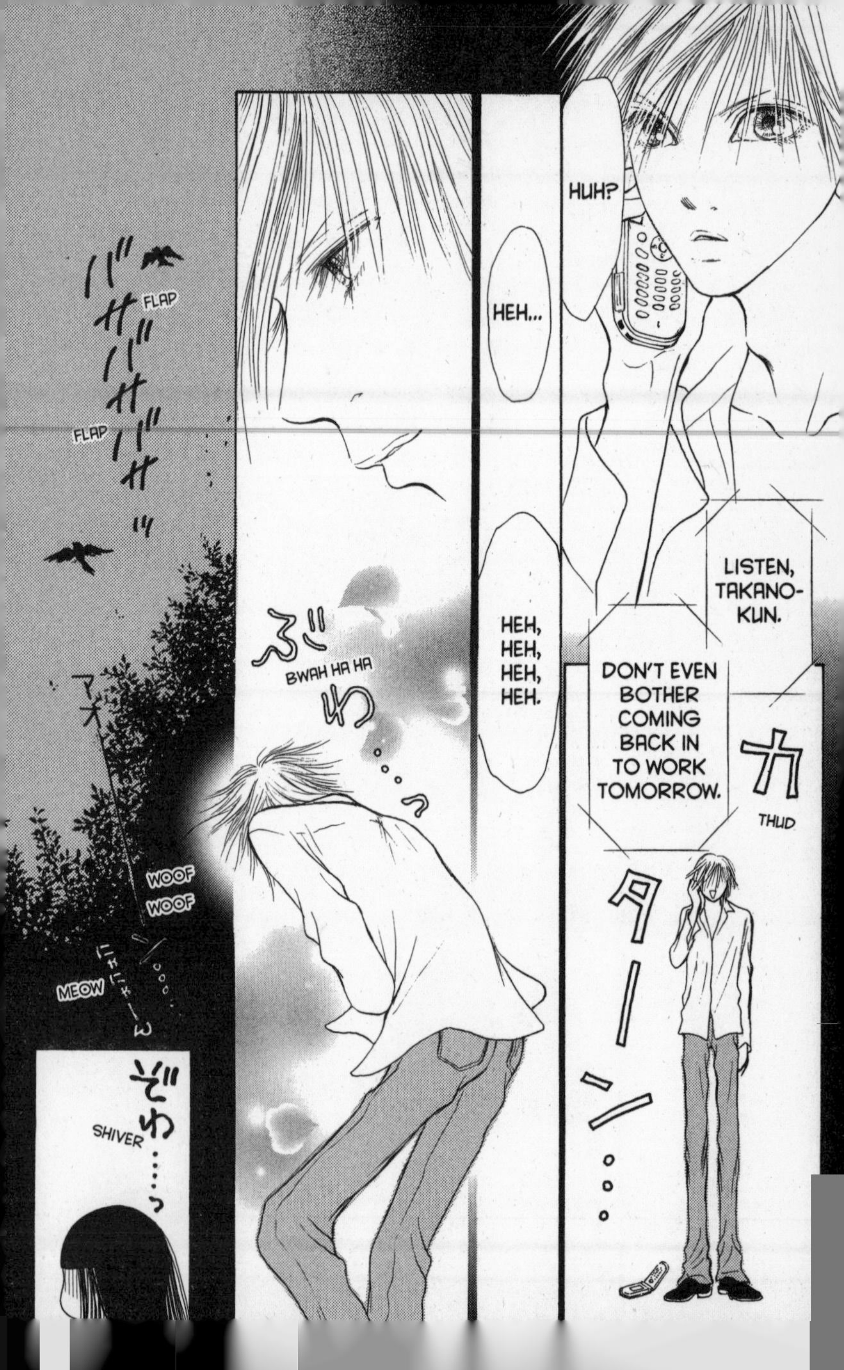
HUH?
LISTEN, TAKANO-KUN.
DON'T EVEN BOTHER COMING BACK IN TO WORK TOMORROW.
THUD
HEH...
HEH, HEH, HEH, HEH.
BWAH HA HA
FLAP
FLAP
WOOF
WOOF
MEOW
SHIVER

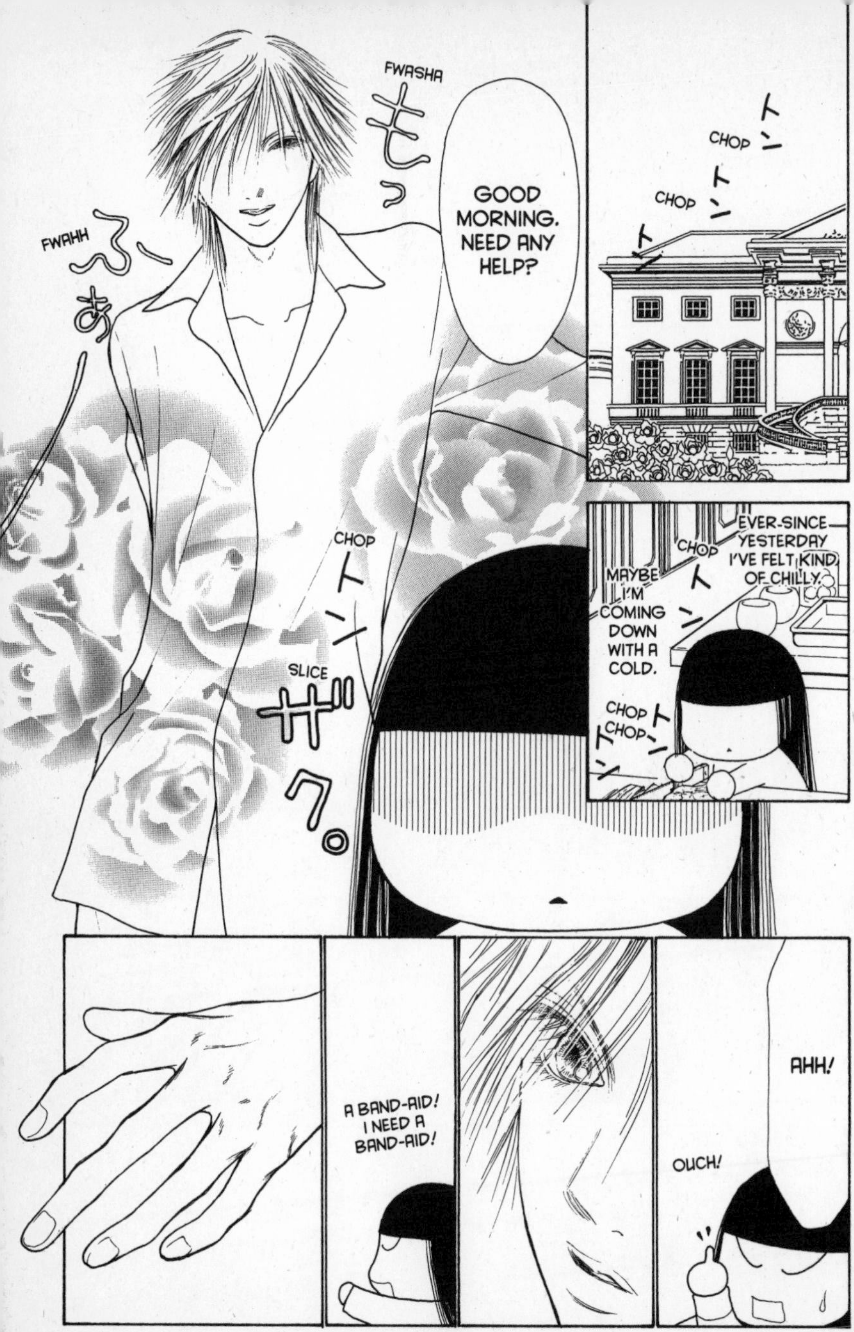
CHOP
トン
CHOP
トン
トン
EVER-SINCE YESTERDAY I'VE FELT KIND OF CHILLY.
CHOP
トン
MAYBE I'M COMING DOWN WITH A COLD.
CHOP
CHOP
トン
トン
FWASHA
GOOD MORNING. NEED ANY HELP?
FWAHH
CHOP
トン
SLICE
ザク。
AHH!
OUCH!
A BAND-AID! I NEED A BAND-AID!

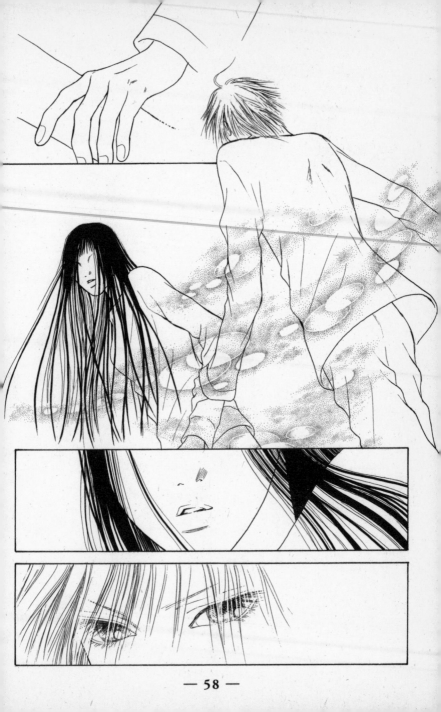

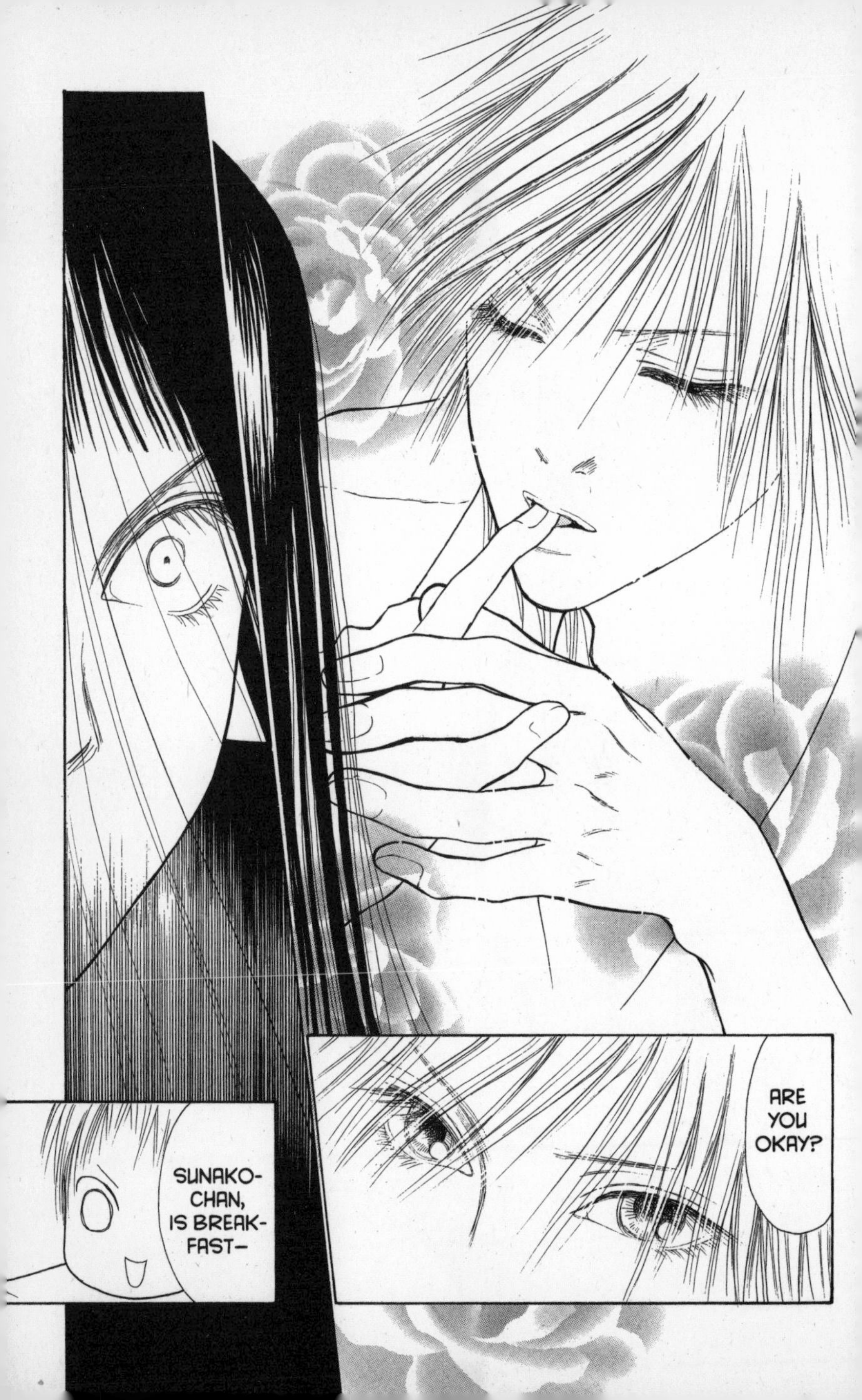
ARE YOU OKAY?
SUNAKO-CHAN, IS BREAK-FAST—

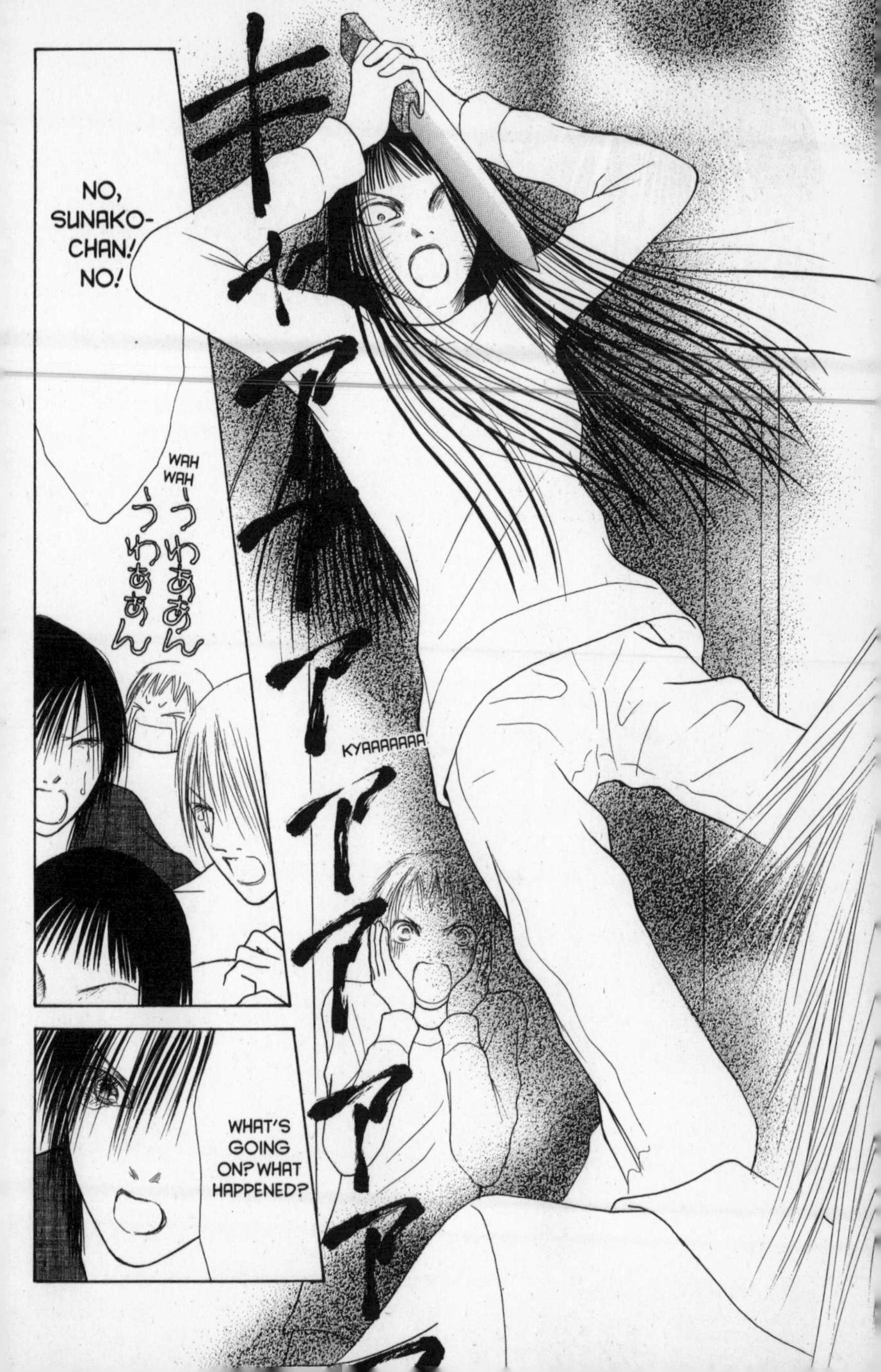
KYAAAAAAA
NO, SUNAKO-CHAN! NO!
WAH WAH
うわああん うわああん
WHAT'S GOING ON? WHAT HAPPENED?

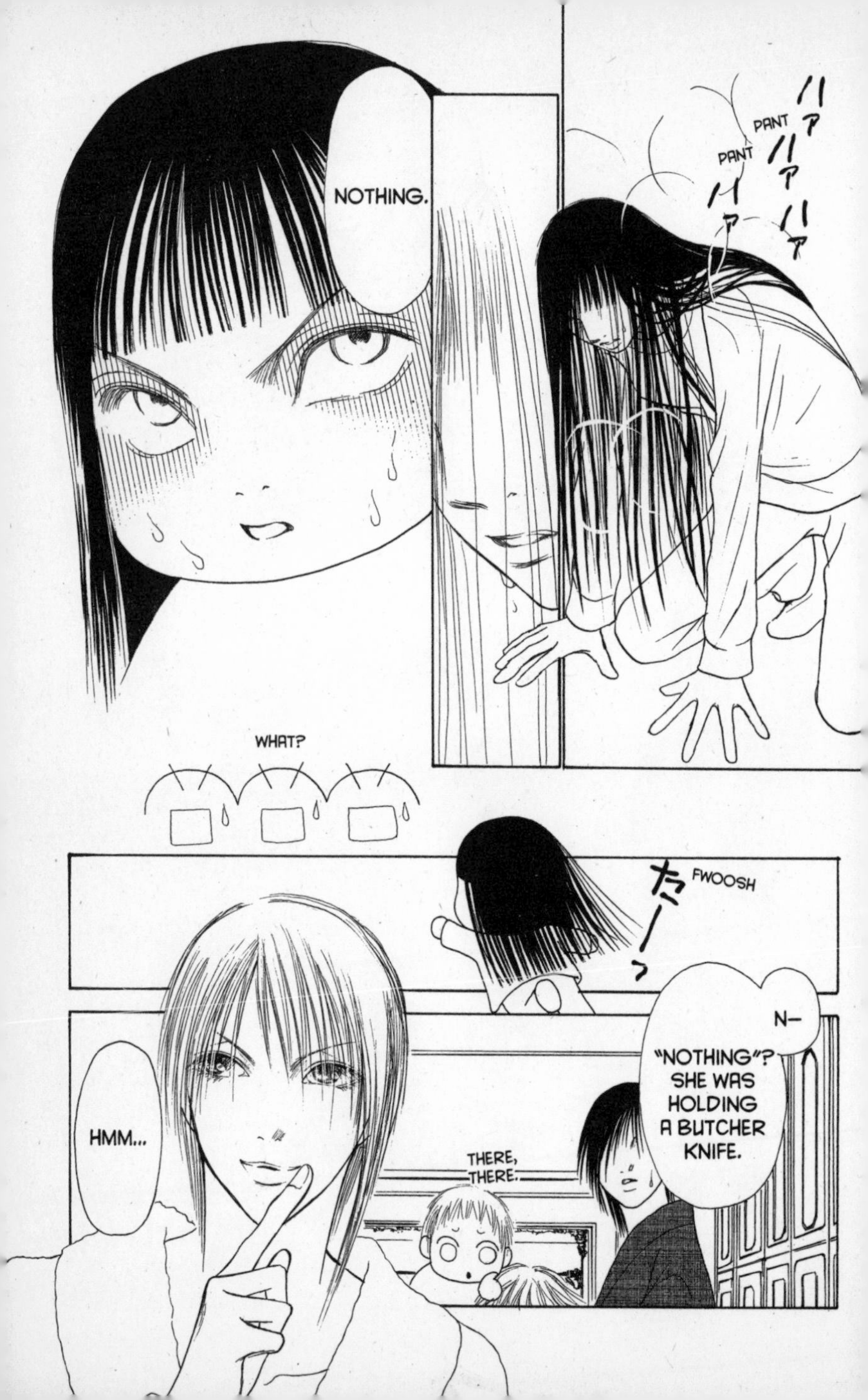
ハァハァハァハァ
PANT
PANT
NOTHING.
WHAT?
たーっ
FWOOSH
N–
"NOTHING"? SHE WAS HOLDING A BUTCHER KNIFE.
THERE, THERE.
HMM...

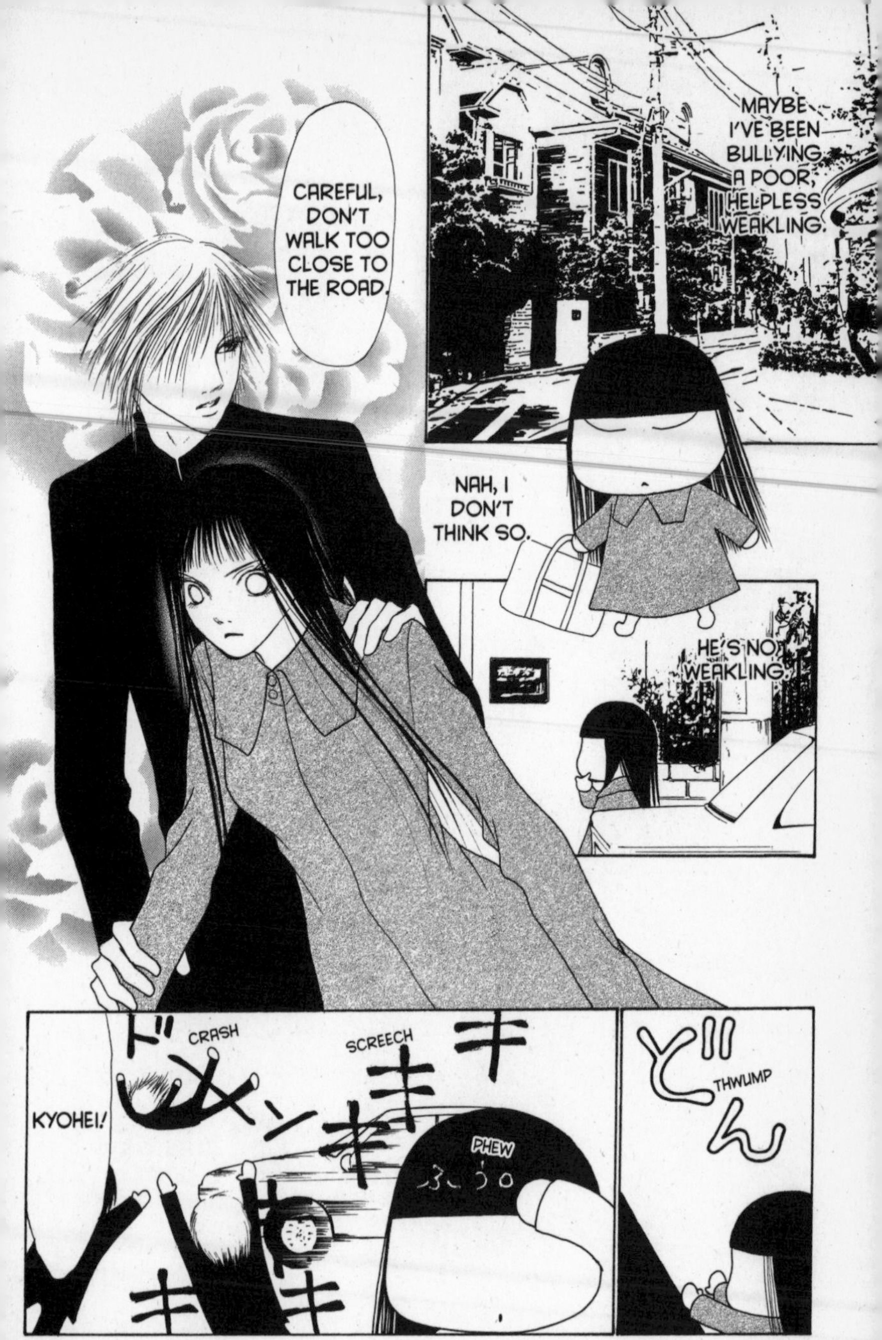
MAYBE I'VE BEEN BULLYING A POOR, HELPLESS WEAKLING.
NAH, I DON'T THINK SO.
HE'S NO WEAKLING.
CAREFUL, DON'T WALK TOO CLOSE TO THE ROAD.
でん
THWUMP
SCREECH
CRASH
KYOHEI!
PHEW

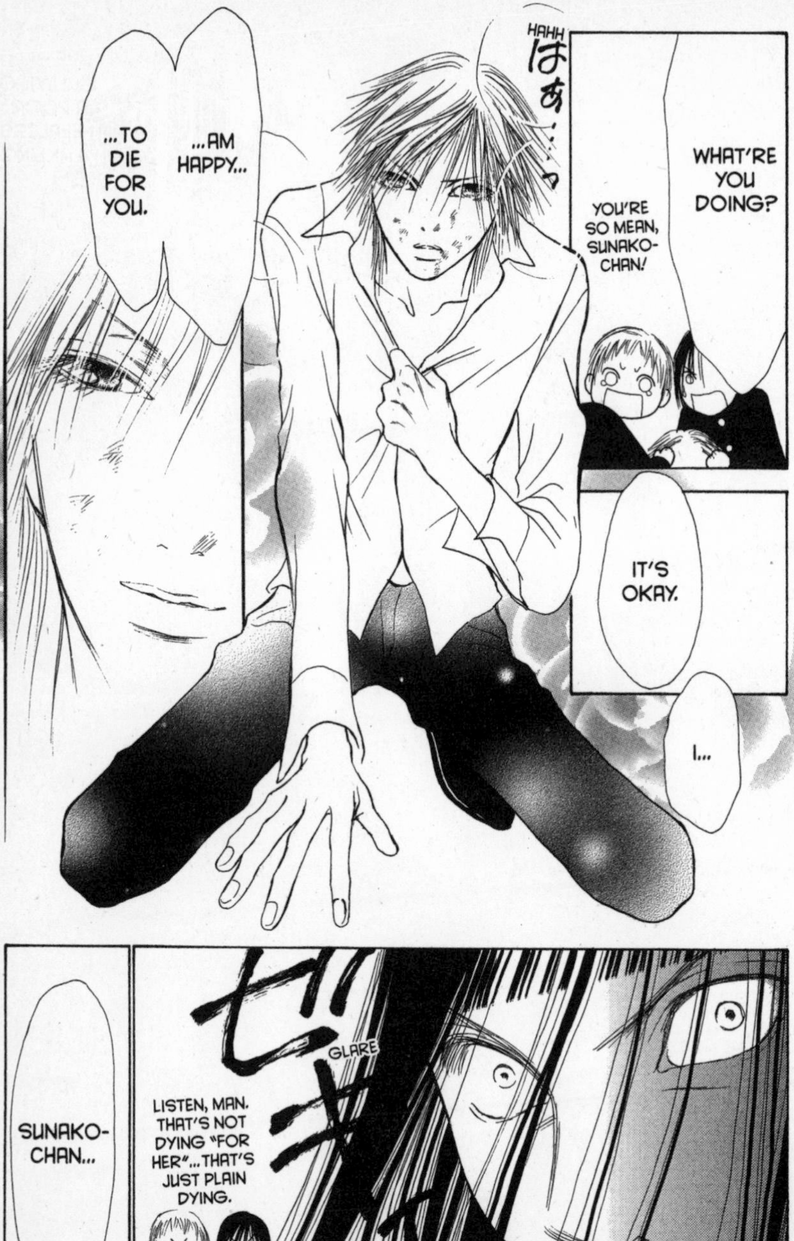

WHAT'RE YOU DOING?
YOU'RE SO MEAN, SUNAKO-CHAN!
IT'S OKAY.
I...
HAHH
はぁ
...AM HAPPY...
...TO DIE FOR YOU.
GLARE
LISTEN, MAN. THAT'S NOT DYING "FOR HER"...THAT'S JUST PLAIN DYING.
SUNAKO-CHAN...

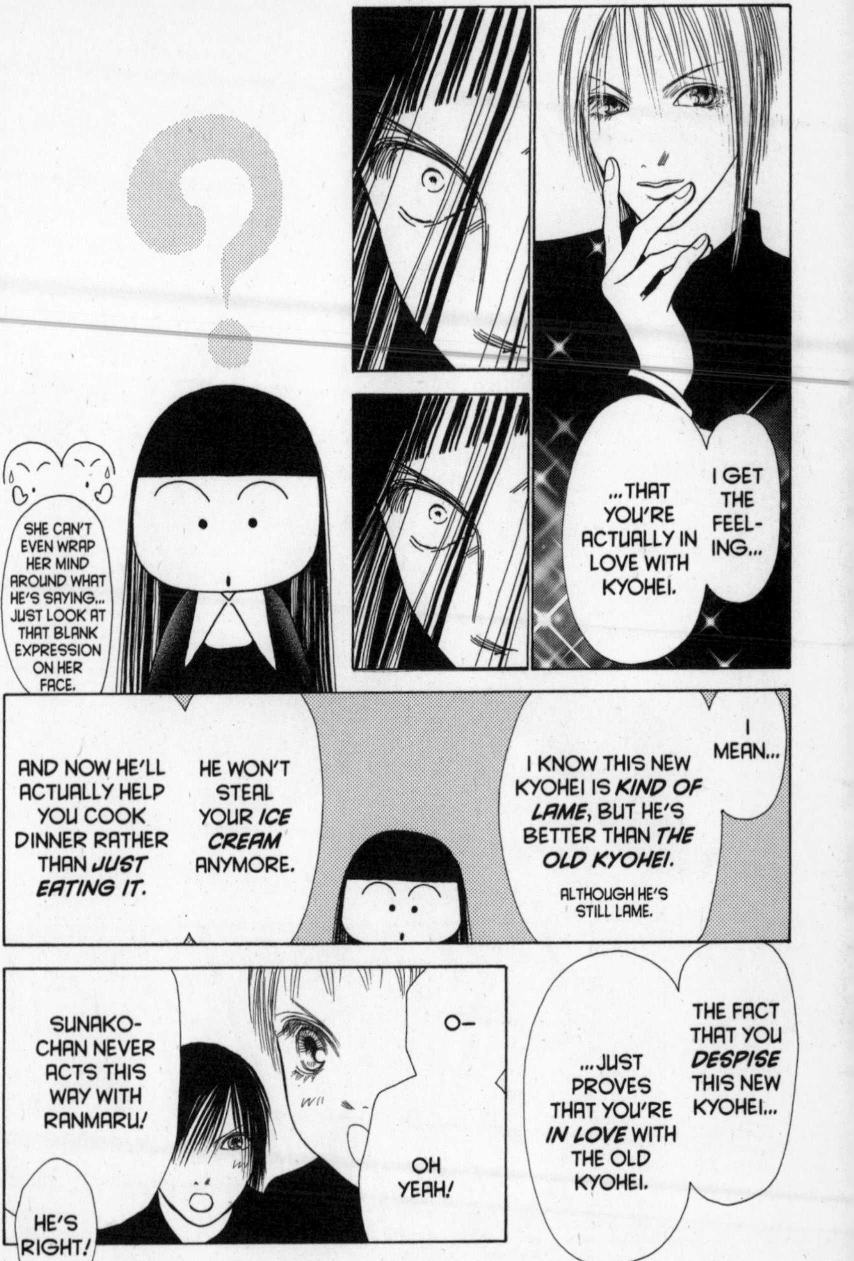
I GET THE FEEL-ING...
...THAT YOU'RE ACTUALLY IN LOVE WITH KYOHEI.
SHE CAN'T EVEN WRAP HER MIND AROUND WHAT HE'S SAYING... JUST LOOK AT THAT BLANK EXPRESSION ON HER FACE.
I MEAN...
I KNOW THIS NEW KYOHEI IS *KIND OF LAME*, BUT HE'S BETTER THAN *THE OLD KYOHEI*.
ALTHOUGH HE'S STILL LAME.
HE WON'T STEAL YOUR *ICE CREAM* ANYMORE.
AND NOW HE'LL ACTUALLY HELP YOU COOK DINNER RATHER THAN *JUST EATING IT*.
THE FACT THAT YOU *DESPISE* THIS NEW KYOHEI...
...JUST PROVES THAT YOU'RE *IN LOVE* WITH THE OLD KYOHEI.
O-
OH YEAH!
SUNAKO-CHAN NEVER ACTS THIS WAY WITH RANMARU!
HE'S RIGHT!

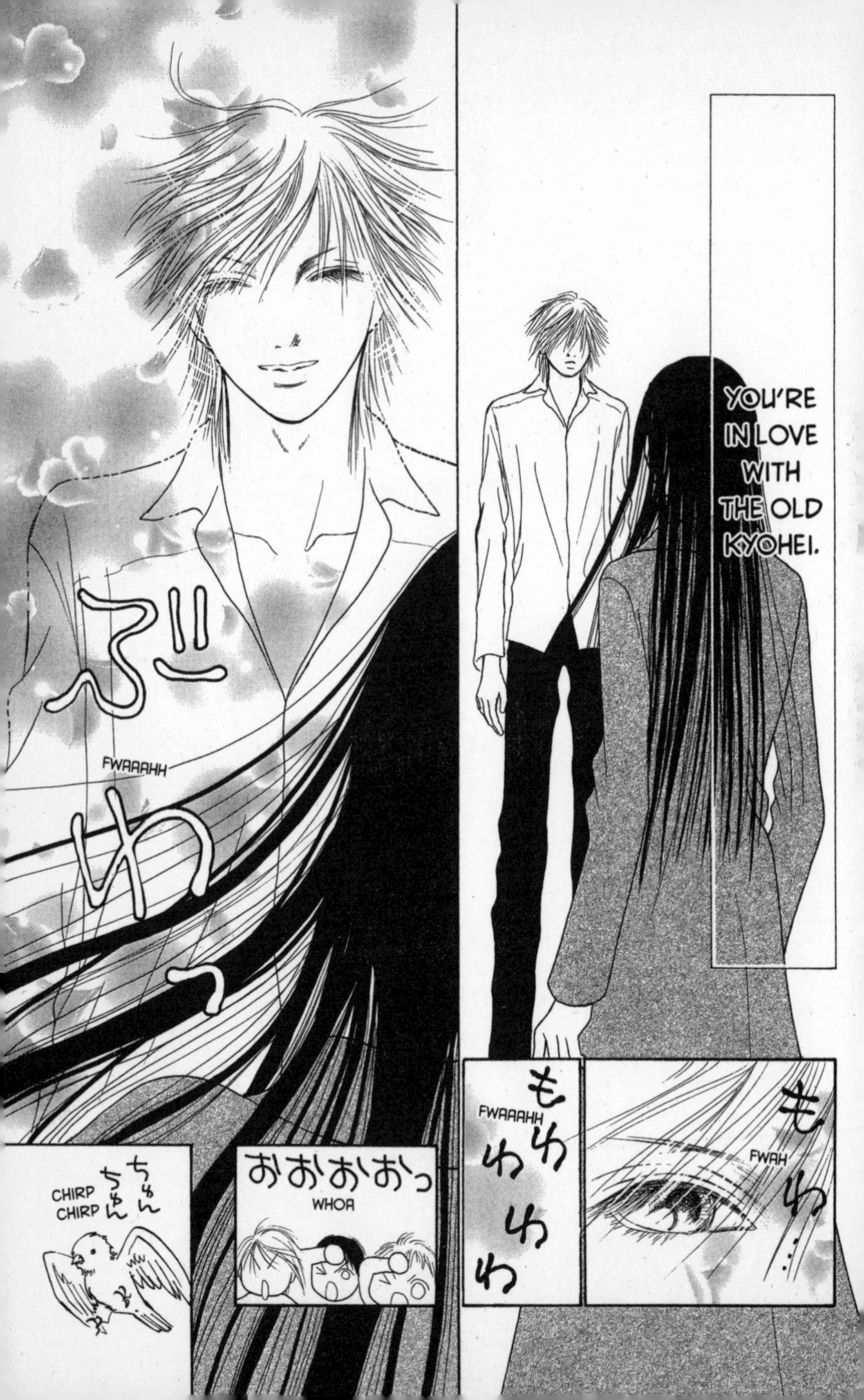

YOU'RE IN LOVE WITH THE OLD KYOHEI.
もわ…
FWAH
もわわわわ
FWAAAHH
ふぃゆっ
FWAAAHH
おおおおっ
WHOA
ちゅんちゅん
CHIRP CHIRP

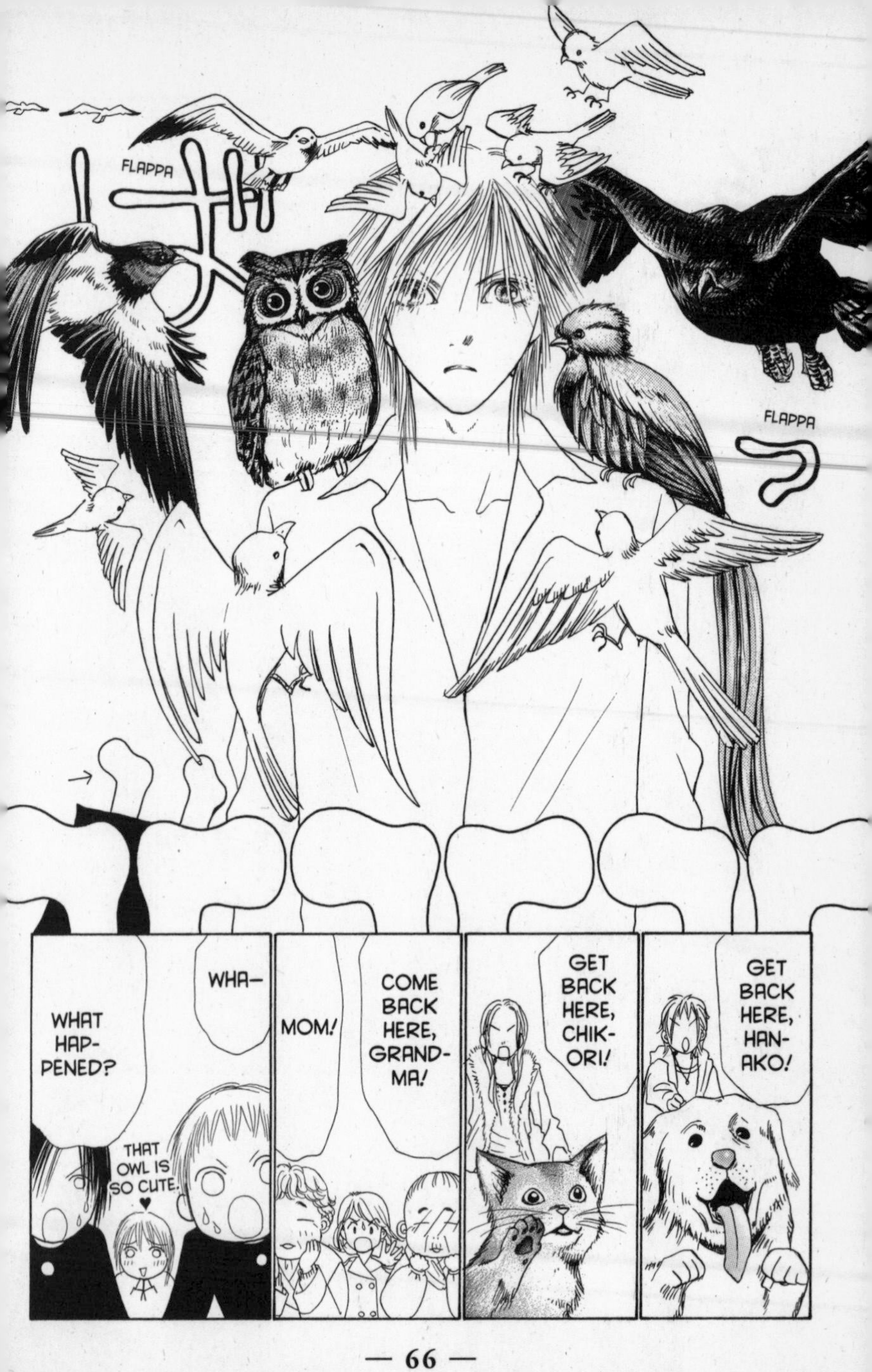
FLAPPA
FLAPPA
GET BACK HERE, HANAKO!
GET BACK HERE, CHIKORI!
COME BACK HERE, GRANDMA!
MOM!
WHA—
WHAT HAPPENED?
THAT OWL IS SO CUTE. ♥

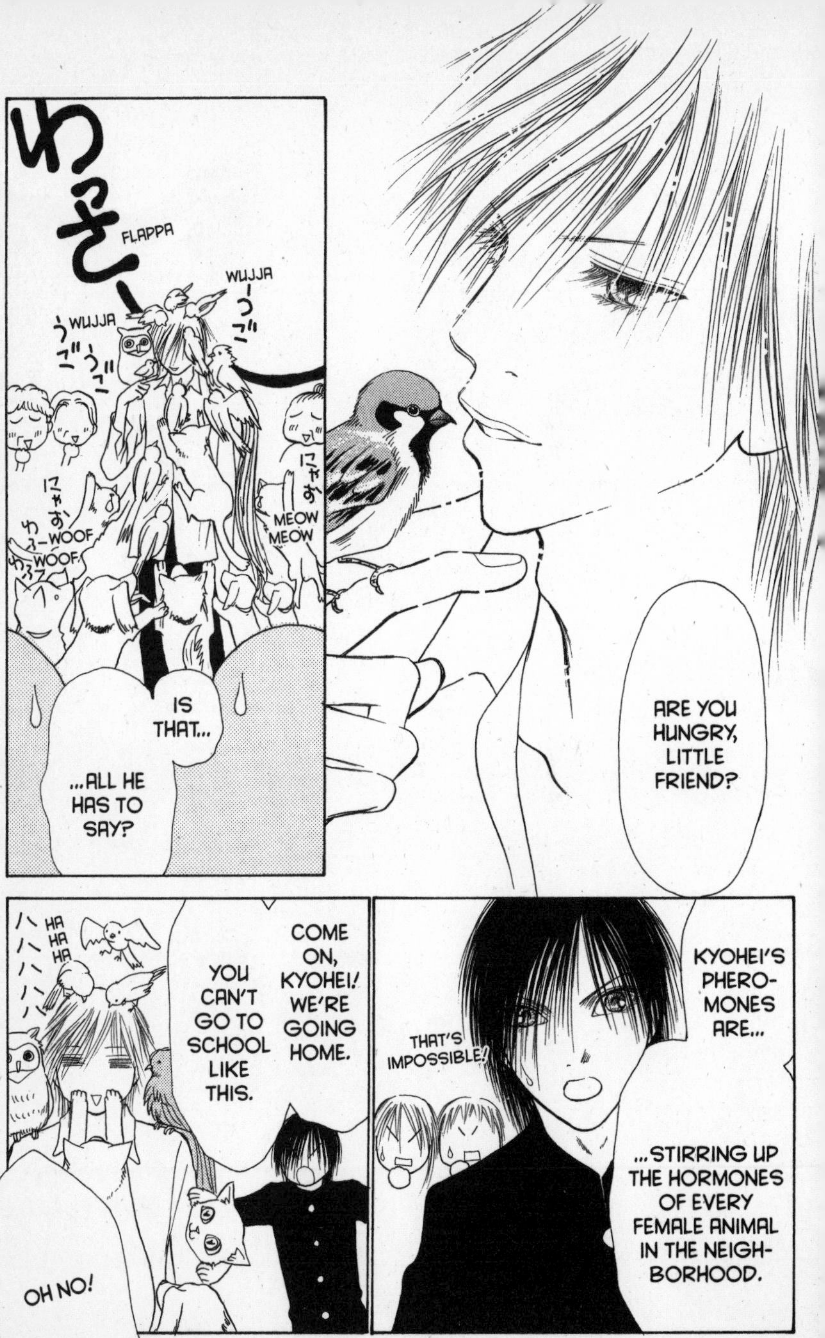
ARE YOU HUNGRY, LITTLE FRIEND?
わっさー
FLAPPA
WUJJA
うごうご
WUJJA
うごうご
にゃお
MEOW MEOW
にゃお
わふ
WOOF WOOF
IS THAT...
...ALL HE HAS TO SAY?
KYOHEI'S PHERO-MONES ARE...
THAT'S IMPOSSIBLE!
...STIRRING UP THE HORMONES OF EVERY FEMALE ANIMAL IN THE NEIGH-BORHOOD.
COME ON, KYOHEI! WE'RE GOING HOME.
YOU CAN'T GO TO SCHOOL LIKE THIS.
ハハハハハ
HA HA HA
OH NO!

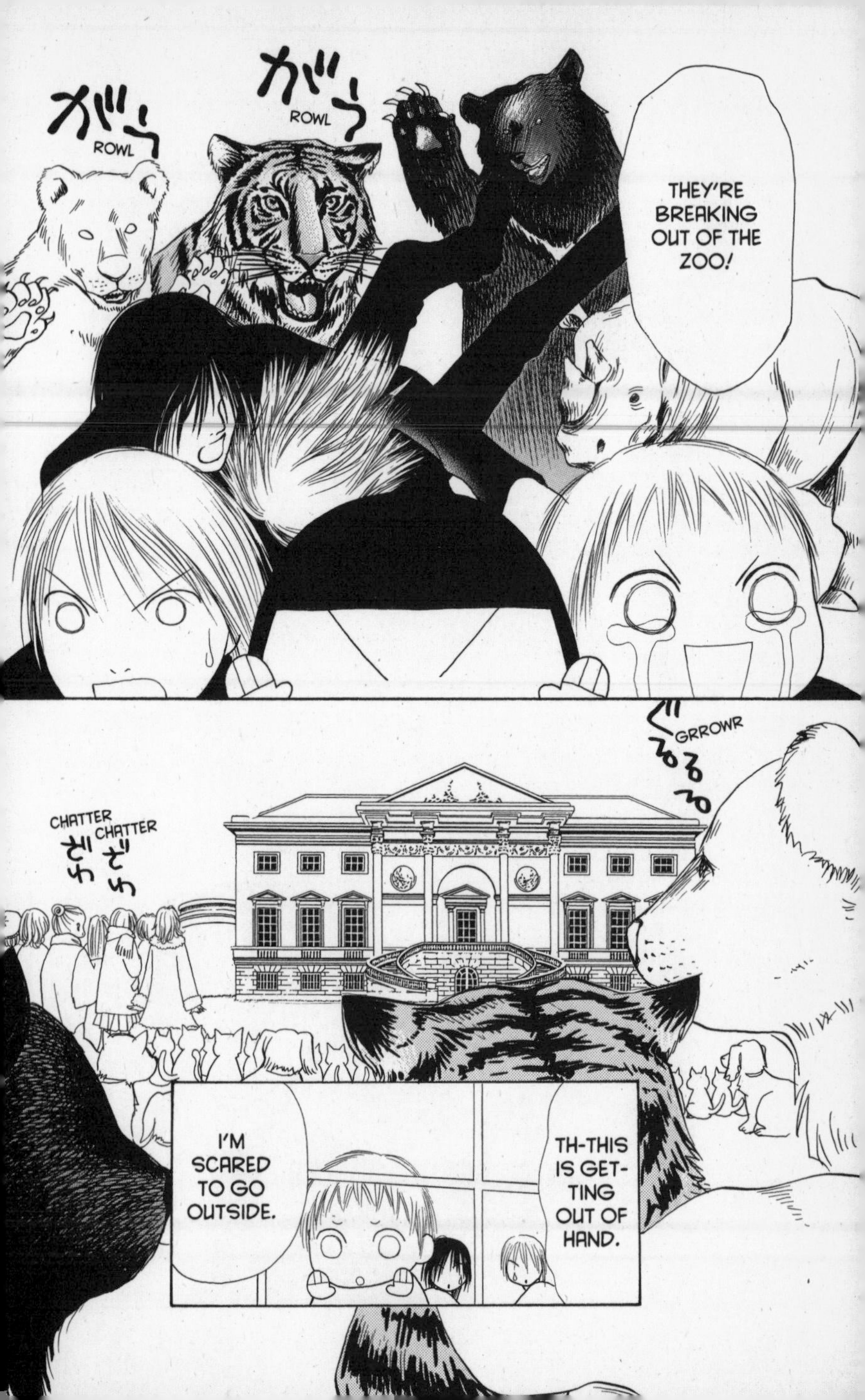
THEY'RE BREAKING OUT OF THE ZOO!
がう
ROWL
がう
ROWL
ぐるる
GRROWR
ざわざわ
CHATTER CHATTER
TH-THIS IS GET-TING OUT OF HAND.
I'M SCARED TO GO OUTSIDE.

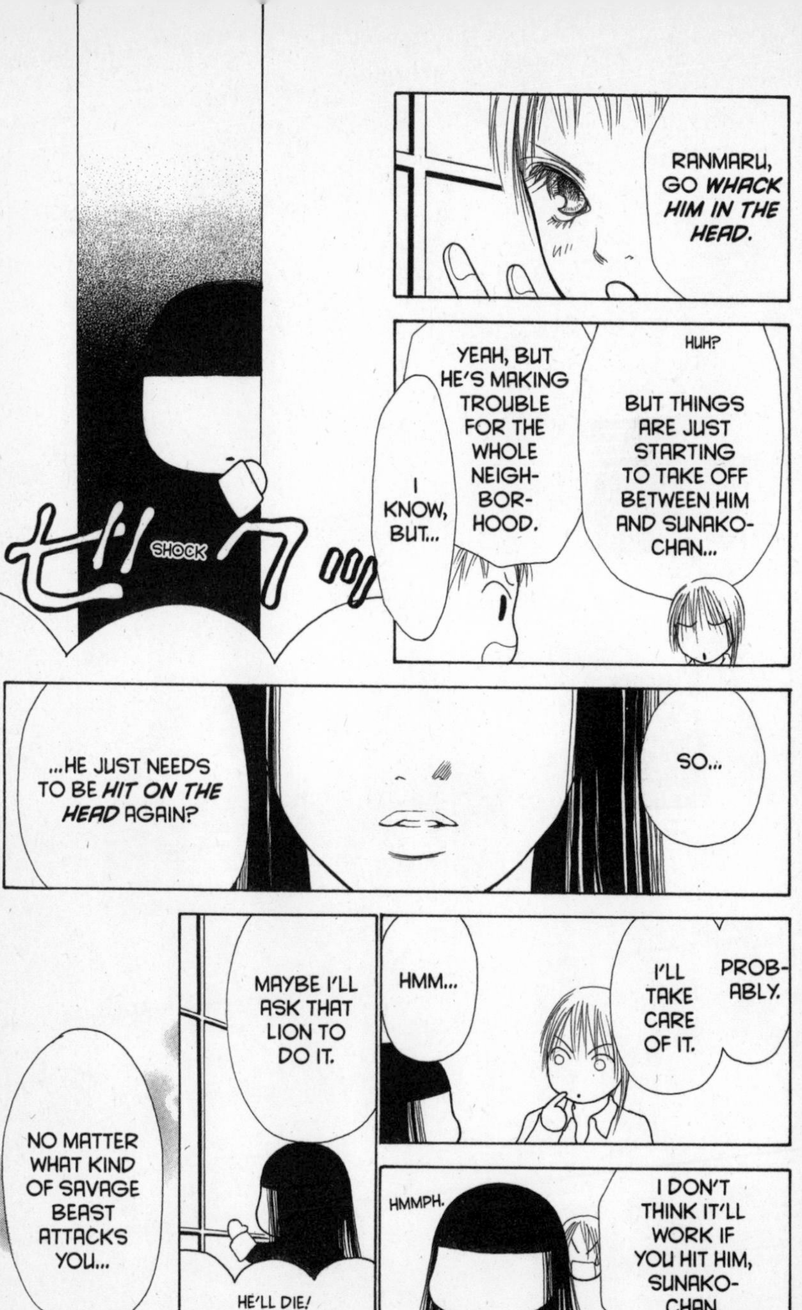
RANMARU, GO *WHACK HIM IN THE HEAD.*
HUH?
BUT THINGS ARE JUST STARTING TO TAKE OFF BETWEEN HIM AND SUNAKO-CHAN...
YEAH, BUT HE'S MAKING TROUBLE FOR THE WHOLE NEIGH-BOR-HOOD.
I KNOW, BUT...
SHOCK
SO...
...HE JUST NEEDS TO BE *HIT ON THE HEAD* AGAIN?
PROB-ABLY.
I'LL TAKE CARE OF IT.
HMM...
I DON'T THINK IT'LL WORK IF YOU HIT HIM, SUNAKO-CHAN.
HMMPH.
MAYBE I'LL ASK THAT LION TO DO IT.
HE'LL DIE!
NO MATTER WHAT KIND OF SAVAGE BEAST ATTACKS YOU...

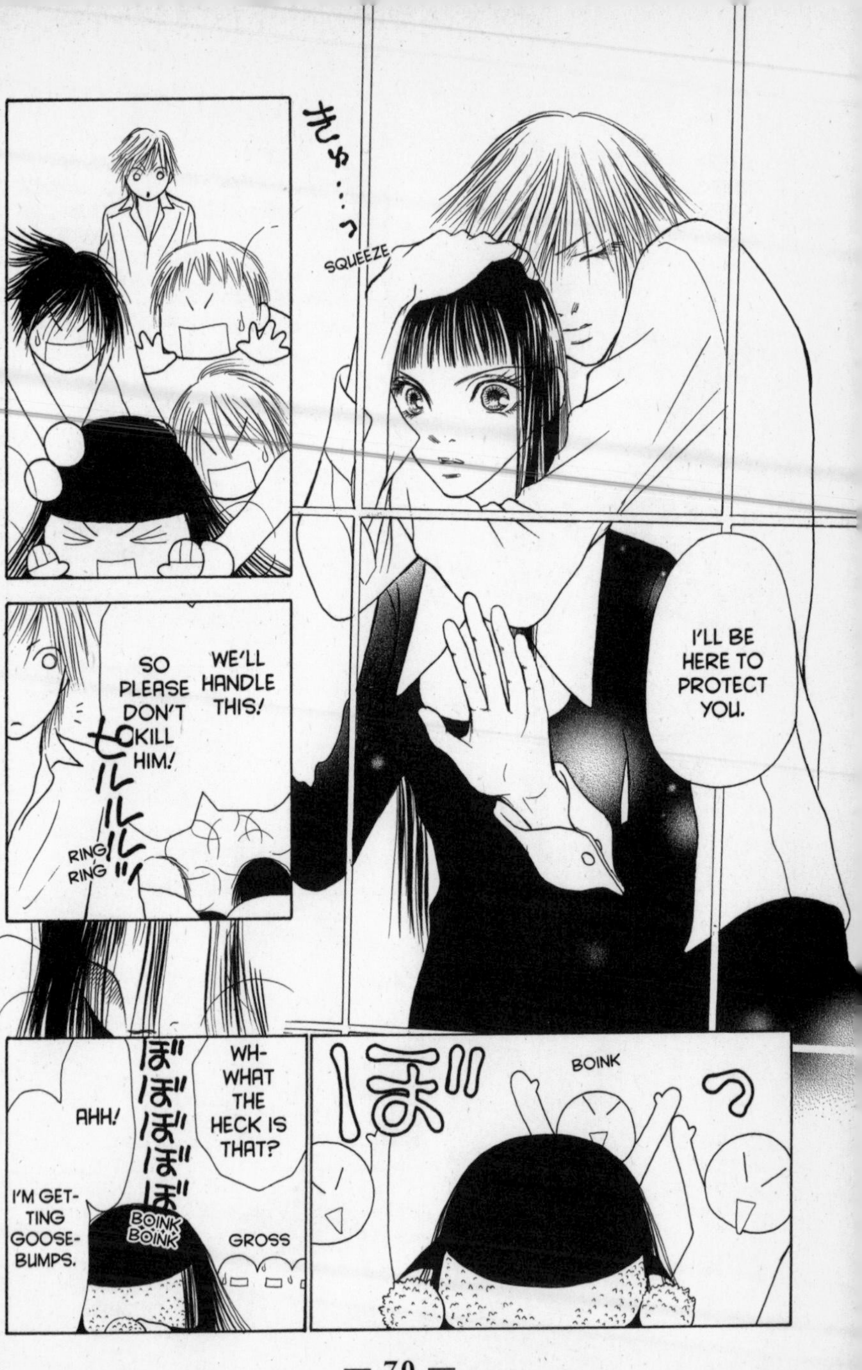
きゅ…っ
SQUEEZE
I'LL BE HERE TO PROTECT YOU.
WE'LL HANDLE THIS!
SO PLEASE DON'T KILL HIM!
ピルルルッ
RING RING
ぽっ
BOINK
WH-WHAT THE HECK IS THAT?
AHH!
ぼぼぼぼぼ
BOINK BOINK
GROSS
I'M GETTING GOOSEBUMPS.

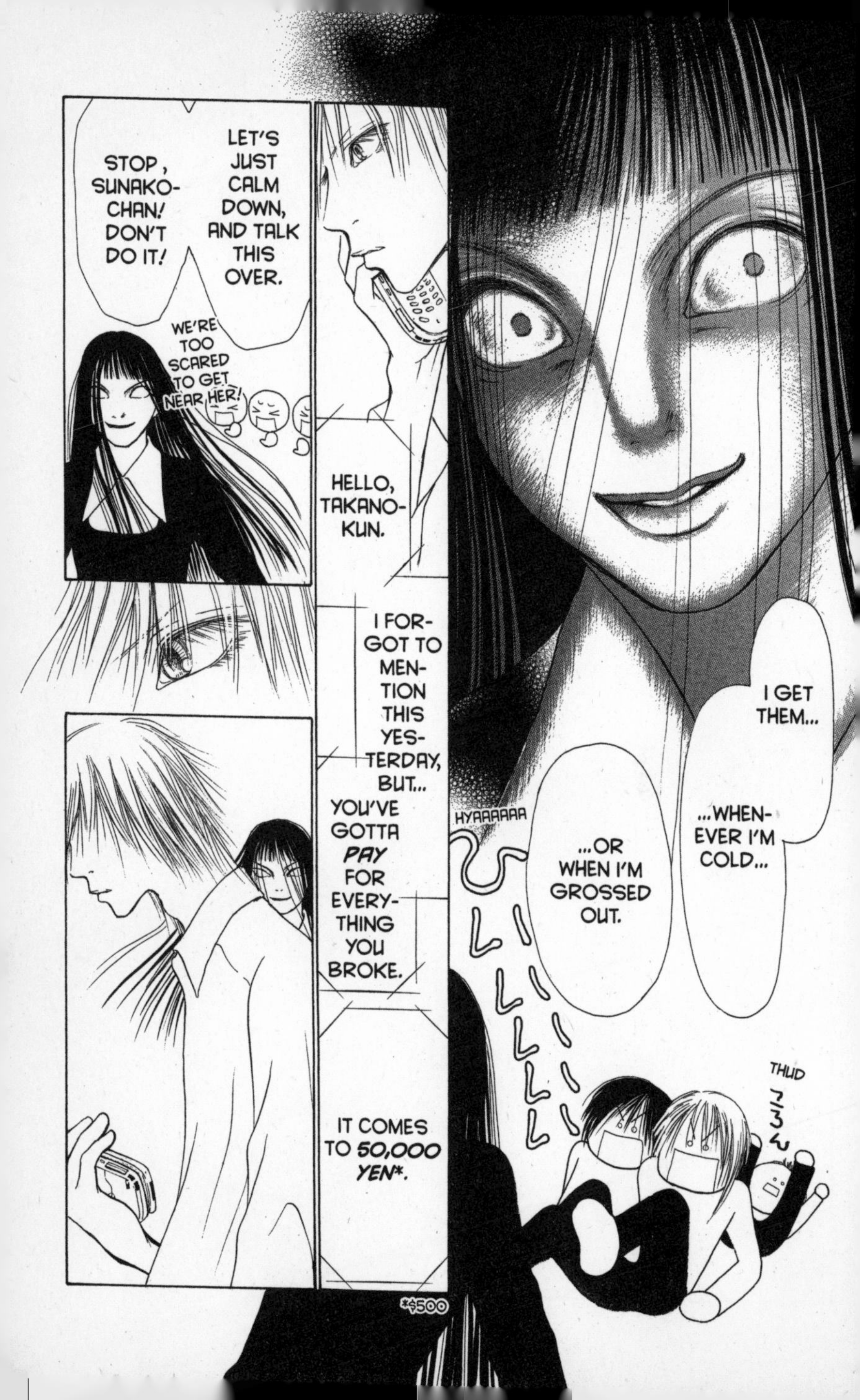
I GET THEM...
...WHENEVER I'M COLD...
...OR WHEN I'M GROSSED OUT.
HYAAAAAA
THUD
LET'S JUST CALM DOWN, AND TALK THIS OVER.
STOP, SUNAKO-CHAN! DON'T DO IT!
WE'RE TOO SCARED TO GET NEAR HER!
HELLO, TAKANO-KUN.
I FORGOT TO MENTION THIS YESTERDAY, BUT...
YOU'VE GOTTA *PAY* FOR EVERYTHING YOU BROKE.
IT COMES TO 50,000 YEN*.
*$500

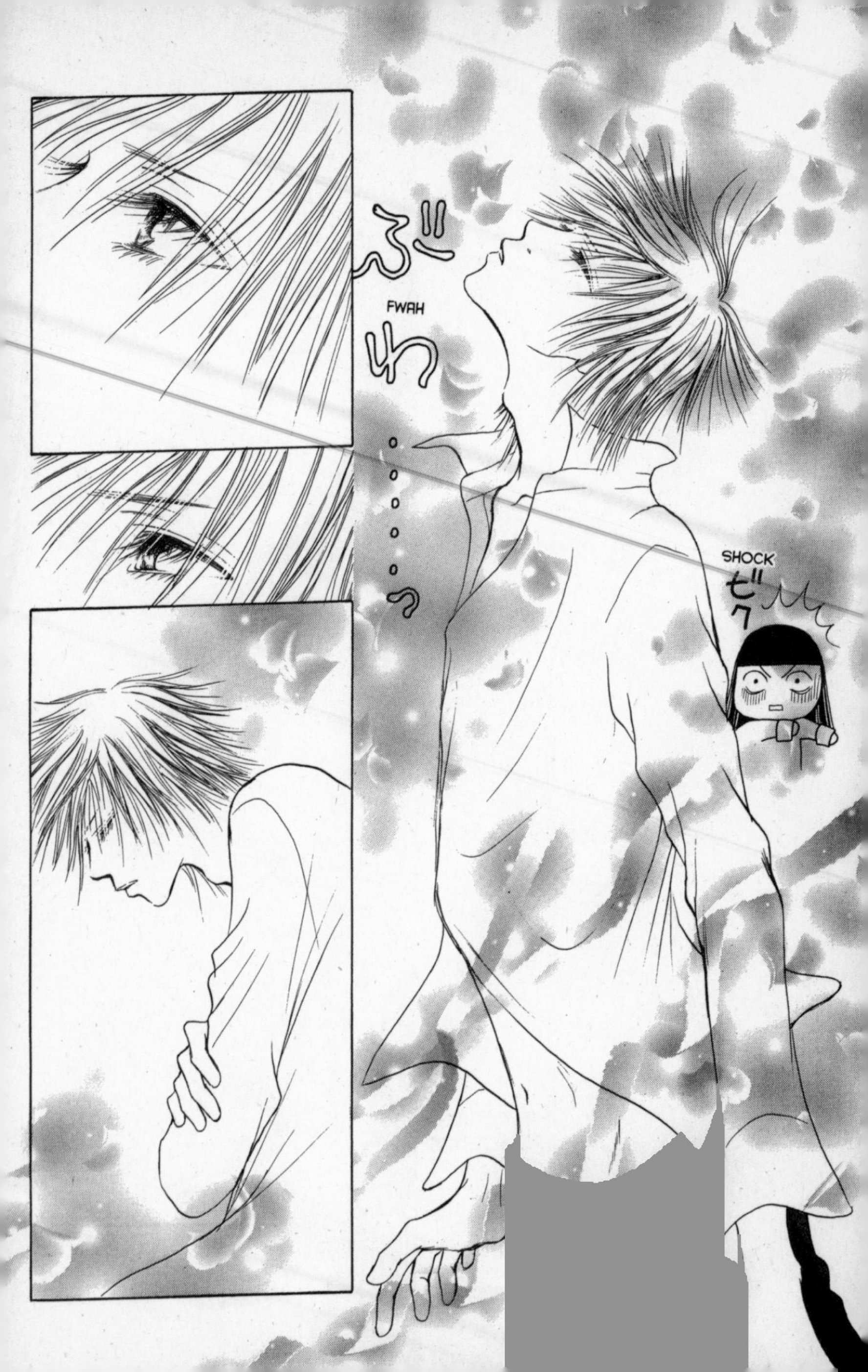
FWAH
SHOCK

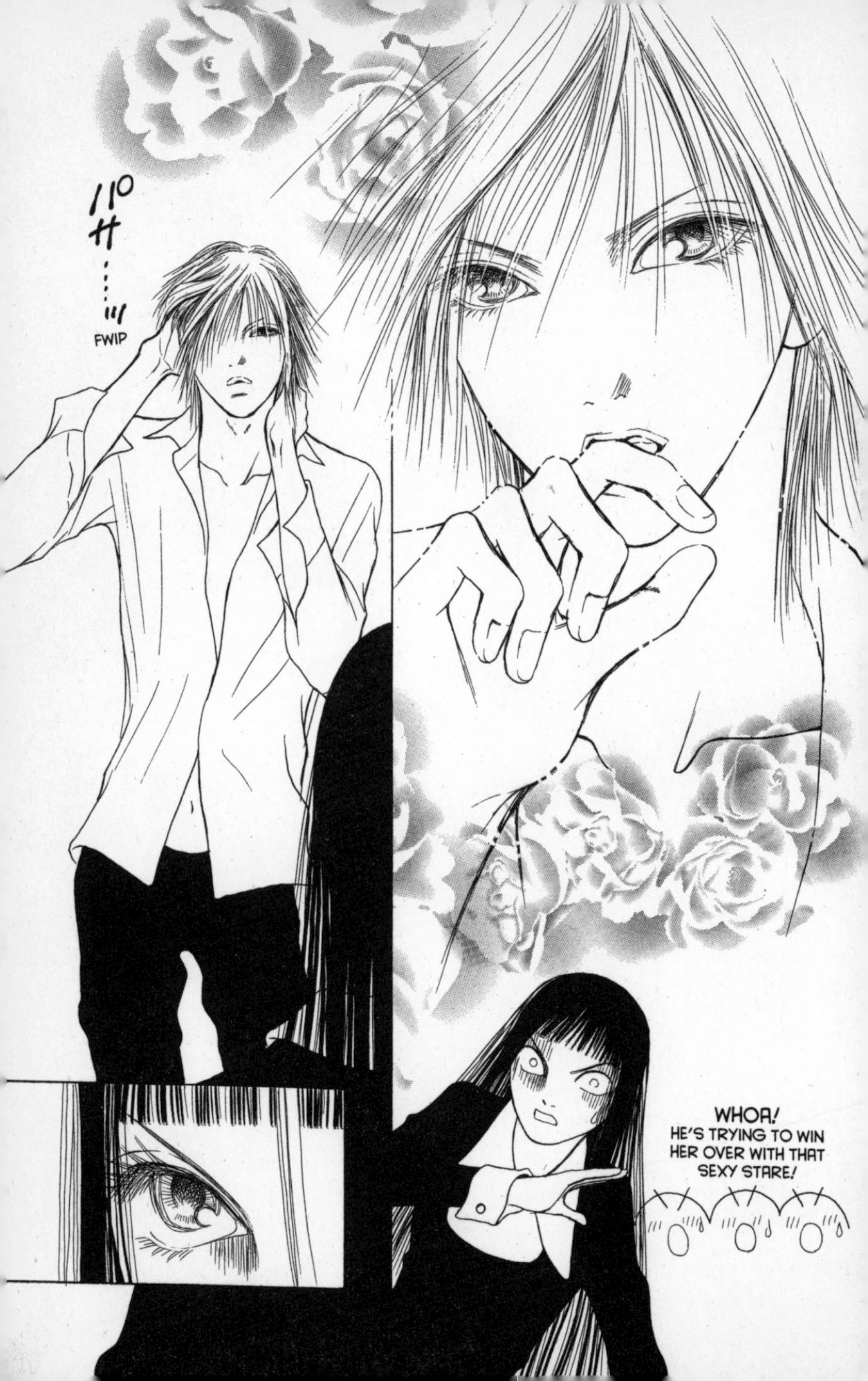
WHOA!
HE'S TRYING TO WIN HER OVER WITH THAT SEXY STARE!
FWIP

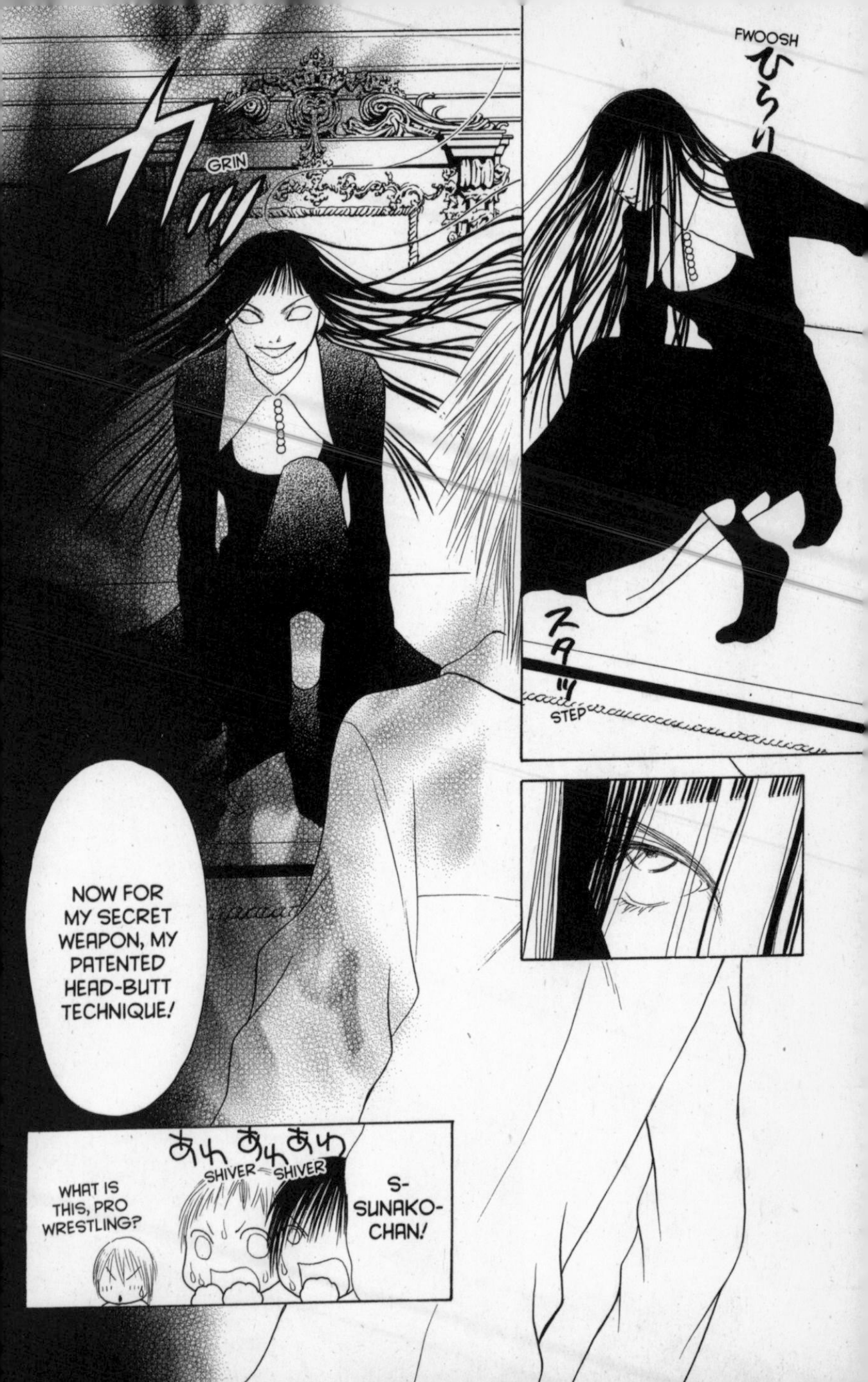
FWOOSH
ひらり
スタッ
STEP
カッ
GRIN
NOW FOR MY SECRET WEAPON, MY PATENTED HEAD-BUTT TECHNIQUE!
S-SUNAKO-CHAN!
あわ あわ あわ
SHIVER SHIVER
WHAT IS THIS, PRO WRESTLING?

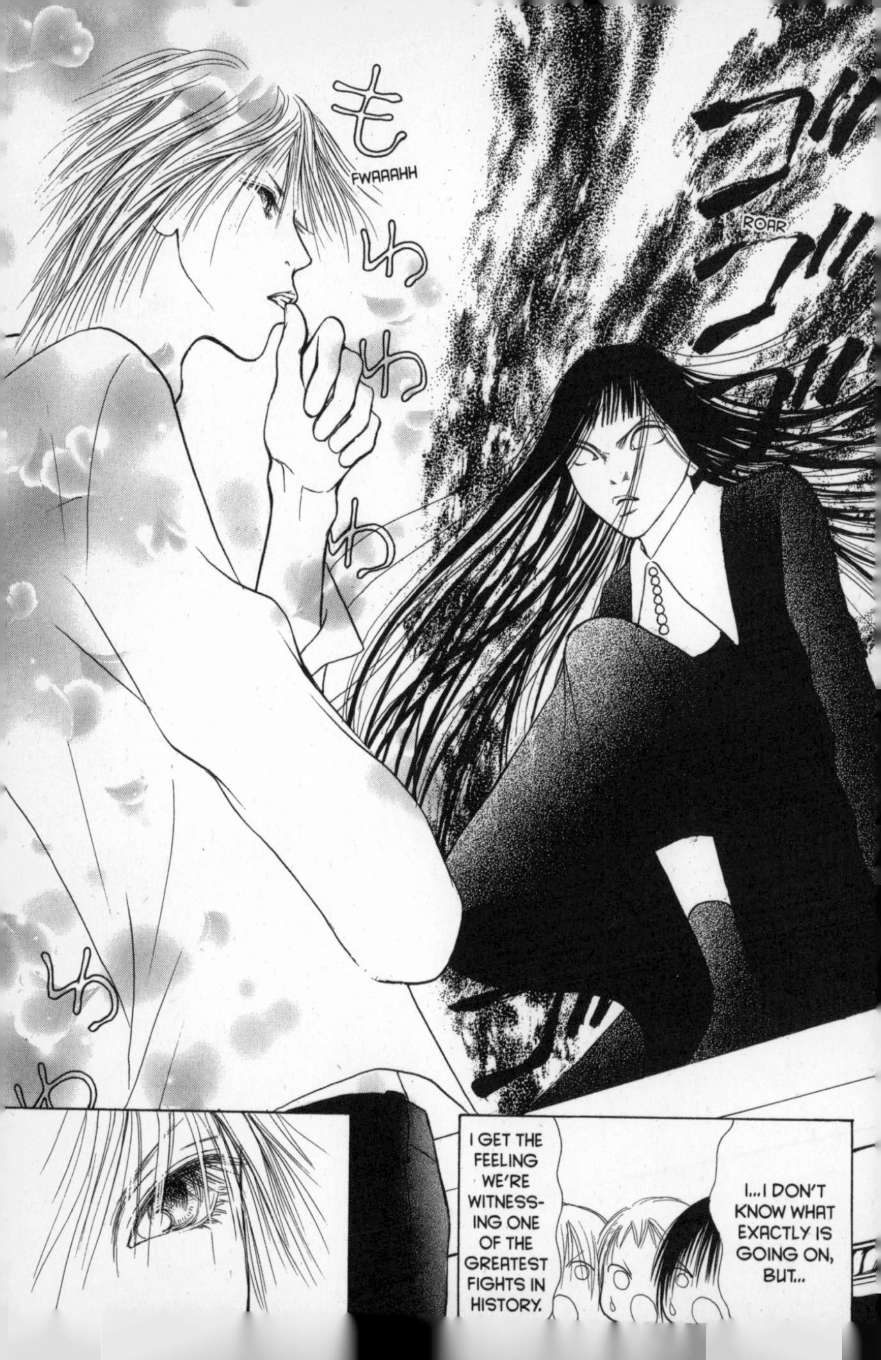
ROAR
FWAAAAHH
I...I DON'T KNOW WHAT EXACTLY IS GOING ON, BUT...
I GET THE FEELING WE'RE WITNESS-ING ONE OF THE GREATEST FIGHTS IN HISTORY.

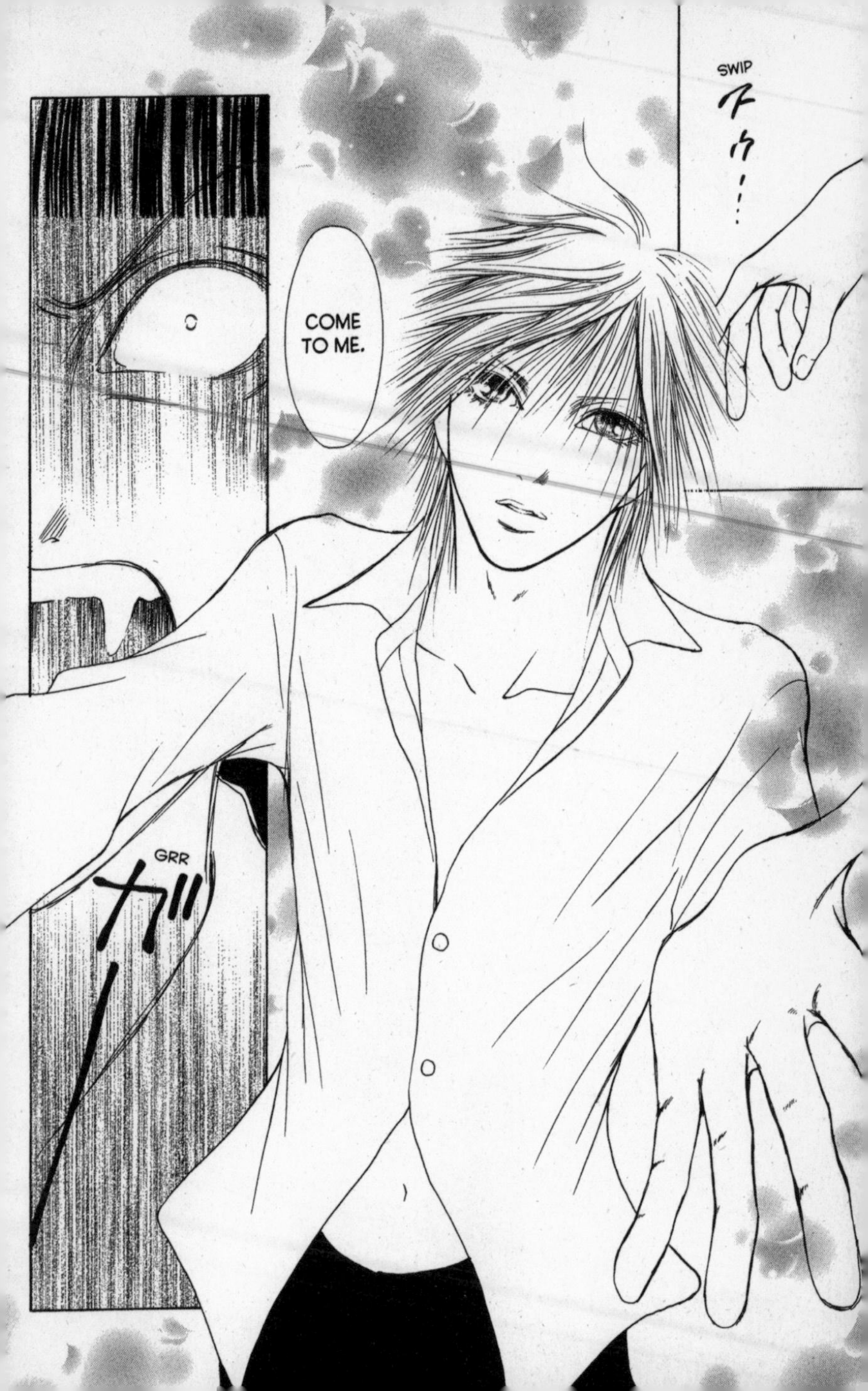
SWIP
COME TO ME.
GRR

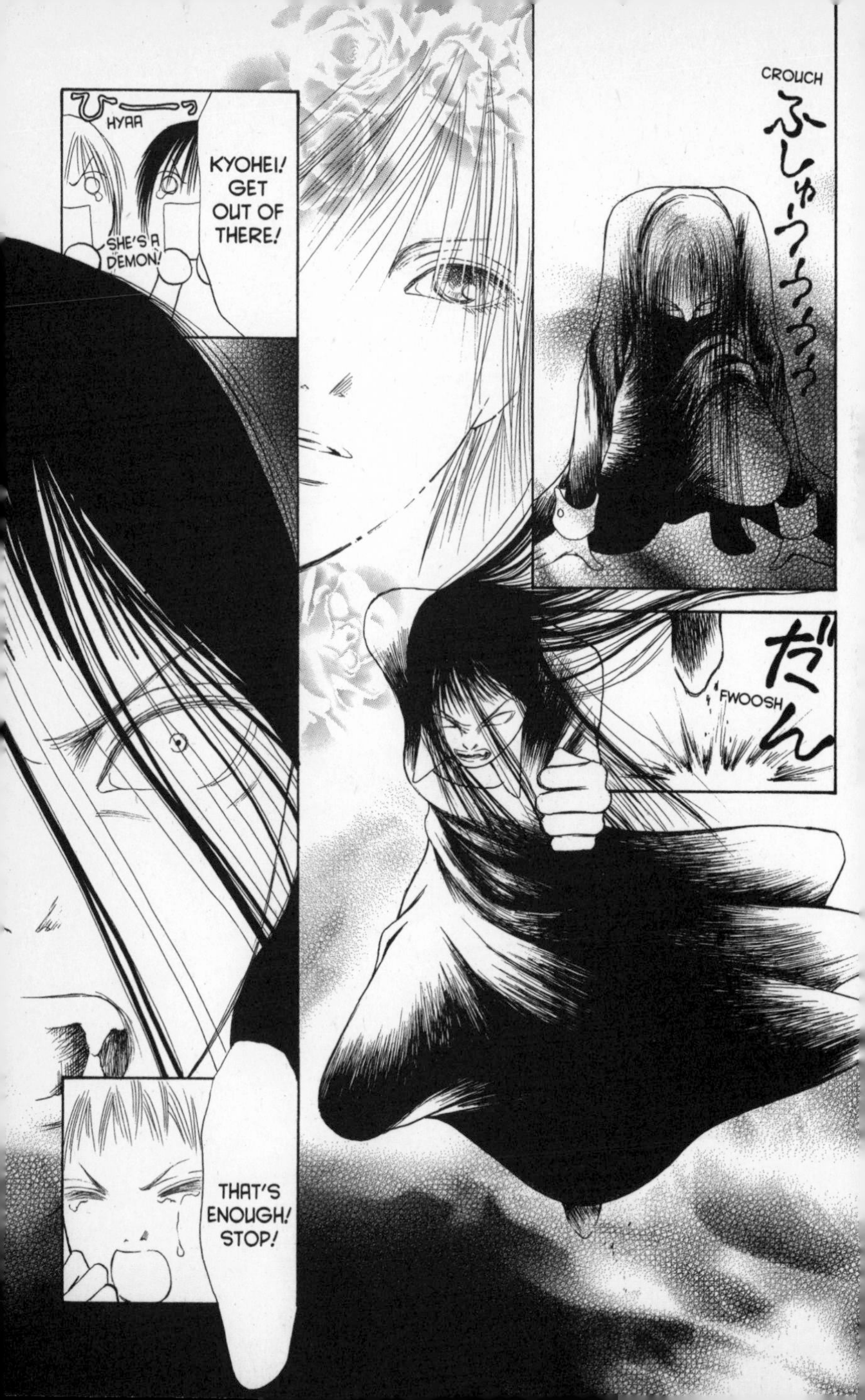
CROUCH
ふしゅううう
ひーっ
HYAA
KYOHEI! GET OUT OF THERE!
SHE'S A DEMON!
だん
FWOOSH
THAT'S ENOUGH! STOP!

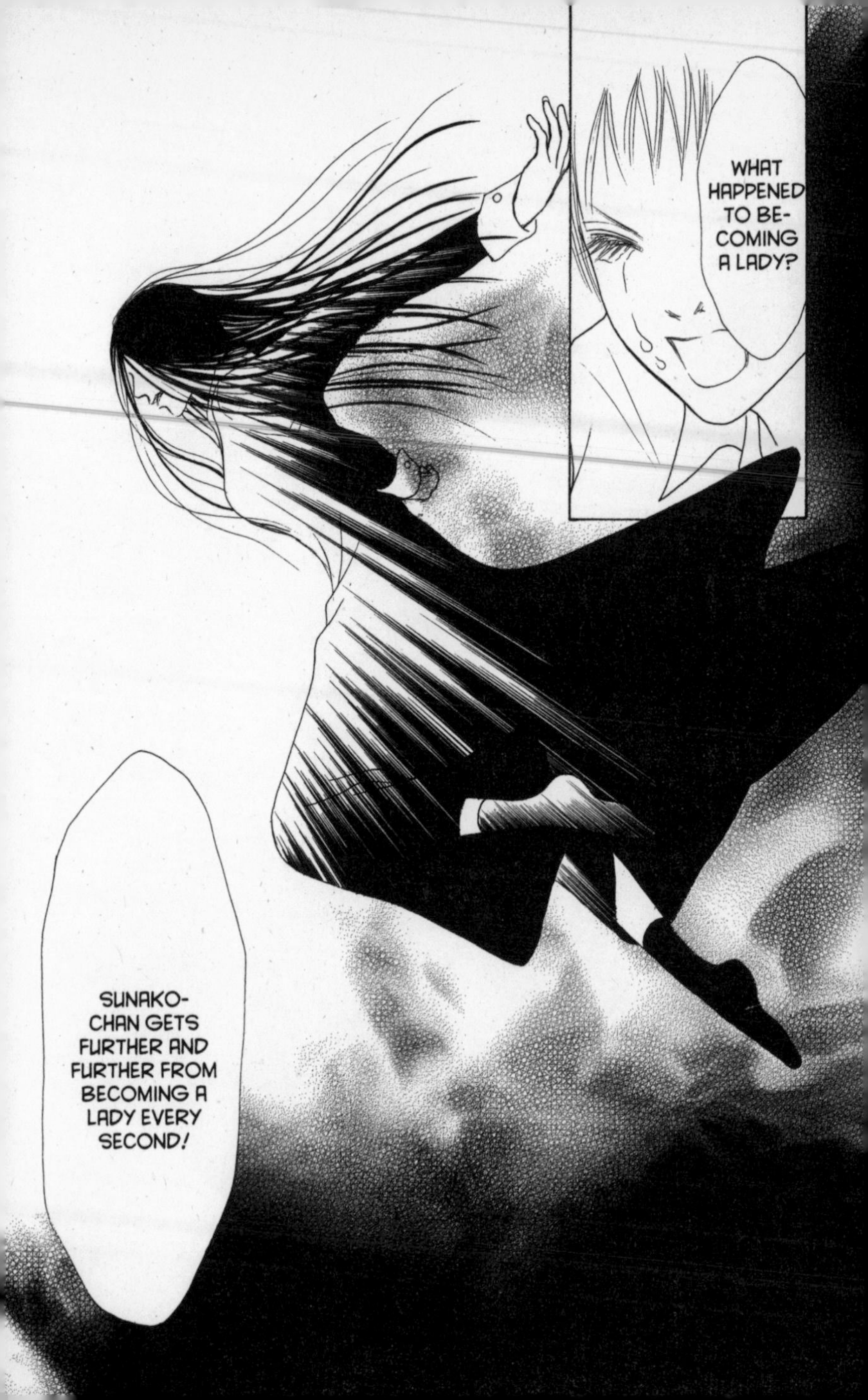
WHAT HAPPENED TO BE-COMING A LADY?
SUNAKO-CHAN GETS FURTHER AND FURTHER FROM BECOMING A LADY EVERY SECOND!

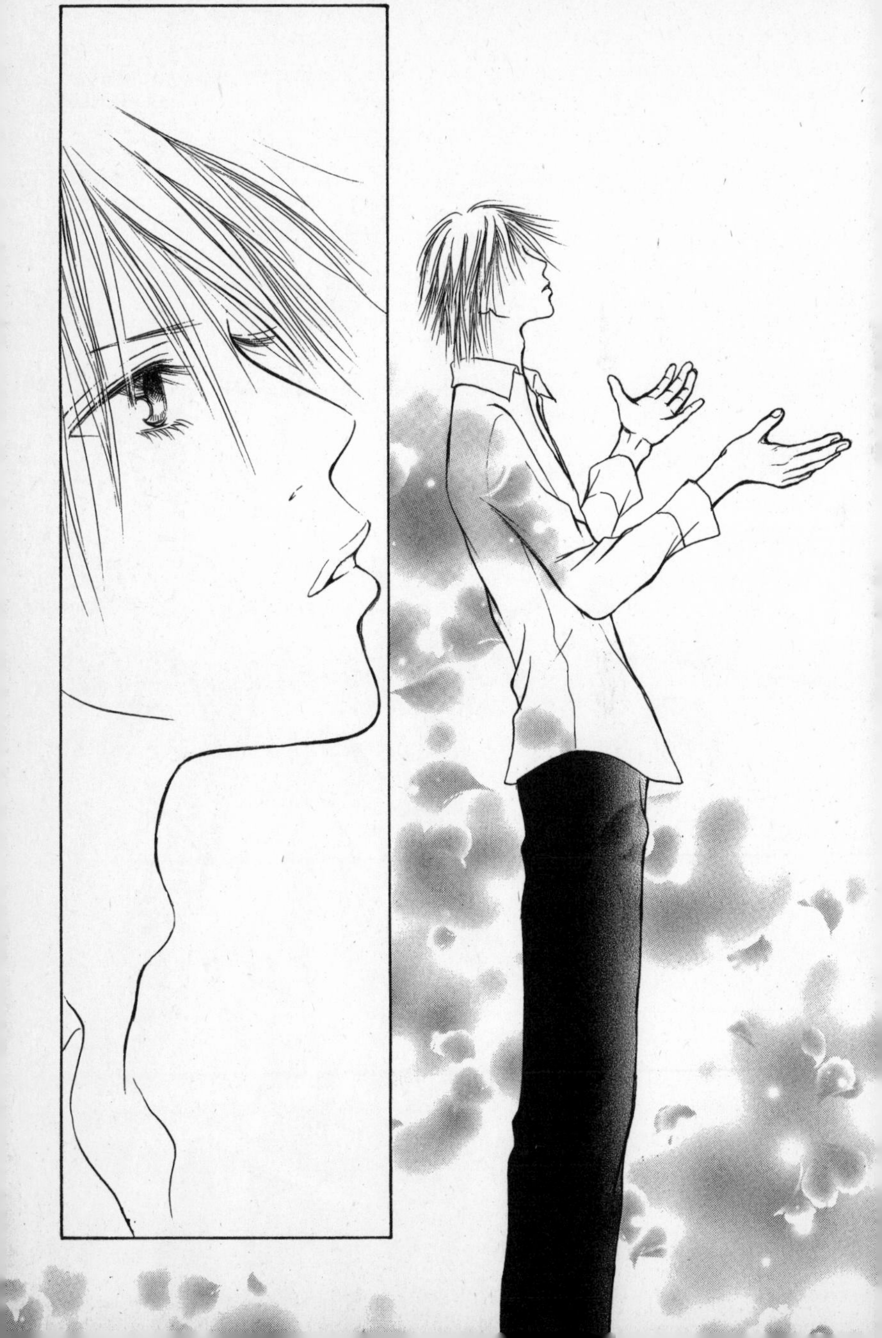

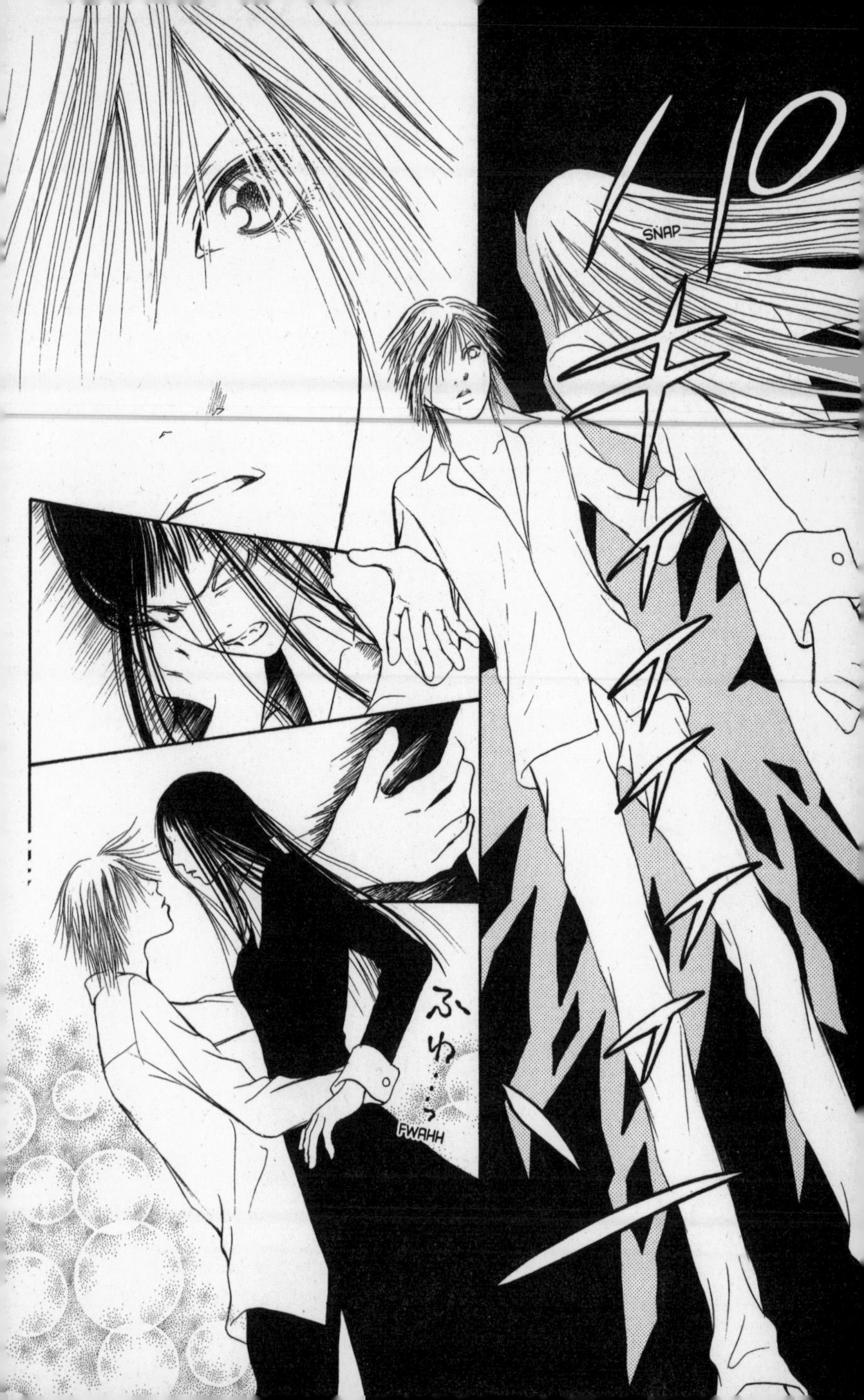
SNAP
ふわ…っ
FWAHH

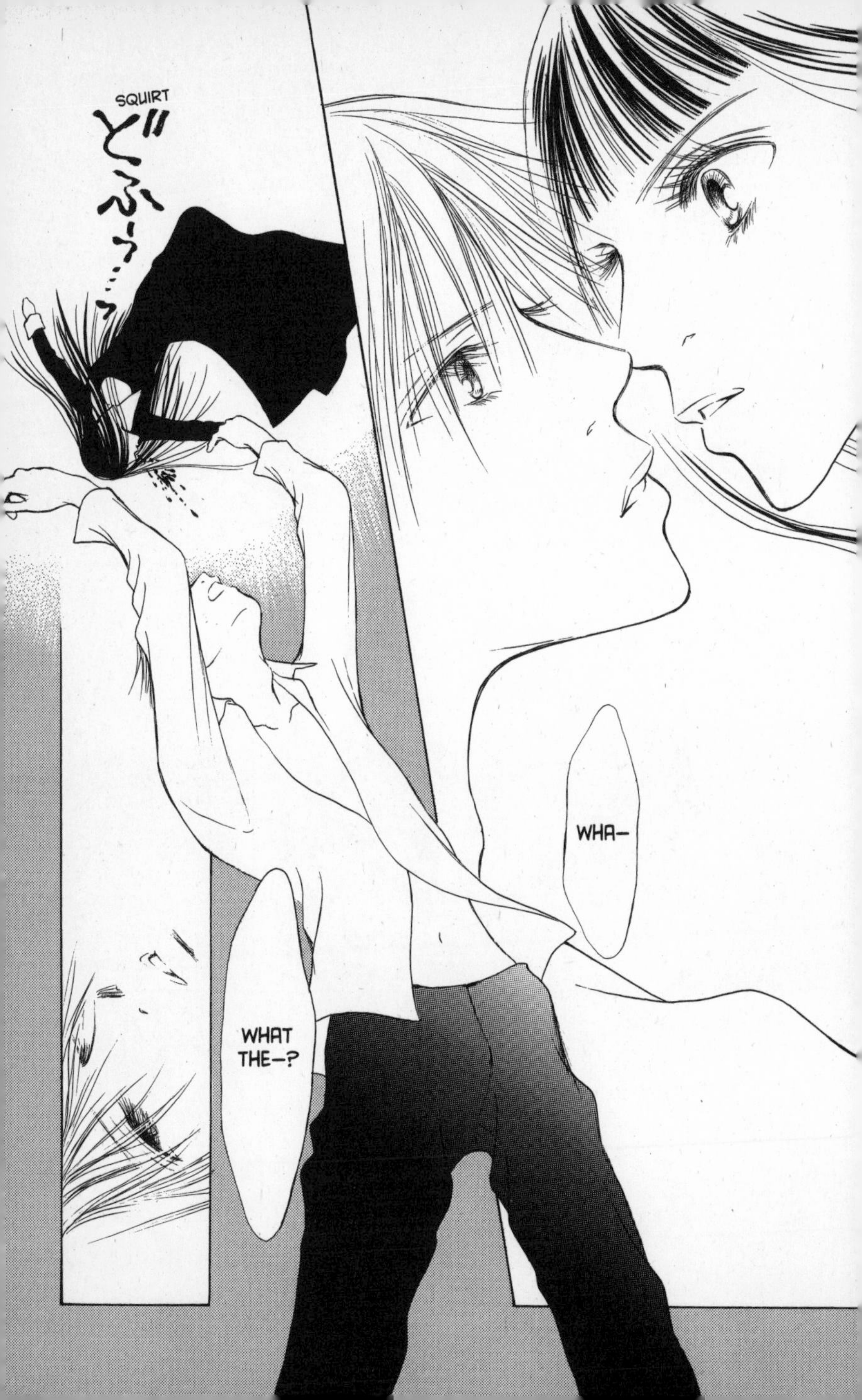
WHA-
SQUIRT
どぷーっ
WHAT THE-?

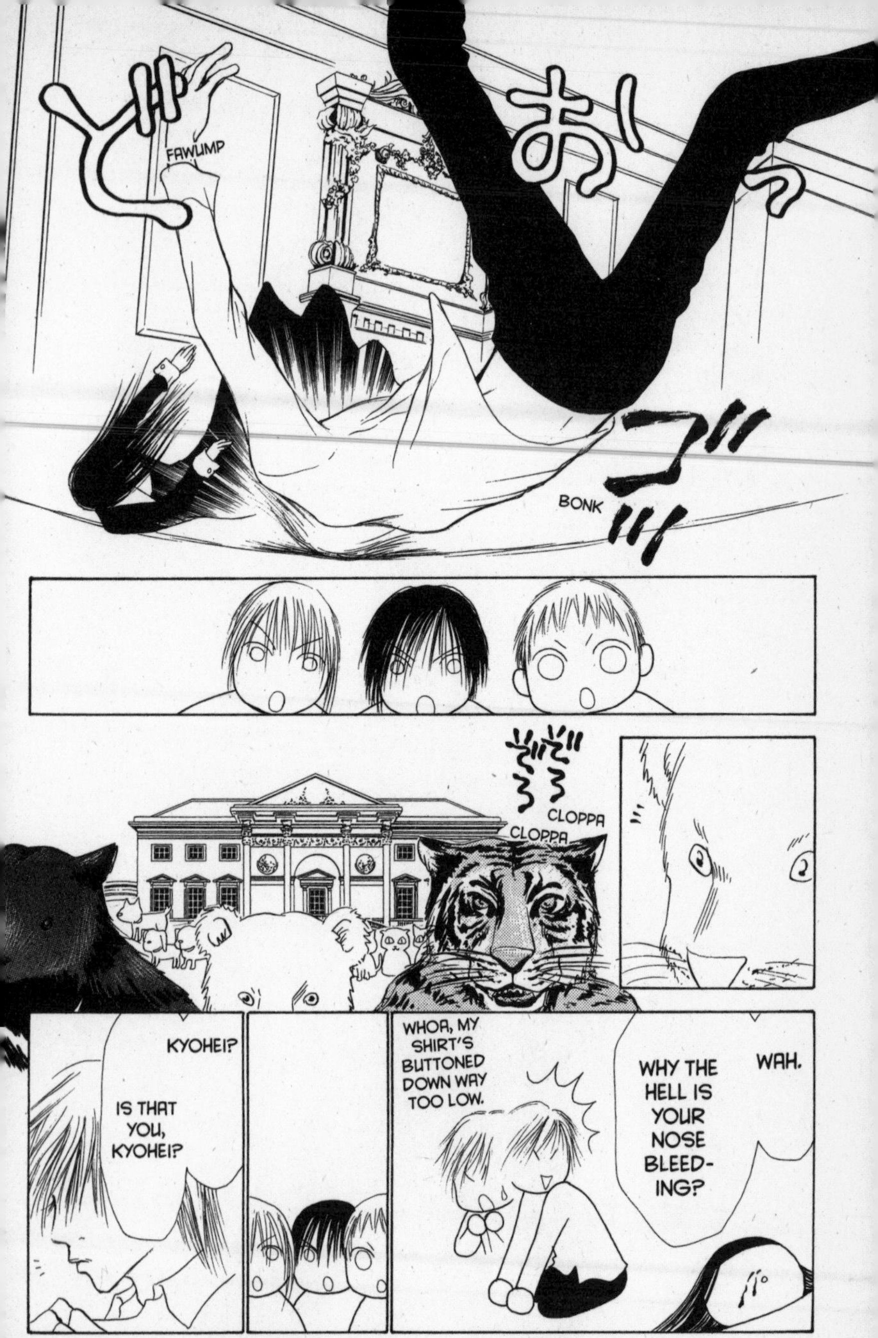
FAWUMP
BONK
CLOPPA
CLOPPA
WAH.
WHY THE HELL IS YOUR NOSE BLEEDING?
WHOA, MY SHIRT'S BUTTONED DOWN WAY TOO LOW.
KYOHEI?
IS THAT YOU, KYOHEI?

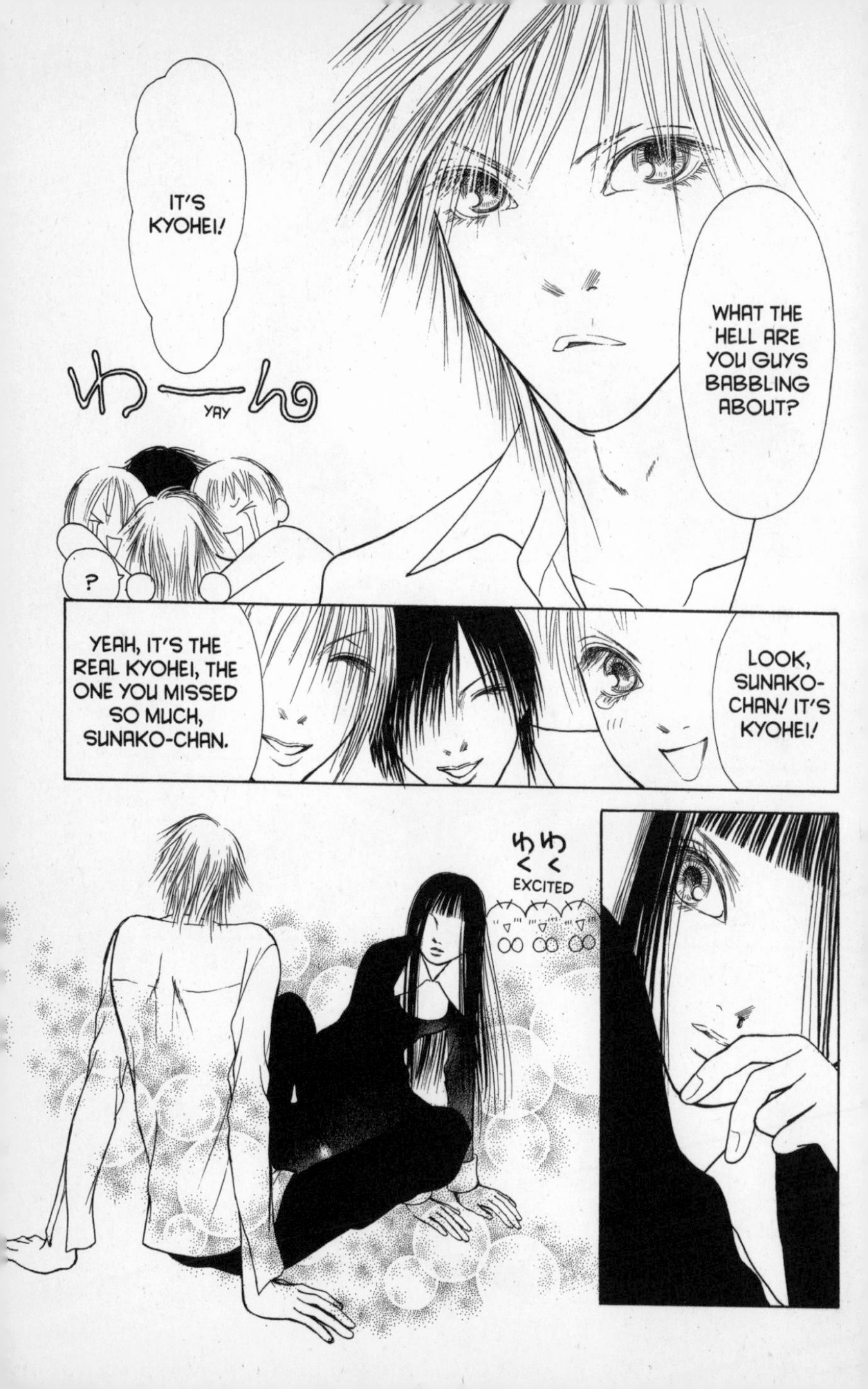

WHAT THE HELL ARE YOU GUYS BABBLING ABOUT?
IT'S KYOHEI!
わーん
YAY
?
LOOK, SUNAKO-CHAN! IT'S KYOHEI!
YEAH, IT'S THE REAL KYOHEI, THE ONE YOU MISSED SO MUCH, SUNAKO-CHAN.
わくわく
EXCITED

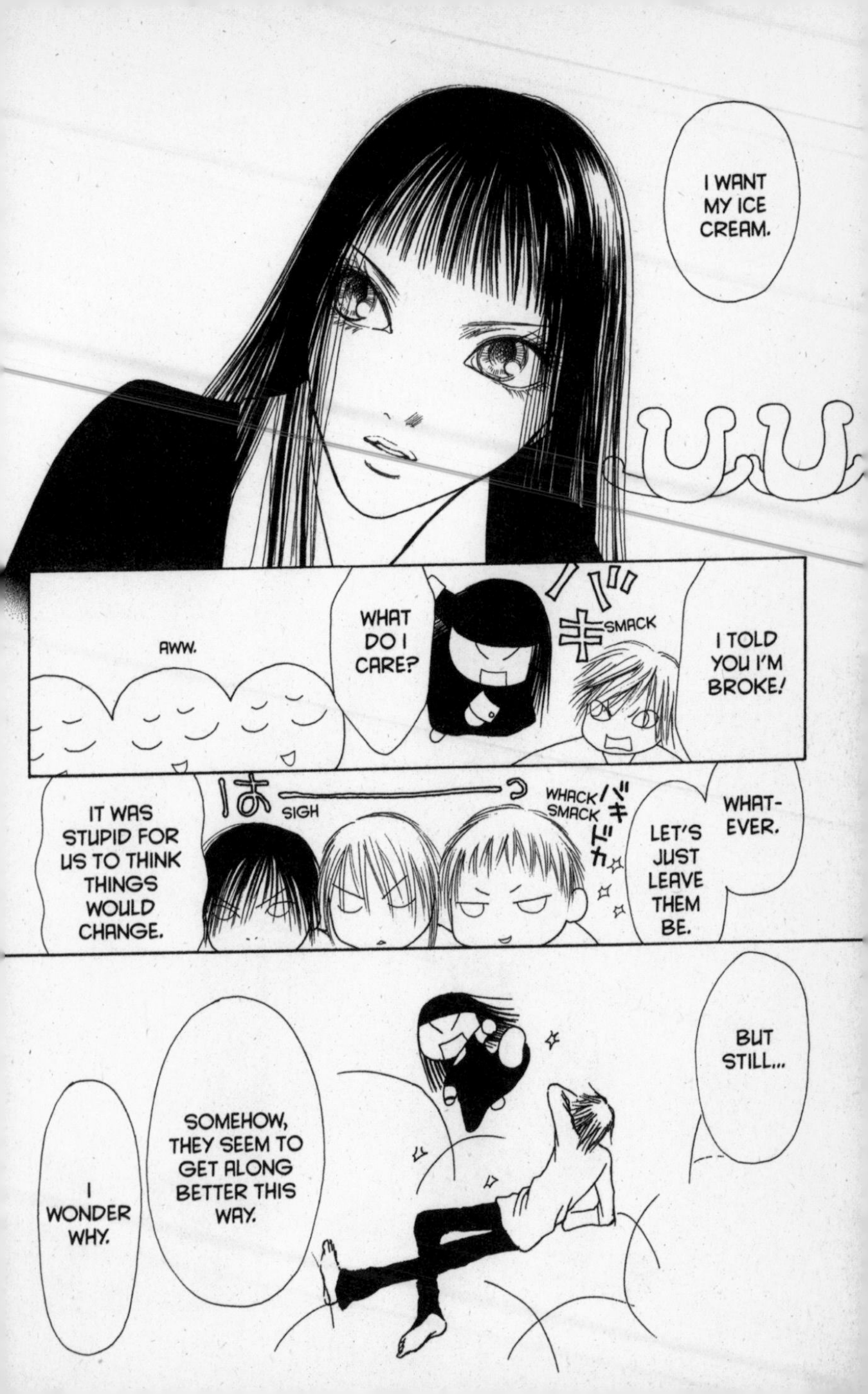
I WANT MY ICE CREAM.
I TOLD YOU I'M BROKE!
バキ
SMACK
WHAT DO I CARE?
AWW.
WHAT-EVER.
LET'S JUST LEAVE THEM BE.
バキ ドカ
WHACK SMACK
はーっ
SIGH
IT WAS STUPID FOR US TO THINK THINGS WOULD CHANGE.
BUT STILL...
SOMEHOW, THEY SEEM TO GET ALONG BETTER THIS WAY.
I WONDER WHY.

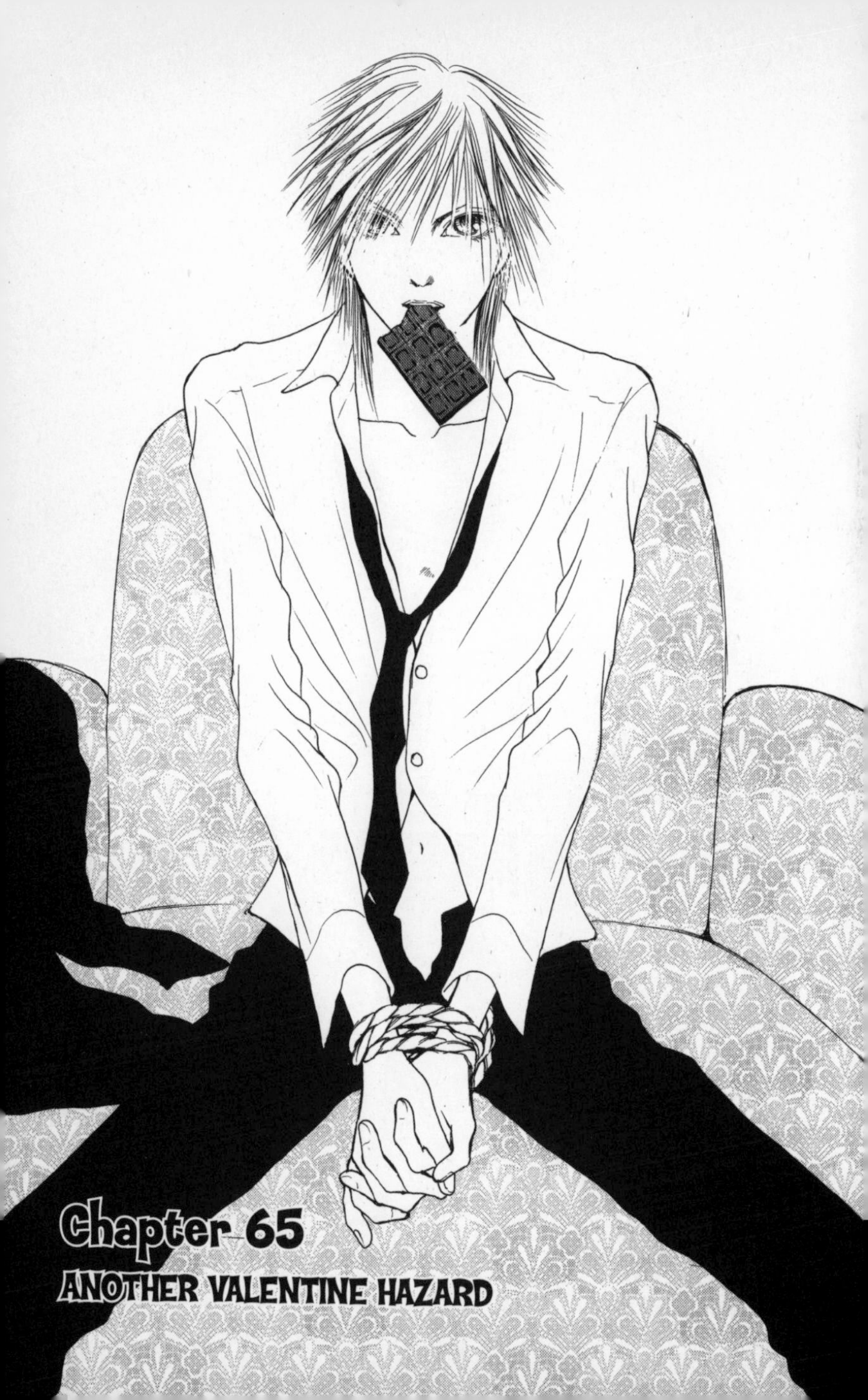

Chapter 65
ANOTHER VALENTINE HAZARD

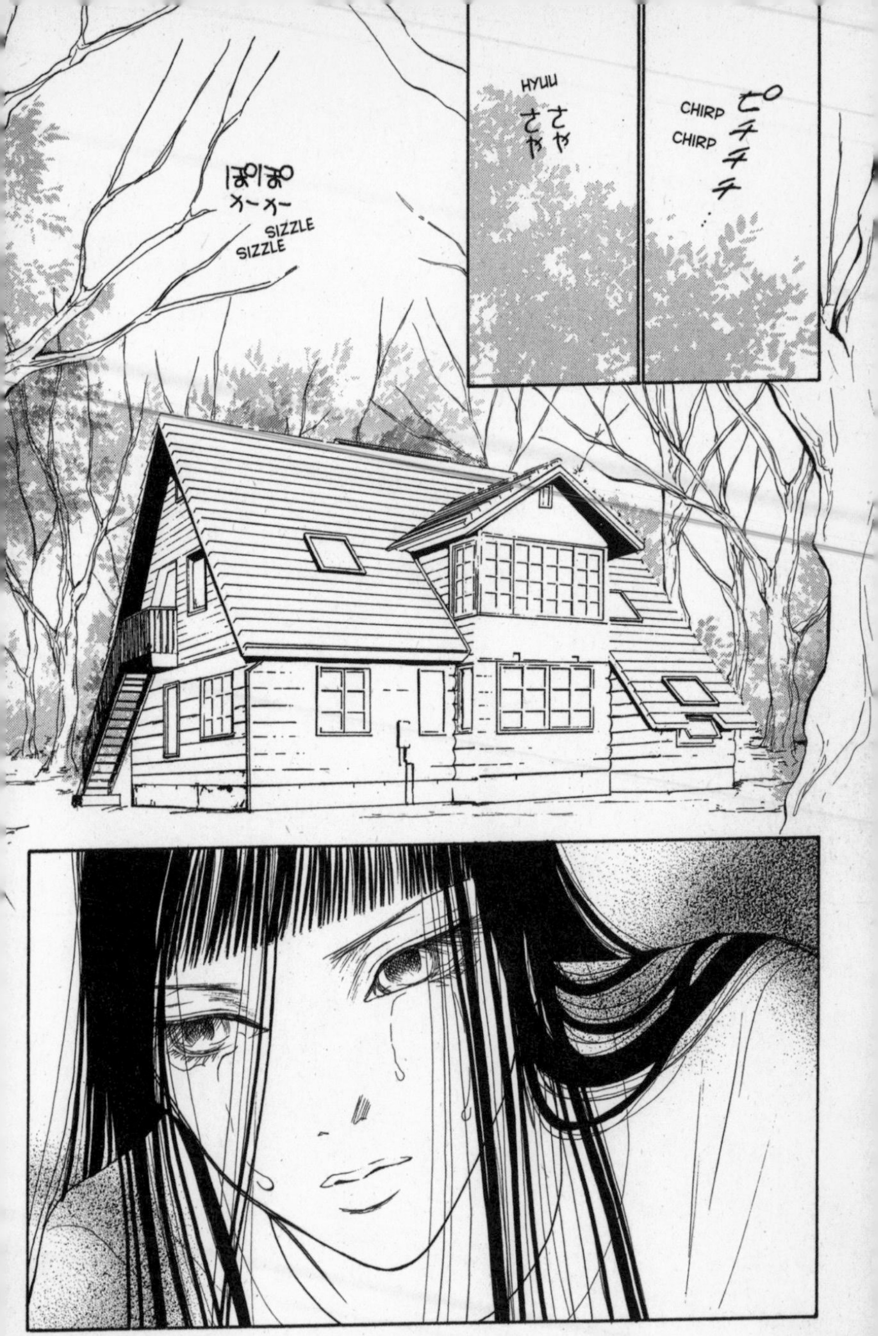
CHIRP
CHIRP
HYUU
SIZZLE
SIZZLE

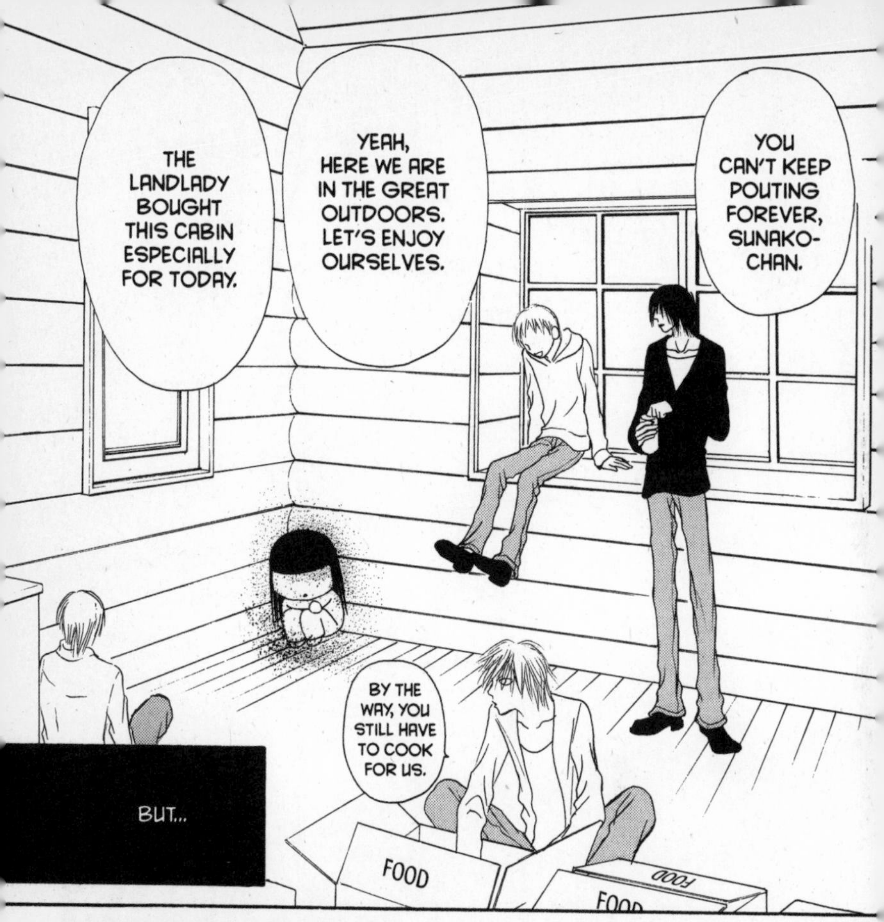
YOU CAN'T KEEP POUTING FOREVER, SUNAKO-CHAN.
YEAH, HERE WE ARE IN THE GREAT OUTDOORS. LET'S ENJOY OURSELVES.
THE LANDLADY BOUGHT THIS CABIN ESPECIALLY FOR TODAY.
BY THE WAY, YOU STILL HAVE TO COOK FOR US.
BUT...
FOOD
FOOD
FOOD

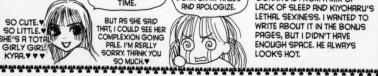

BEHIND THE SCENES

WHEN I WAS WRITING THIS STORY, I WAS FACED WITH A REALLY TOUGH DEADLINE. I THOUGHT MY STORY WOULD GET DROPPED (AND NOT MAKE IT INTO THE MAGAZINE).

MOST OF MY ASSISTANTS WERE BUSY WITH OTHER JOBS, SO I DID PRETTY MUCH THE WHOLE STORY WITH ONLY ONE OTHER PERSON HELPING.

▼

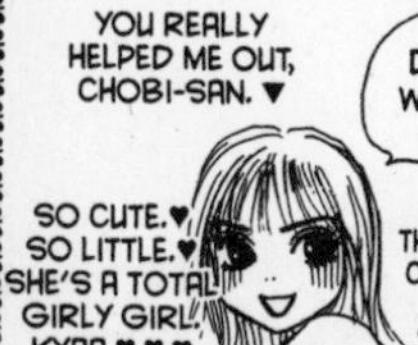
YOU REALLY HELPED ME OUT, CHOBI-SAN. ▼
SO CUTE.♥ SO LITTLE.♥ SHE'S A TOTAL GIRLY GIRL. KYAA.♥ ♥ ♥
DON'T WORRY. WE'LL FINISH ON TIME.
BUT AS SHE SAID THAT, I COULD SEE HER COMPLEXION GOING PALE. I'M REALLY SORRY. THANK YOU SO MUCH.♥

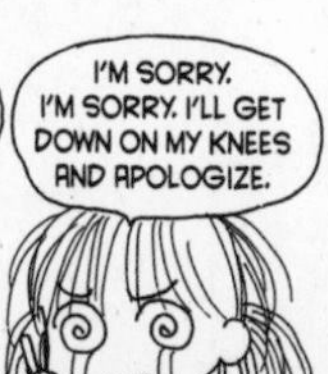
I'M SORRY. I'M SORRY. I'LL GET DOWN ON MY KNEES AND APOLOGIZE.

I DIDN'T SLEEP FOR THREE DAYS, AND WHEN I FINISHED, I WENT STRAIGHT TO A KIYOHARU-SAMA CONCERT. I THOUGHT I WAS GONNA DIE FROM A MIX OF LACK OF SLEEP AND KIYOHARU'S LETHAL SEXINESS. I WANTED TO WRITE ABOUT IT IN THE BONUS PAGES, BUT I DIDN'T HAVE ENOUGH SPACE. HE ALWAYS LOOKS HOT.

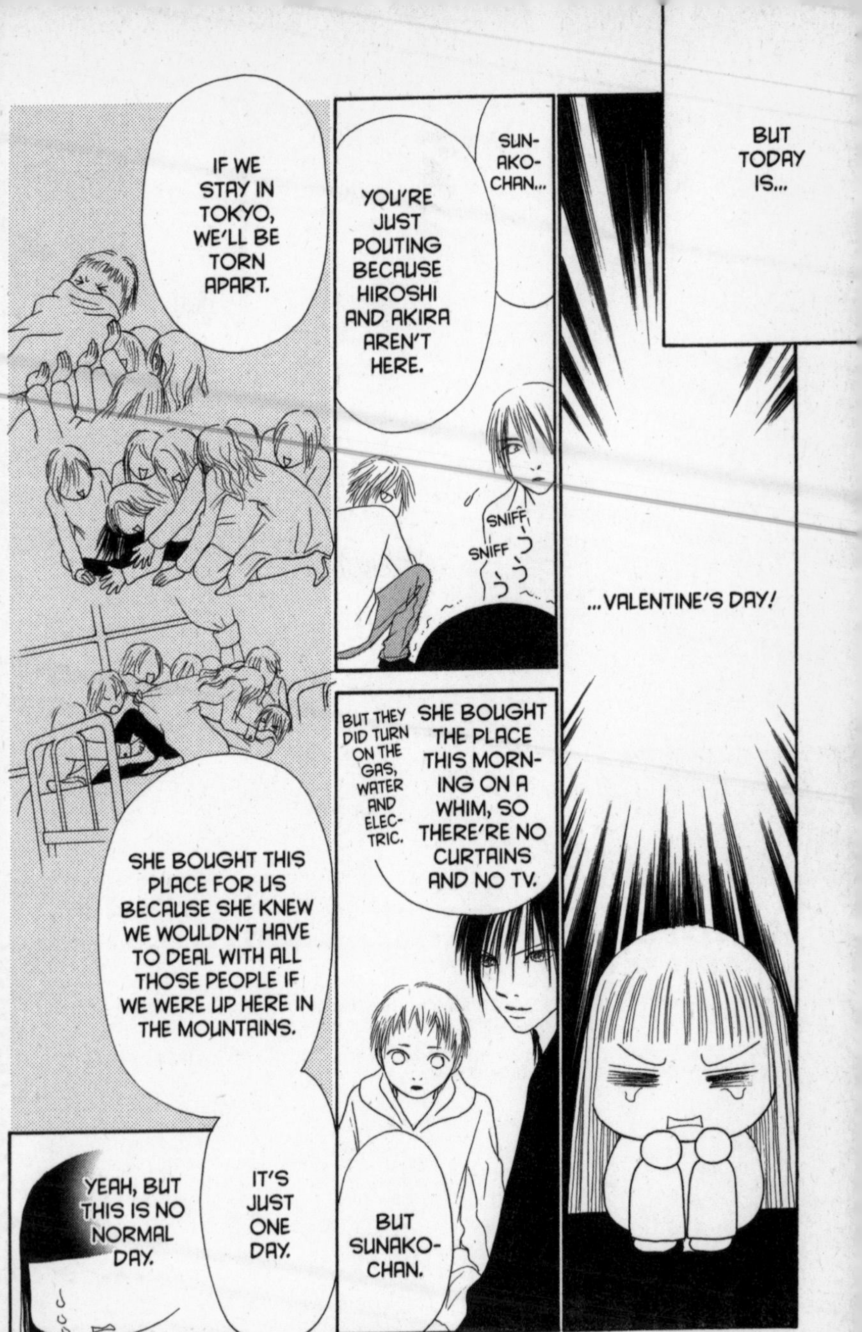
BUT TODAY IS...
...VALENTINE'S DAY!
SUN-AKO-CHAN...
YOU'RE JUST POUTING BECAUSE HIROSHI AND AKIRA AREN'T HERE.
SNIFF SNIFF
SHE BOUGHT THE PLACE THIS MORN-ING ON A WHIM, SO THERE'RE NO CURTAINS AND NO TV.
BUT THEY DID TURN ON THE GAS, WATER AND ELEC-TRIC.
BUT SUNAKO-CHAN.
IF WE STAY IN TOKYO, WE'LL BE TORN APART.
SHE BOUGHT THIS PLACE FOR US BECAUSE SHE KNEW WE WOULDN'T HAVE TO DEAL WITH ALL THOSE PEOPLE IF WE WERE UP HERE IN THE MOUNTAINS.
IT'S JUST ONE DAY.
YEAH, BUT THIS IS NO NORMAL DAY.

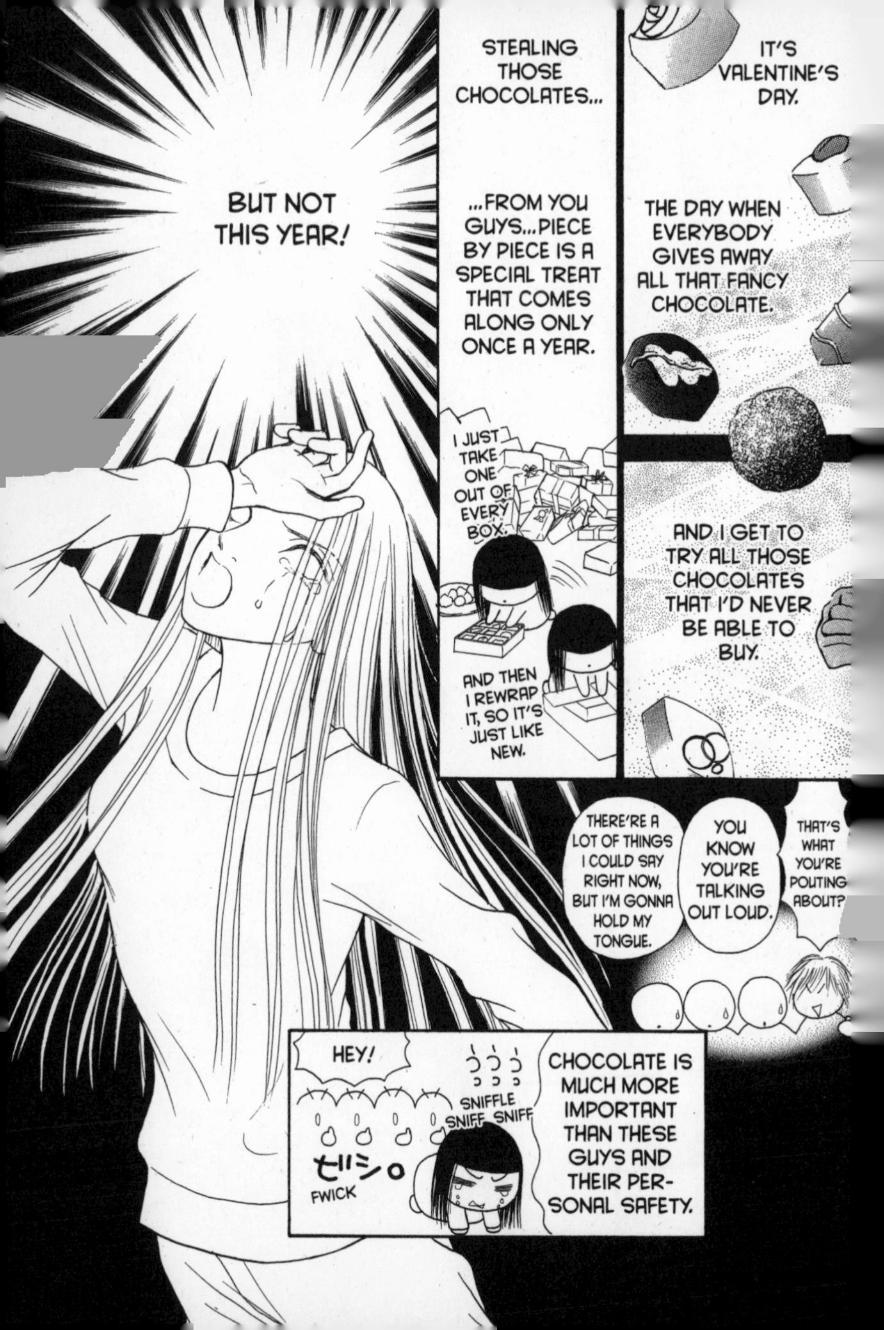
IT'S VALENTINE'S DAY.
THE DAY WHEN EVERYBODY GIVES AWAY ALL THAT FANCY CHOCOLATE.
AND I GET TO TRY ALL THOSE CHOCOLATES THAT I'D NEVER BE ABLE TO BUY.
STEALING THOSE CHOCOLATES...
...FROM YOU GUYS...PIECE BY PIECE IS A SPECIAL TREAT THAT COMES ALONG ONLY ONCE A YEAR.
I JUST TAKE ONE OUT OF EVERY BOX.
AND THEN I REWRAP IT, SO IT'S JUST LIKE NEW.
BUT NOT THIS YEAR!
THAT'S WHAT YOU'RE POUTING ABOUT?
YOU KNOW YOU'RE TALKING OUT LOUD.
THERE'RE A LOT OF THINGS I COULD SAY RIGHT NOW, BUT I'M GONNA HOLD MY TONGUE.
CHOCOLATE IS MUCH MORE IMPORTANT THAN THESE GUYS AND THEIR PER-SONAL SAFETY.
SNIFFLE SNIFF SNIFF
HEY!
FWICK

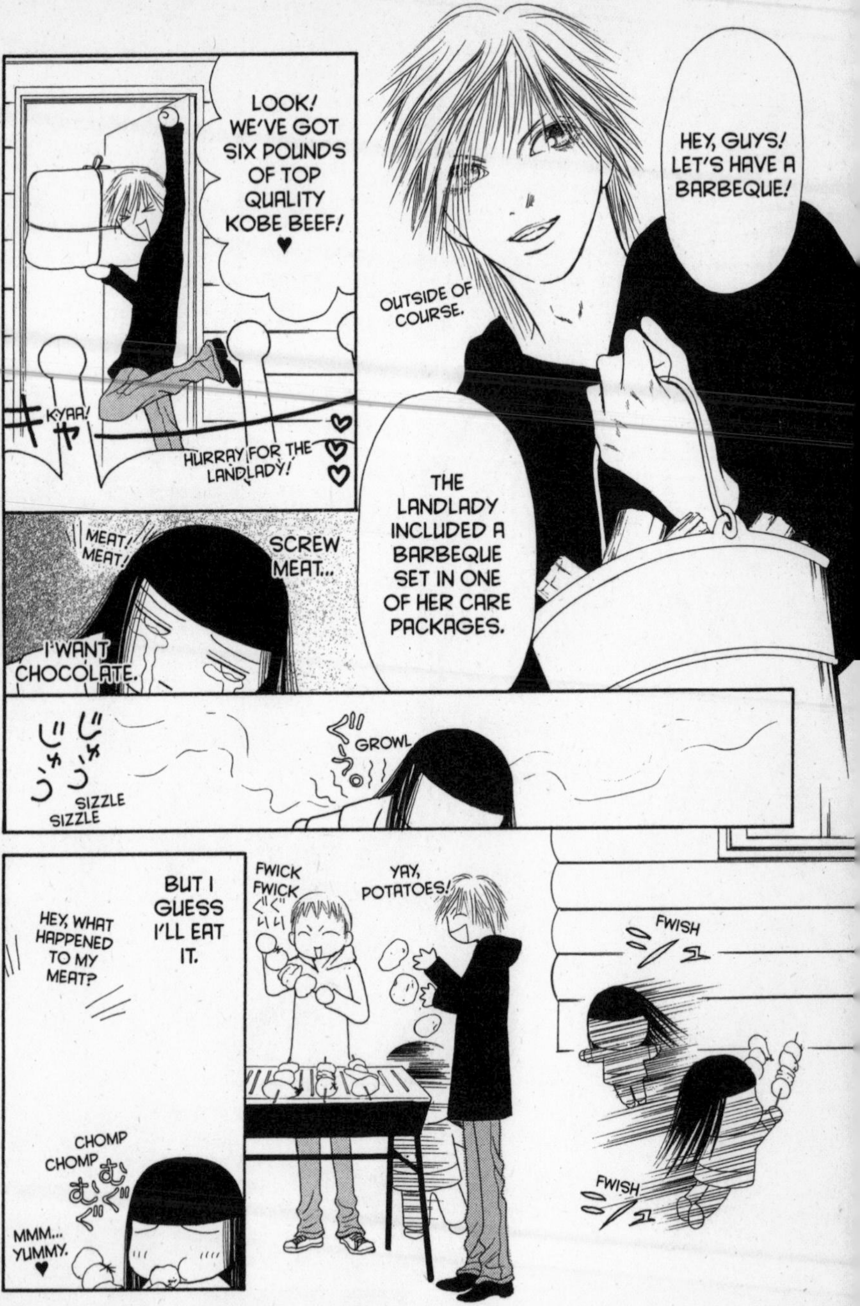
HEY, GUYS! LET'S HAVE A BARBEQUE!
OUTSIDE OF COURSE.
THE LANDLADY INCLUDED A BARBEQUE SET IN ONE OF HER CARE PACKAGES.
LOOK! WE'VE GOT SIX POUNDS OF TOP QUALITY KOBE BEEF! ♥
KYAA!
HURRAY FOR THE LANDLADY! ♥♥♥
SCREW MEAT...
MEAT! MEAT!
I WANT CHOCOLATE.
GROWL
SIZZLE SIZZLE
FWISH
FWISH
YAY, POTATOES!
FWICK FWICK
BUT I GUESS I'LL EAT IT.
HEY, WHAT HAPPENED TO MY MEAT?
CHOMP CHOMP
MMM... YUMMY. ♥

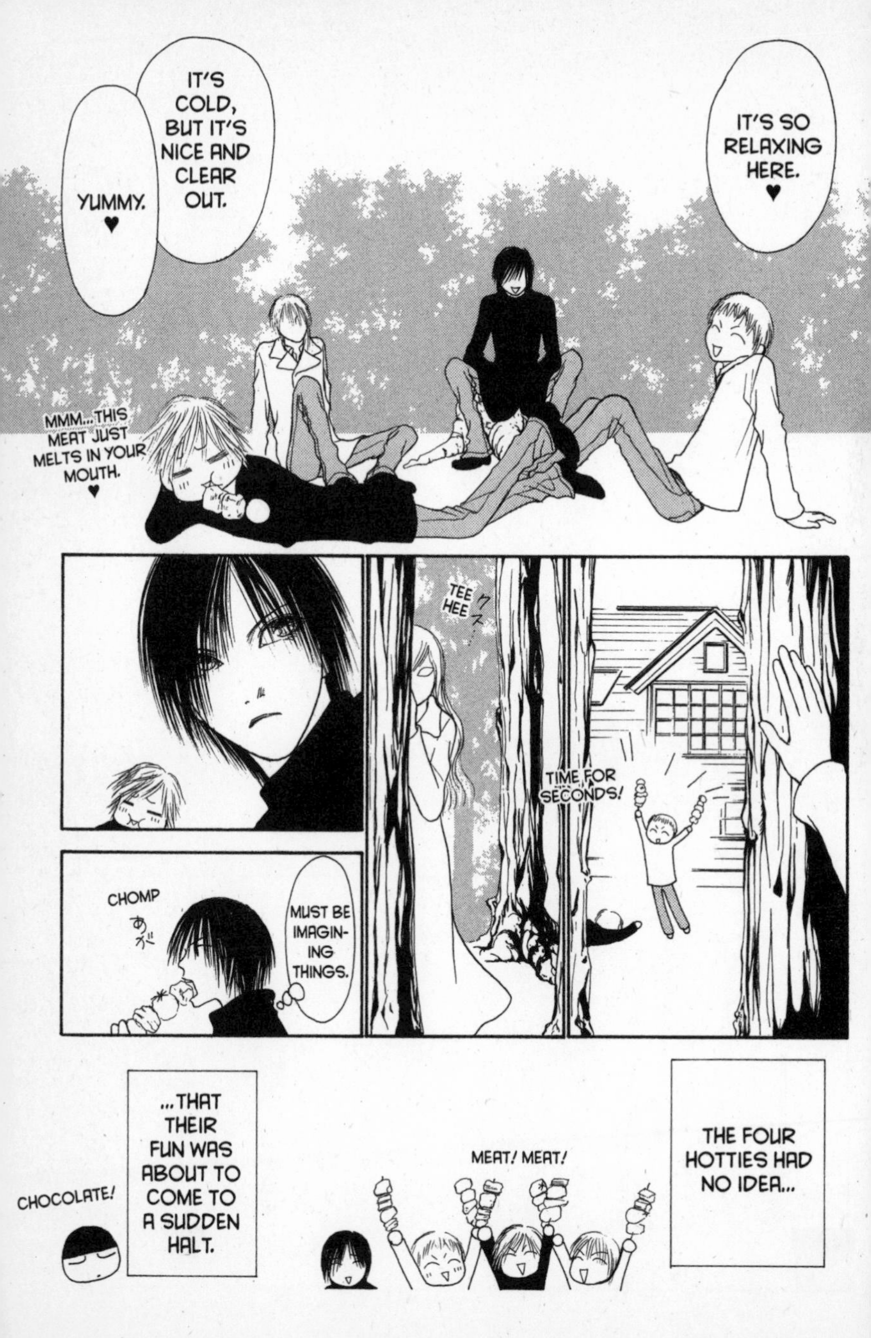
IT'S SO RELAXING HERE. ♥
IT'S COLD, BUT IT'S NICE AND CLEAR OUT.
YUMMY. ♥
MMM...THIS MEAT JUST MELTS IN YOUR MOUTH. ♥
TIME FOR SECONDS!
TEE HEE
MUST BE IMAGINING THINGS.
CHOMP
THE FOUR HOTTIES HAD NO IDEA...
MEAT! MEAT!
...THAT THEIR FUN WAS ABOUT TO COME TO A SUDDEN HALT.
CHOCOLATE!

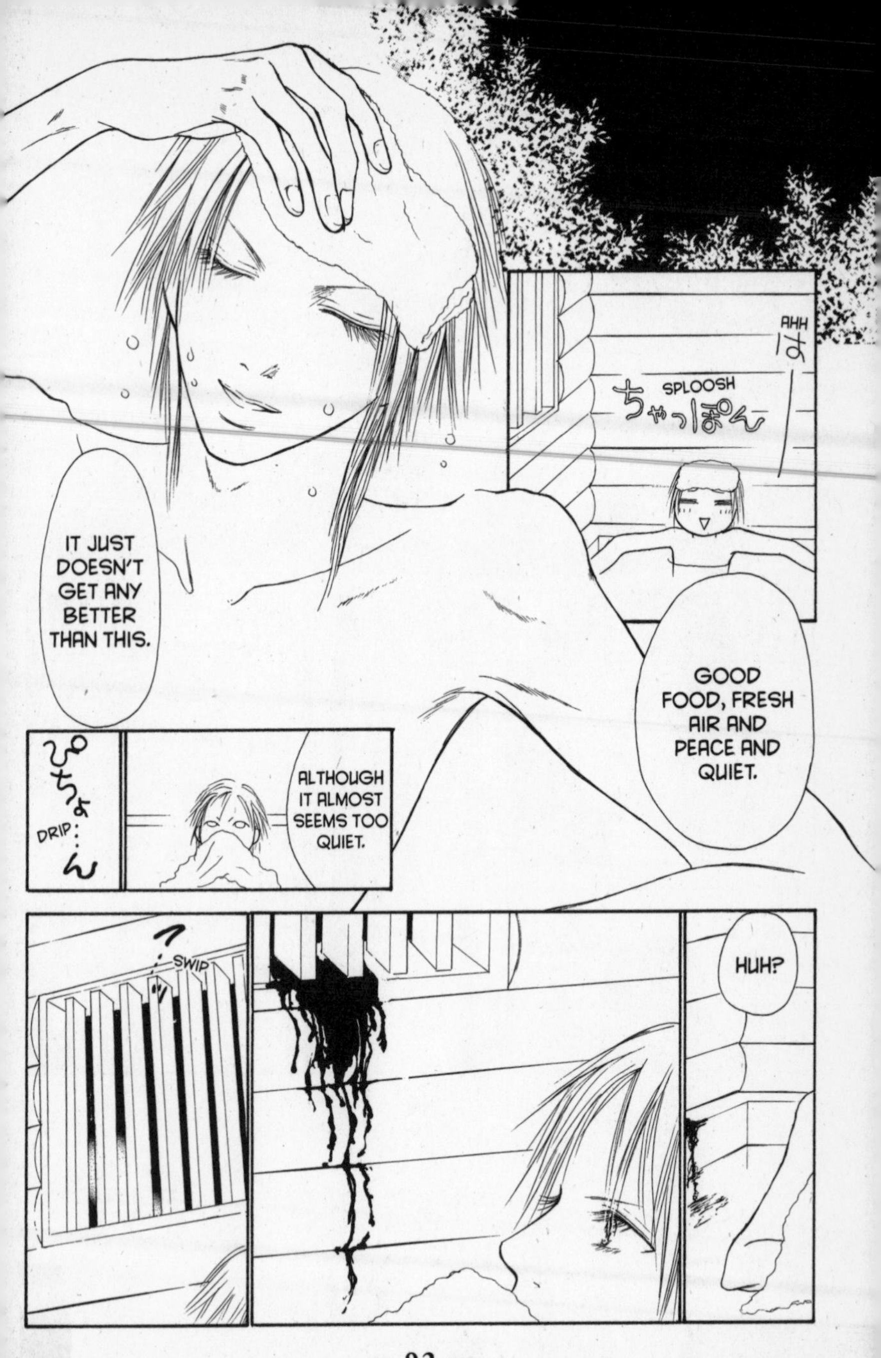

AHH
はー
SPLOOSH
ちゃっぽん
GOOD FOOD, FRESH AIR AND PEACE AND QUIET.
IT JUST DOESN'T GET ANY BETTER THAN THIS.
ALTHOUGH IT ALMOST SEEMS TOO QUIET.
ぴちょ…ん
DRIP...
HUH?
SWIP

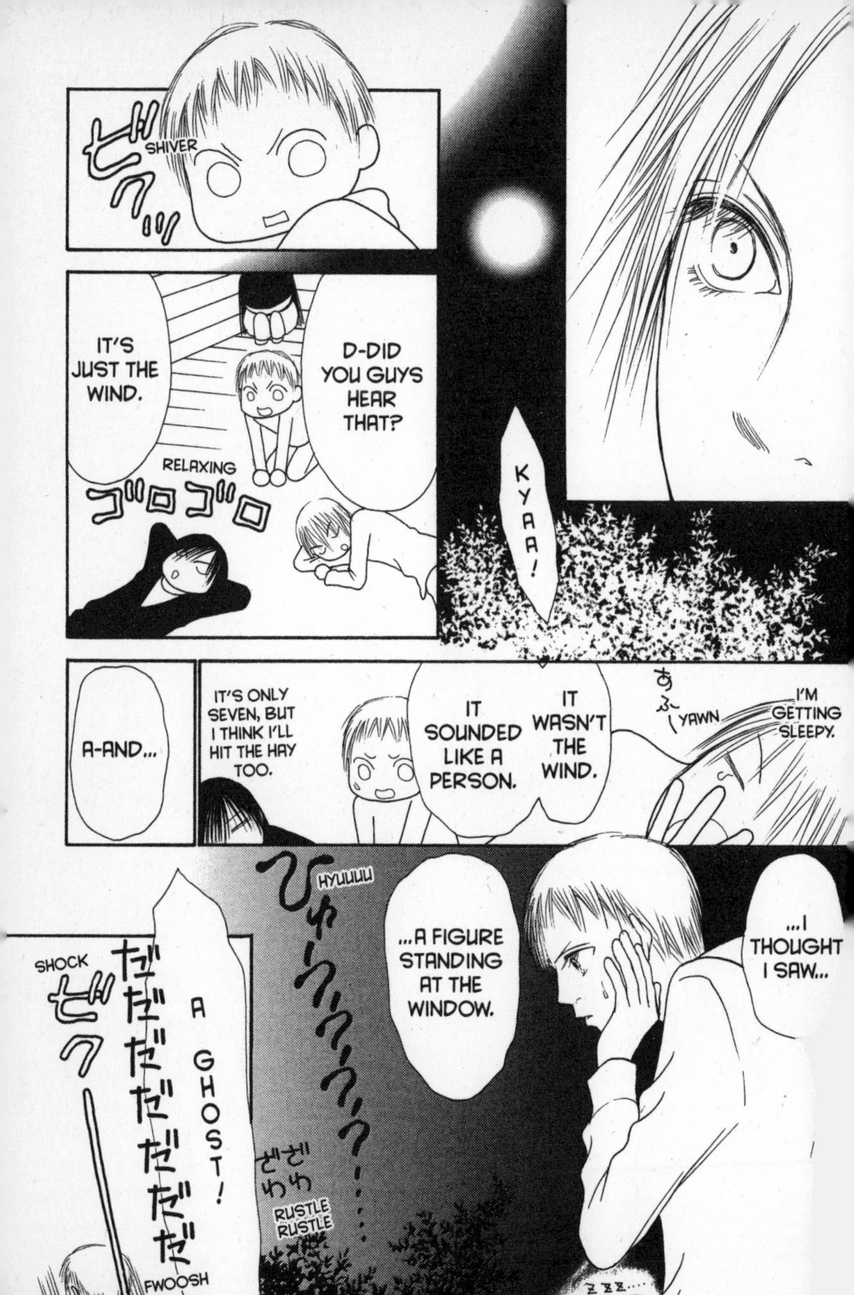
KYAA!
SHIVER
D-DID YOU GUYS HEAR THAT?
IT'S JUST THE WIND.
RELAXING
YAWN
I'M GETTING SLEEPY.
IT WASN'T THE WIND.
IT SOUNDED LIKE A PERSON.
IT'S ONLY SEVEN, BUT I THINK I'LL HIT THE HAY TOO.
A-AND...
...I THOUGHT I SAW...
...A FIGURE STANDING AT THE WINDOW.
HYUUUU
RUSTLE RUSTLE
ZZZ...
A GHOST!
SHOCK
FWOOSH

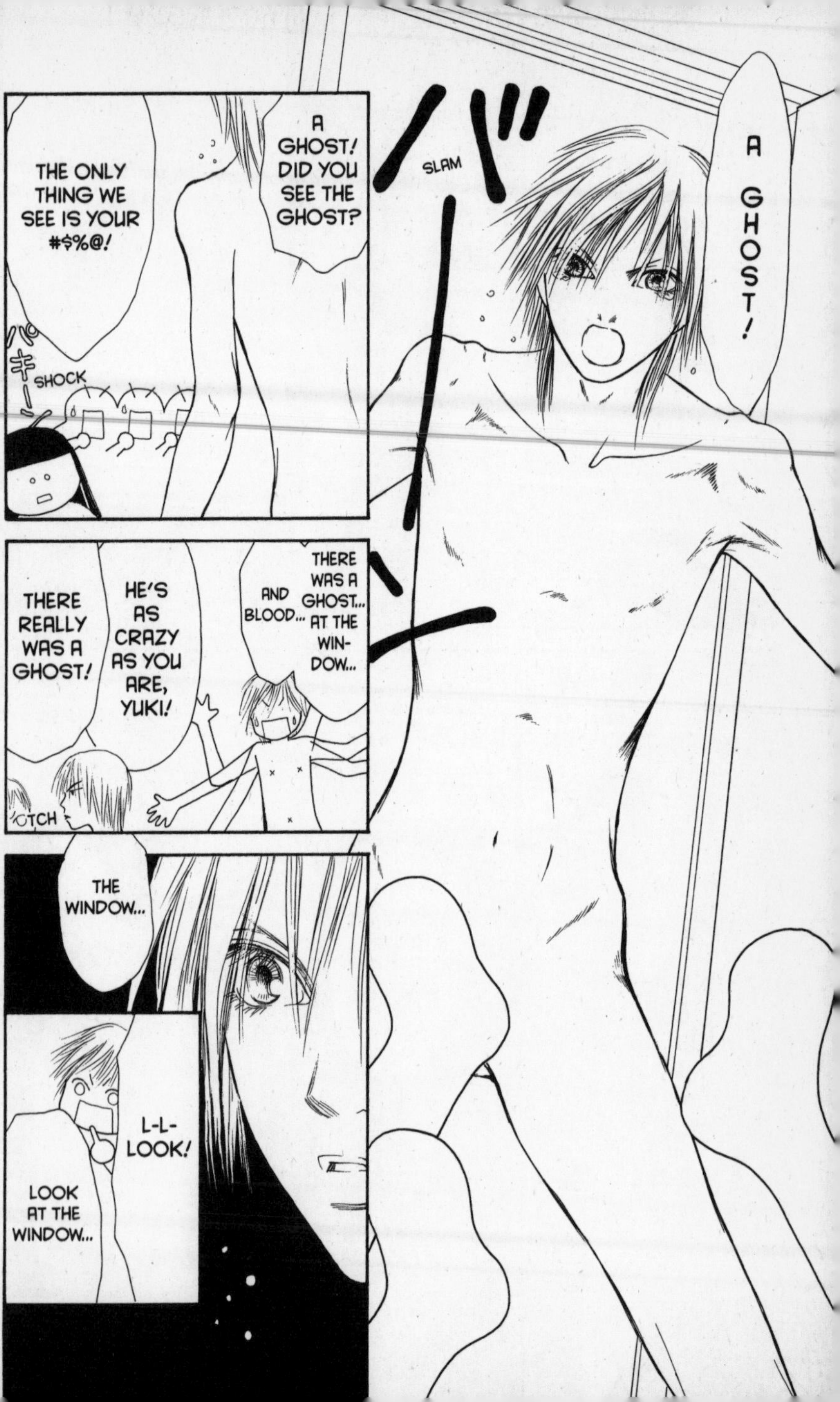
A GHOST!
SLAM
A GHOST! DID YOU SEE THE GHOST?
THE ONLY THING WE SEE IS YOUR #$%@!
SHOCK
THERE WAS A GHOST... AT THE WIN-DOW...
AND BLOOD...
HE'S AS CRAZY AS YOU ARE, YUKI!
THERE REALLY WAS A GHOST!
THE WINDOW...
L-L-LOOK!
LOOK AT THE WINDOW...

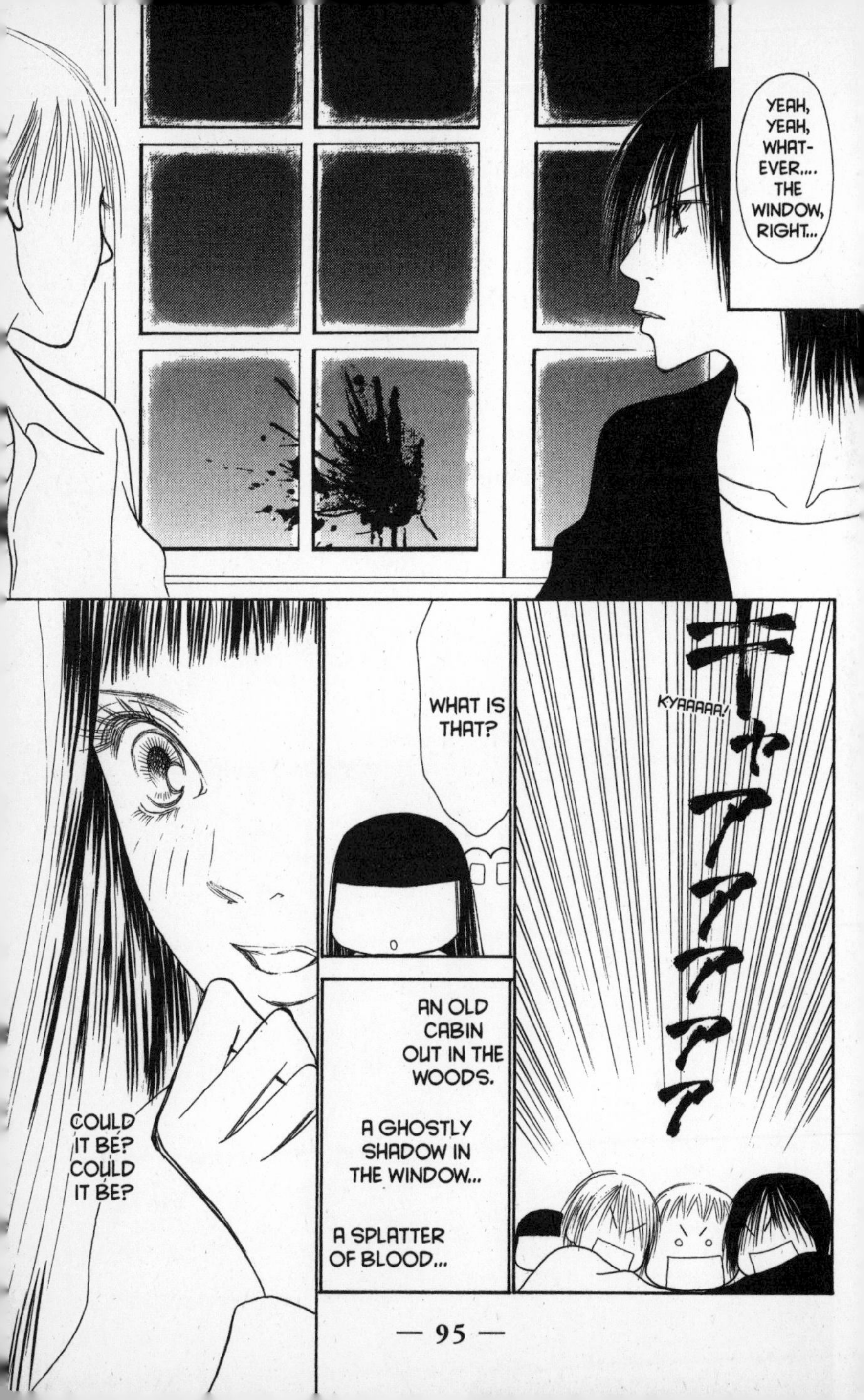
YEAH, YEAH, WHATEVER.... THE WINDOW, RIGHT...
キャアアアアア
KYAAAAAA!
WHAT IS THAT?
AN OLD CABIN OUT IN THE WOODS.
A GHOSTLY SHADOW IN THE WINDOW...
A SPLATTER OF BLOOD...
COULD IT BE? COULD IT BE?

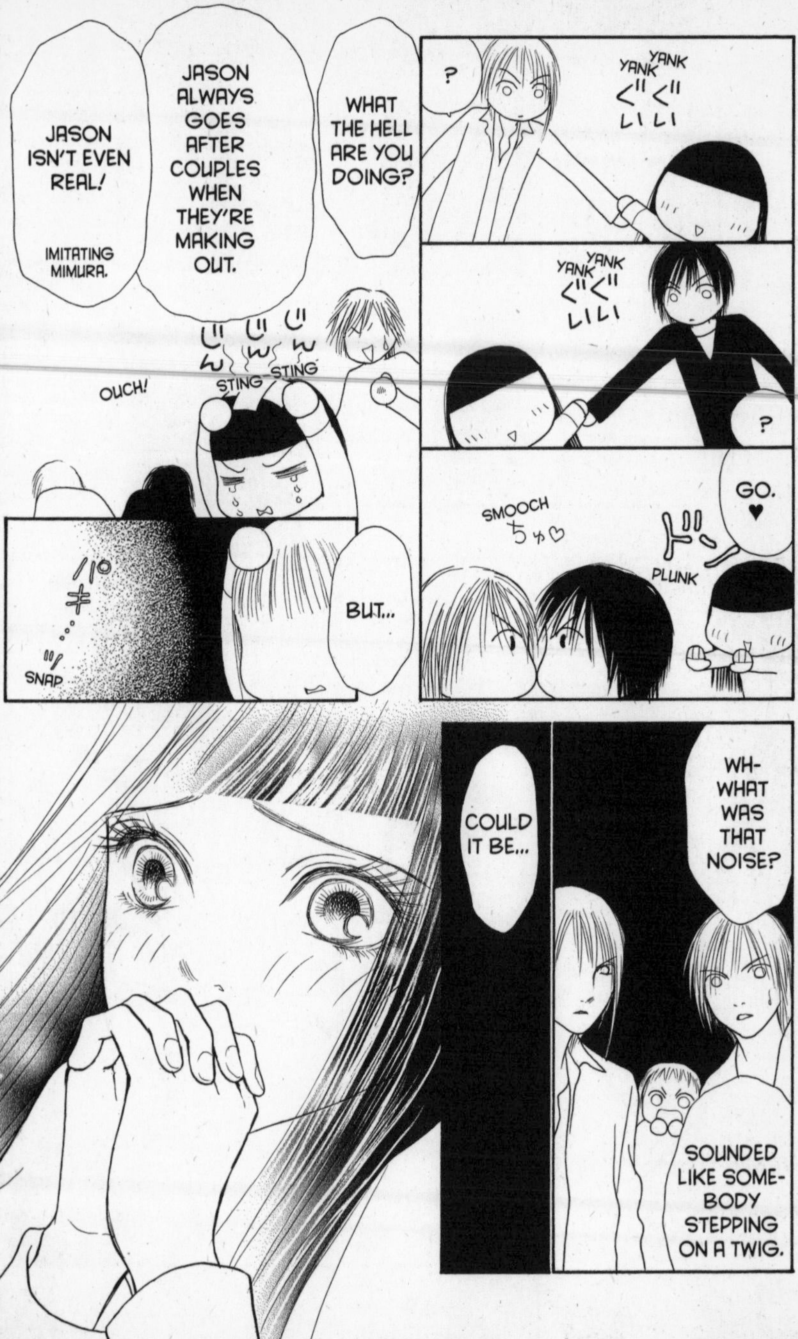
?
YANK YANK
ぐぐいい
YANK YANK
ぐぐいい
?
GO. ♥
SMOOCH
ちゅ♡
ドン
PLUNK
WHAT THE HELL ARE YOU DOING?
JASON ALWAYS GOES AFTER COUPLES WHEN THEY'RE MAKING OUT.
JASON ISN'T EVEN REAL!
IMITATING MIMURA.
じんじんじん
STING STING
OUCH!
BUT...
パキ…ッ
SNAP
WH-WHAT WAS THAT NOISE?
SOUNDED LIKE SOME-BODY STEPPING ON A TWIG.
COULD IT BE...

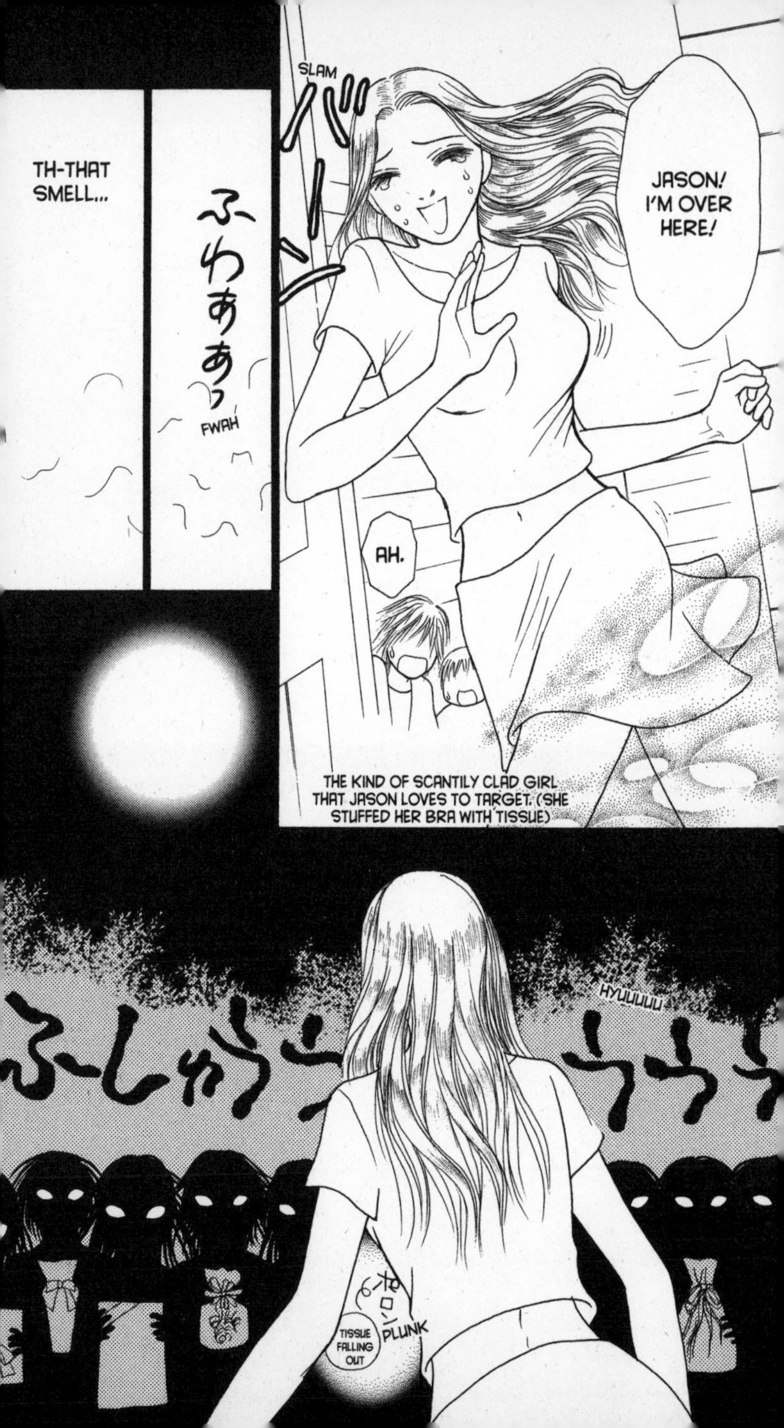
SLAM
JASON! I'M OVER HERE!
AH.
THE KIND OF SCANTILY CLAD GIRL THAT JASON LOVES TO TARGET. (SHE STUFFED HER BRA WITH TISSUE)
FWAH
TH-THAT SMELL...
HYUUUUU
PLUNK
TISSUE FALLING OUT

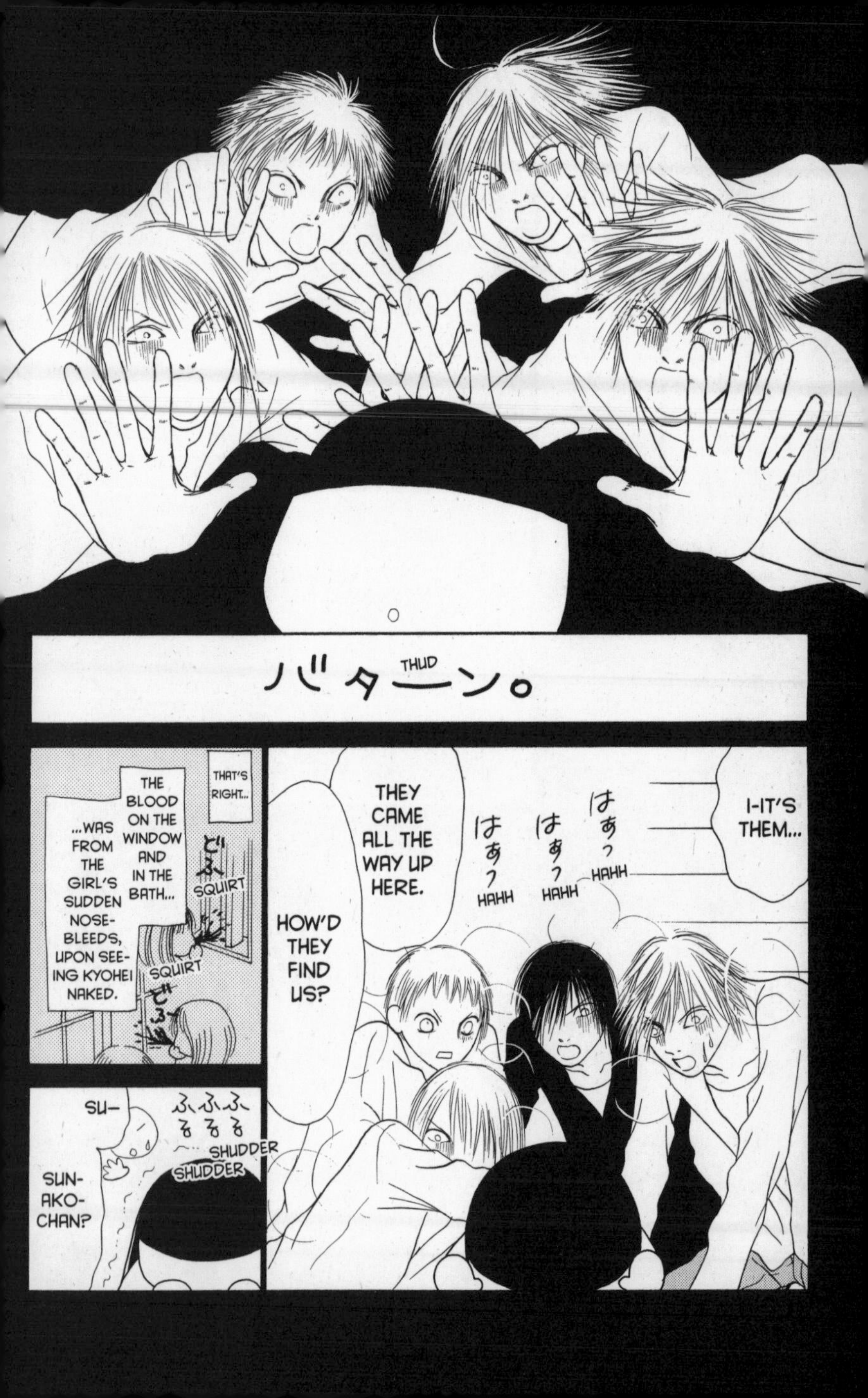
バターン。
THUD
I-IT'S THEM...
はぁっ
HAHH
はぁっ
HAHH
はぁっ
HAHH
THEY CAME ALL THE WAY UP HERE.
HOW'D THEY FIND US?
THAT'S RIGHT...
THE BLOOD ON THE WINDOW AND IN THE BATH...
...WAS FROM THE GIRL'S SUDDEN NOSE-BLEEDS, UPON SEEING KYOHEI NAKED.
どぶ
SQUIRT
どぶ
SQUIRT
SU-
ふるふるふる…
SHUDDER
SHUDDER
SUNAKO-CHAN?

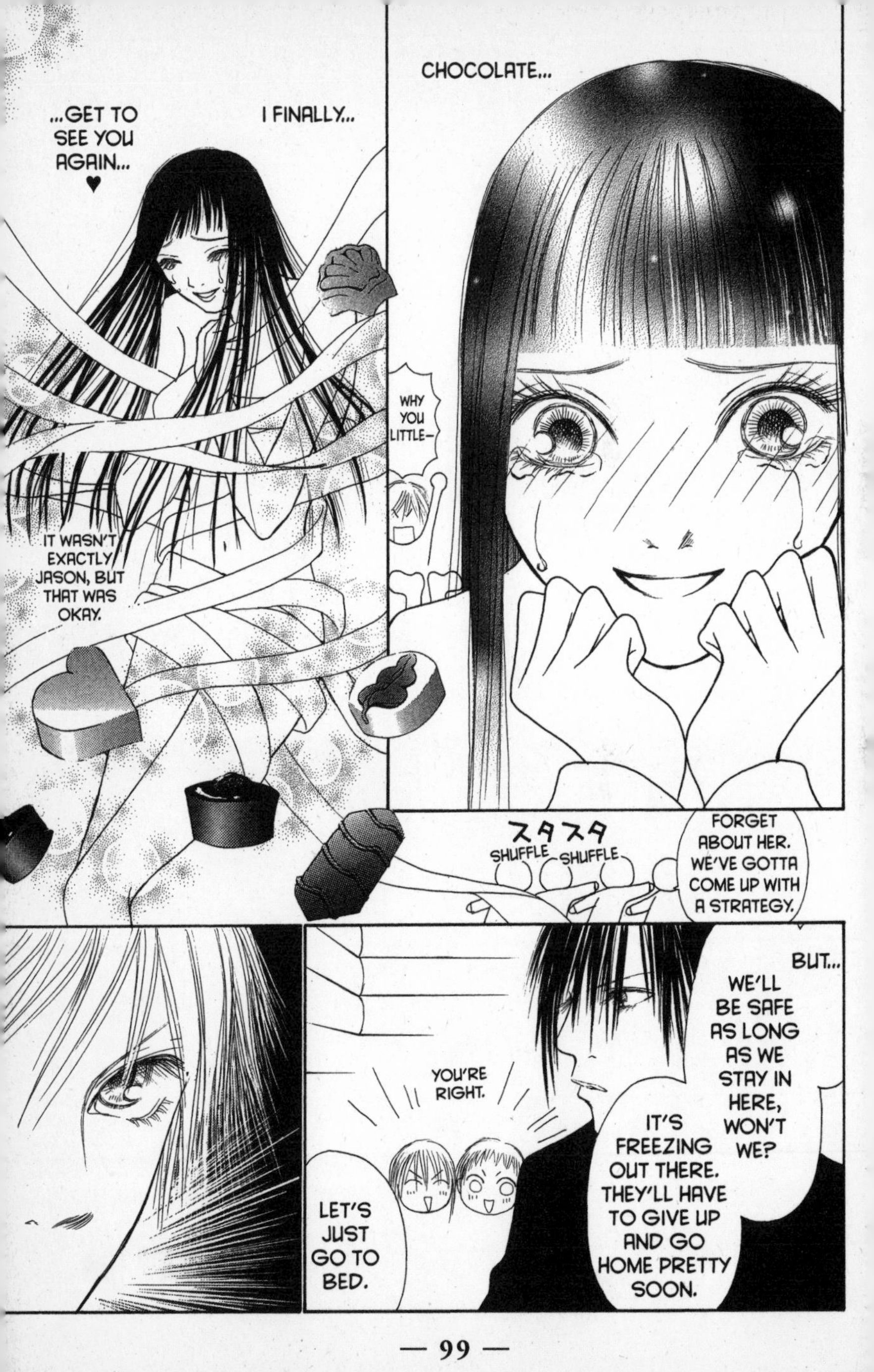
CHOCOLATE...
WHY YOU LITTLE—
スタスタ
SHUFFLE SHUFFLE
FORGET ABOUT HER. WE'VE GOTTA COME UP WITH A STRATEGY.
I FINALLY...
...GET TO SEE YOU AGAIN... ♥
IT WASN'T EXACTLY JASON, BUT THAT WAS OKAY.
BUT...
WE'LL BE SAFE AS LONG AS WE STAY IN HERE, WON'T WE?
IT'S FREEZING OUT THERE. THEY'LL HAVE TO GIVE UP AND GO HOME PRETTY SOON.
YOU'RE RIGHT.
LET'S JUST GO TO BED.

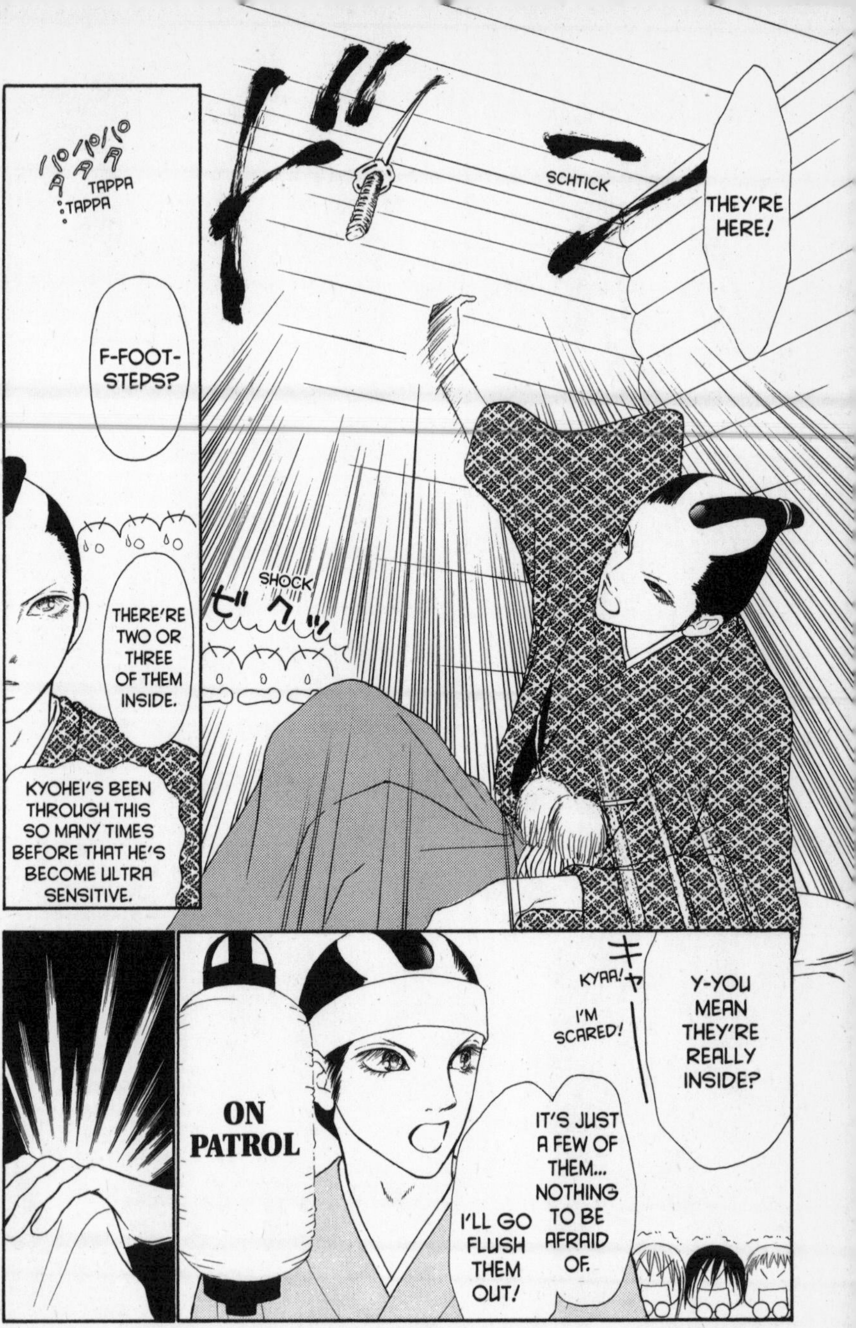

SCHTICK
THEY'RE HERE!
SHOCK
TAPPA TAPPA
F-FOOT-STEPS?
THERE'RE TWO OR THREE OF THEM INSIDE.
KYOHEI'S BEEN THROUGH THIS SO MANY TIMES BEFORE THAT HE'S BECOME ULTRA SENSITIVE.
KYAA! I'M SCARED!
Y-YOU MEAN THEY'RE REALLY INSIDE?
IT'S JUST A FEW OF THEM... NOTHING TO BE AFRAID OF.
I'LL GO FLUSH THEM OUT!
ON PATROL

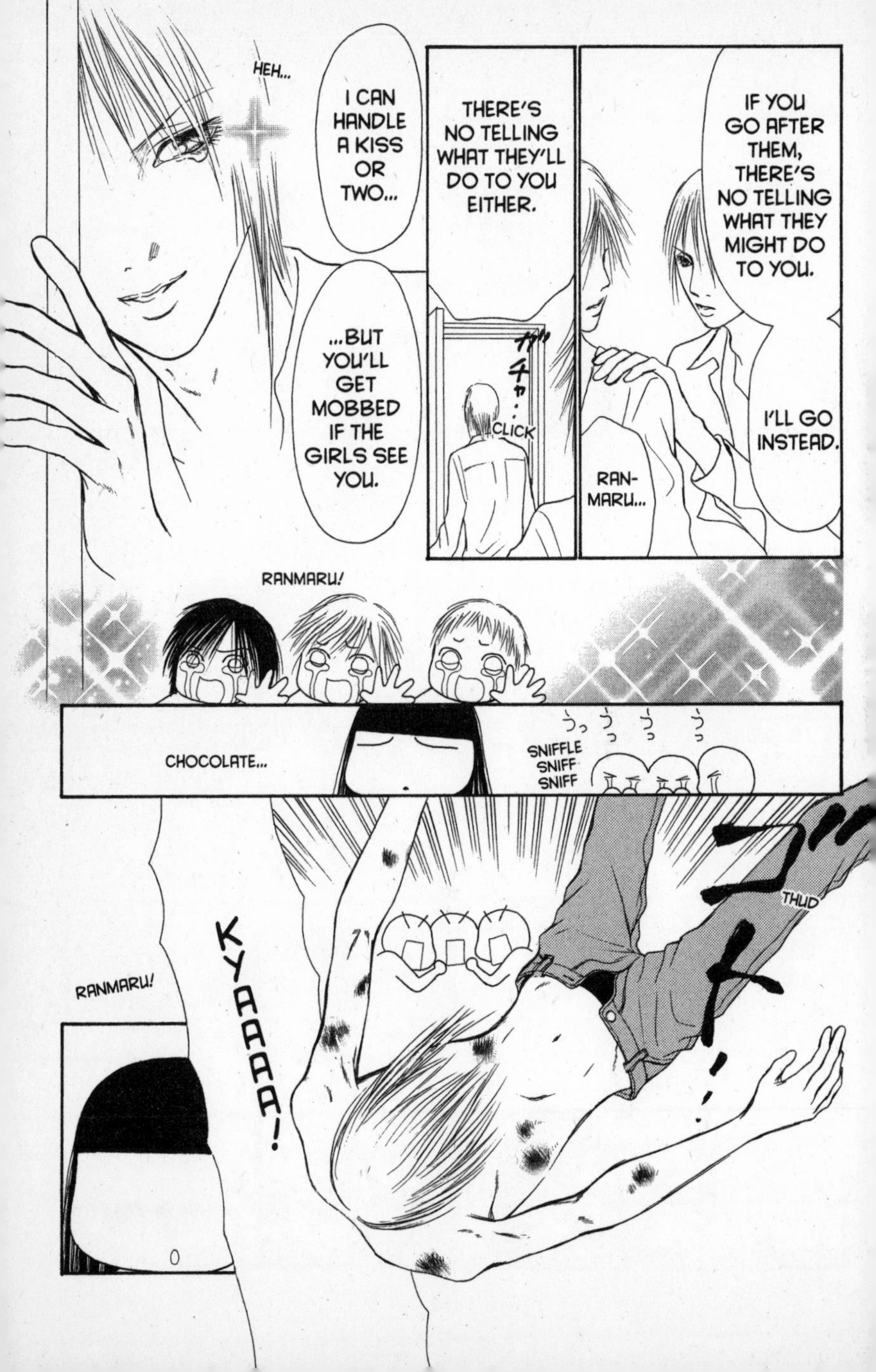
IF YOU GO AFTER THEM, THERE'S NO TELLING WHAT THEY MIGHT DO TO YOU.
I'LL GO INSTEAD.
RAN-MARU...
THERE'S NO TELLING WHAT THEY'LL DO TO YOU EITHER.
CLICK
HEH...
I CAN HANDLE A KISS OR TWO...
...BUT YOU'LL GET MOBBED IF THE GIRLS SEE YOU.
RANMARU!
SNIFFLE SNIFF SNIFF
CHOCOLATE...
THUD
KYAAAAA!
RANMARU!

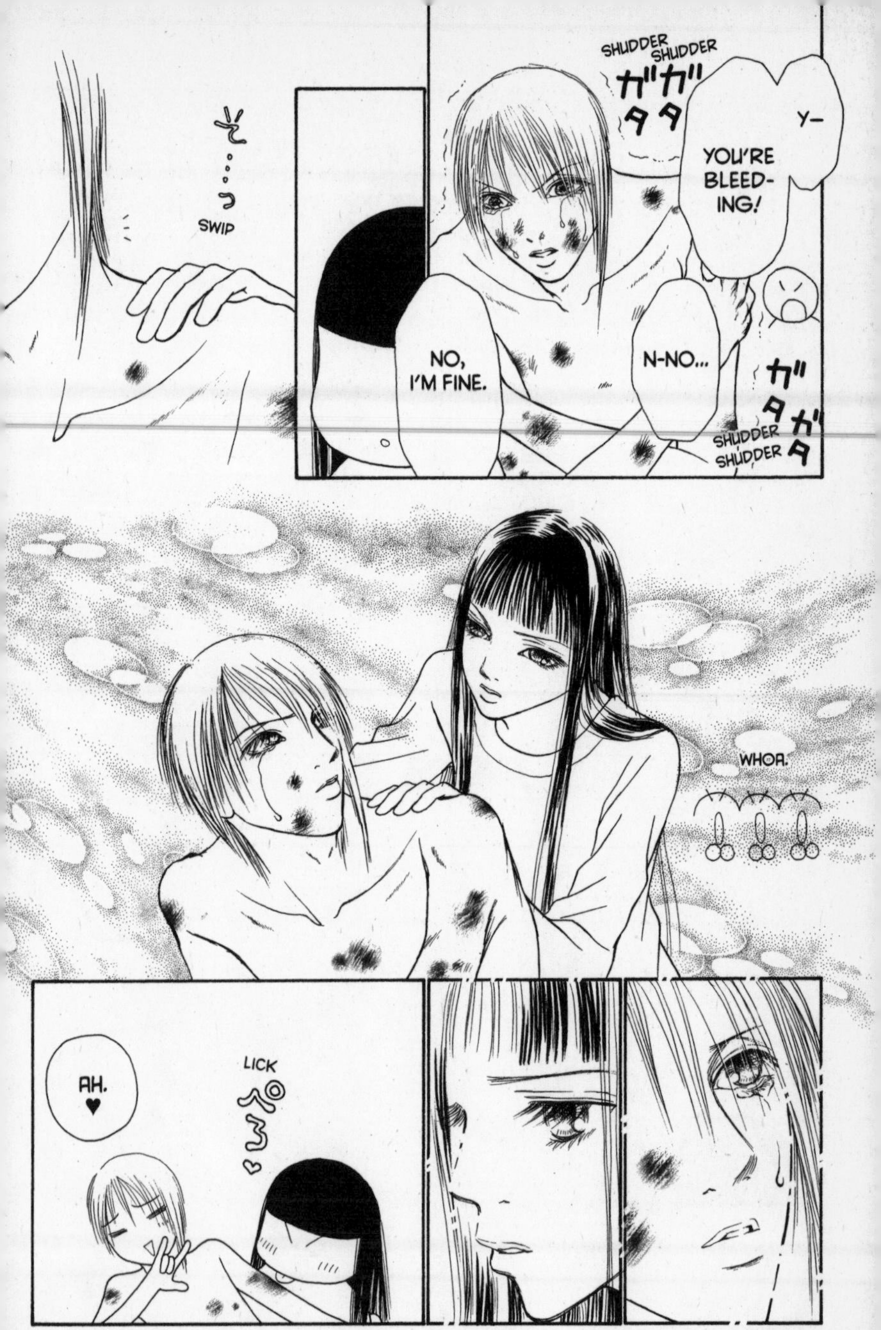
SHUDDER SHUDDER
ガタガタ
Y—
YOU'RE BLEEDING!
N-NO...
NO, I'M FINE.
ガタガタ
SHUDDER SHUDDER
そ…っ
SWIP
WHOA.
AH. ♥
ぺろ
LICK

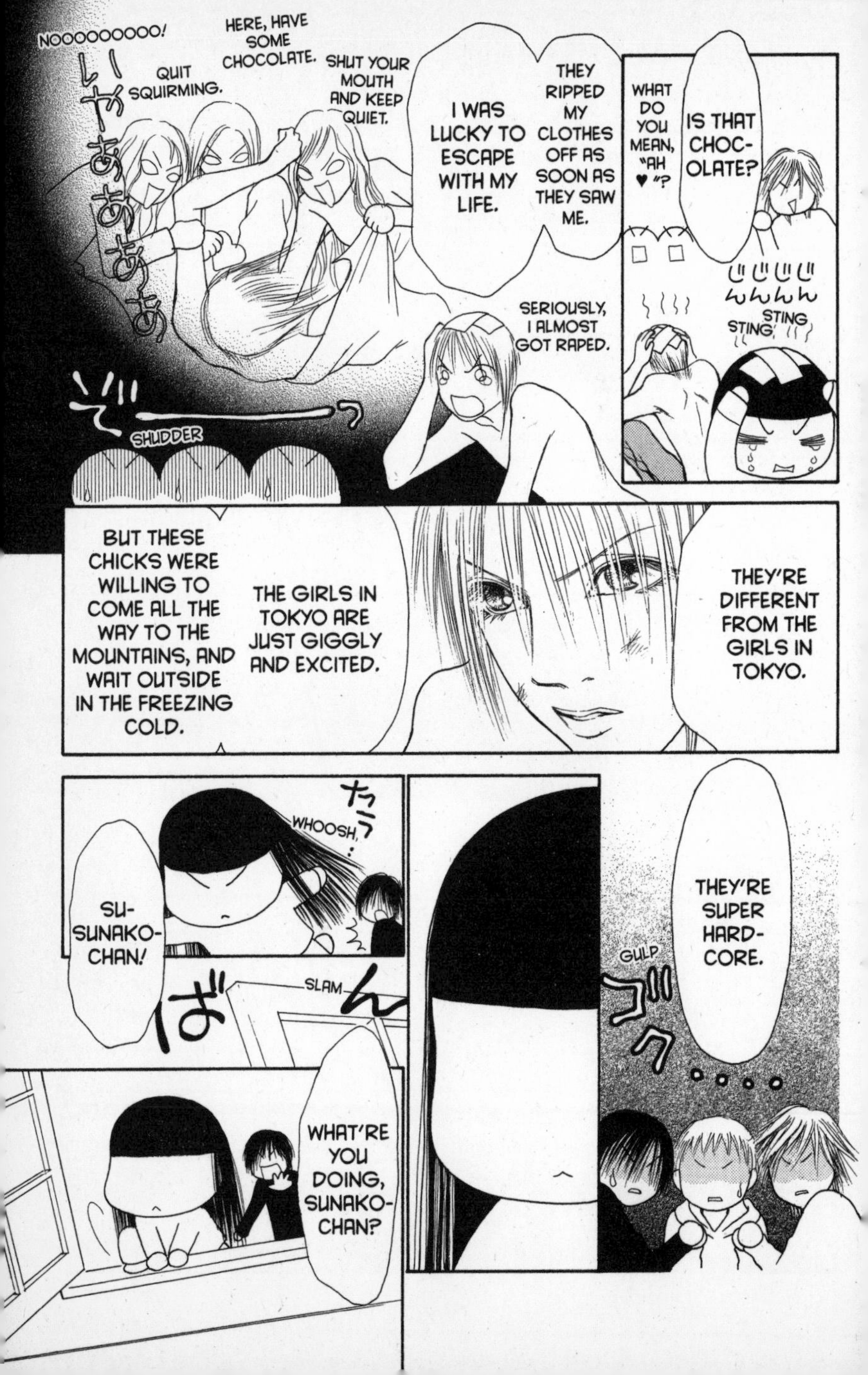

IS THAT CHOCOLATE?
WHAT DO YOU MEAN, "AH ♥"?
STING STING
THEY RIPPED MY CLOTHES OFF AS SOON AS THEY SAW ME.
I WAS LUCKY TO ESCAPE WITH MY LIFE.
SHUT YOUR MOUTH AND KEEP QUIET.
HERE, HAVE SOME CHOCOLATE.
QUIT SQUIRMING.
NOOOOOOOOO!
SERIOUSLY, I ALMOST GOT RAPED.
SHUDDER
THEY'RE DIFFERENT FROM THE GIRLS IN TOKYO.
THE GIRLS IN TOKYO ARE JUST GIGGLY AND EXCITED.
BUT THESE CHICKS WERE WILLING TO COME ALL THE WAY TO THE MOUNTAINS, AND WAIT OUTSIDE IN THE FREEZING COLD.
THEY'RE SUPER HARD-CORE.
GULP
....
WHOOSH
SU-SUNAKO-CHAN!
SLAM
WHAT'RE YOU DOING, SUNAKO-CHAN?

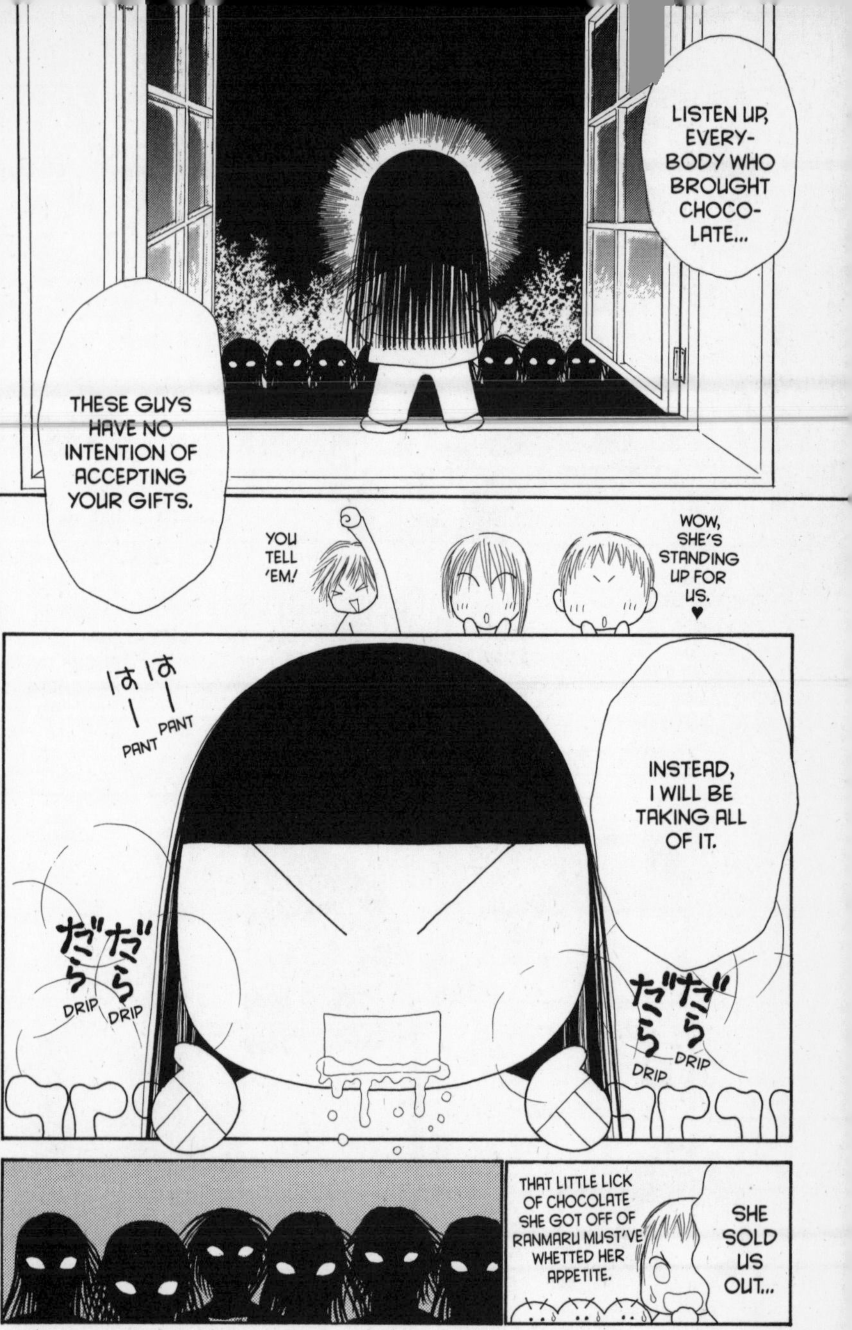
LISTEN UP, EVERYBODY WHO BROUGHT CHOCOLATE...
THESE GUYS HAVE NO INTENTION OF ACCEPTING YOUR GIFTS.
WOW, SHE'S STANDING UP FOR US. ♥
YOU TELL 'EM!
INSTEAD, I WILL BE TAKING ALL OF IT.
だらだら DRIP DRIP
はーはー PANT PANT
だらだら DRIP DRIP
SHE SOLD US OUT...
THAT LITTLE LICK OF CHOCOLATE SHE GOT OFF OF RANMARU MUST'VE WHETTED HER APPETITE.

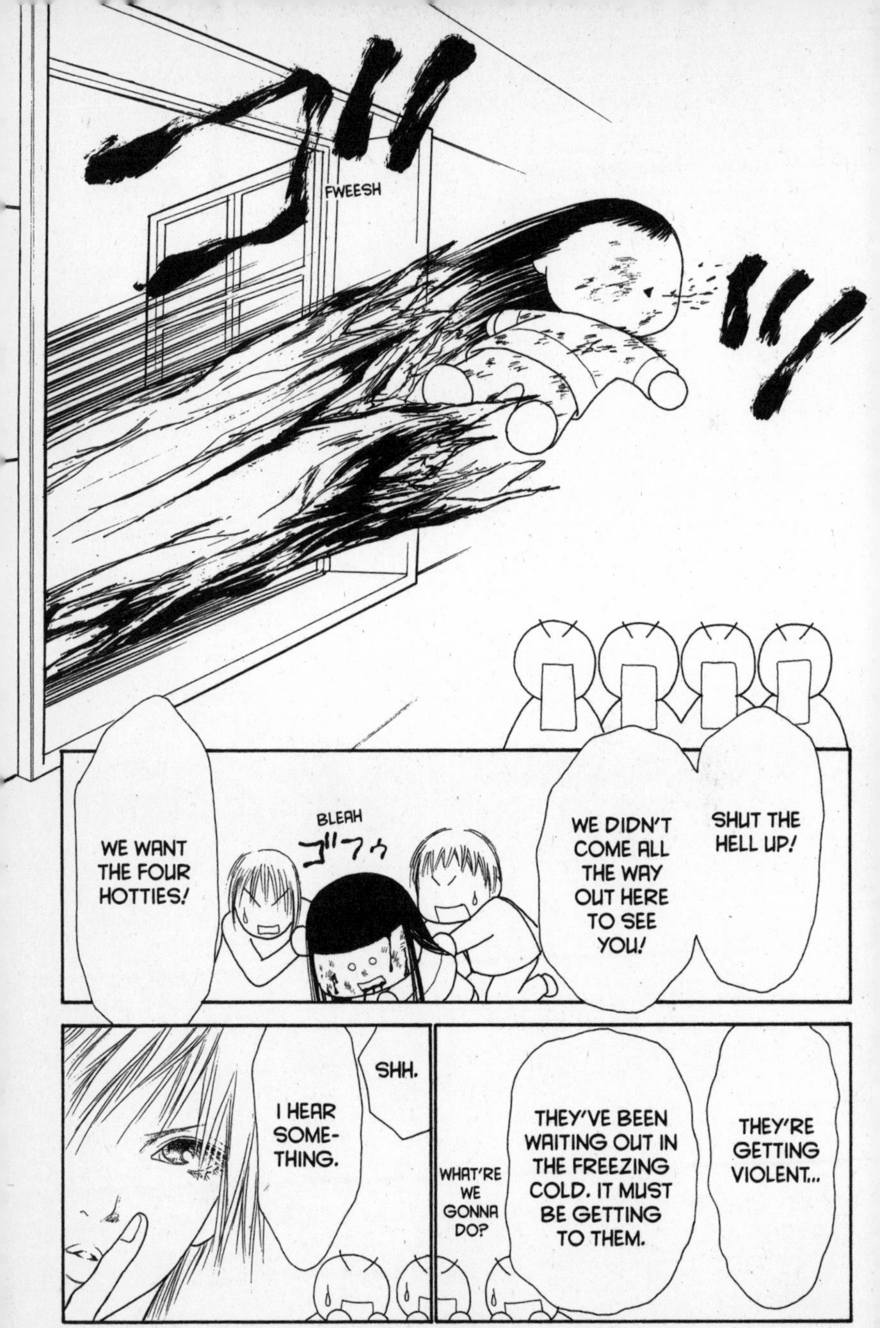
FWEESH
SHUT THE HELL UP!
WE DIDN'T COME ALL THE WAY OUT HERE TO SEE YOU!
BLEAH
ゴフゥ
WE WANT THE FOUR HOTTIES!
THEY'RE GETTING VIOLENT...
THEY'VE BEEN WAITING OUT IN THE FREEZING COLD. IT MUST BE GETTING TO THEM.
WHAT'RE WE GONNA DO?
SHH.
I HEAR SOME-THING.

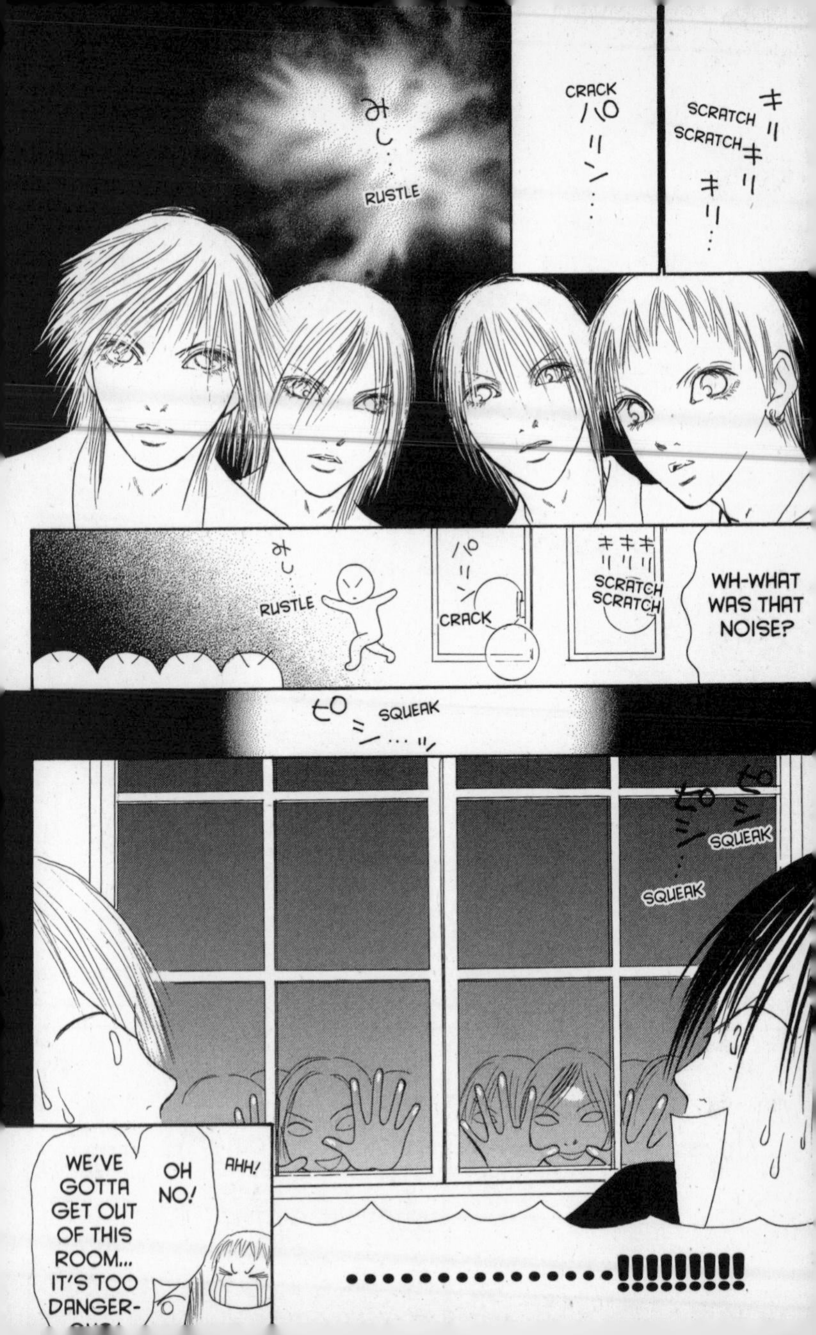

SCRATCH SCRATCH
キリキリキリ…
CRACK
パリン…
みし…
RUSTLE
WH-WHAT WAS THAT NOISE?
キキキ リリリ
SCRATCH SCRATCH
パリン
CRACK
みし…
RUSTLE
SQUEAK
SQUEAK
SQUEAK
…………………!!!!!!!!
AHH!
OH NO!
WE'VE GOTTA GET OUT OF THIS ROOM... IT'S TOO DANGER-

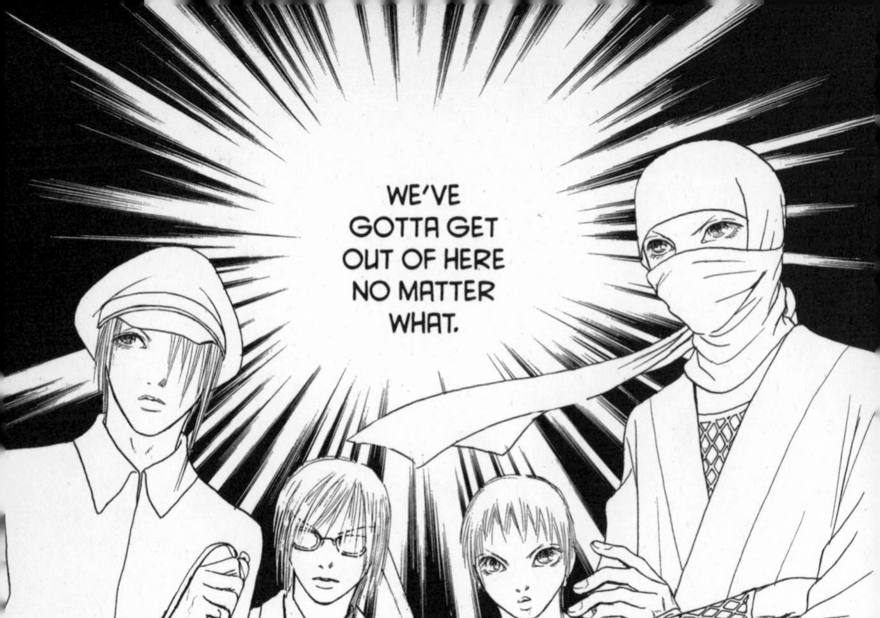
WE'VE GOTTA GET OUT OF HERE NO MATTER WHAT.
※DRAMATIZATION

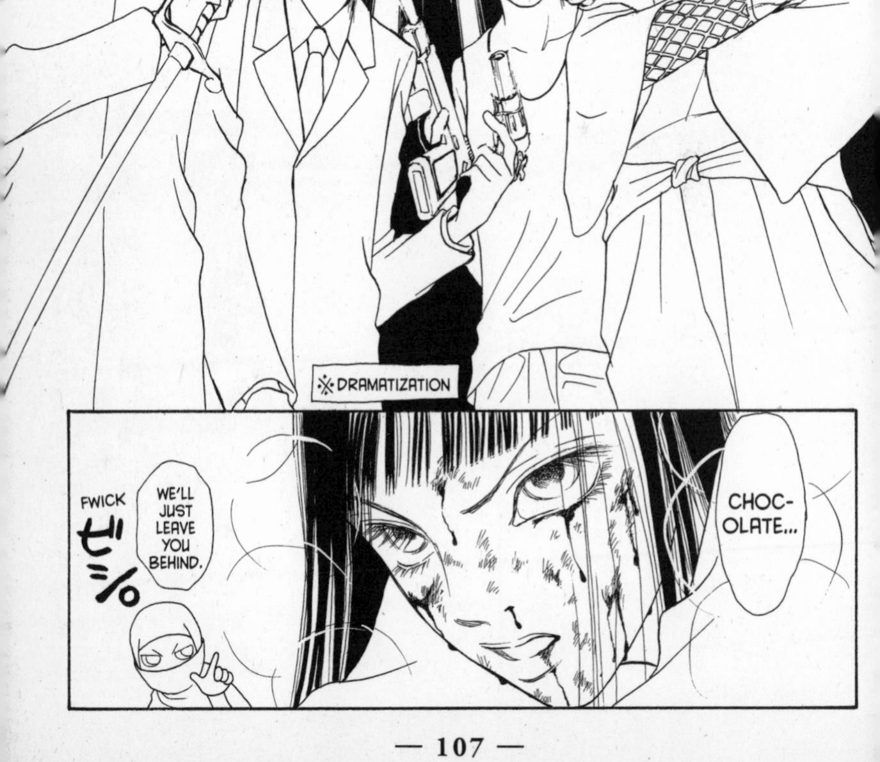
CHOC-OLATE...
WE'LL JUST LEAVE YOU BEHIND.
FWICK

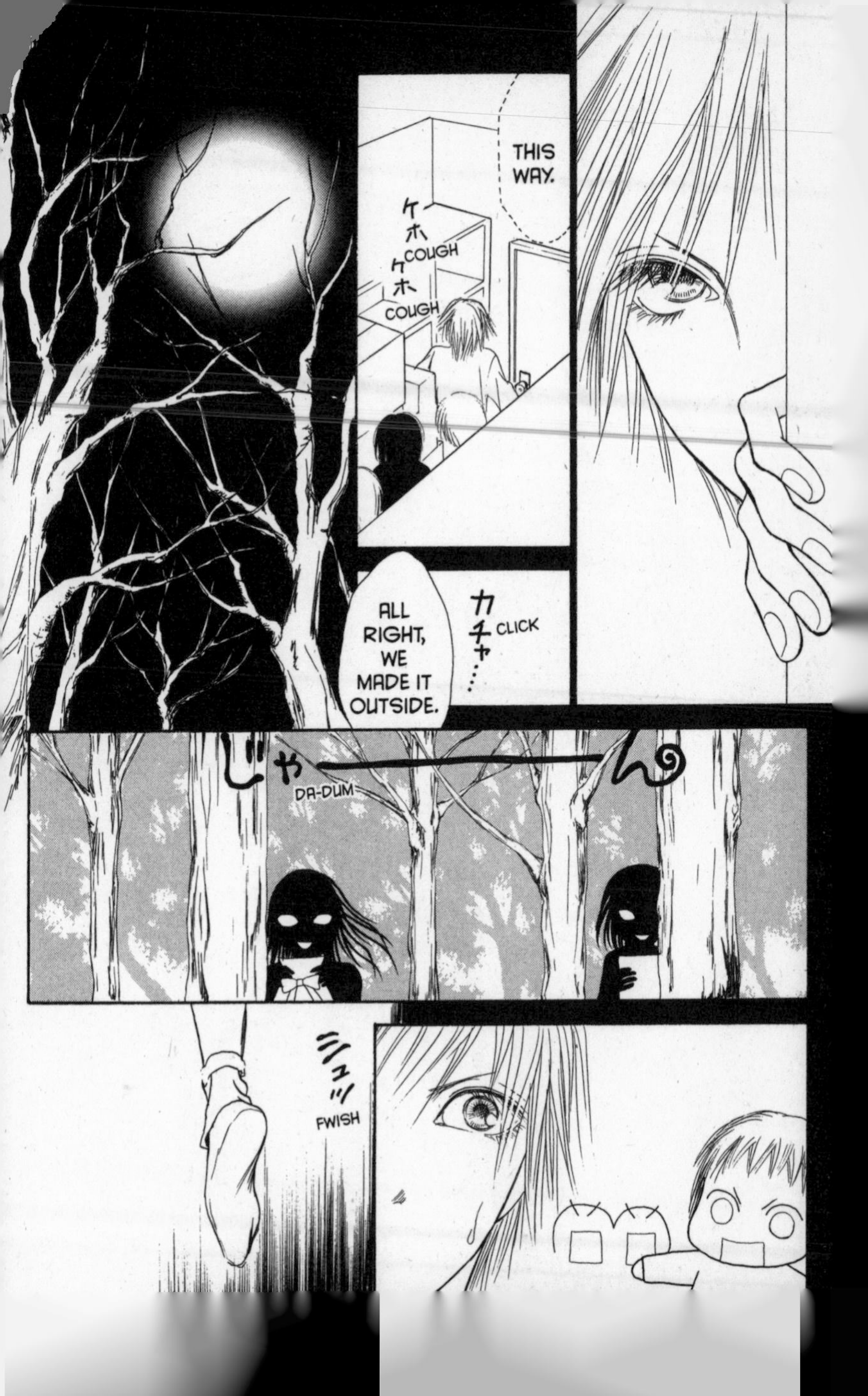
THIS WAY.
ケホ COUGH
ケホ COUGH
ALL RIGHT, WE MADE IT OUTSIDE.
カチャ… CLICK
じゃーん DA-DUM
シュッ FWISH

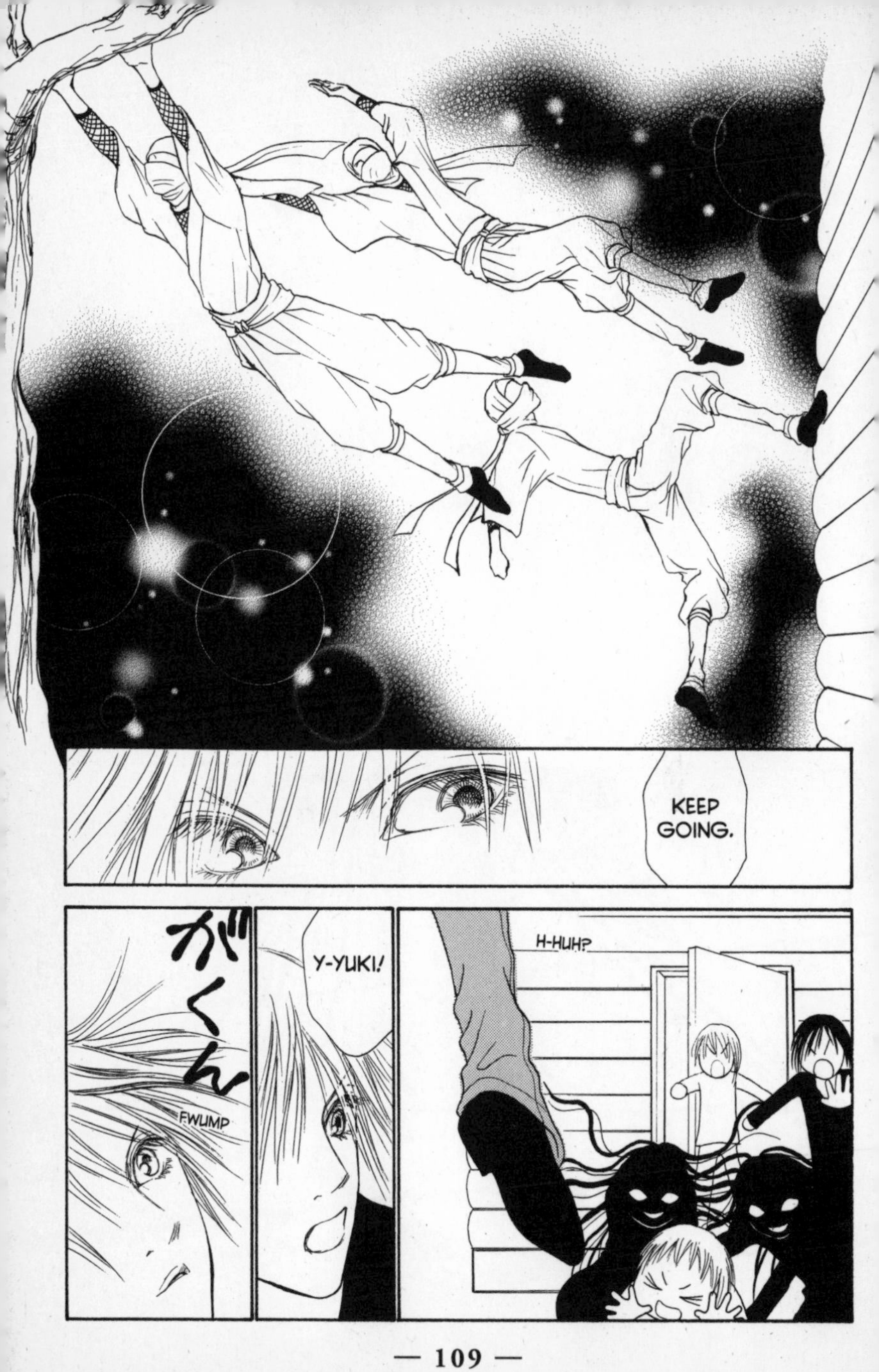
KEEP GOING.
H-HUH?
Y-YUKI!
がくん
FWUMP

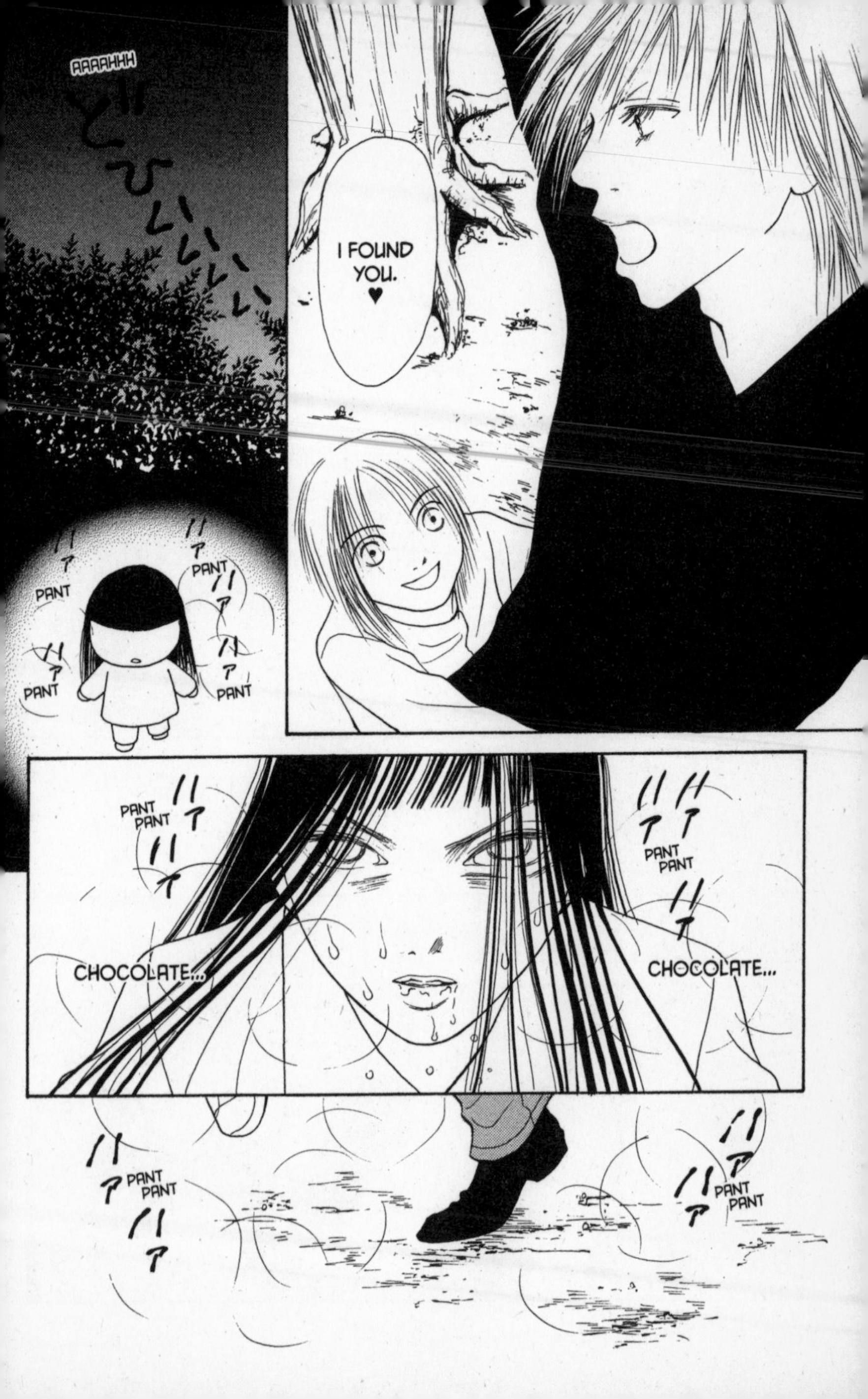
I FOUND YOU. ♥
AAAAHHH
PANT
PANT
PANT
PANT
CHOCOLATE...
CHOCOLATE...
PANT PANT
PANT PANT
PANT PANT
PANT PANT

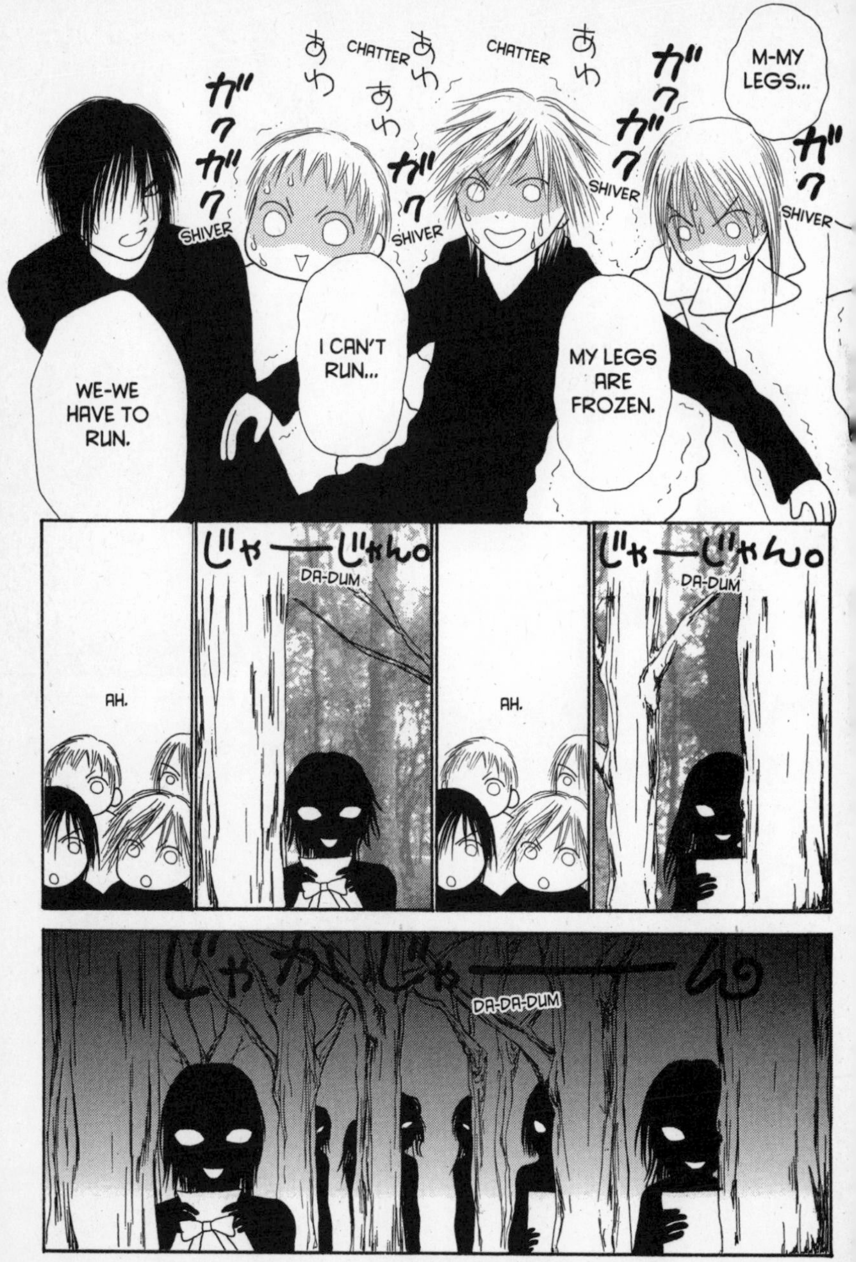
M-MY LEGS...
SHIVER
SHIVER
MY LEGS ARE FROZEN.
CHATTER
SHIVER
CHATTER
SHIVER
I CAN'T RUN...
WE-WE HAVE TO RUN.
DA-DUM
AH.
DA-DUM
AH.
DA-DA-DUM

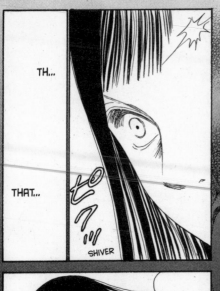

TH...

THAT...

SHIVER

KYRAAAA

THAT AROMA... ♥♥♥

CRUNCH CRUNCH

HUH?

AH, IT'S SUNAKO NAKA-HARA.

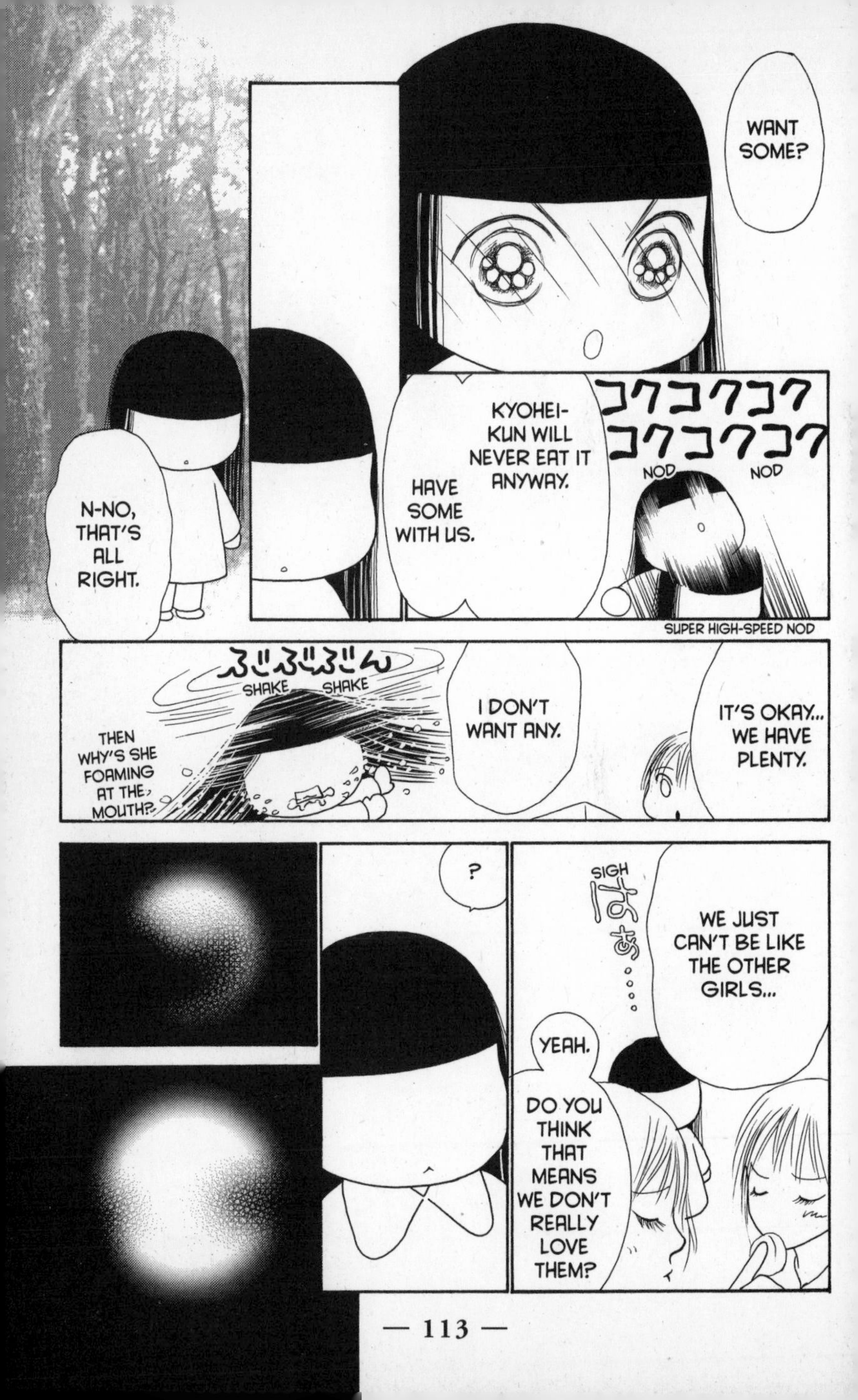
WANT SOME?
KYOHEI-KUN WILL NEVER EAT IT ANYWAY.
HAVE SOME WITH US.
コクコクコク コクコクコク
NOD NOD
SUPER HIGH-SPEED NOD
N-NO, THAT'S ALL RIGHT.
IT'S OKAY... WE HAVE PLENTY.
I DON'T WANT ANY.
ぶぶぶん
SHAKE SHAKE
THEN WHY'S SHE FOAMING AT THE MOUTH?
SIGH
はぁ……
WE JUST CAN'T BE LIKE THE OTHER GIRLS...
YEAH.
DO YOU THINK THAT MEANS WE DON'T REALLY LOVE THEM?
?

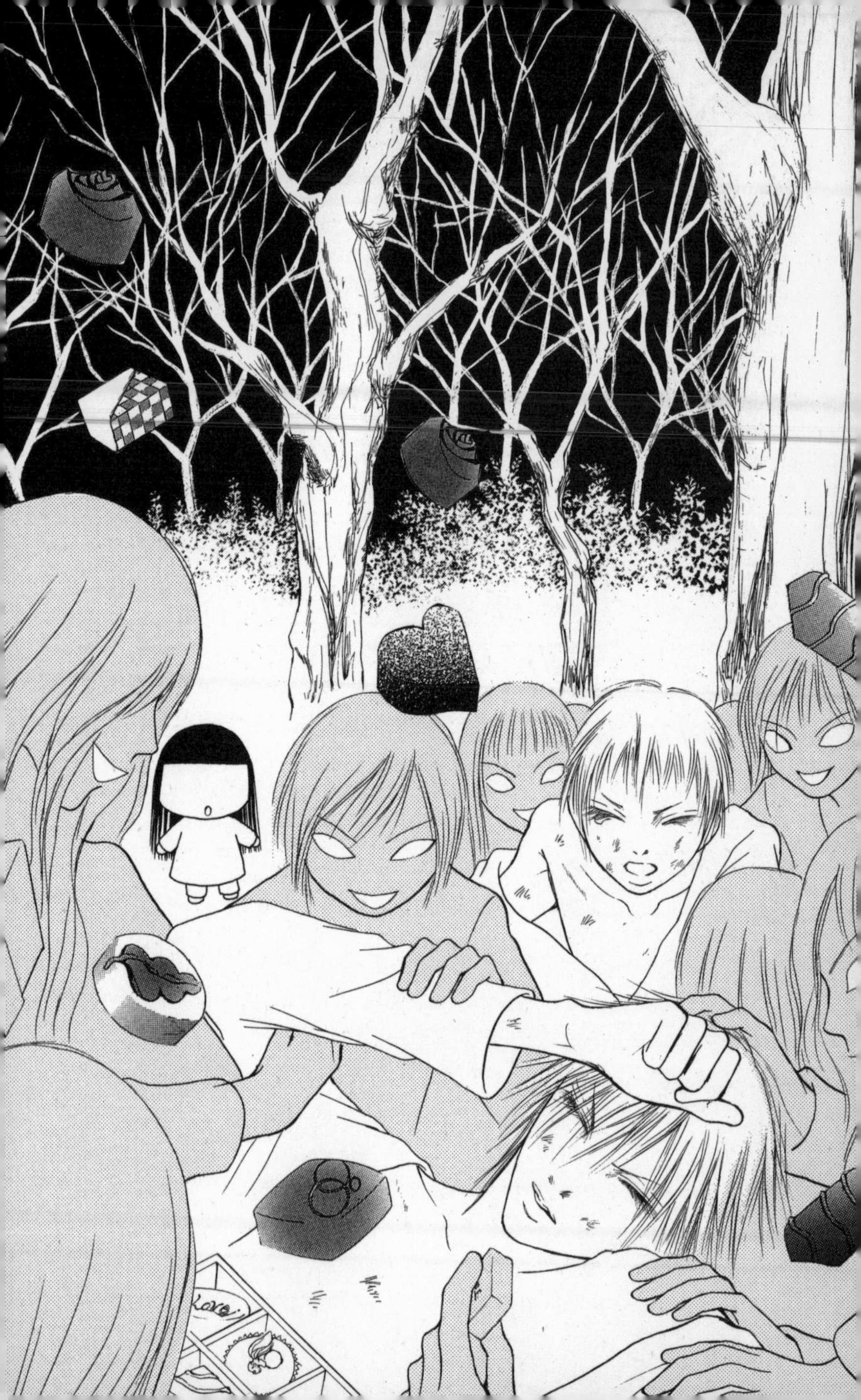
Love

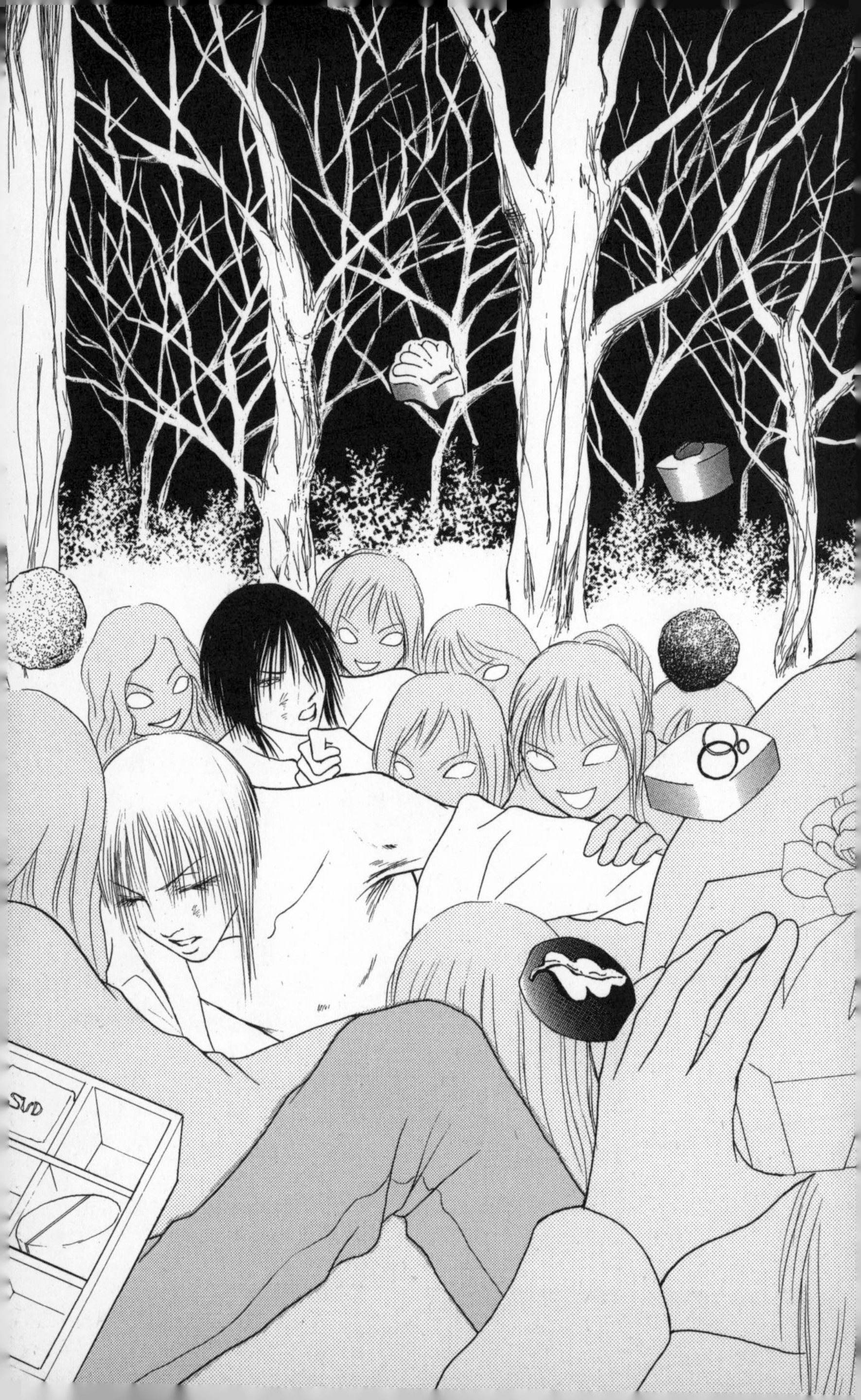

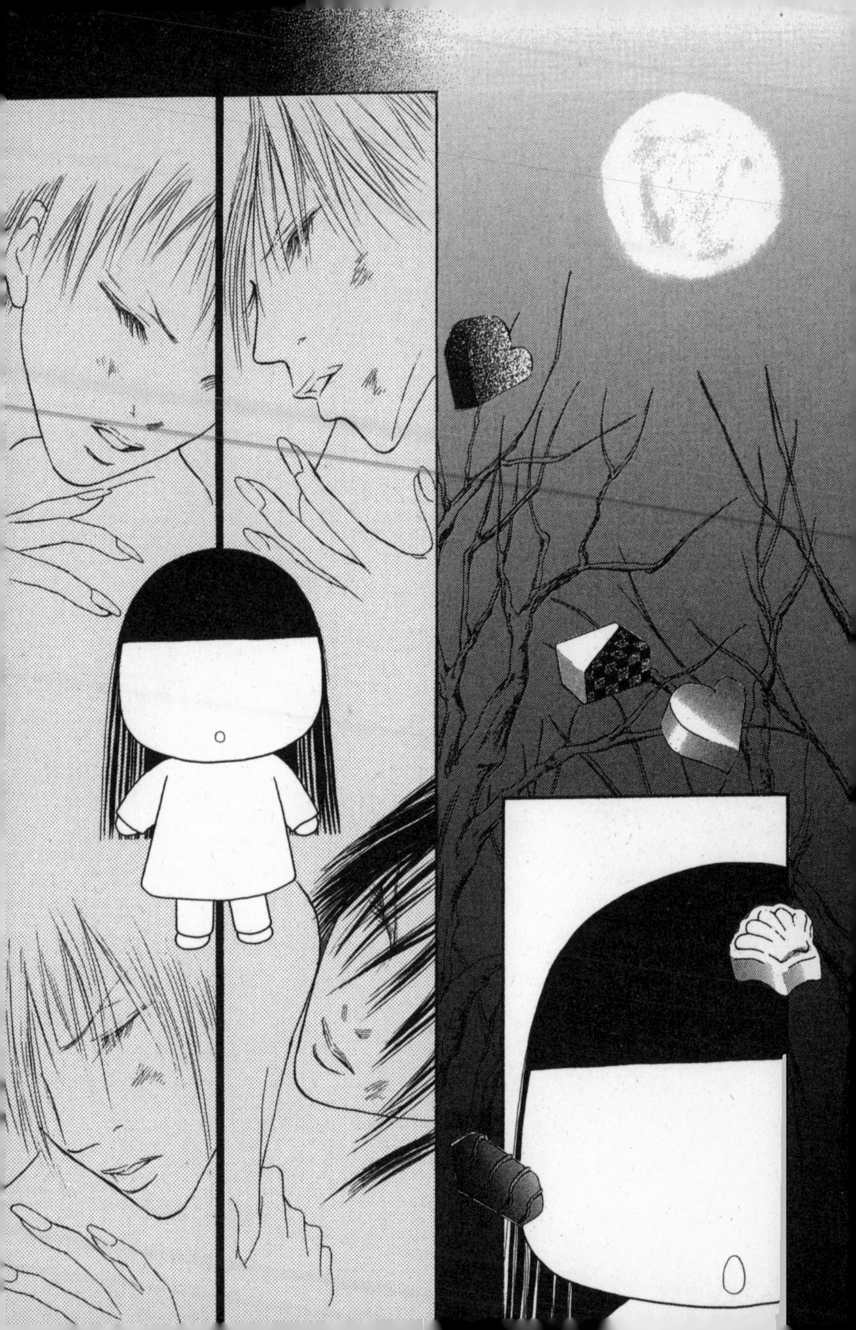

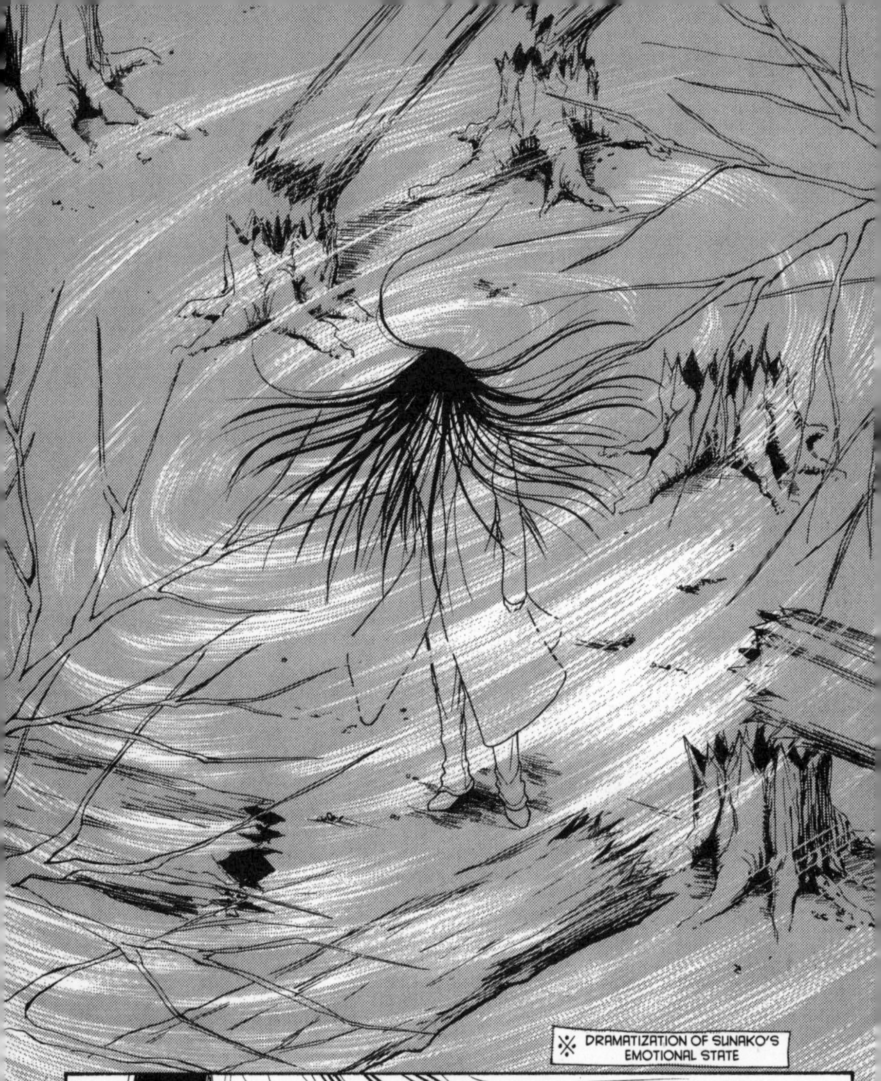
※ DRAMATIZATION OF SUNAKO'S EMOTIONAL STATE

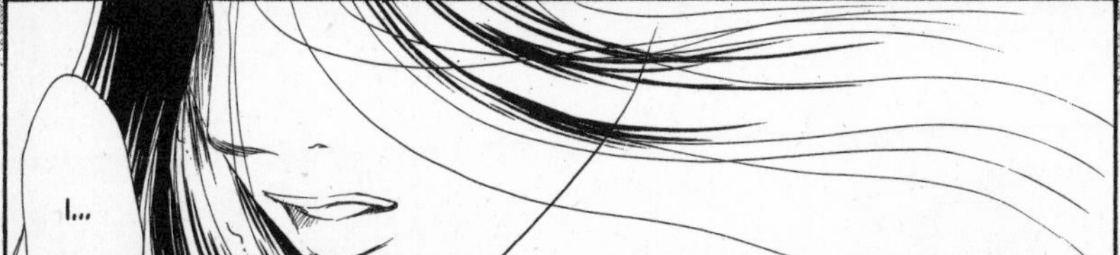
I...

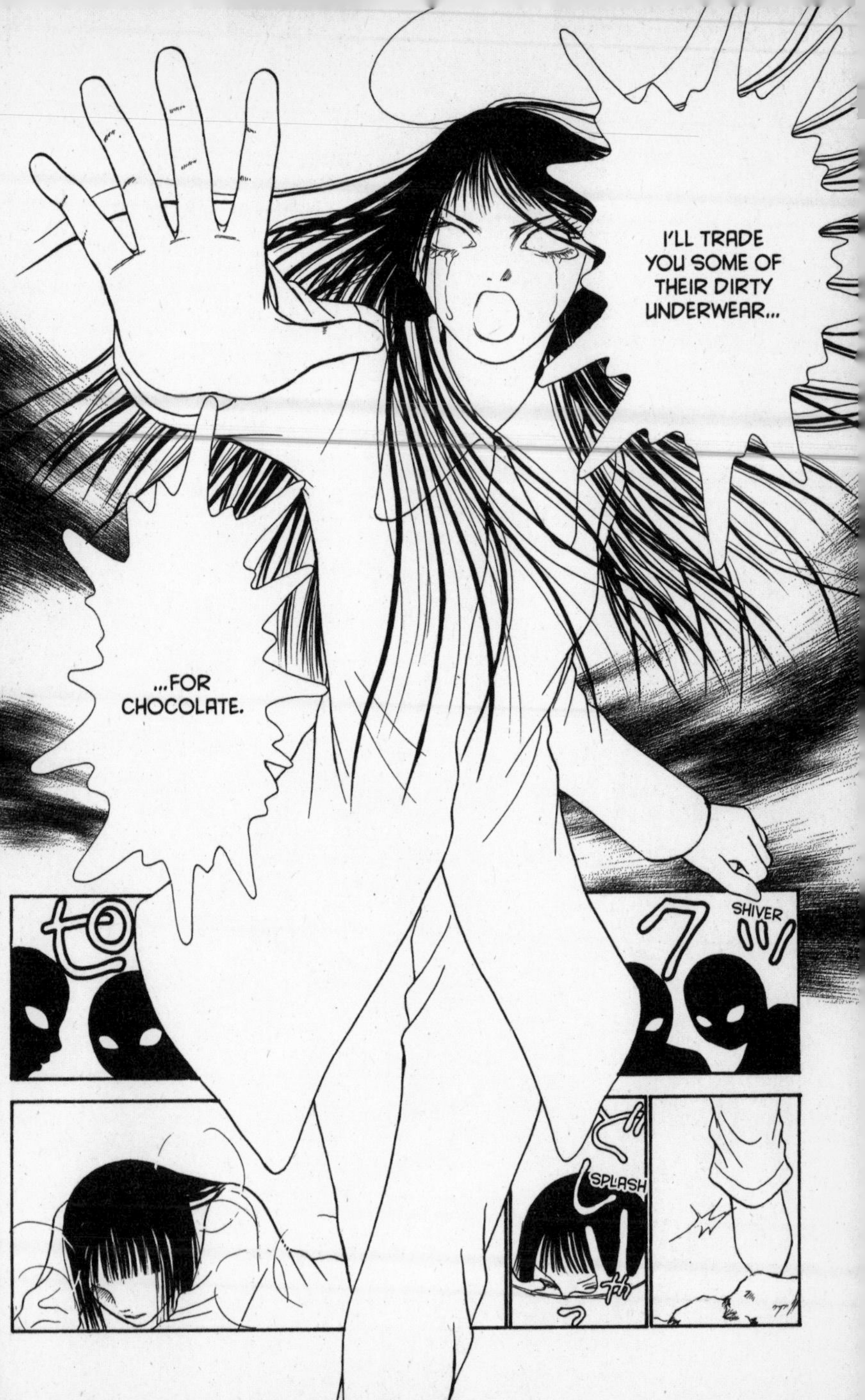
I'LL TRADE YOU SOME OF THEIR DIRTY UNDERWEAR...
...FOR CHOCOLATE.
SHIVER
SPLASH

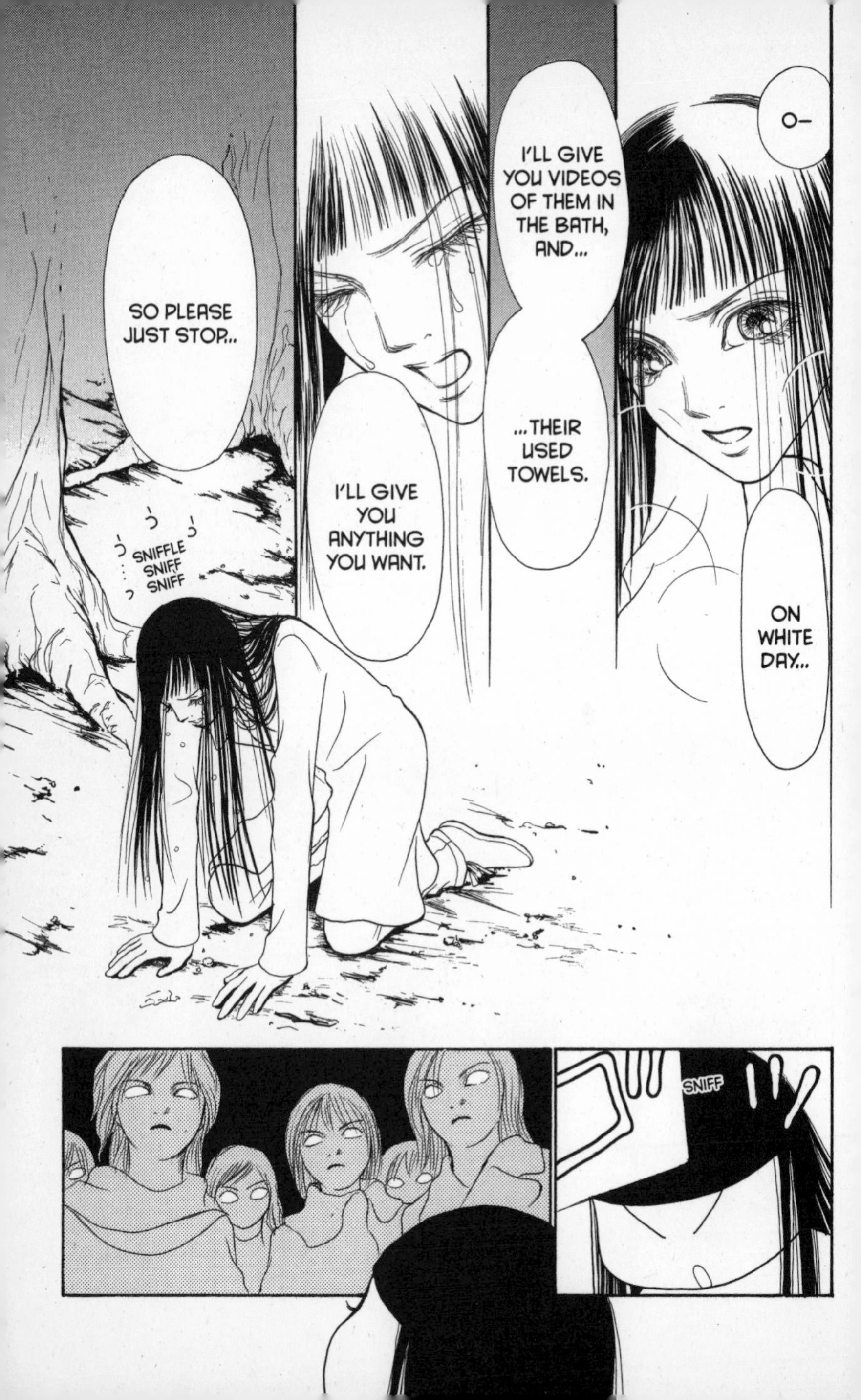
O-
ON WHITE DAY...
I'LL GIVE YOU VIDEOS OF THEM IN THE BATH, AND...
...THEIR USED TOWELS.
I'LL GIVE YOU ANYTHING YOU WANT.
SO PLEASE JUST STOP...
SNIFFLE SNIFF SNIFF
SNIFF

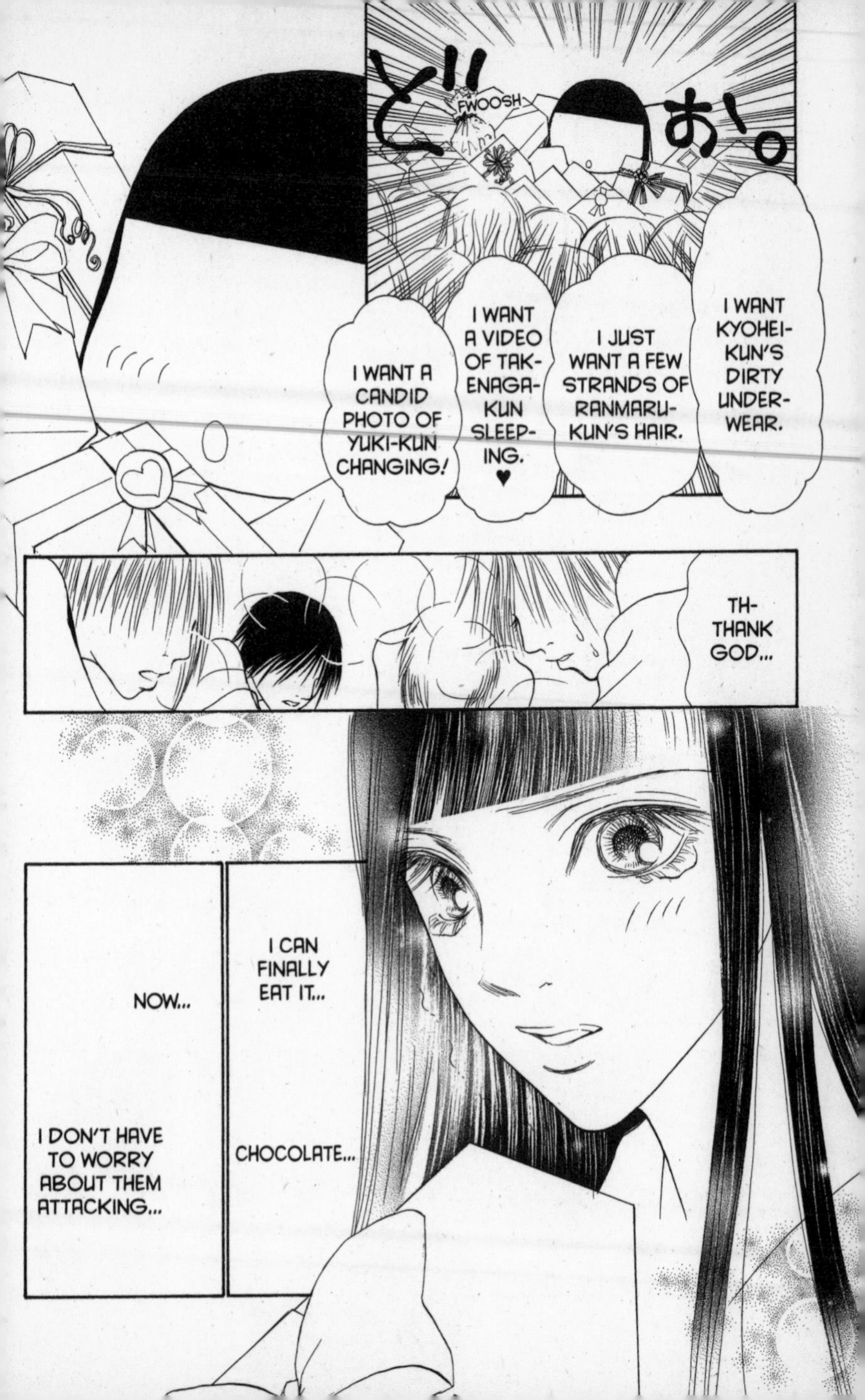
FWOOSH
I WANT KYOHEI-KUN'S DIRTY UNDER-WEAR.
I JUST WANT A FEW STRANDS OF RANMARU-KUN'S HAIR.
I WANT A VIDEO OF TAK-ENAGA-KUN SLEEP-ING. ♥
I WANT A CANDID PHOTO OF YUKI-KUN CHANGING!
TH-THANK GOD...
I CAN FINALLY EAT IT...
CHOCOLATE...
NOW...
I DON'T HAVE TO WORRY ABOUT THEM ATTACKING...

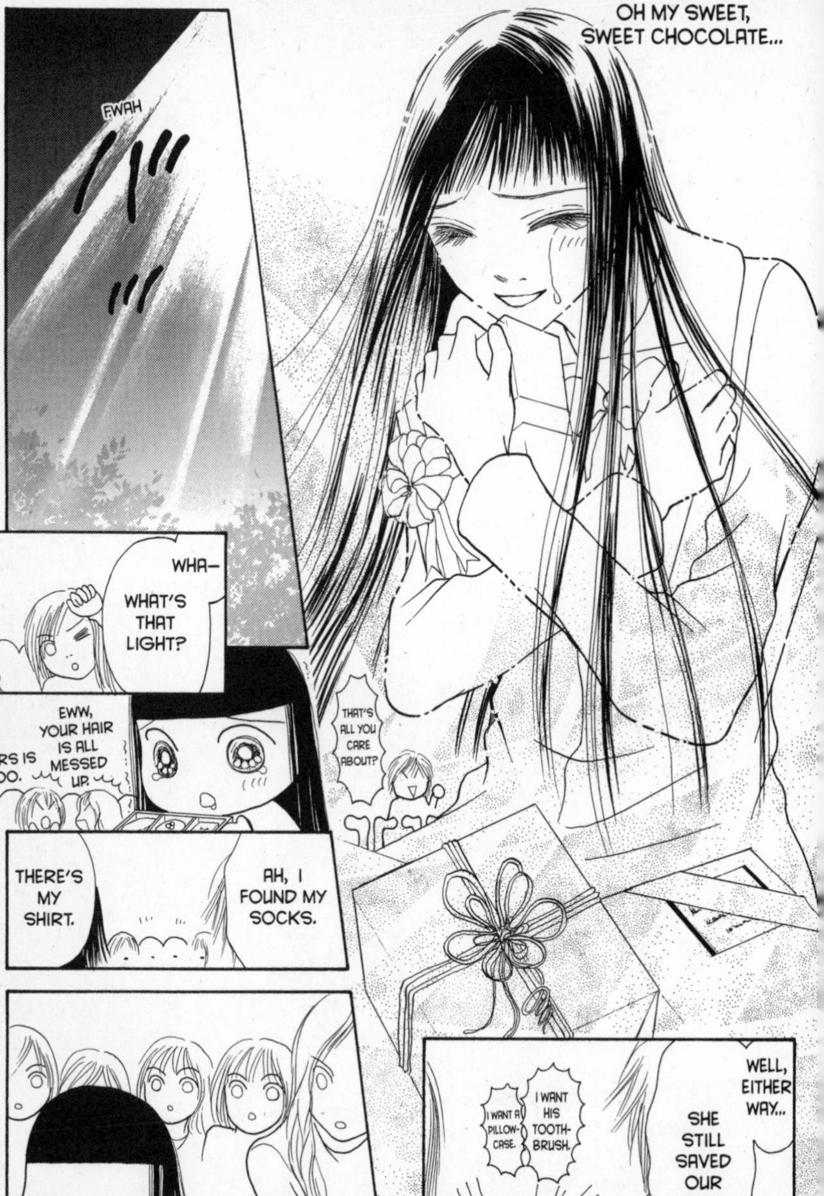
OH MY SWEET, SWEET CHOCOLATE...
THAT'S ALL YOU CARE ABOUT?
FWAH
WHA-
WHAT'S THAT LIGHT?
EWW, YOUR HAIR IS ALL MESSED UP.
YOURS IS TOO.
AH, I FOUND MY SOCKS.
THERE'S MY SHIRT.
WELL, EITHER WAY...
SHE STILL SAVED OUR SKIN.
I WANT HIS TOOTH-BRUSH.
I WANT A PILLOW-CASE.

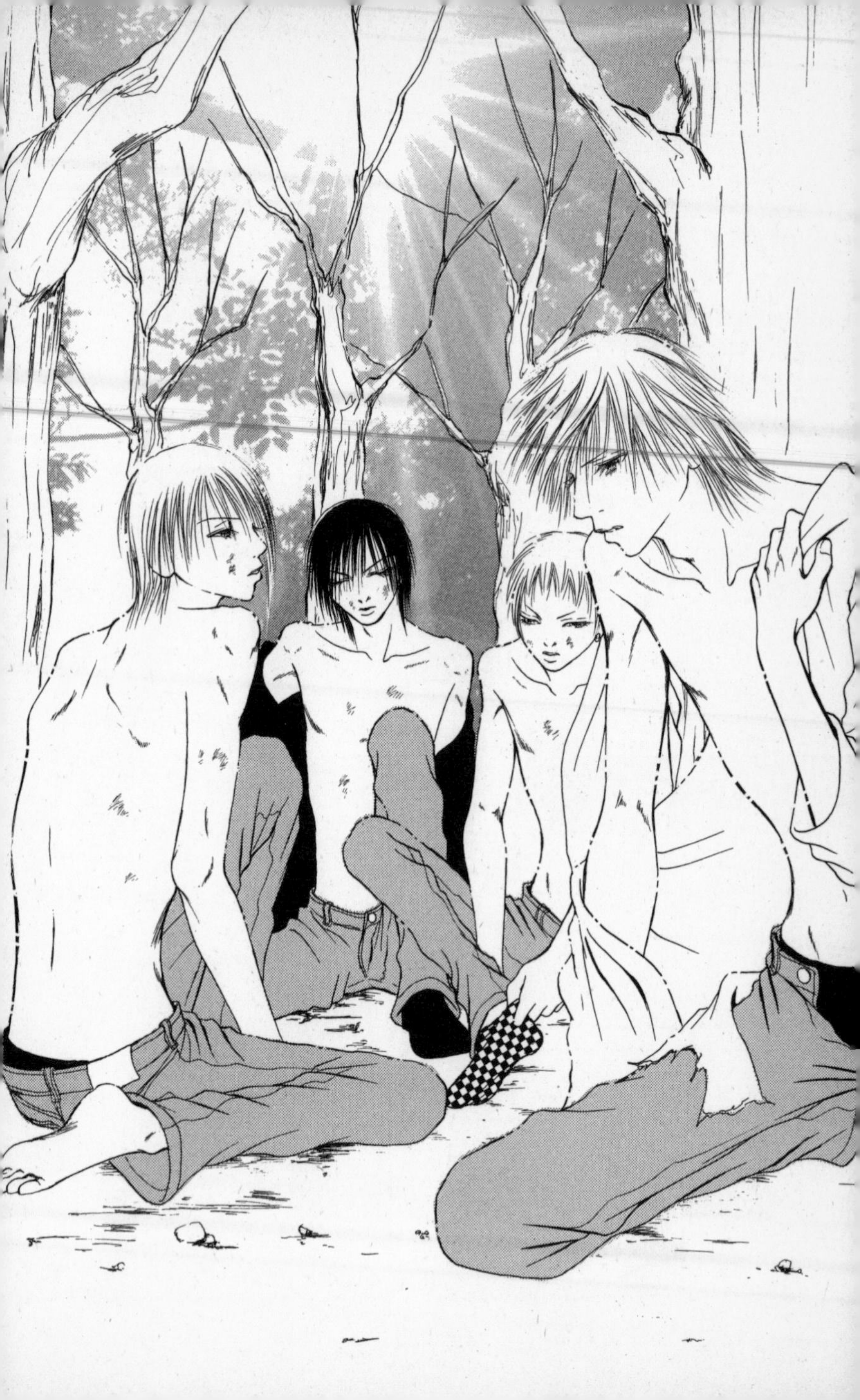

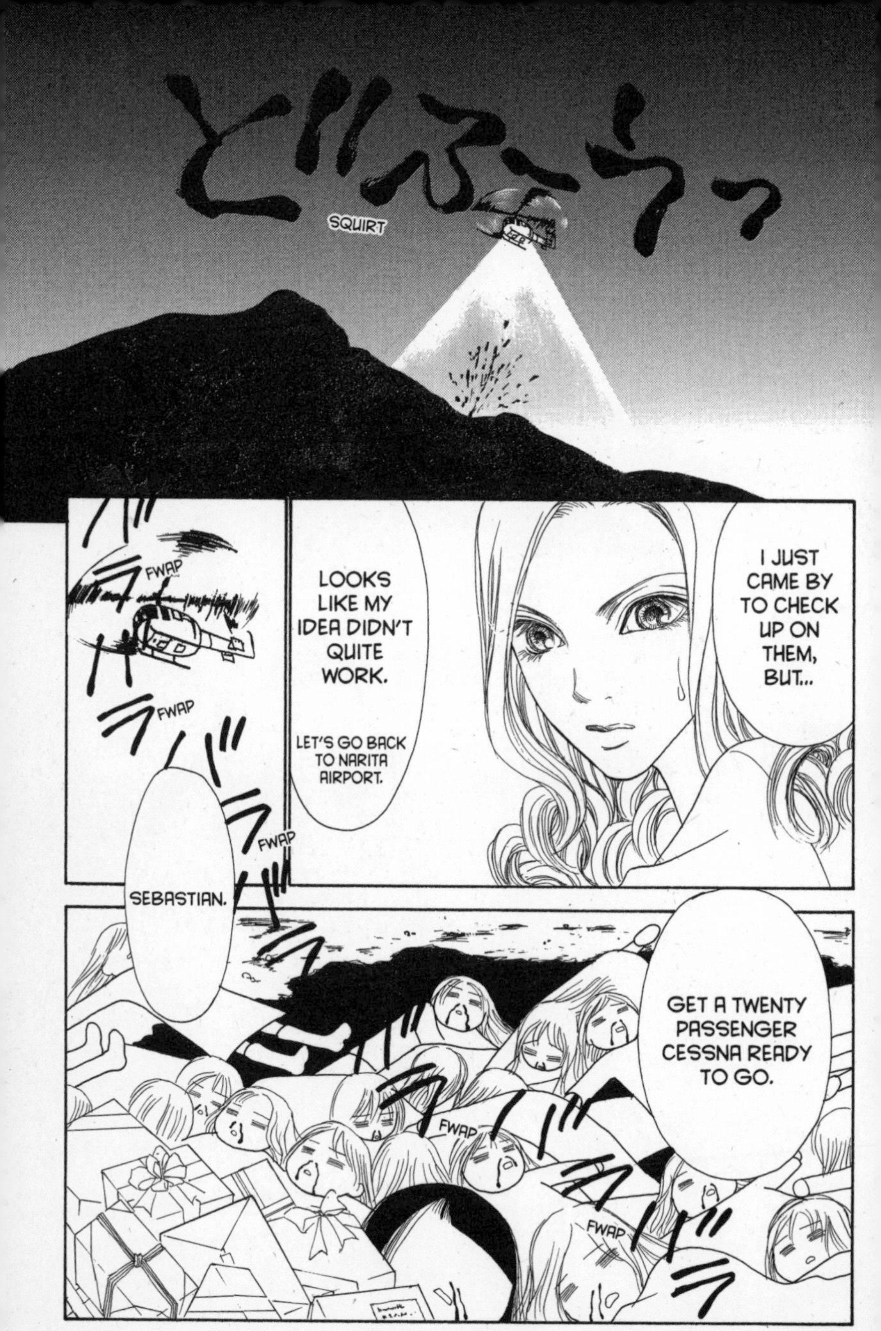
SQUIRT
I JUST CAME BY TO CHECK UP ON THEM, BUT...
LOOKS LIKE MY IDEA DIDN'T QUITE WORK.
LET'S GO BACK TO NARITA AIRPORT.
FWAP
FWAP
FWAP
SEBASTIAN.
GET A TWENTY PASSENGER CESSNA READY TO GO.
FWAP
FWAP

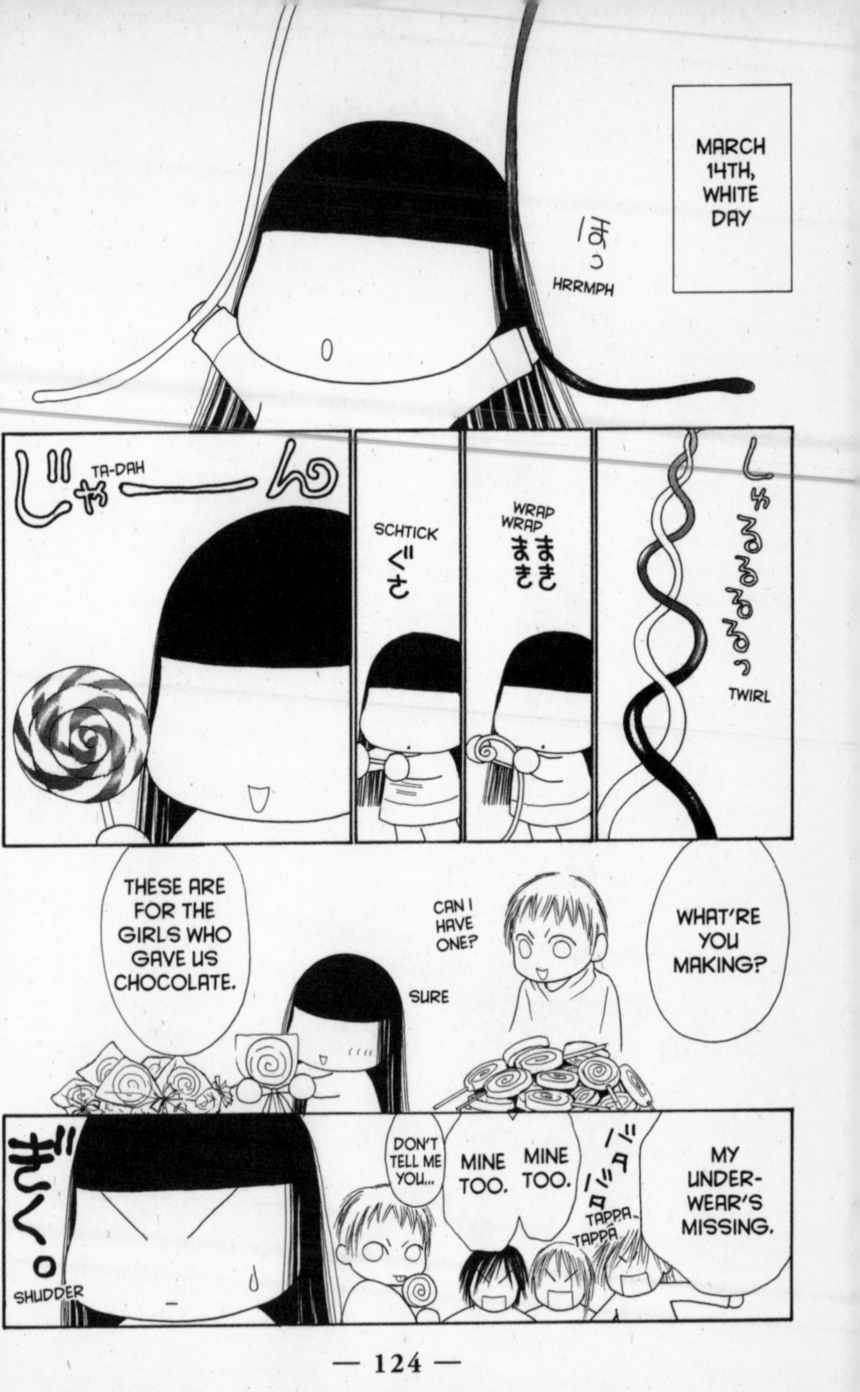
MARCH 14TH, WHITE DAY
ほっ
HRRMPH
しゅるるるっ
TWIRL
まきまき
WRAP WRAP
ぐさ
SCHTICK
じゃーん
TA-DAH
WHAT'RE YOU MAKING?
THESE ARE FOR THE GIRLS WHO GAVE US CHOCOLATE.
CAN I HAVE ONE?
SURE
MY UNDER-WEAR'S MISSING.
バタバタ
TAPPA TAPPA
MINE TOO.
MINE TOO.
DON'T TELL ME YOU...
ぎくっ
SHUDDER

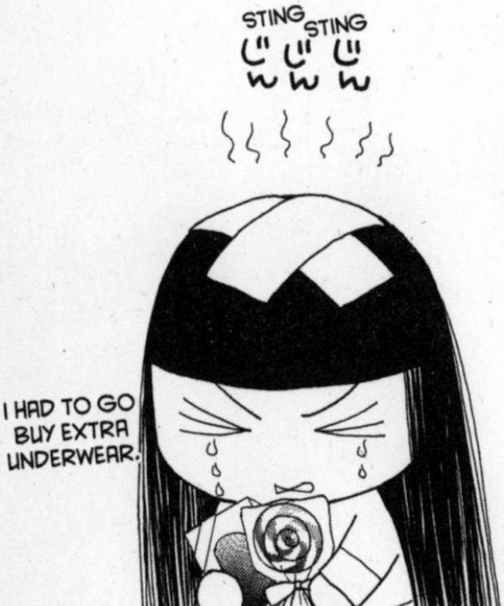
STING STING
じんじんじん
I HAD TO GO BUY EXTRA UNDERWEAR.

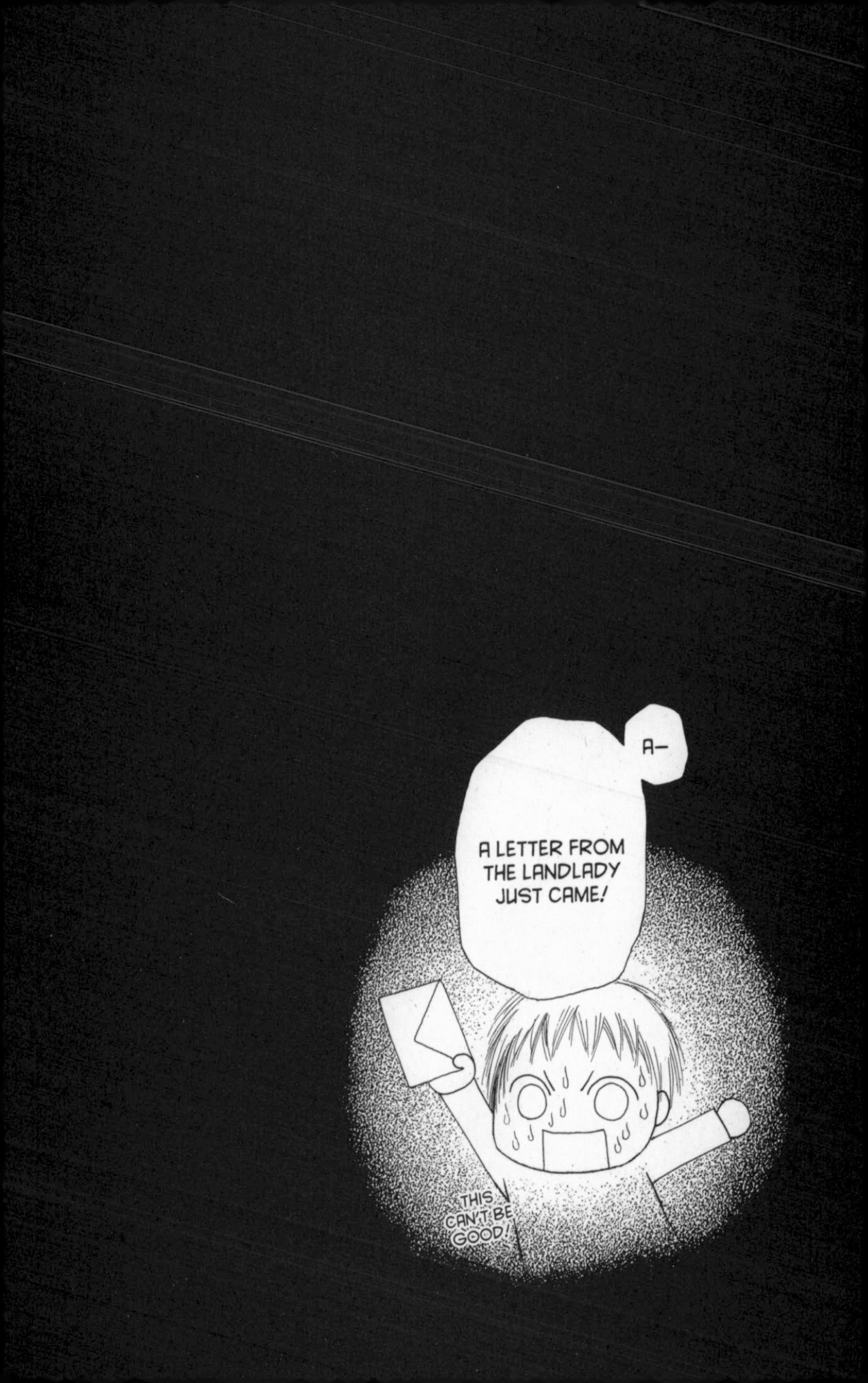
A—
A LETTER FROM THE LANDLADY JUST CAME!
THIS CAN'T BE GOOD!

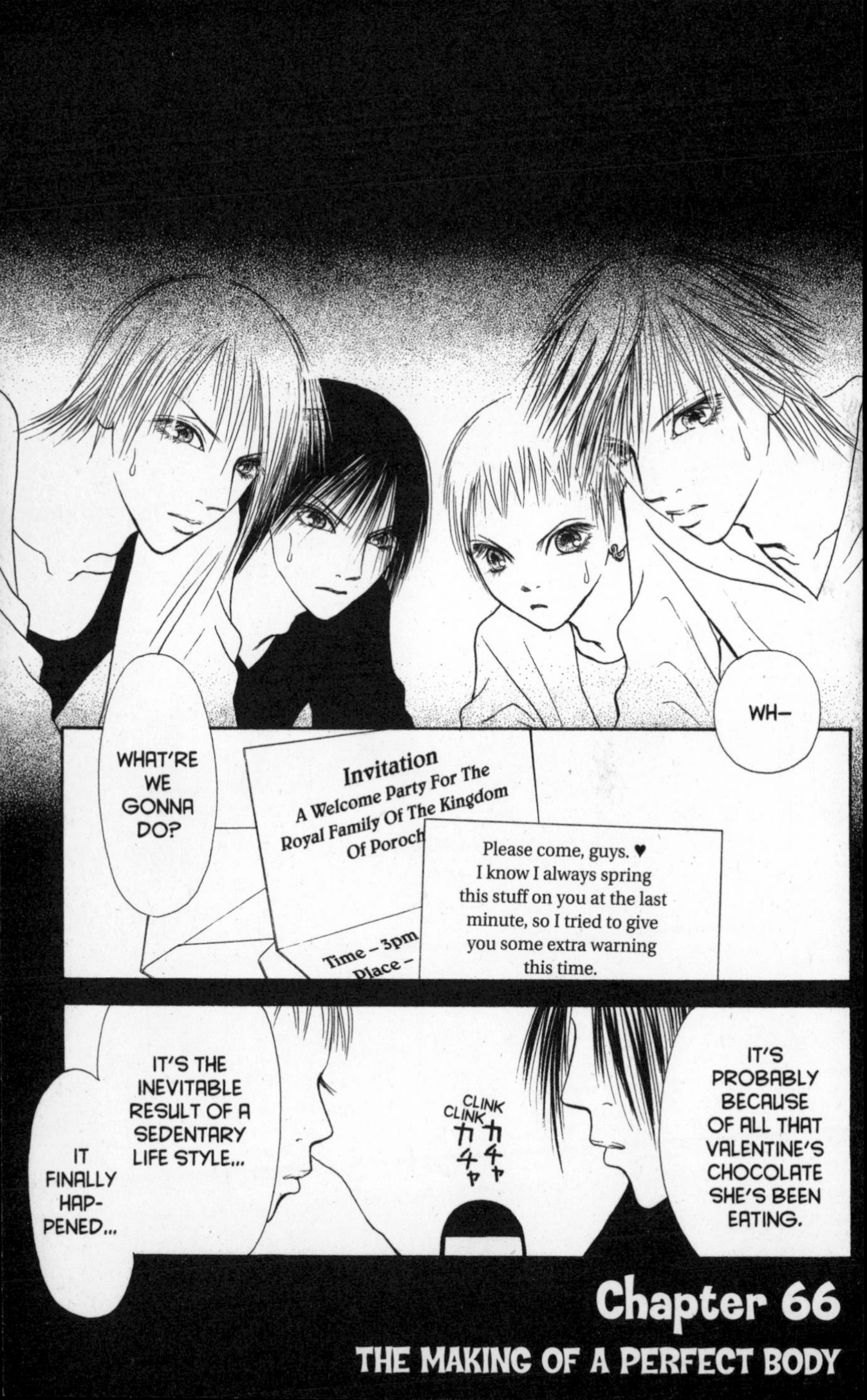
WH–
WHAT'RE WE GONNA DO?
Invitation
A Welcome Party For The Royal Family Of The Kingdom Of Poroch
Time – 3pm
Place –
Please come, guys. ♥ I know I always spring this stuff on you at the last minute, so I tried to give you some extra warning this time.
IT'S PROBABLY BECAUSE OF ALL THAT VALENTINE'S CHOCOLATE SHE'S BEEN EATING.
CLINK CLINK
IT'S THE INEVITABLE RESULT OF A SEDENTARY LIFE STYLE...
IT FINALLY HAP-PENED...
Chapter 66
THE MAKING OF A PERFECT BODY

Chapter 66

THE MAKING OF A PERFECT BODY

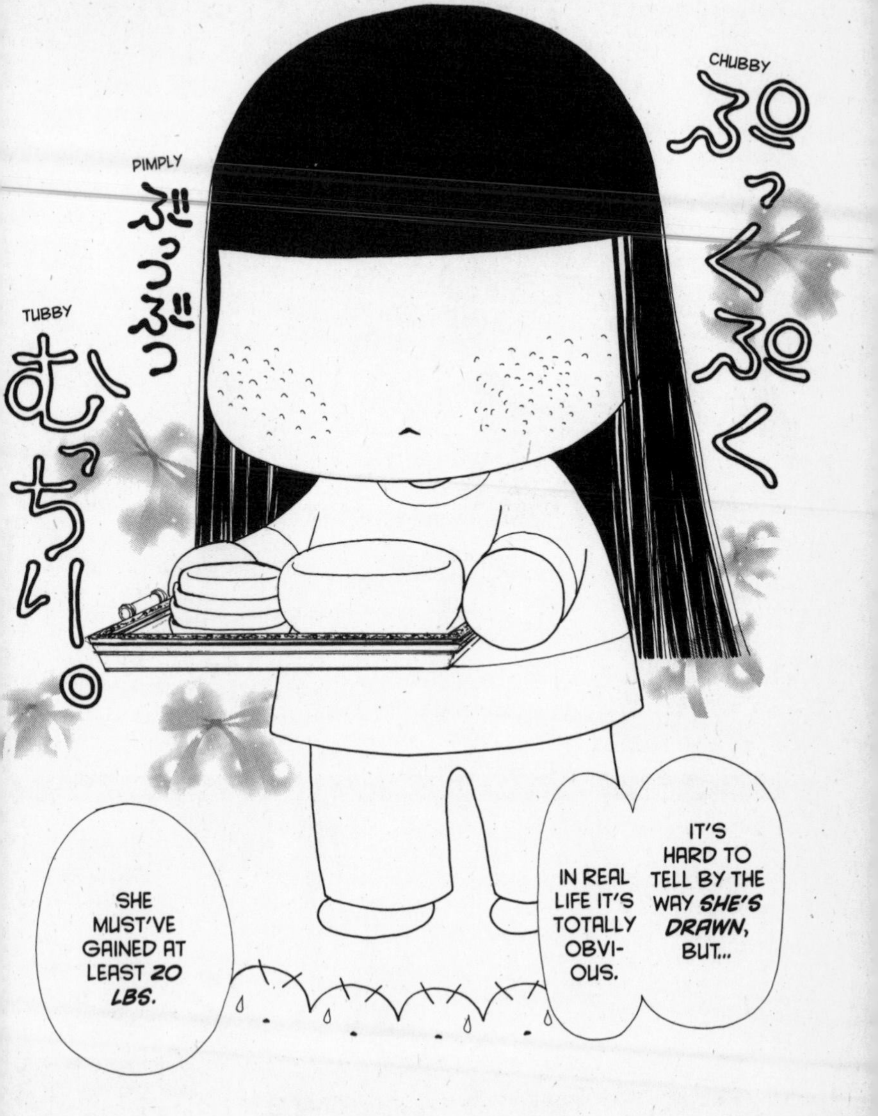
CHUBBY
ふっくふっく
PIMPLY
TUBBY
むっちー。
IT'S HARD TO TELL BY THE WAY *SHE'S DRAWN*, BUT...
IN REAL LIFE IT'S TOTALLY OBVI-OUS.
SHE MUST'VE GAINED AT LEAST *20 LBS.*

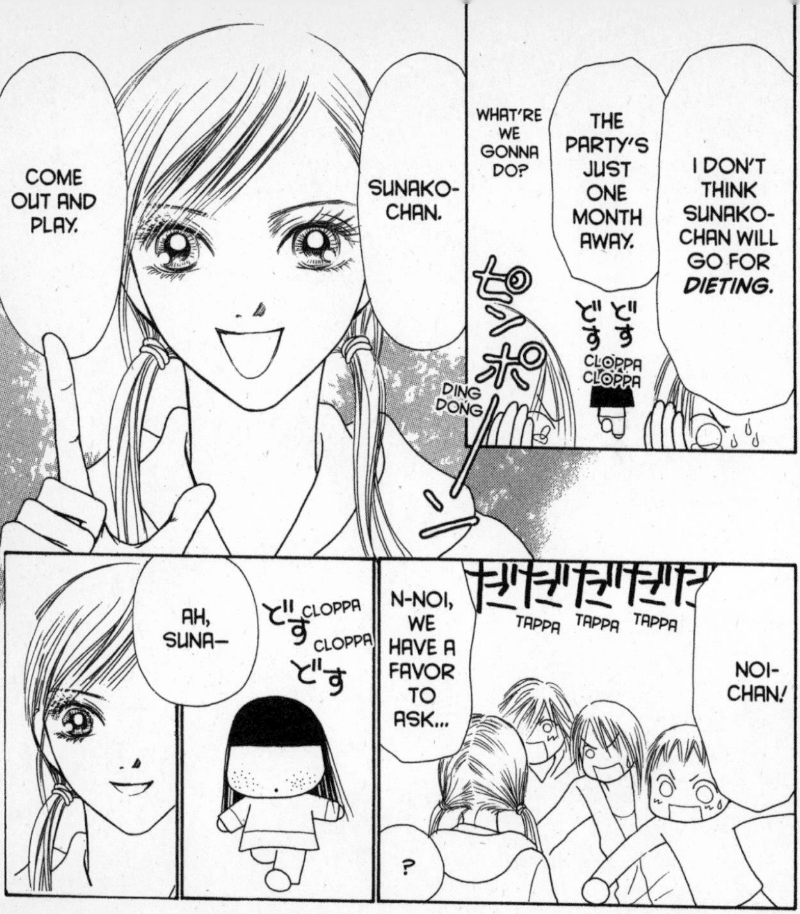
I DON'T THINK SUNAKO-CHAN WILL GO FOR *DIETING*.
THE PARTY'S JUST ONE MONTH AWAY.
WHAT'RE WE GONNA DO?
どすどす
CLOPPA CLOPPA
DING DONG
SUNAKO-CHAN.
COME OUT AND PLAY.
NOI-CHAN!
TAPPA TAPPA TAPPA
N-NOI, WE HAVE A FAVOR TO ASK...
?
どすどす
CLOPPA CLOPPA
AH, SUNA-

BEHIND THE SCENES

"STRENGTH TRAINING" IS A PHRASE THAT HAS PRETTY MUCH NOTHING TO DO WITH MY LIFE. I'D LIKE TO TRY IT, BUT I HAVE NO ENERGY AND NO MUSCLE TONE.

...BUT IF I DON'T BUILD UP SOME MUSCLE SOON, I'LL BE IN REAL TROUBLE. I'M GETTING REALLY CHUBBY.

JUST BEFORE MY DEADLINE FOR THIS STORY, THE BAND MERRY PUT ON A TWO-DAY CONCERT. ♥ ♥ ♥

I COULDN'T GO...

I CRIED WHILE I WORKED.

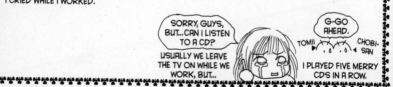

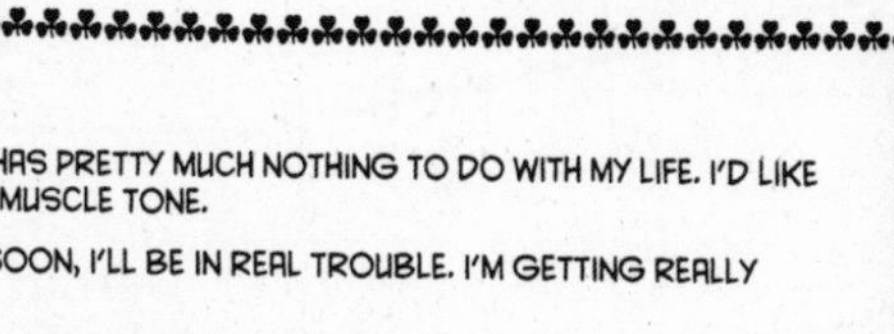
SORRY, GUYS, BUT...CAN I LISTEN TO A CD?
USUALLY WE LEAVE THE TV ON WHILE WE WORK, BUT...
G-GO AHEAD.
TOMII
CHOBI-SAN
I PLAYED FIVE MERRY CDS IN A ROW.

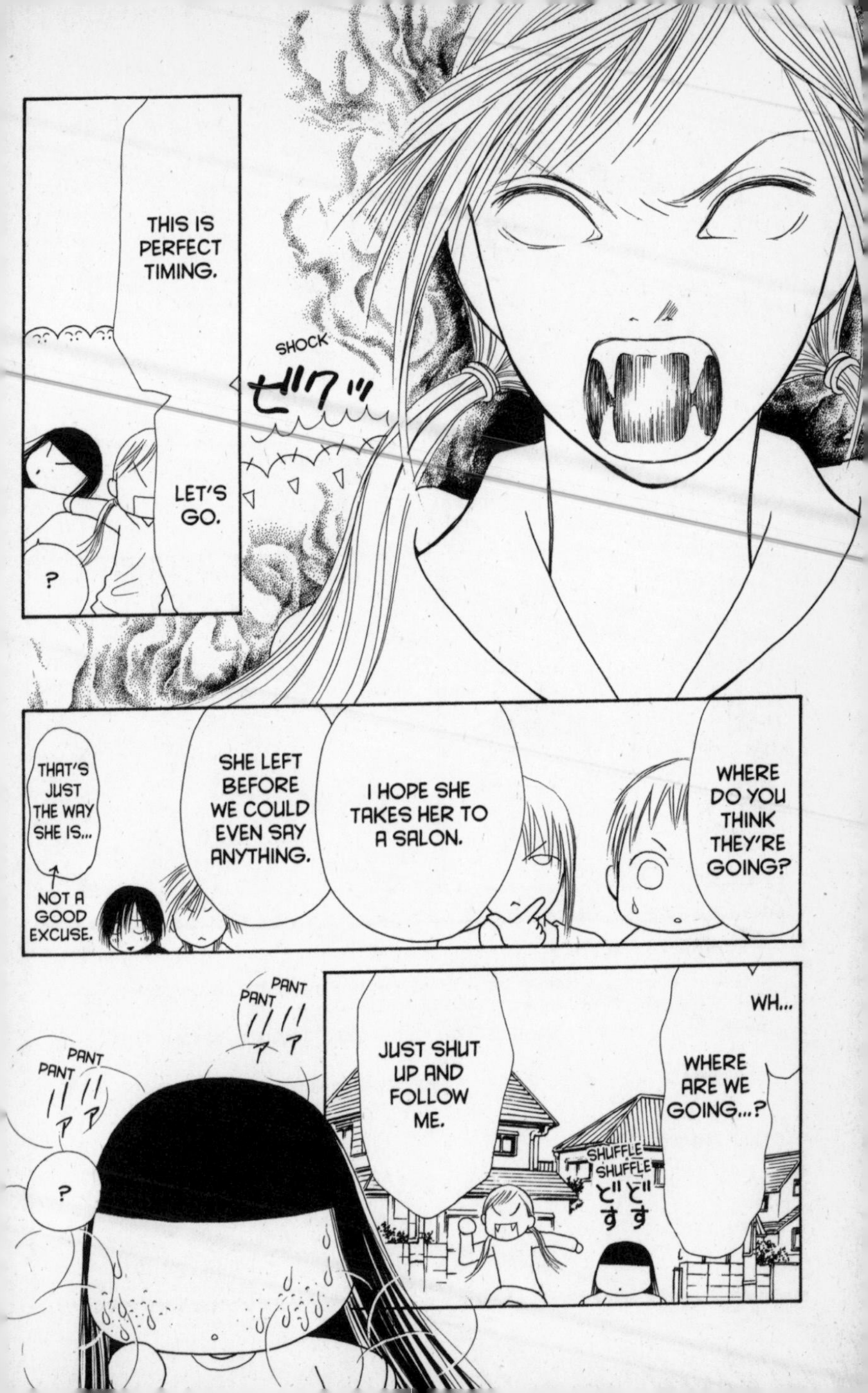
SHOCK
THIS IS PERFECT TIMING.
LET'S GO.
?
WHERE DO YOU THINK THEY'RE GOING?
I HOPE SHE TAKES HER TO A SALON.
SHE LEFT BEFORE WE COULD EVEN SAY ANYTHING.
THAT'S JUST THE WAY SHE IS...
NOT A GOOD EXCUSE.
WH...
WHERE ARE WE GOING...?
JUST SHUT UP AND FOLLOW ME.
SHUFFLE SHUFFLE
どすどす
PANT PANT
ハァハァ
PANT PANT
ハァハァ
?

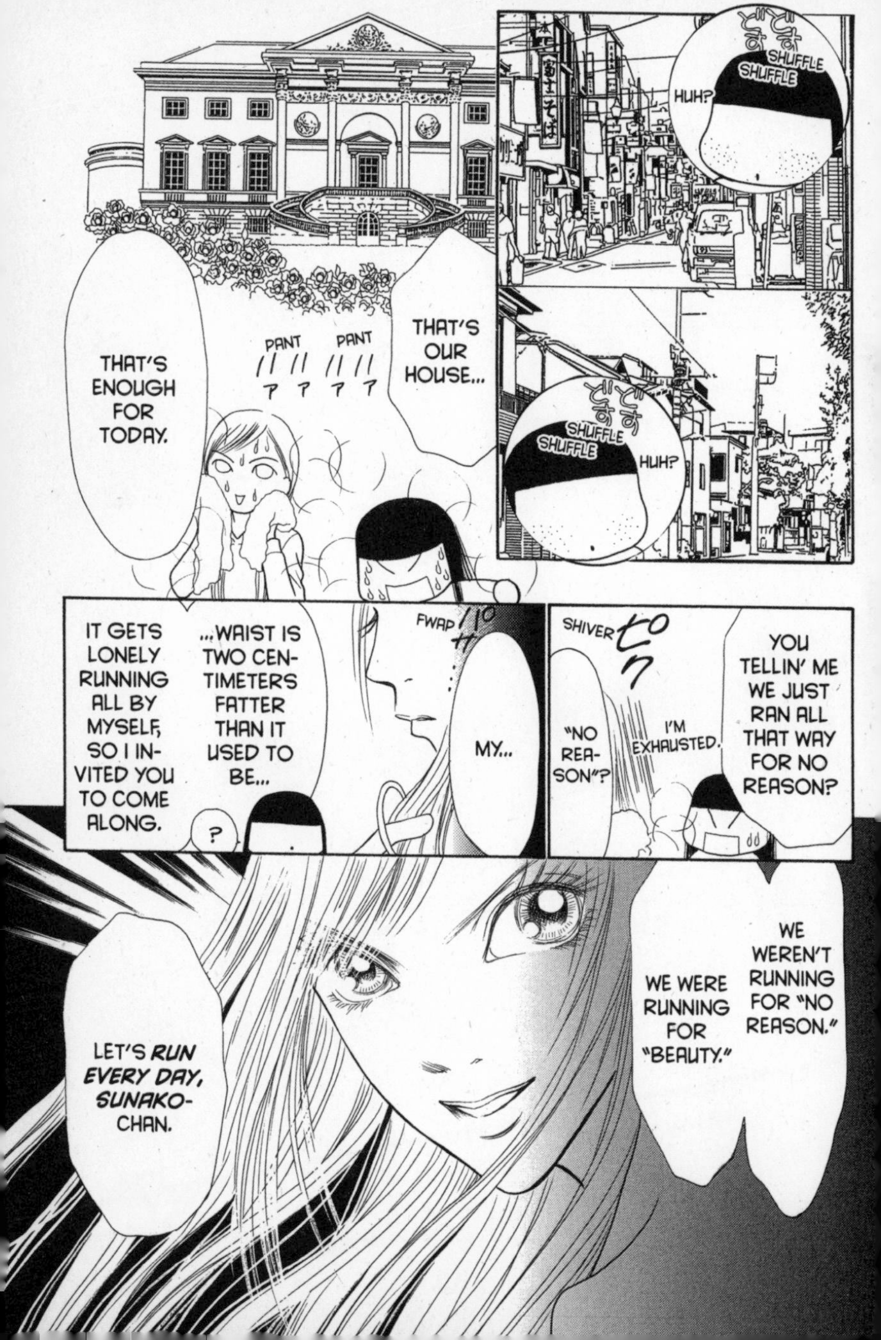
どすどす
SHUFFLE SHUFFLE
HUH?
どすどす
SHUFFLE SHUFFLE
HUH?
THAT'S OUR HOUSE...
PANT PANT
ハァハァ
THAT'S ENOUGH FOR TODAY.
YOU TELLIN' ME WE JUST RAN ALL THAT WAY FOR NO REASON?
SHIVER
I'M EXHAUSTED.
"NO REASON"?
FWAP
MY...
...WAIST IS TWO CENTIMETERS FATTER THAN IT USED TO BE...
IT GETS LONELY RUNNING ALL BY MYSELF, SO I INVITED YOU TO COME ALONG.
?
WE WEREN'T RUNNING FOR "NO REASON."
WE WERE RUNNING FOR "BEAUTY."
LET'S *RUN EVERY DAY, SUNAKO-CHAN.*

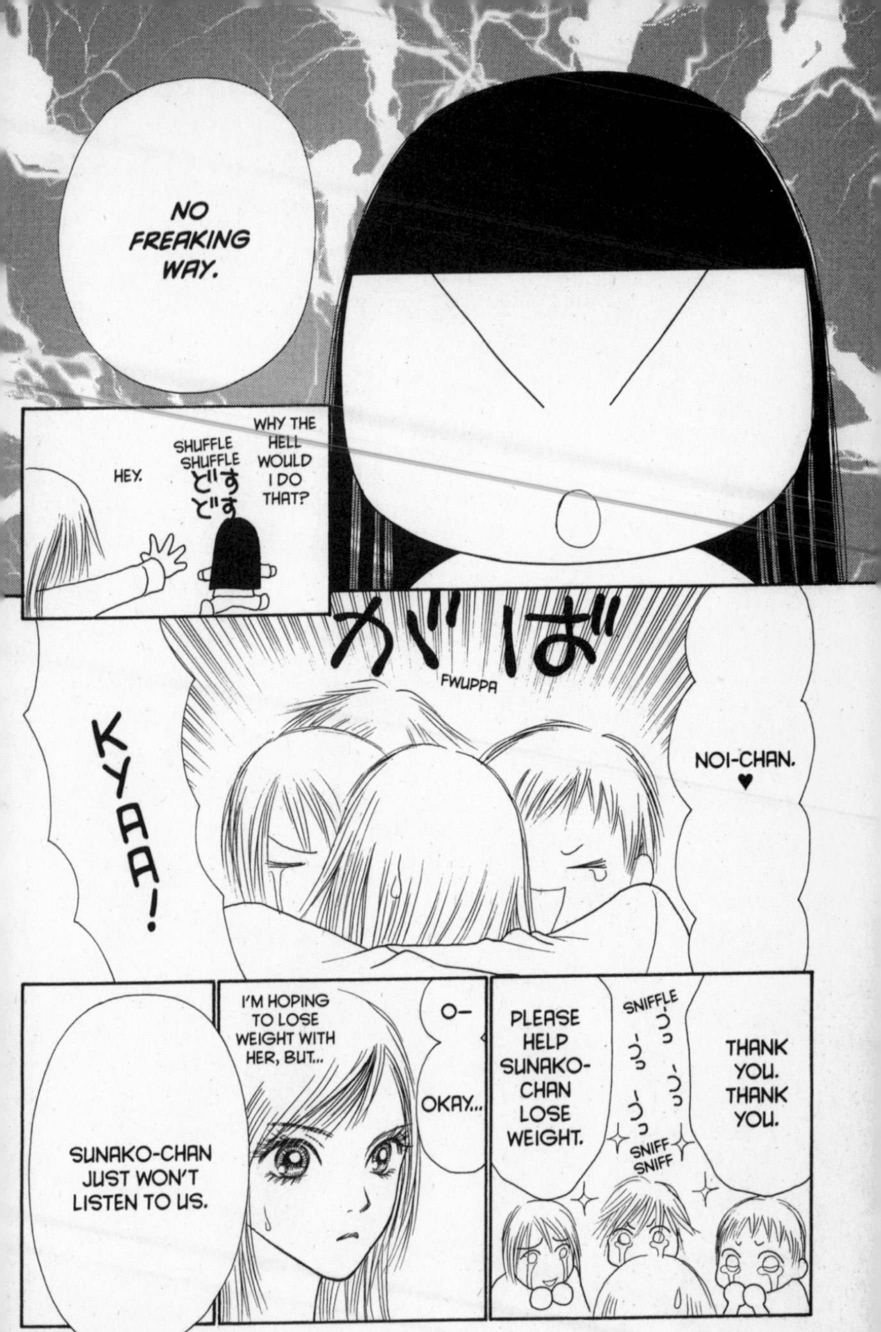
NO FREAKING WAY.
WHY THE HELL WOULD I DO THAT?
SHUFFLE SHUFFLE どすどす
HEY.
NOI-CHAN. ♥
がば
FWUPPA
KYAA!
THANK YOU. THANK YOU.
SNIFFLE
PLEASE HELP SUNAKO-CHAN LOSE WEIGHT.
SNIFF SNIFF
O-
OKAY...
I'M HOPING TO LOSE WEIGHT WITH HER, BUT...
SUNAKO-CHAN JUST WON'T LISTEN TO US.

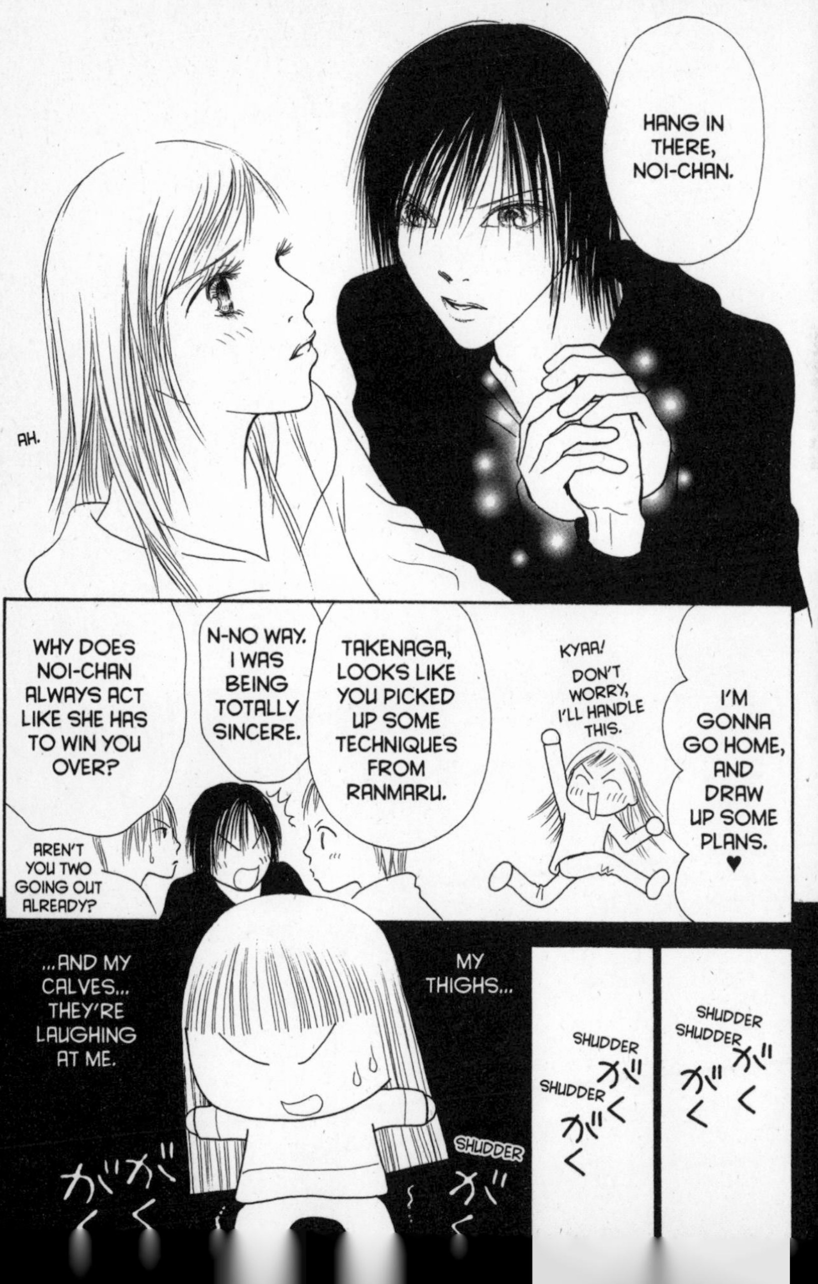
HANG IN THERE, NOI-CHAN.
AH.
I'M GONNA GO HOME, AND DRAW UP SOME PLANS. ♥
KYAA!
DON'T WORRY, I'LL HANDLE THIS.
TAKENAGA, LOOKS LIKE YOU PICKED UP SOME TECHNIQUES FROM RANMARU.
N-NO WAY. I WAS BEING TOTALLY SINCERE.
WHY DOES NOI-CHAN ALWAYS ACT LIKE SHE HAS TO WIN YOU OVER?
AREN'T YOU TWO GOING OUT ALREADY?
SHUDDER
SHUDDER
がくがく
SHUDDER
SHUDDER
がくがく
MY THIGHS...
...AND MY CALVES... THEY'RE LAUGHING AT ME.
SHUDDER
がく
がくがく

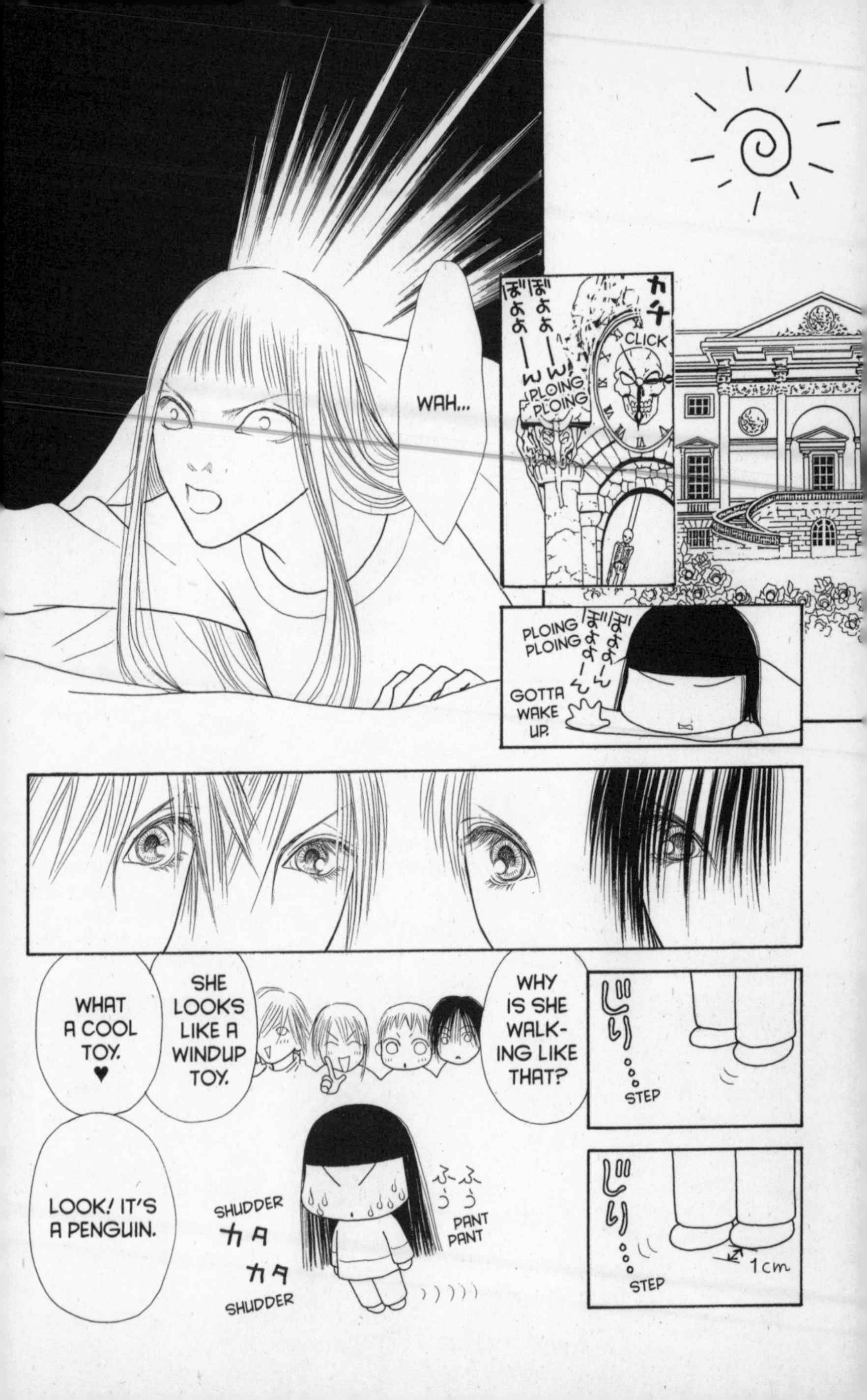

カチ
CLICK
ぼよよーん ぼよよーん
PLOING PLOING
ぼよよーん ぼよよーん
PLOING PLOING
GOTTA WAKE UP.
WAH...
じり。。。
STEP
じり。。。
STEP
1cm
WHY IS SHE WALKING LIKE THAT?
SHE LOOKS LIKE A WINDUP TOY.
WHAT A COOL TOY. ♥
ふうふう
PANT PANT
SHUDDER
カタ
カタ
SHUDDER
LOOK! IT'S A PENGUIN.

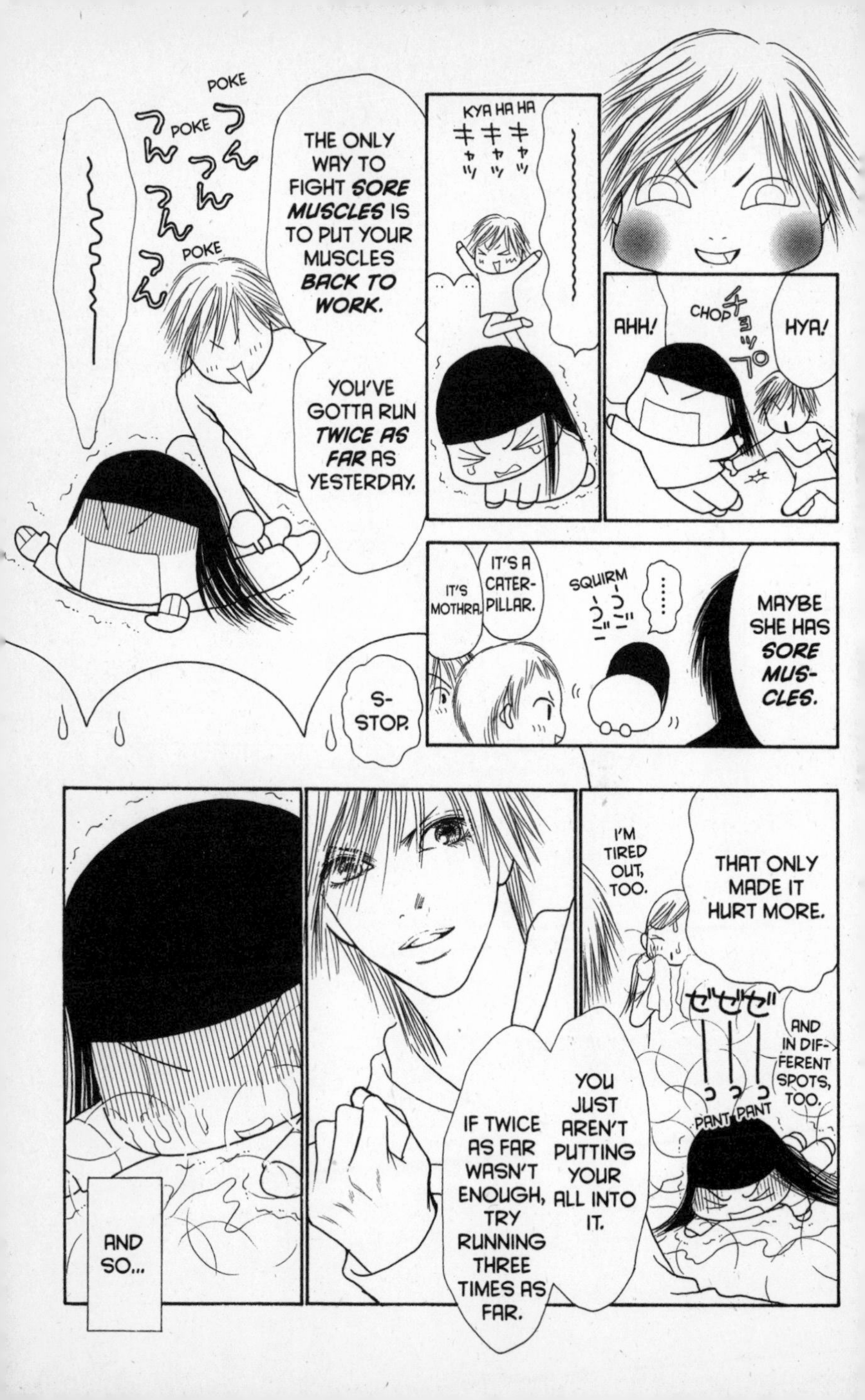

HYA!
CHOP
AHH!
KYA HA HA
THE ONLY WAY TO FIGHT SORE MUSCLES IS TO PUT YOUR MUSCLES BACK TO WORK.
YOU'VE GOTTA RUN TWICE AS FAR AS YESTERDAY.
POKE
POKE
POKE
MAYBE SHE HAS SORE MUS-CLES.
......
SQUIRM
IT'S A CATER-PILLAR.
IT'S MOTHRA.
S-STOP.
THAT ONLY MADE IT HURT MORE.
I'M TIRED OUT, TOO.
AND IN DIF-FERENT SPOTS, TOO.
PANT PANT
YOU JUST AREN'T PUTTING YOUR ALL INTO IT.
IF TWICE AS FAR WASN'T ENOUGH, TRY RUNNING THREE TIMES AS FAR.
AND SO...

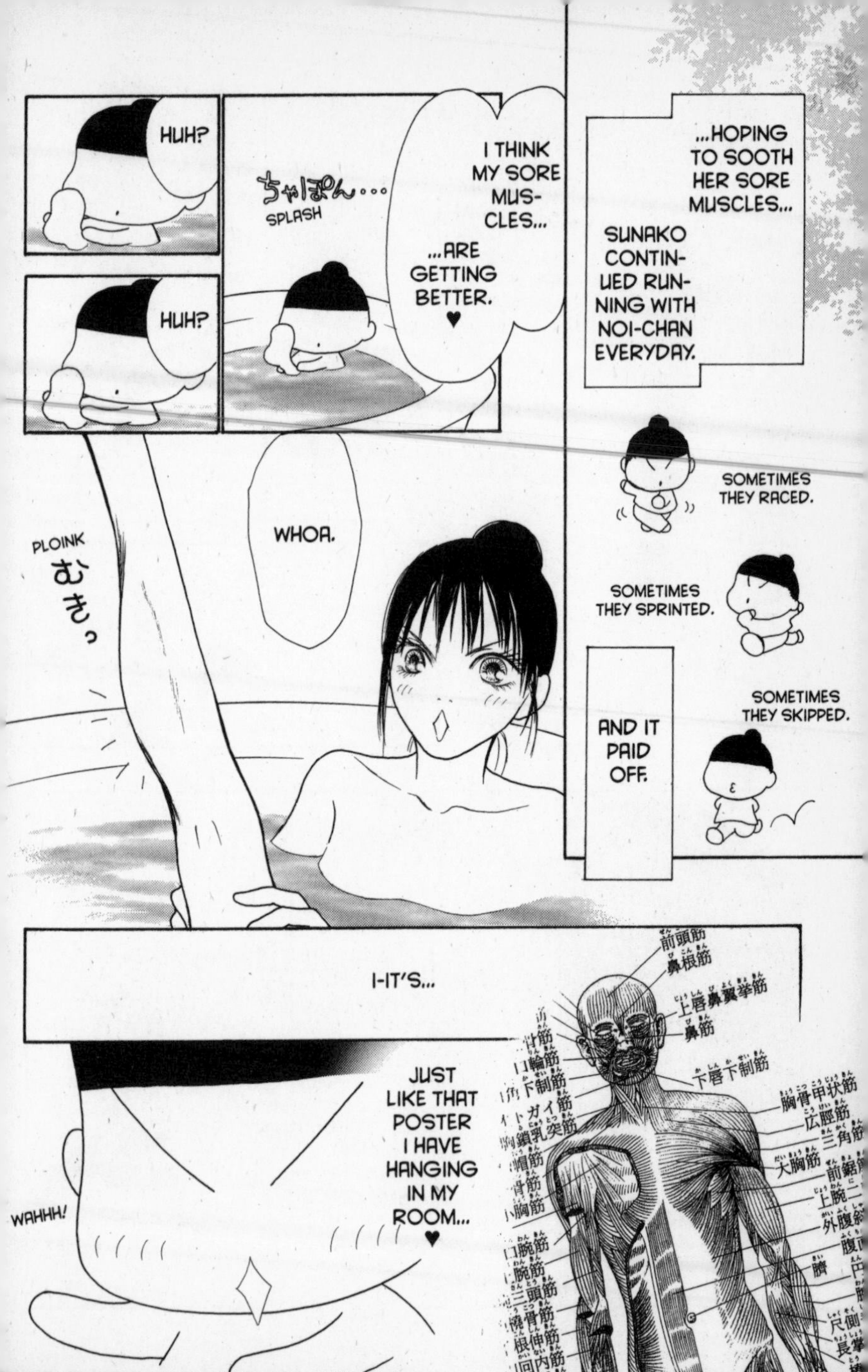
...HOPING TO SOOTH HER SORE MUSCLES...
SUNAKO CONTINUED RUNNING WITH NOI-CHAN EVERYDAY.
SOMETIMES THEY RACED.
SOMETIMES THEY SPRINTED.
SOMETIMES THEY SKIPPED.
AND IT PAID OFF.
I THINK MY SORE MUSCLES...
...ARE GETTING BETTER. ♥
ちゃぽん・・・
SPLASH
HUH?
HUH?
WHOA.
PLOINK
むきっ
I-IT'S...
JUST LIKE THAT POSTER I HAVE HANGING IN MY ROOM... ♥
WAHHH!
前頭筋
鼻根筋
上唇鼻翼挙筋
鼻筋
下唇下制筋
胸骨甲状筋
広頸筋
大胸筋
臍
REFERENCE MATERIAL "KIHON JINTAI KAIBOZU" (AN ILLUSTRATED BOOK OF HUMAN ANATOMY) PUBLISHED BY KINENSHA

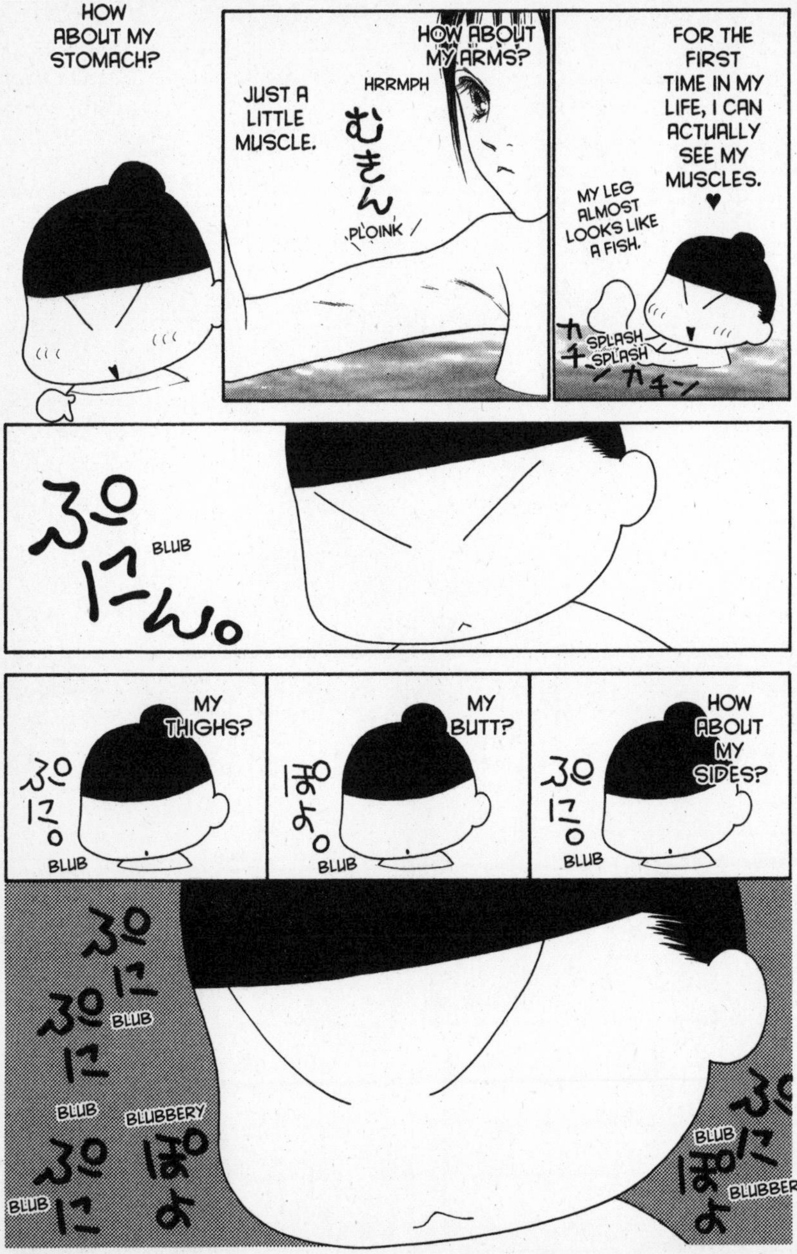
FOR THE FIRST TIME IN MY LIFE, I CAN ACTUALLY SEE MY MUSCLES. ♥
MY LEG ALMOST LOOKS LIKE A FISH.
カチ
SPLASH
SPLASH
カチン
HOW ABOUT MY ARMS?
JUST A LITTLE MUSCLE.
HRRMPH
むきん
PLOINK
HOW ABOUT MY STOMACH?
ぷにーん。
BLUB
HOW ABOUT MY SIDES?
ぷに。
BLUB
MY BUTT?
ぽよ。
BLUB
MY THIGHS?
ぷに。
BLUB
ぷにぽよ
BLUB
BLUBBERY
ぽよ
BLUBBERY
ぷにぷに
BLUB
ぷにぷに
BLUB
BLUB

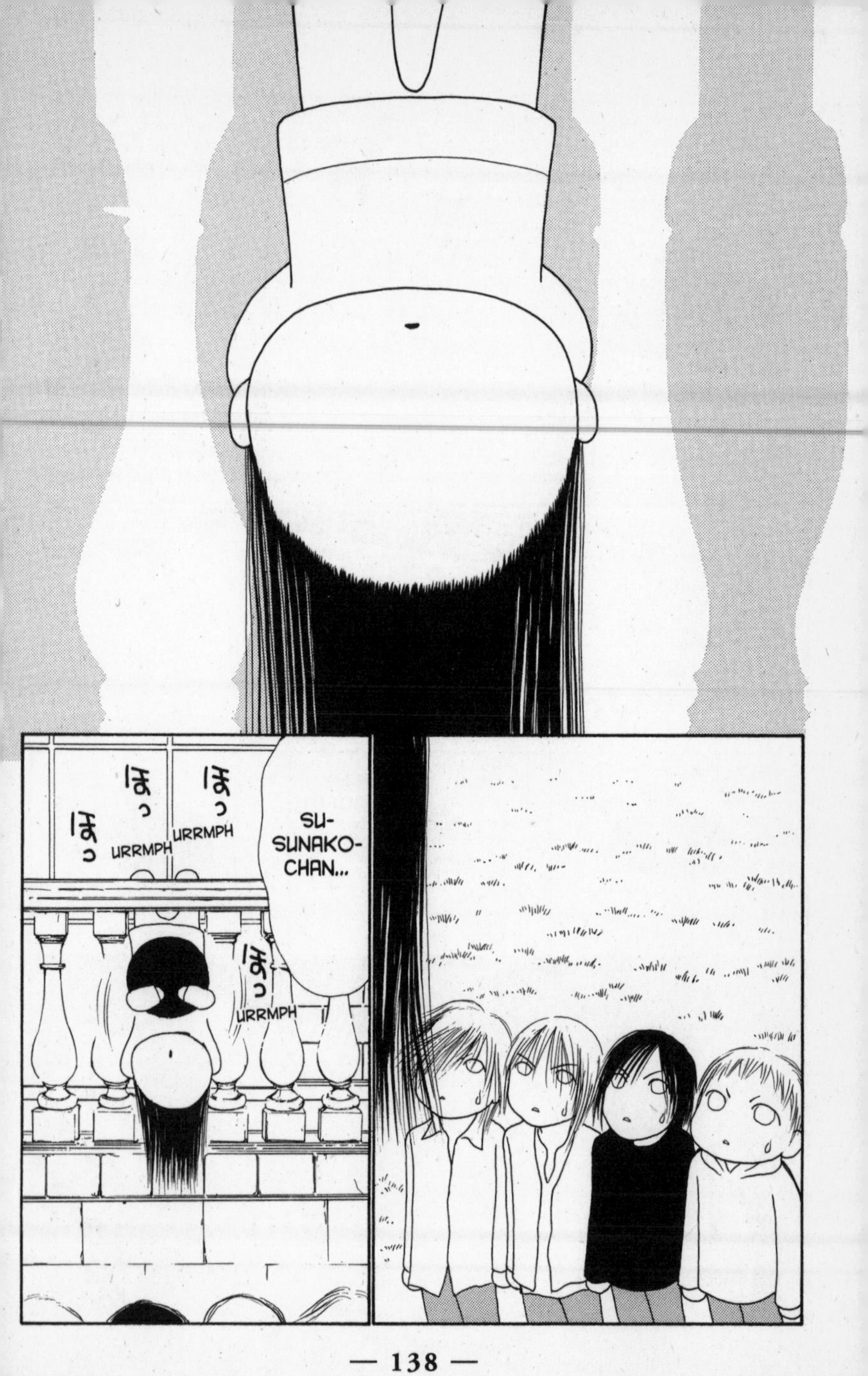
SU-SUNAKO-CHAN...
ほっ
URRMPH
ほっ
URRMPH
ほっ
ほっ
URRMPH

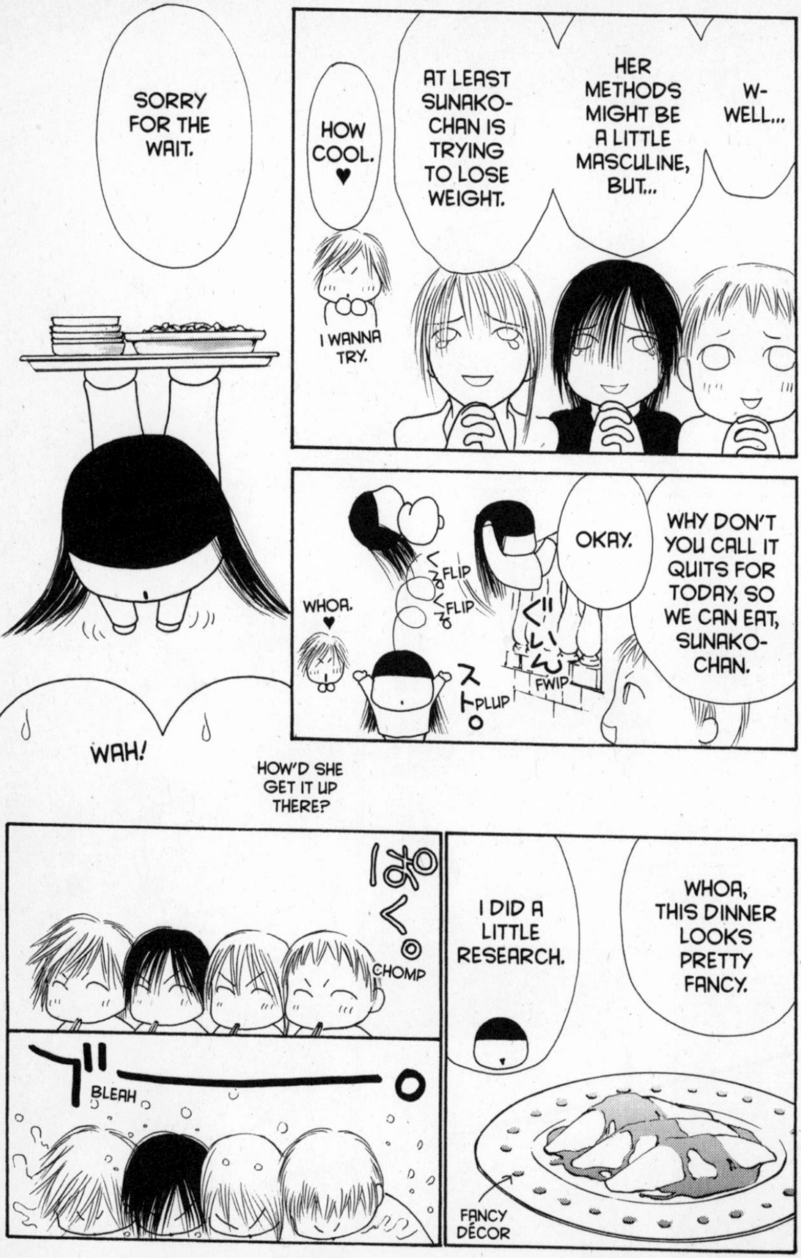
W-WELL...
HER METHODS MIGHT BE A LITTLE MASCULINE, BUT...
AT LEAST SUNAKO-CHAN IS TRYING TO LOSE WEIGHT.
HOW COOL. ♥
I WANNA TRY.
WHY DON'T YOU CALL IT QUITS FOR TODAY, SO WE CAN EAT, SUNAKO-CHAN.
OKAY.
FWIP
FLIP
FLIP
WHOA. ♥
PLUP
SORRY FOR THE WAIT.
WAH!
HOW'D SHE GET IT UP THERE?
WHOA, THIS DINNER LOOKS PRETTY FANCY.
I DID A LITTLE RESEARCH.
FANCY DÉCOR
CHOMP
BLEAH

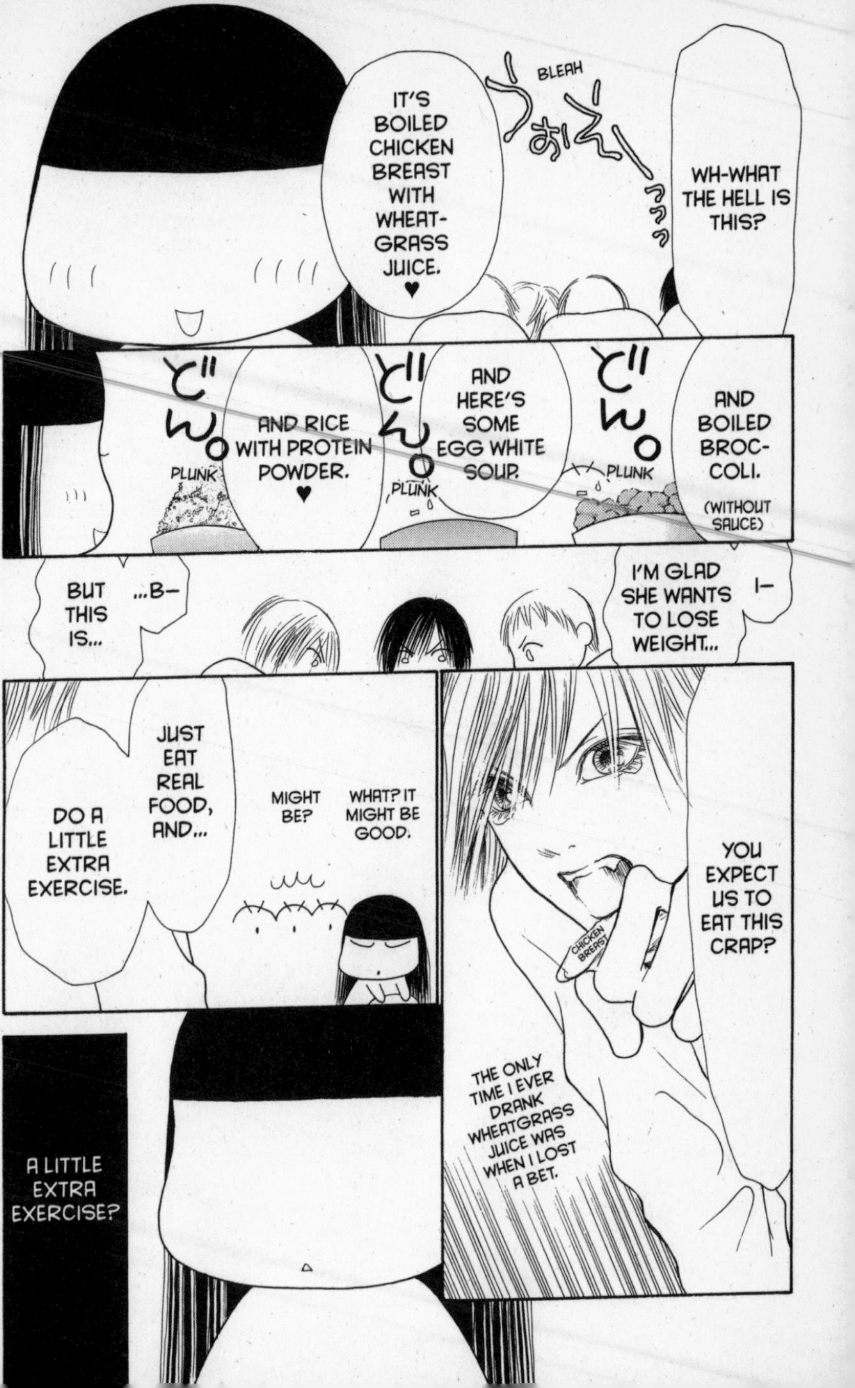

WH-WHAT THE HELL IS THIS?
BLEAH
IT'S BOILED CHICKEN BREAST WITH WHEAT-GRASS JUICE. ♥
AND BOILED BROC-COLI.
(WITHOUT SAUCE)
PLUNK
AND HERE'S SOME EGG WHITE SOUP.
PLUNK
AND RICE WITH PROTEIN POWDER. ♥
PLUNK
I—
I'M GLAD SHE WANTS TO LOSE WEIGHT...
...B—
BUT THIS IS...
YOU EXPECT US TO EAT THIS CRAP?
CHICKEN BREAST
THE ONLY TIME I EVER DRANK WHEATGRASS JUICE WAS WHEN I LOST A BET.
WHAT? IT MIGHT BE GOOD.
MIGHT BE?
JUST EAT REAL FOOD, AND...
DO A LITTLE EXTRA EXERCISE.
A LITTLE EXTRA EXERCISE?

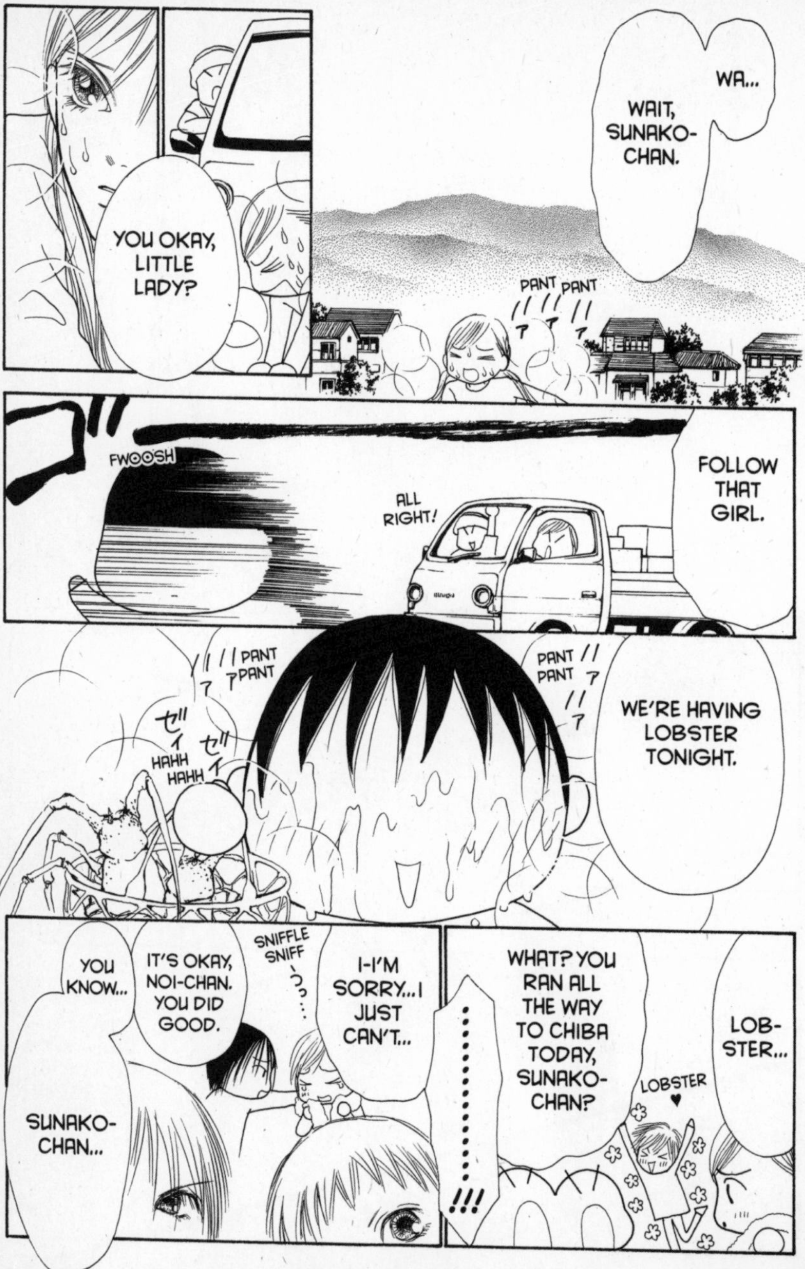
WA...
WAIT, SUNAKO-CHAN.
PANT PANT
YOU OKAY, LITTLE LADY?
FOLLOW THAT GIRL.
ALL RIGHT!
FWOOSH
WE'RE HAVING LOBSTER TONIGHT.
PANT PANT
PANT PANT
ゼイ ゼイ
HAHH HAHH
LOB-STER...
LOBSTER ♥
WHAT? YOU RAN ALL THE WAY TO CHIBA TODAY, SUNAKO-CHAN?
........!!!
I-I'M SORRY...I JUST CAN'T...
SNIFFLE SNIFF
IT'S OKAY, NOI-CHAN. YOU DID GOOD.
YOU KNOW...
SUNAKO-CHAN...

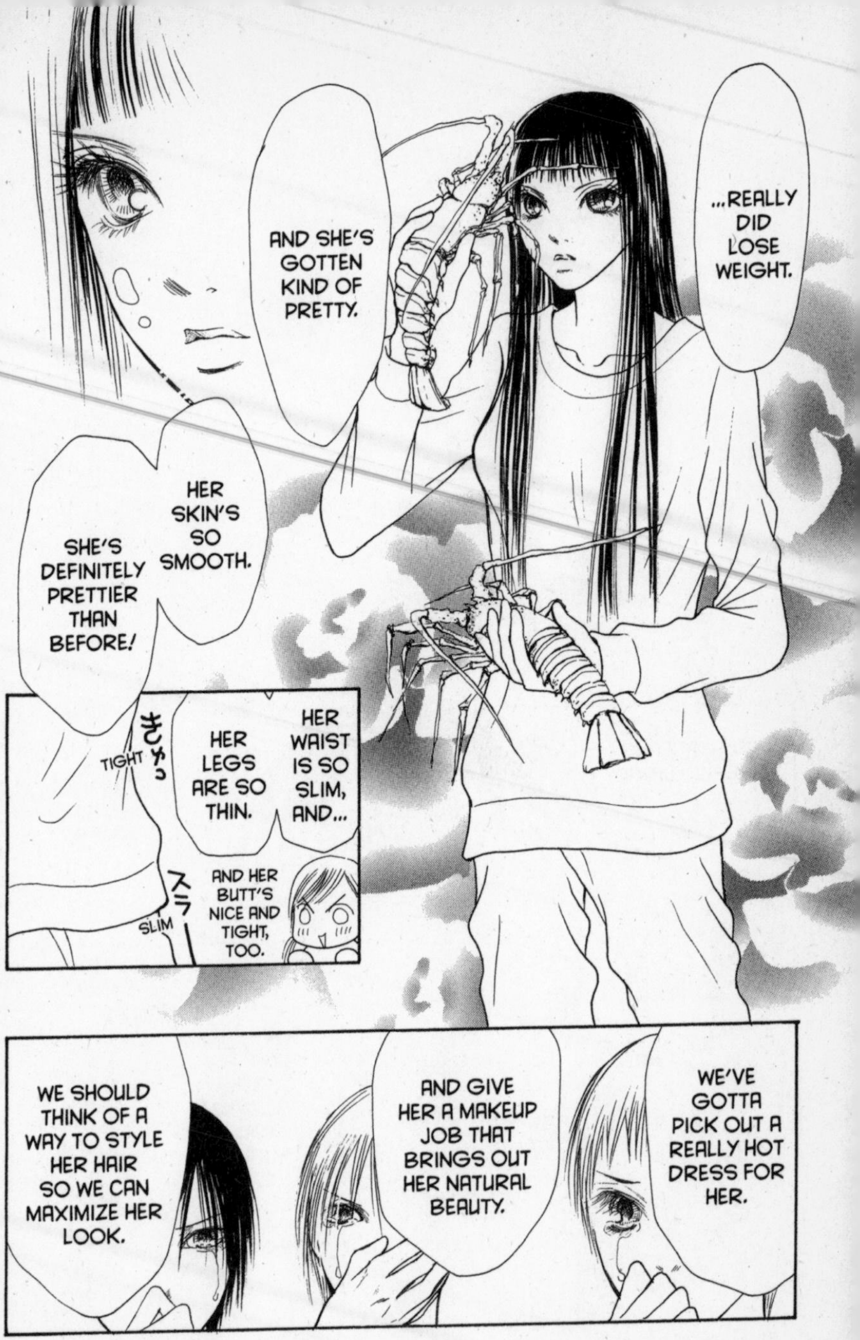
...REALLY DID LOSE WEIGHT.
AND SHE'S GOTTEN KIND OF PRETTY.
HER SKIN'S SO SMOOTH.
SHE'S DEFINITELY PRETTIER THAN BEFORE!
HER WAIST IS SO SLIM, AND...
HER LEGS ARE SO THIN.
きゅっ
TIGHT
AND HER BUTT'S NICE AND TIGHT, TOO.
スラ
SLIM
WE'VE GOTTA PICK OUT A REALLY HOT DRESS FOR HER.
AND GIVE HER A MAKEUP JOB THAT BRINGS OUT HER NATURAL BEAUTY.
WE SHOULD THINK OF A WAY TO STYLE HER HAIR SO WE CAN MAXIMIZE HER LOOK.

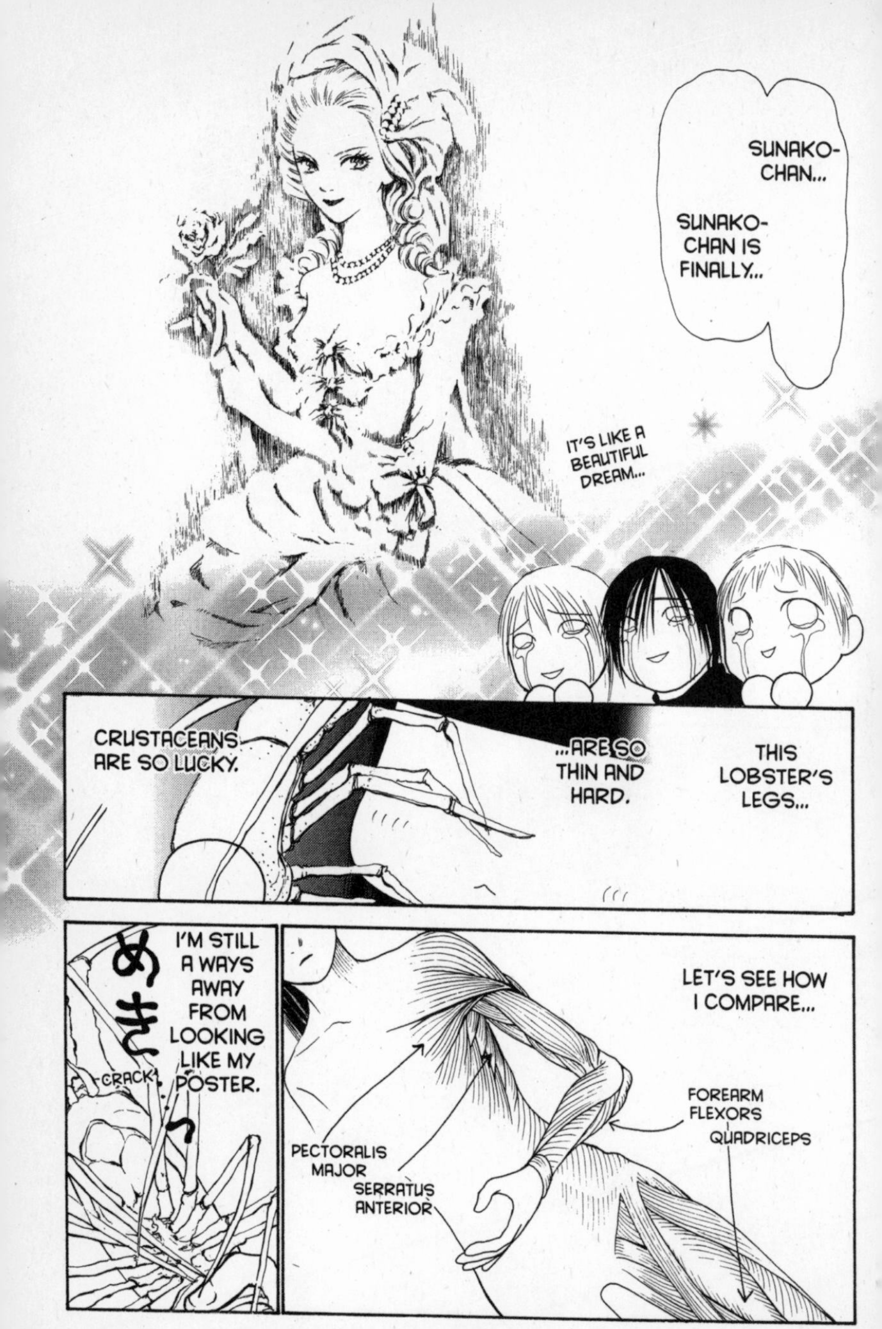
SUNAKO-CHAN...
SUNAKO-CHAN IS FINALLY...
IT'S LIKE A BEAUTIFUL DREAM...
THIS LOBSTER'S LEGS...
...ARE SO THIN AND HARD.
CRUSTACEANS ARE SO LUCKY.
LET'S SEE HOW I COMPARE...
FOREARM FLEXORS
QUADRICEPS
PECTORALIS MAJOR
SERRATUS ANTERIOR
I'M STILL A WAYS AWAY FROM LOOKING LIKE MY POSTER.
めき
CRACK

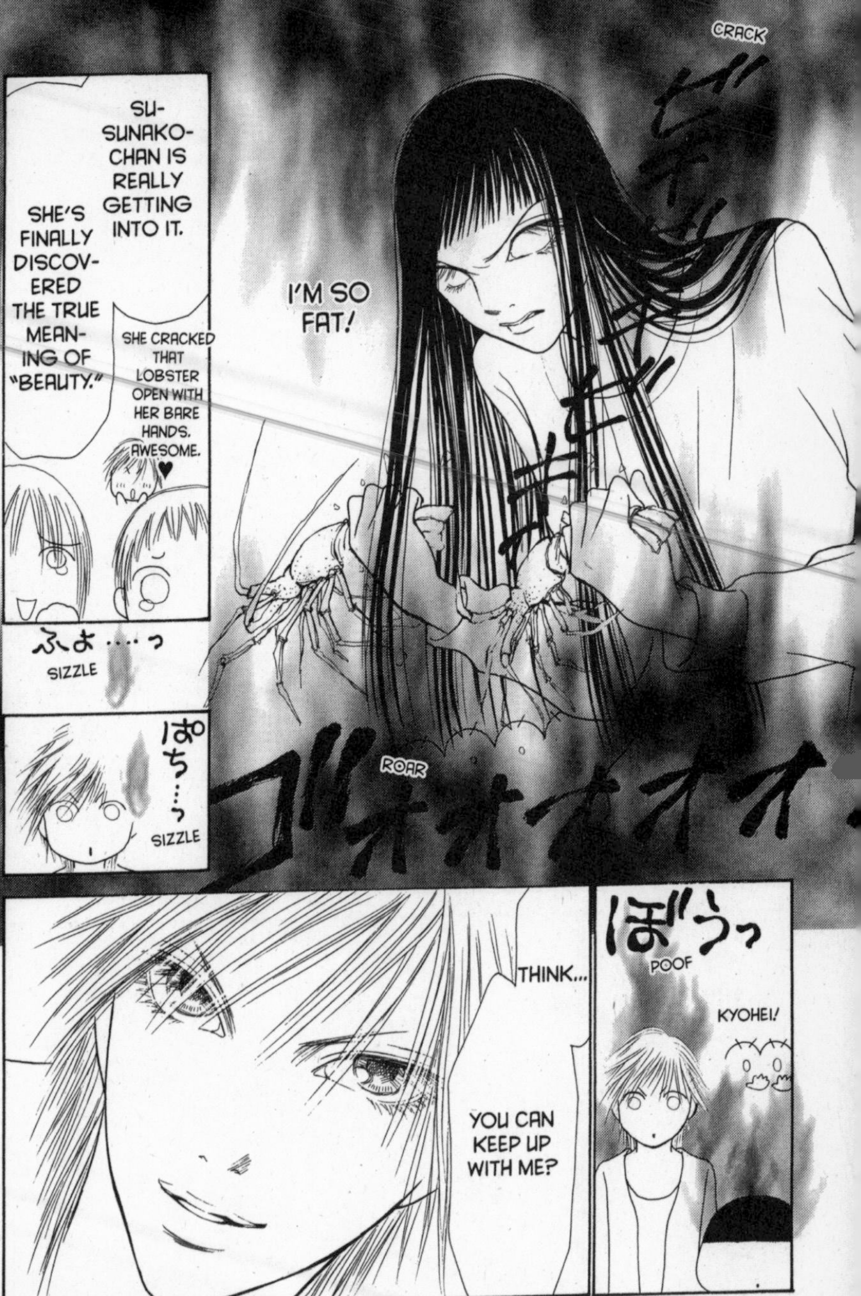
CRACK
I'M SO FAT!
ROAR
SU-SUNAKO-CHAN IS REALLY GETTING INTO IT.
SHE'S FINALLY DISCOVERED THE TRUE MEANING OF "BEAUTY."
SHE CRACKED THAT LOBSTER OPEN WITH HER BARE HANDS. AWESOME. ♥
ふよ…っ
SIZZLE
ぱち…っ
SIZZLE
ぼうっ
POOF
KYOHEI!
THINK...
YOU CAN KEEP UP WITH ME?

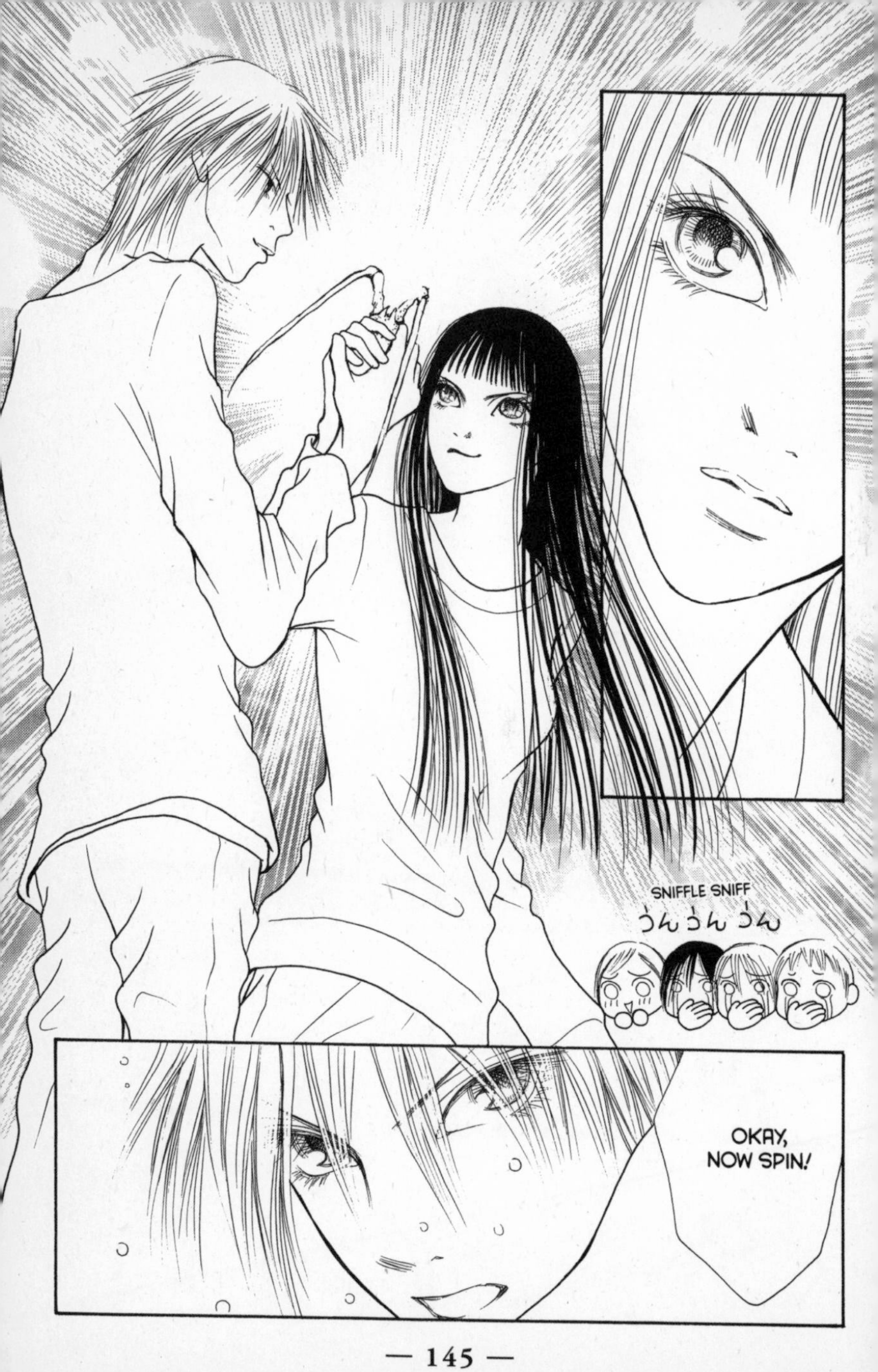
SNIFFLE SNIFF
うんうんうん
OKAY,
NOW SPIN!

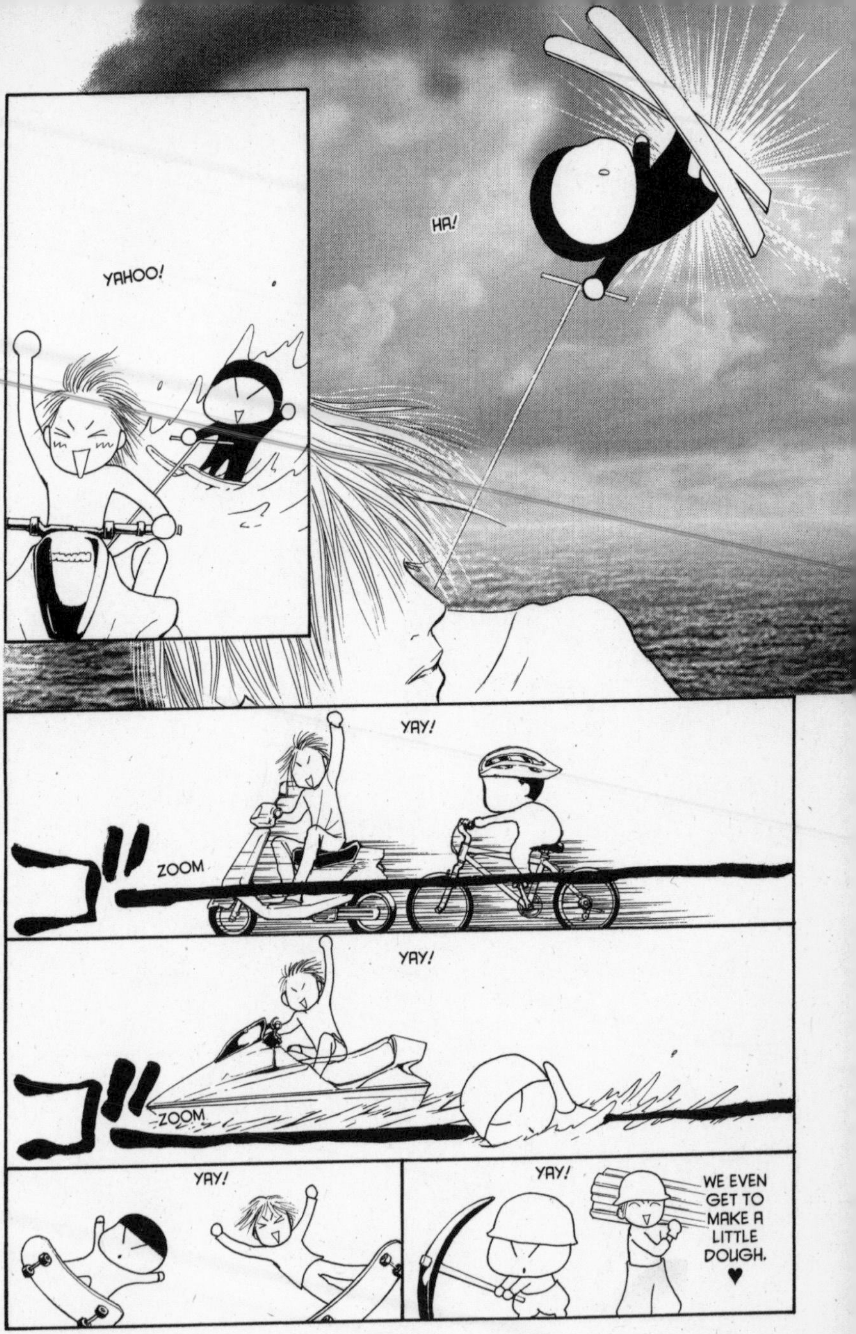
HA!
YAHOO!
YAY!
ゴ
ZOOM
YAY!
ゴ
ZOOM
YAY!
WE EVEN GET TO MAKE A LITTLE DOUGH. ♥
YAY!

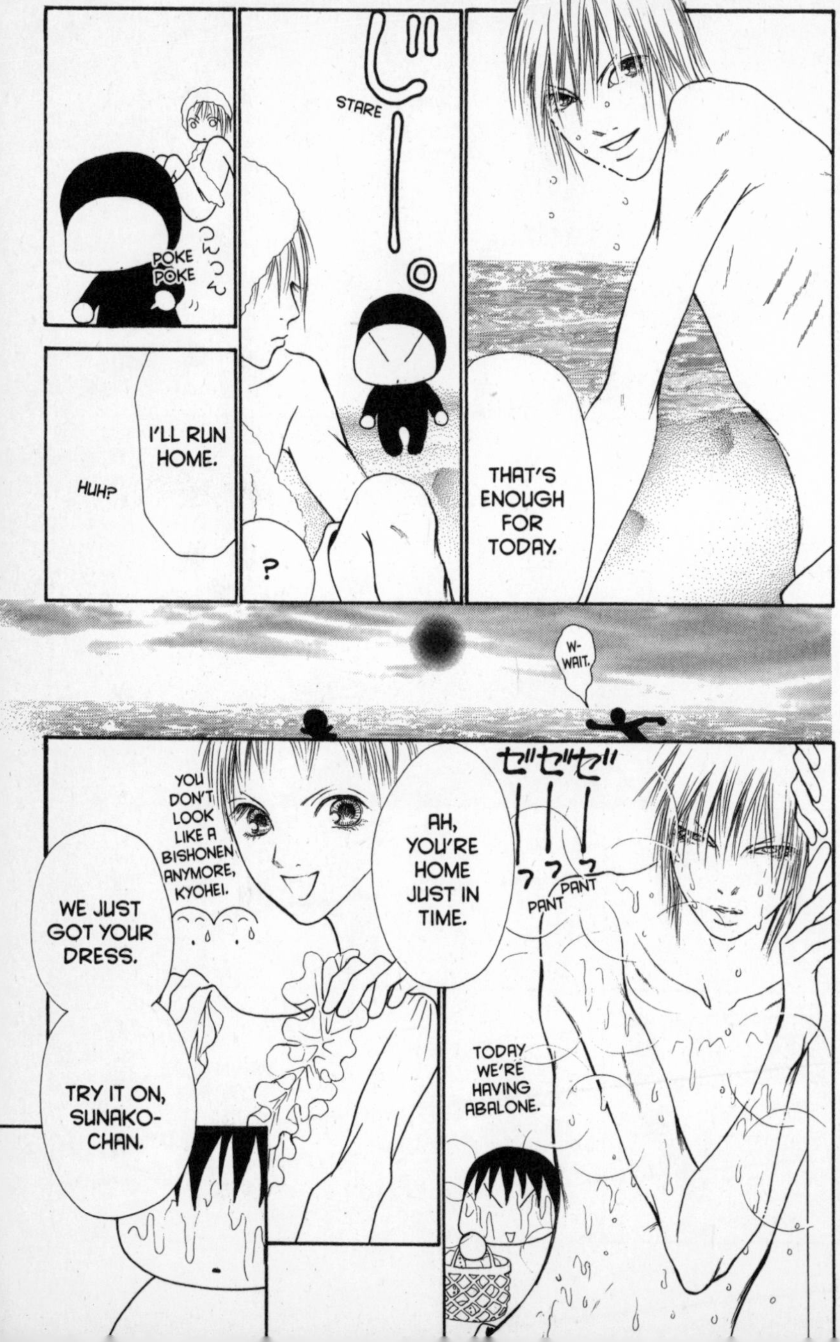
THAT'S ENOUGH FOR TODAY.
STARE
?
POKE POKE
I'LL RUN HOME.
HUH?
W-WAIT.
PANT PANT
TODAY WE'RE HAVING ABALONE.
AH, YOU'RE HOME JUST IN TIME.
YOU DON'T LOOK LIKE A BISHONEN ANYMORE, KYOHEI.
WE JUST GOT YOUR DRESS.
TRY IT ON, SUNAKO-CHAN.

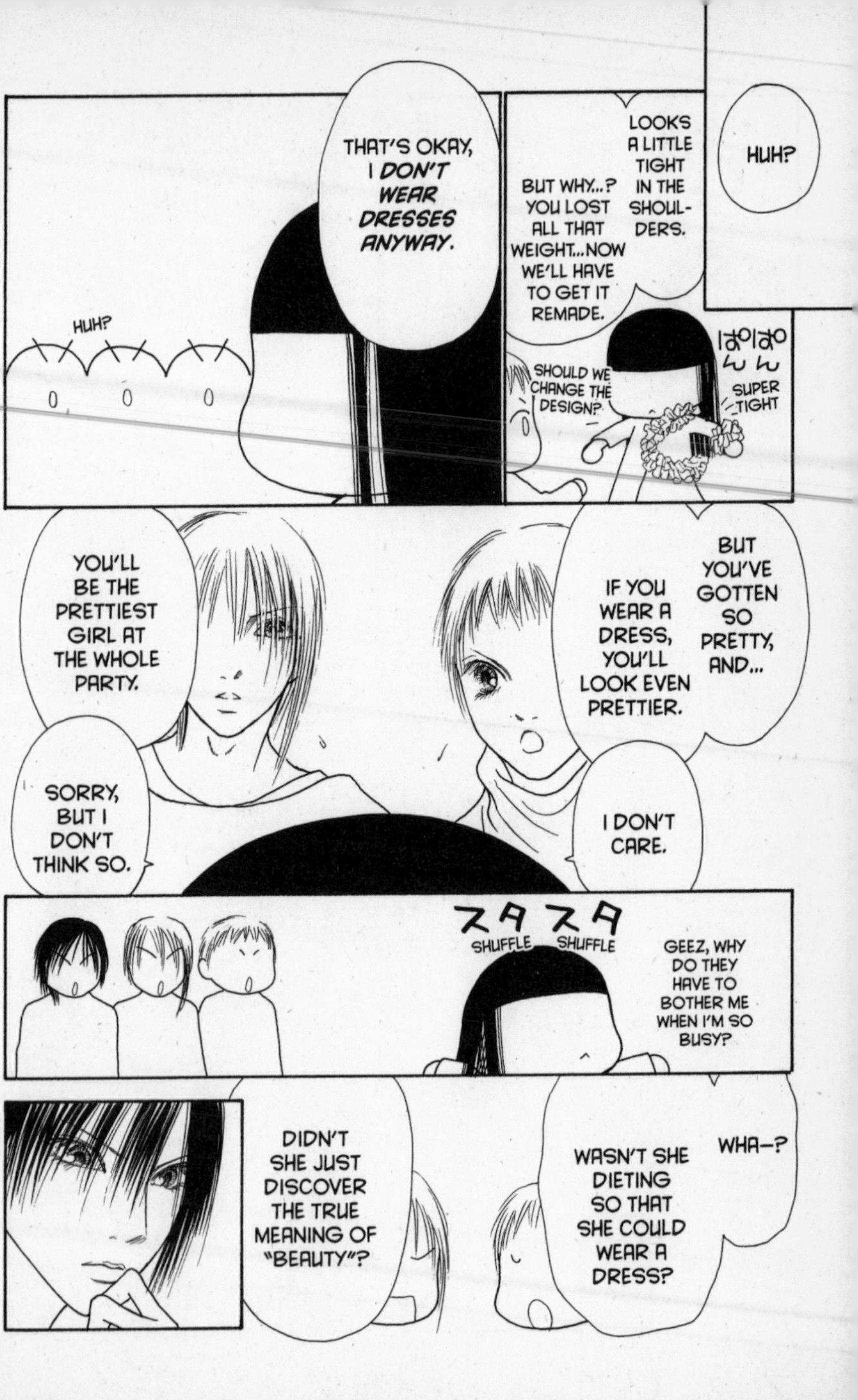
HUH?
LOOKS A LITTLE TIGHT IN THE SHOUL-DERS.
BUT WHY...? YOU LOST ALL THAT WEIGHT...NOW WE'LL HAVE TO GET IT REMADE.
ぱんぱん
SUPER TIGHT
SHOULD WE CHANGE THE DESIGN?
THAT'S OKAY, I *DON'T WEAR DRESSES ANYWAY.*
HUH?
BUT YOU'VE GOTTEN SO PRETTY, AND...
IF YOU WEAR A DRESS, YOU'LL LOOK EVEN PRETTIER.
YOU'LL BE THE PRETTIEST GIRL AT THE WHOLE PARTY.
I DON'T CARE.
SORRY, BUT I DON'T THINK SO.
GEEZ, WHY DO THEY HAVE TO BOTHER ME WHEN I'M SO BUSY?
スタスタ
SHUFFLE SHUFFLE
WHA—?
WASN'T SHE DIETING SO THAT SHE COULD WEAR A DRESS?
DIDN'T SHE JUST DISCOVER THE TRUE MEANING OF "BEAUTY"?

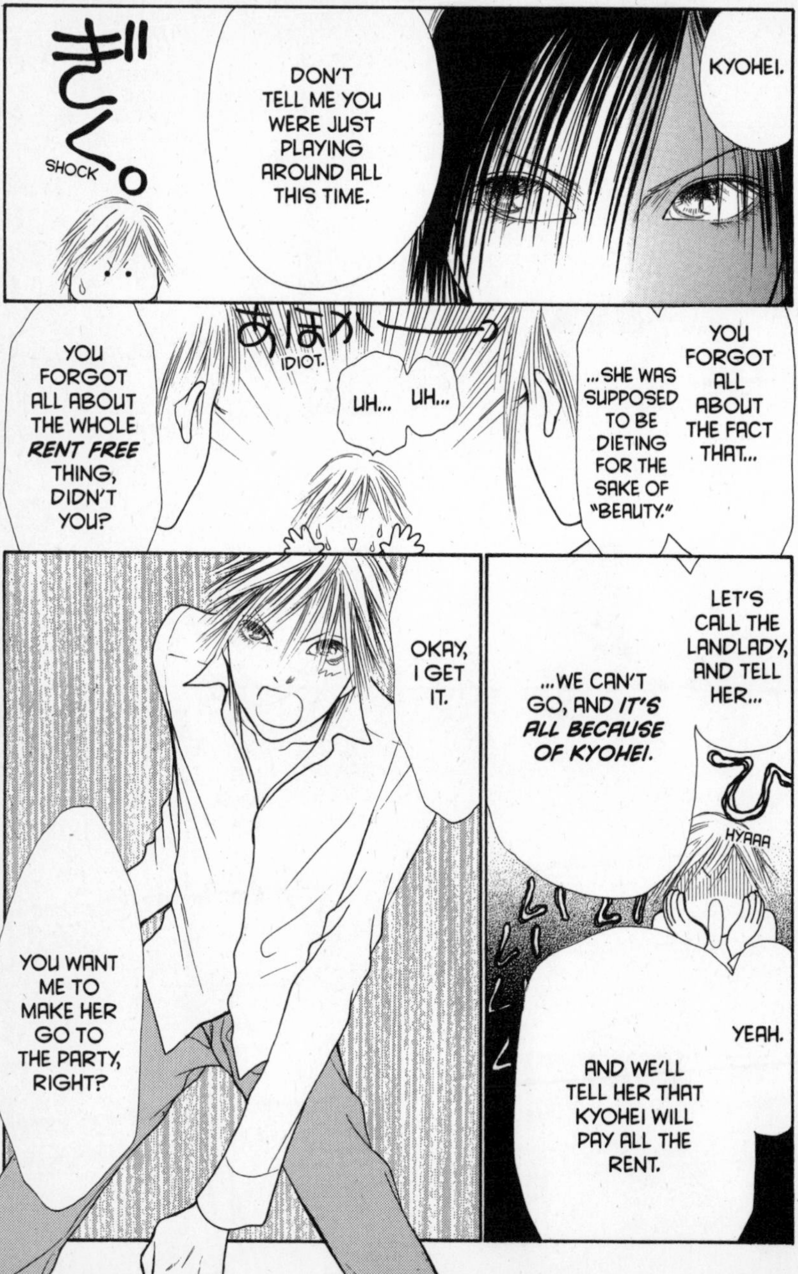
KYOHEI.
DON'T TELL ME YOU WERE JUST PLAYING AROUND ALL THIS TIME.
ぎく。
SHOCK
YOU FORGOT ALL ABOUT THE FACT THAT...
...SHE WAS SUPPOSED TO BE DIETING FOR THE SAKE OF "BEAUTY."
あほかーっ
IDIOT.
UH... UH...
YOU FORGOT ALL ABOUT THE WHOLE *RENT FREE* THING, DIDN'T YOU?
LET'S CALL THE LANDLADY, AND TELL HER...
...WE CAN'T GO, AND *IT'S ALL BECAUSE OF KYOHEI.*
HYAAA
YEAH.
AND WE'LL TELL HER THAT KYOHEI WILL PAY ALL THE RENT.
OKAY, I GET IT.
YOU WANT ME TO MAKE HER GO TO THE PARTY, RIGHT?

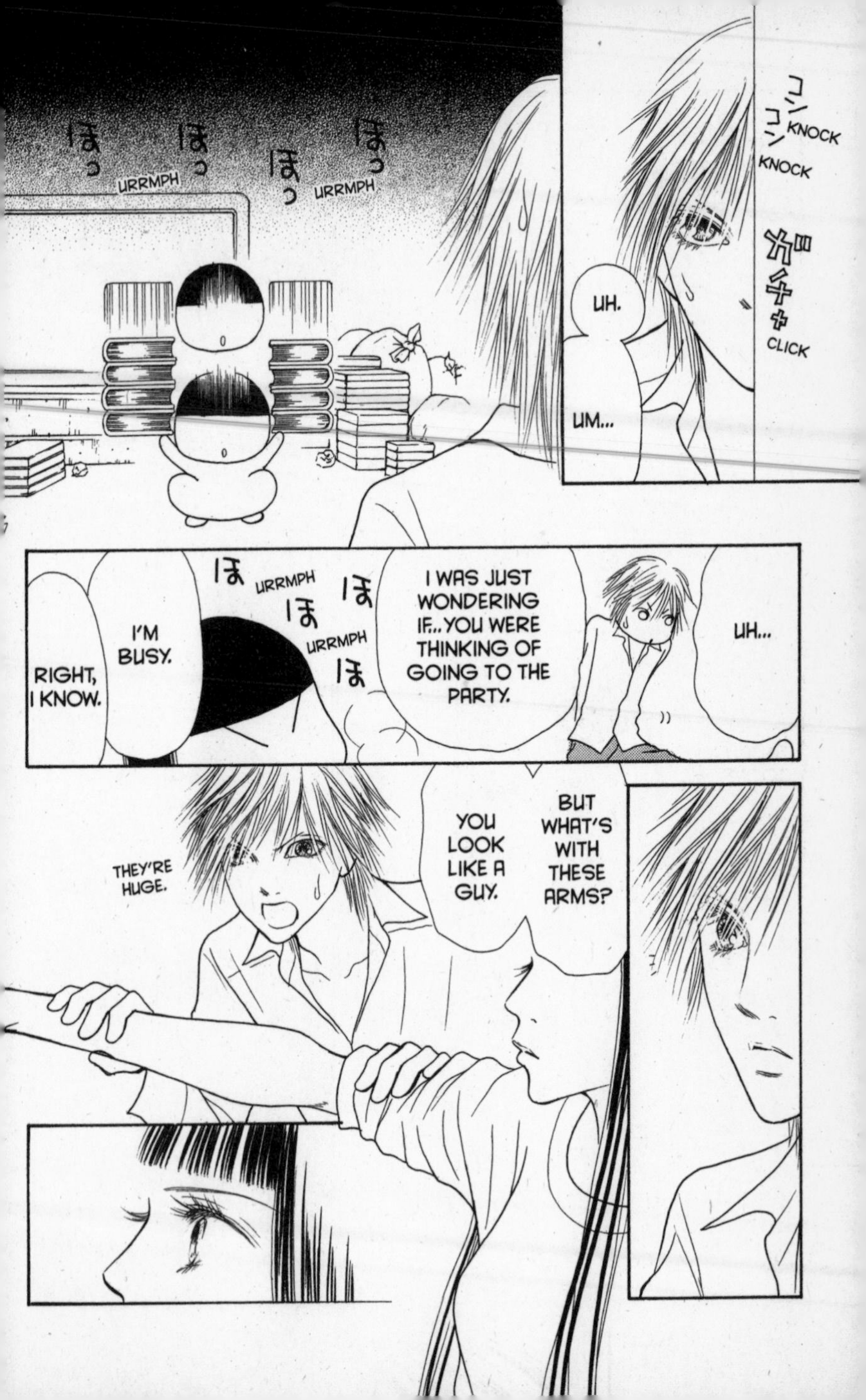
コンコン
KNOCK
KNOCK
ガチャ
CLICK
UH.
UM...
ほっ
ほっ
ほっ
ほっ
URRMPH
URRMPH
UH...
I WAS JUST WONDERING IF... YOU WERE THINKING OF GOING TO THE PARTY.
ほ
URRMPH
ほ
ほ
URRMPH
ほ
I'M BUSY.
RIGHT, I KNOW.
BUT WHAT'S WITH THESE ARMS?
YOU LOOK LIKE A GUY.
THEY'RE HUGE.

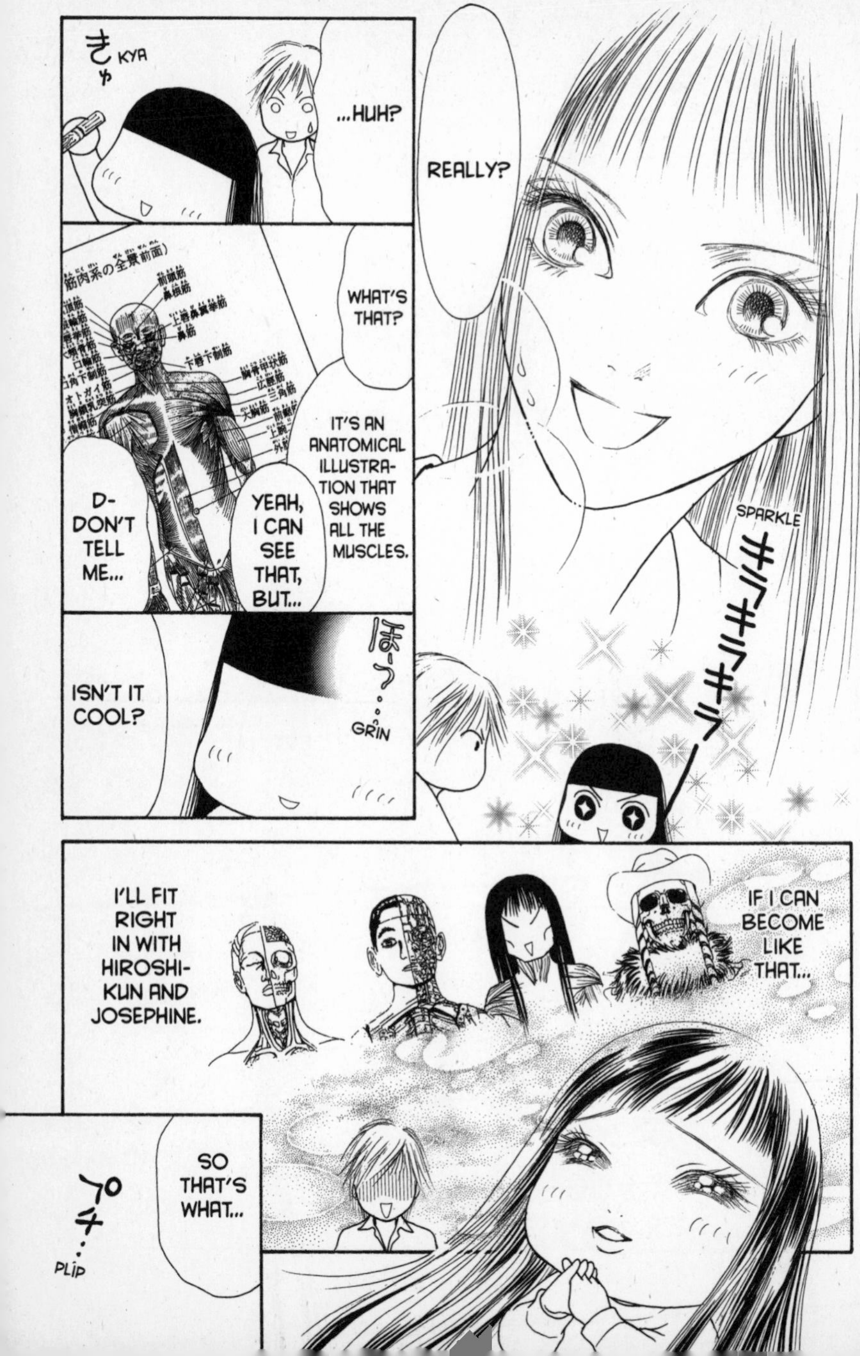

REALLY?
キラキラキラ
SPARKLE
...HUH?
きゅ
KYA
WHAT'S THAT?
IT'S AN ANATOMICAL ILLUSTRATION THAT SHOWS ALL THE MUSCLES.
YEAH, I CAN SEE THAT, BUT...
D-DON'T TELL ME...
ほーっ...
GRIN
ISN'T IT COOL?
IF I CAN BECOME LIKE THAT...
I'LL FIT RIGHT IN WITH HIROSHI-KUN AND JOSEPHINE.
SO THAT'S WHAT...
プチ...
PLIP

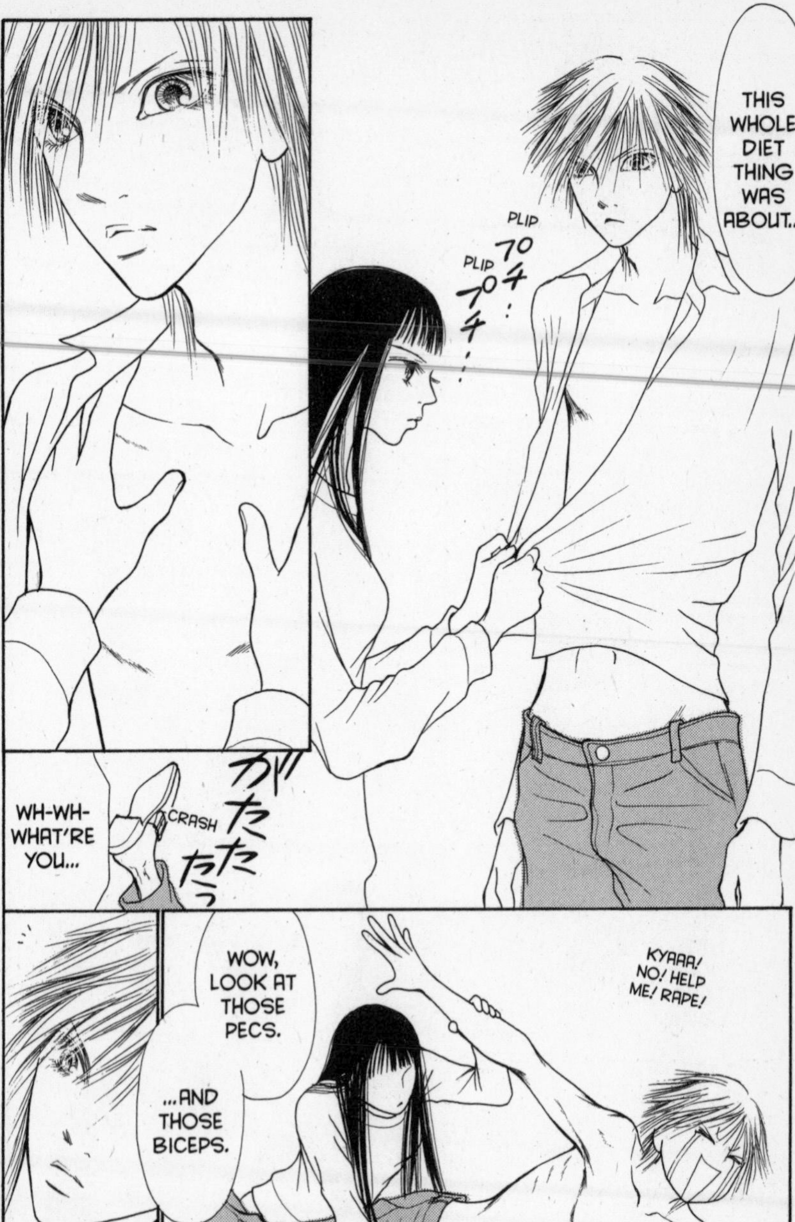
THIS WHOLE DIET THING WAS ABOUT...
PLIP
プチ…
PLIP
プチ…
WH-WH-WHAT'RE YOU...
CRASH
がたたたっ
KYAAA! NO! HELP ME! RAPE!
WOW, LOOK AT THOSE PECS.
...AND THOSE BICEPS.

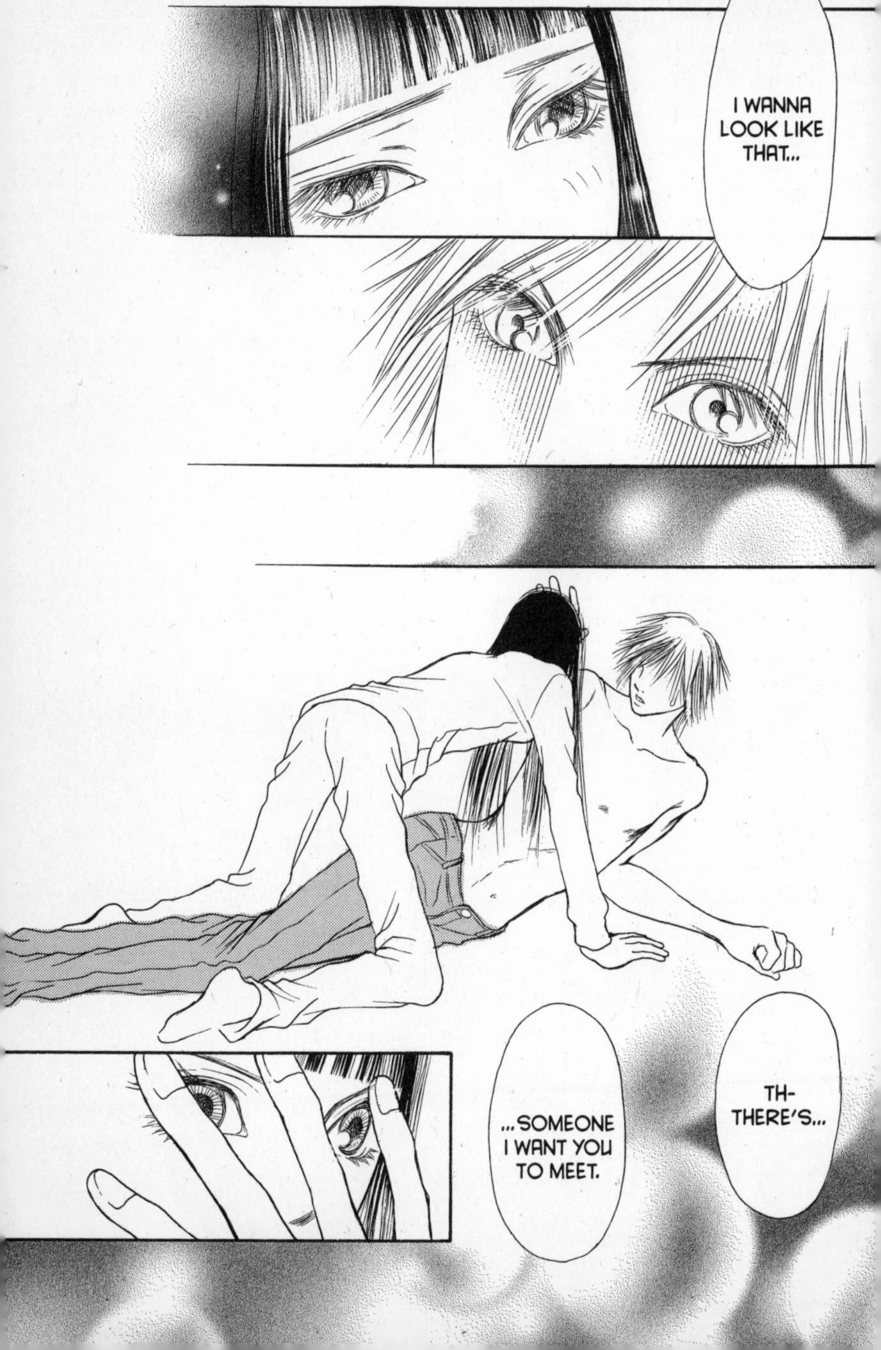
I WANNA LOOK LIKE THAT...
TH- THERE'S...
...SOMEONE I WANT YOU TO MEET.

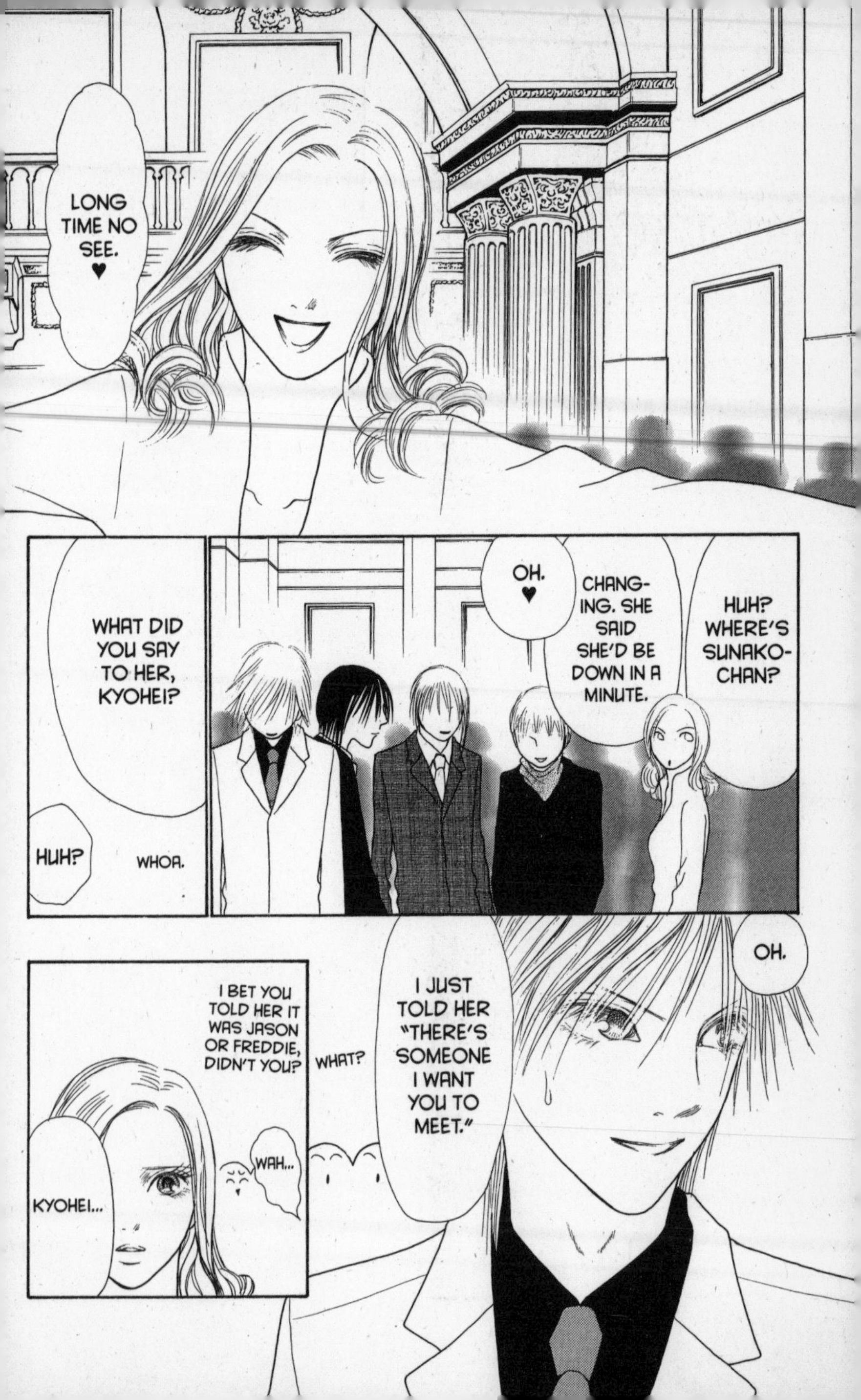
LONG TIME NO SEE. ♥
HUH? WHERE'S SUNAKO-CHAN?
CHANG-ING. SHE SAID SHE'D BE DOWN IN A MINUTE.
OH. ♥
WHAT DID YOU SAY TO HER, KYOHEI?
WHOA.
HUH?
OH.
I JUST TOLD HER "THERE'S SOMEONE I WANT YOU TO MEET."
WHAT?
I BET YOU TOLD HER IT WAS JASON OR FREDDIE, DIDN'T YOU?
WAH...
KYOHEI...

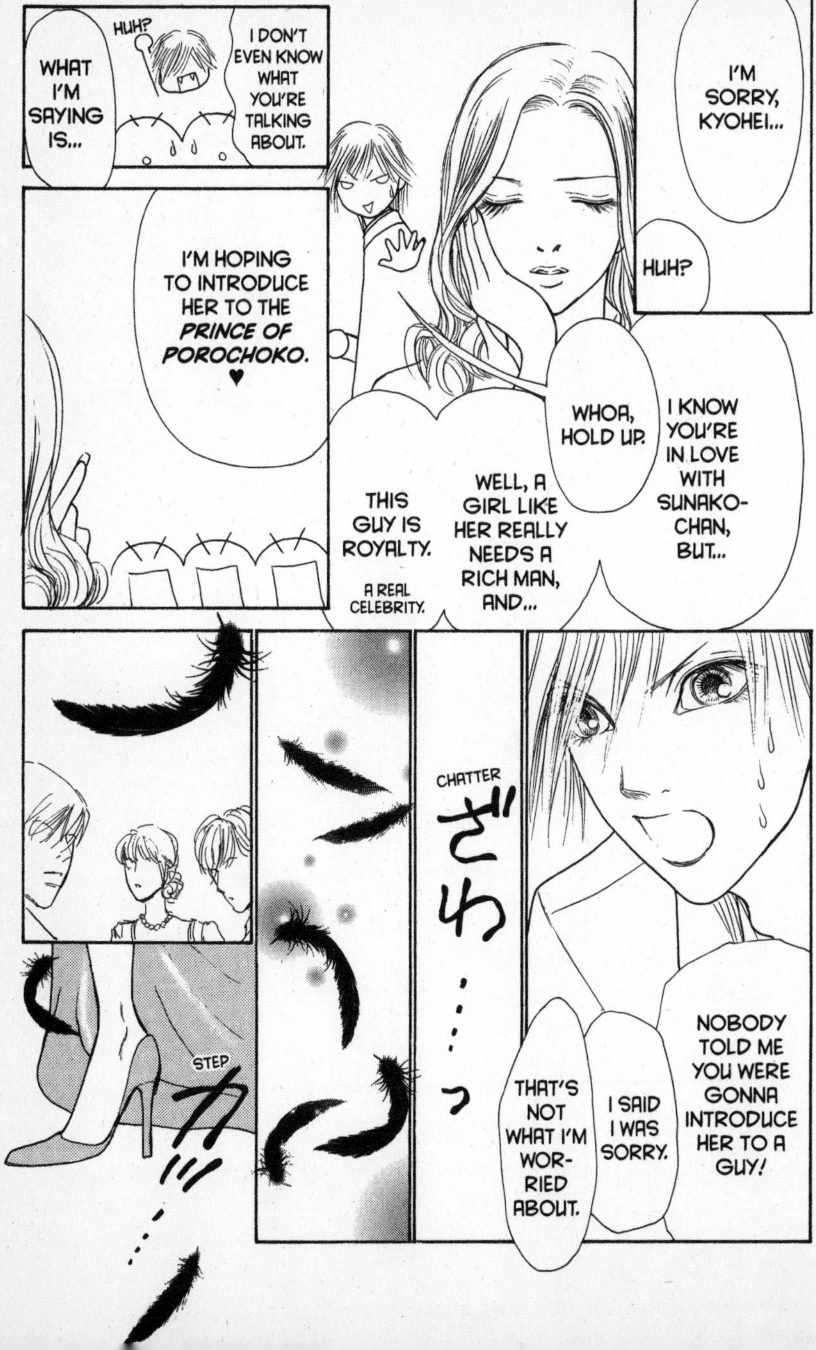
I'M SORRY, KYOHEI...
HUH?
I DON'T EVEN KNOW WHAT YOU'RE TALKING ABOUT.
HUH?
WHAT I'M SAYING IS...
I'M HOPING TO INTRODUCE HER TO THE *PRINCE OF POROCHOKO.* ♥
I KNOW YOU'RE IN LOVE WITH SUNAKO-CHAN, BUT...
WHOA, HOLD UP.
WELL, A GIRL LIKE HER REALLY NEEDS A RICH MAN, AND...
THIS GUY IS ROYALTY.
A REAL CELEBRITY.
NOBODY TOLD ME YOU WERE GONNA INTRODUCE HER TO A GUY!
I SAID I WAS SORRY.
THAT'S NOT WHAT I'M WOR-RIED ABOUT.
CHATTER
ざわ…っ
STEP
カツ…

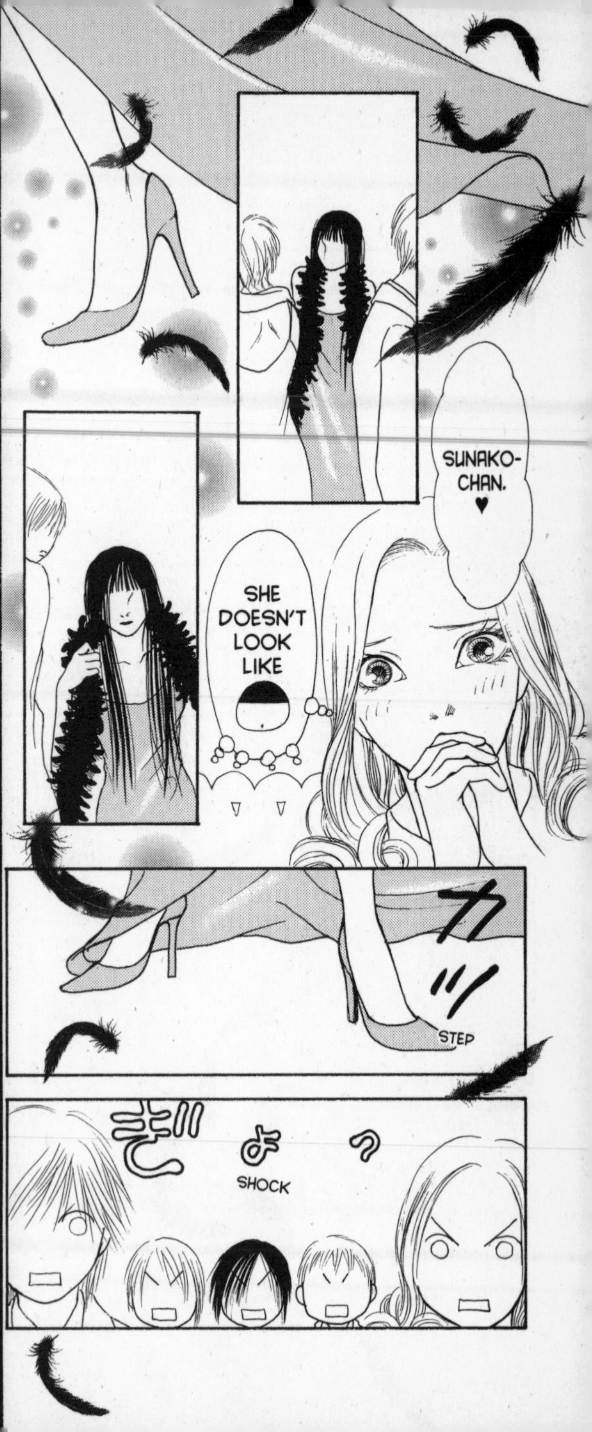
SUNAKO-CHAN. ♥
SHE DOESN'T LOOK LIKE
カッ
STEP
ぎょっ
SHOCK

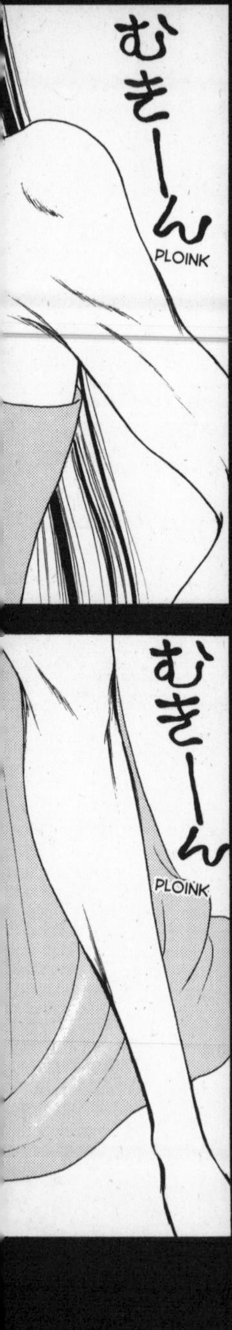
むきーん
PLOINK
むきーん
PLOINK

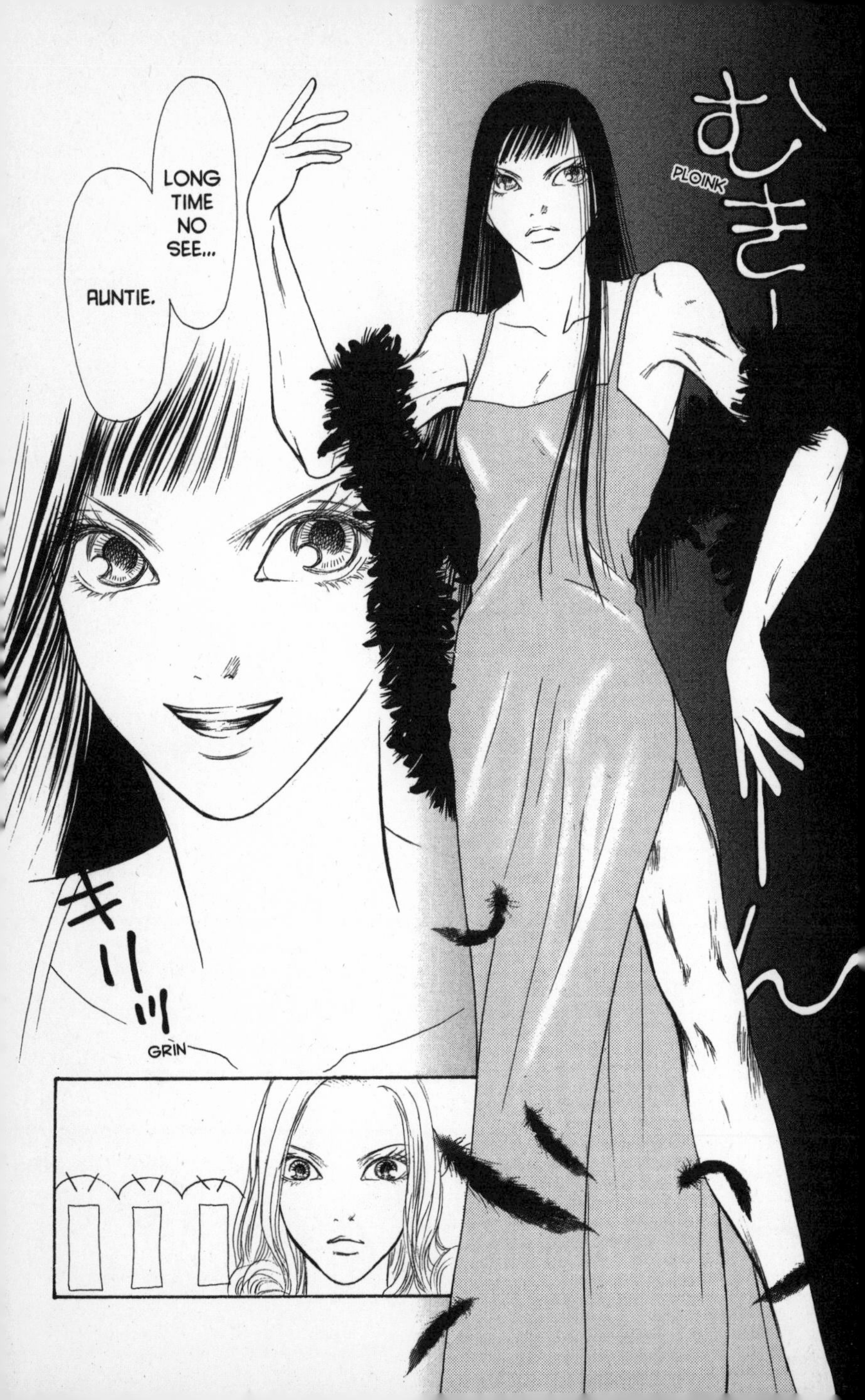
むきーん〜
PLOINK
LONG TIME NO SEE...
AUNTIE.
キリッ
GRIN

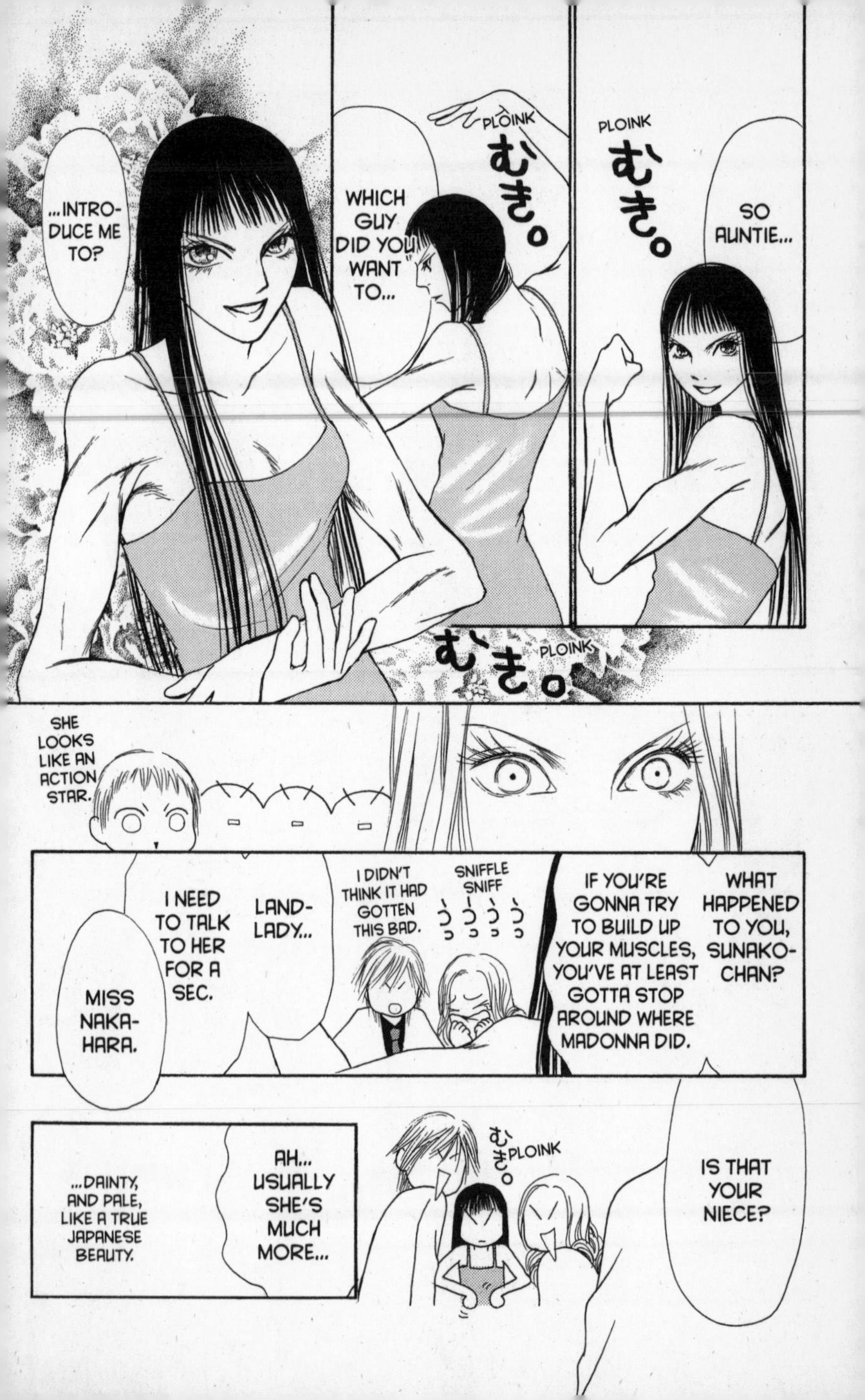
SO AUNTIE...
PLOINK
むき。
WHICH GUY DID YOU WANT TO...
PLOINK
むき。
...INTRODUCE ME TO?
むき。
PLOINK
SHE LOOKS LIKE AN ACTION STAR.
WHAT HAPPENED TO YOU, SUNAKO-CHAN?
IF YOU'RE GONNA TRY TO BUILD UP YOUR MUSCLES, YOU'VE AT LEAST GOTTA STOP AROUND WHERE MADONNA DID.
SNIFFLE SNIFF
うううう
I DIDN'T THINK IT HAD GOTTEN THIS BAD.
LANDLADY...
I NEED TO TALK TO HER FOR A SEC.
MISS NAKAHARA.
IS THAT YOUR NIECE?
むき。
PLOINK
AH... USUALLY SHE'S MUCH MORE...
...DAINTY, AND PALE, LIKE A TRUE JAPANESE BEAUTY.

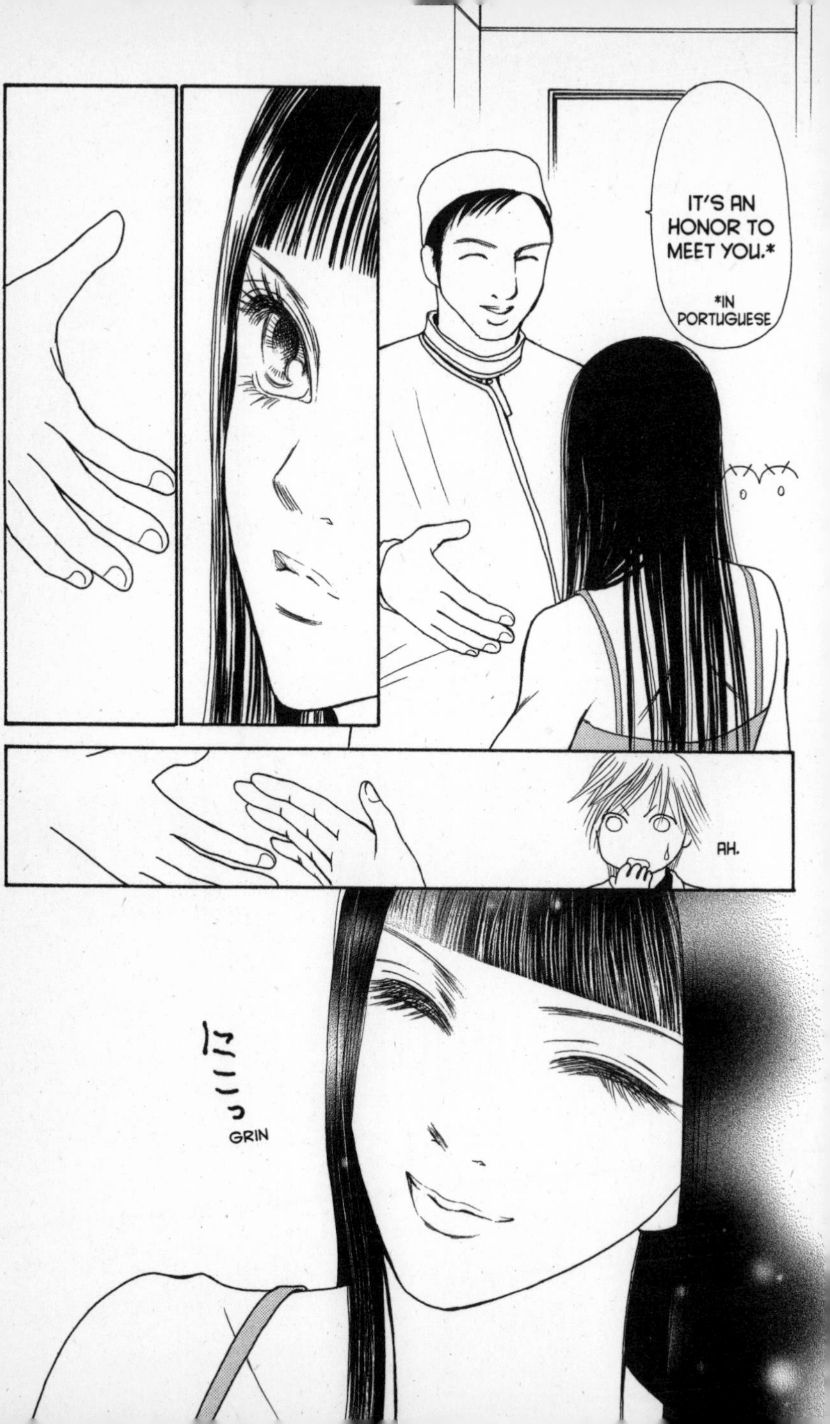
IT'S AN HONOR TO MEET YOU.*
*IN PORTUGUESE
AH.
にこっ
GRIN

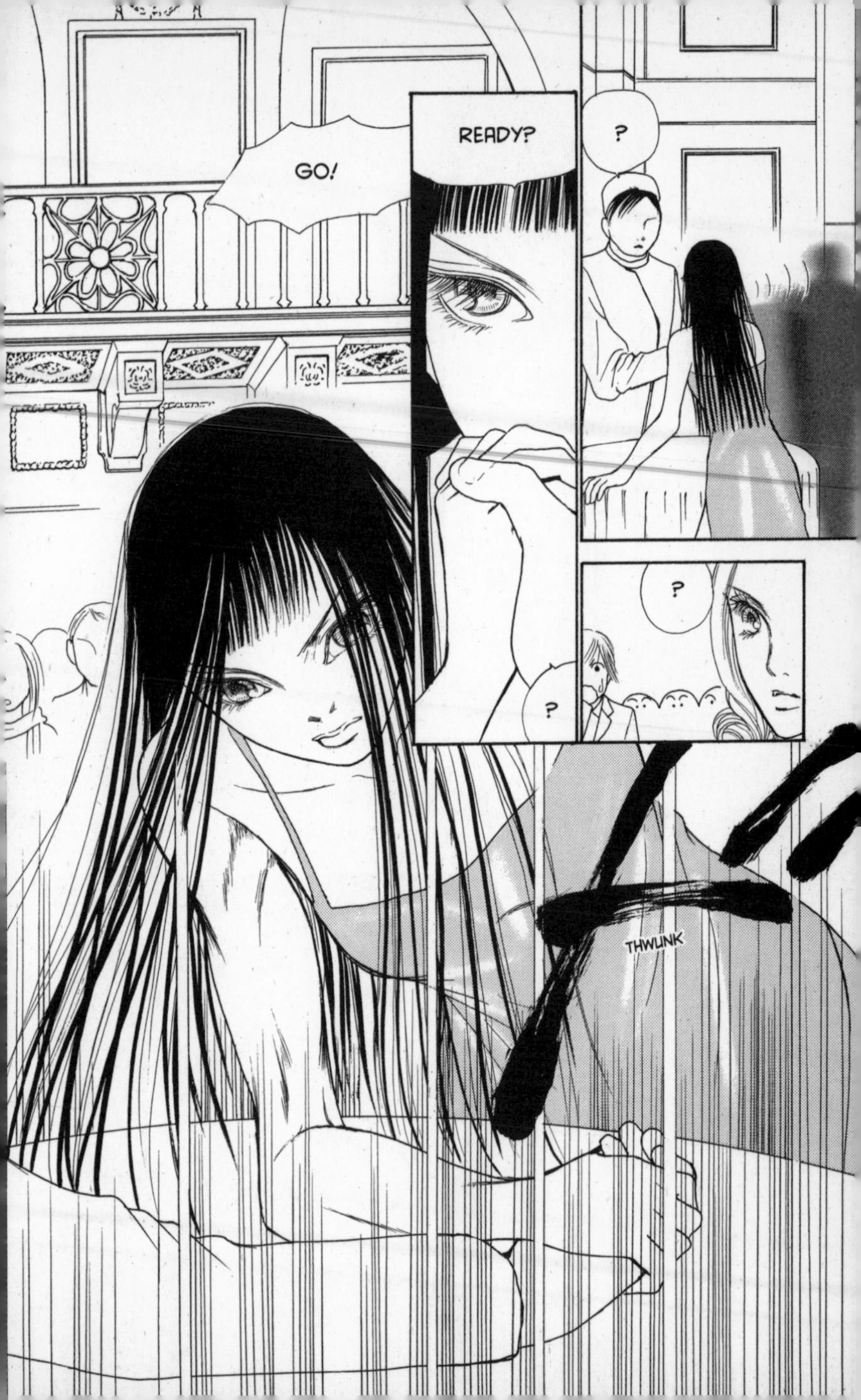
?
?
READY?
?
GO!
THWUNK

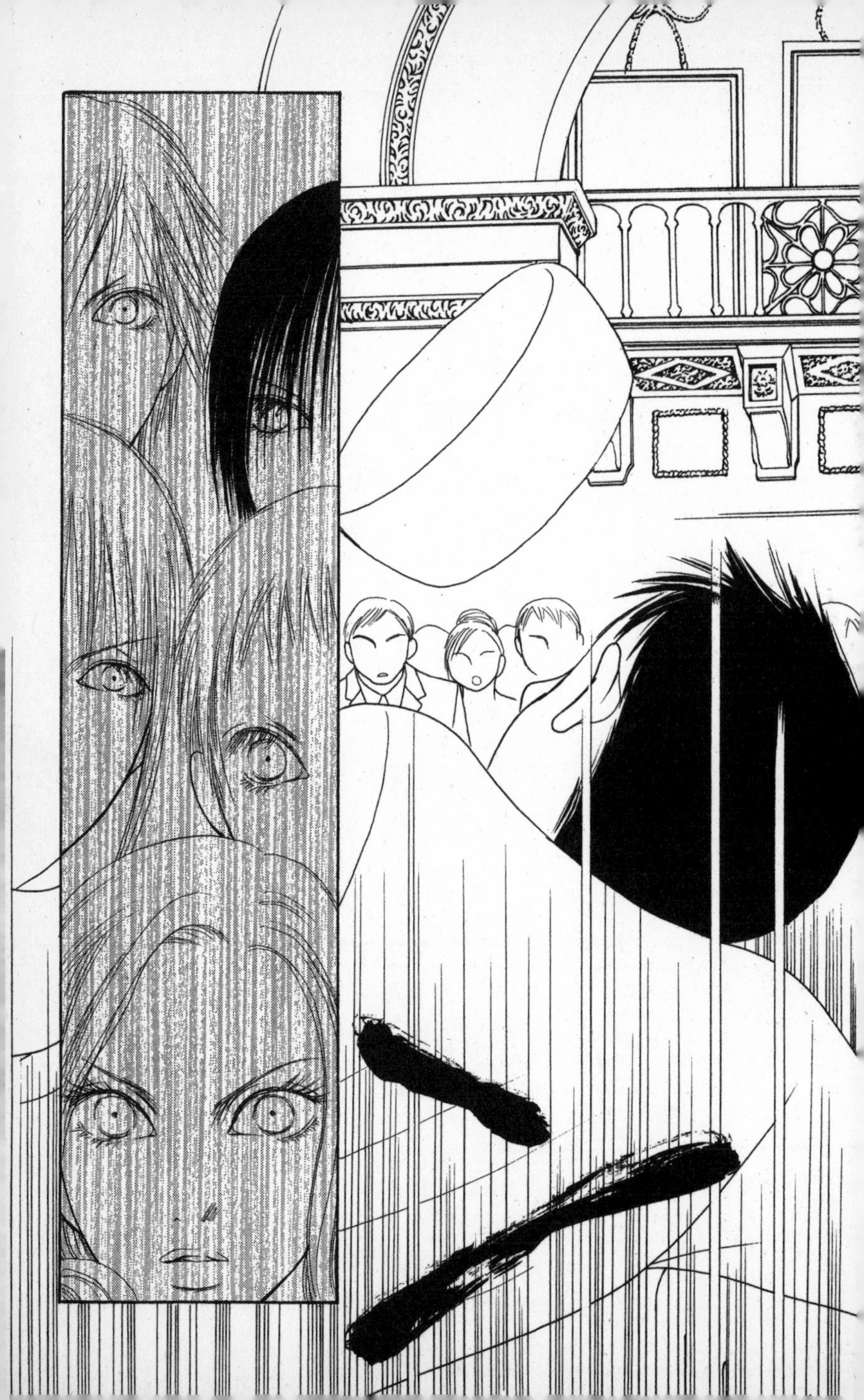

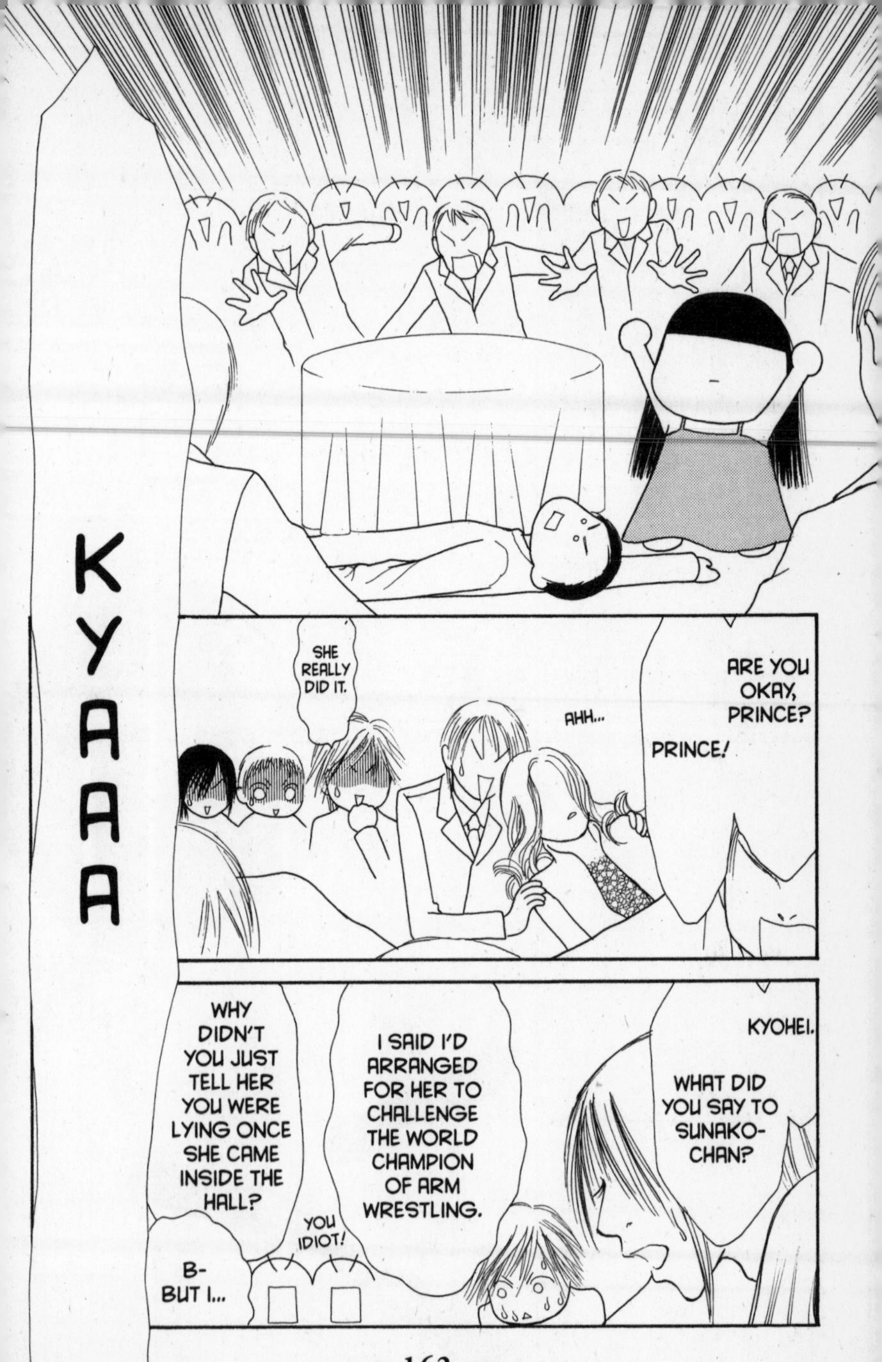
KYAAA
ARE YOU OKAY, PRINCE?
PRINCE!
AHH...
SHE REALLY DID IT.
KYOHEI.
WHAT DID YOU SAY TO SUNAKO-CHAN?
I SAID I'D ARRANGED FOR HER TO CHALLENGE THE WORLD CHAMPION OF ARM WRESTLING.
WHY DIDN'T YOU JUST TELL HER YOU WERE LYING ONCE SHE CAME INSIDE THE HALL?
YOU IDIOT!
B- BUT I...

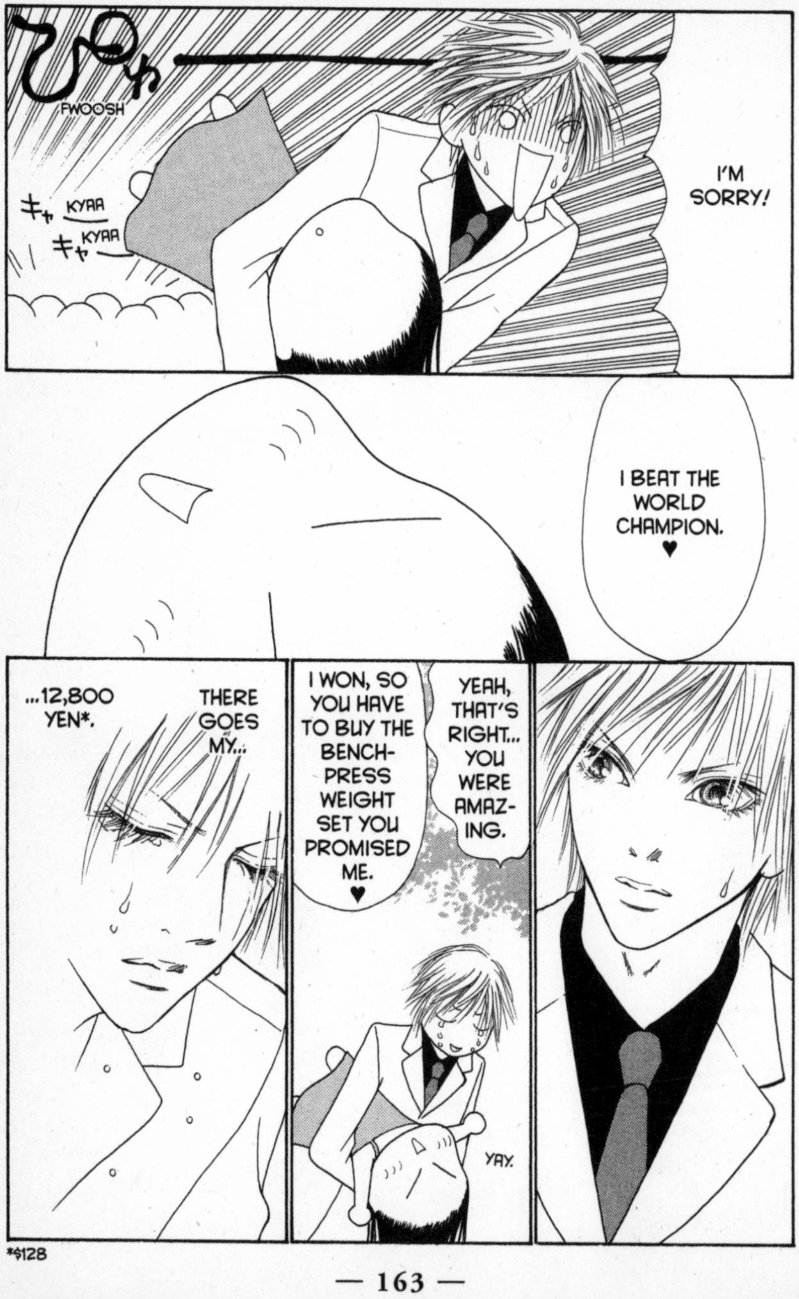
ひゅ
FWOOSH
I'M SORRY!
キャ KYAA
キャ KYAA
I BEAT THE WORLD CHAMPION. ♥
YEAH, THAT'S RIGHT... YOU WERE AMAZ-ING.
I WON, SO YOU HAVE TO BUY THE BENCH-PRESS WEIGHT SET YOU PROMISED ME. ♥
YAY.
THERE GOES MY...
...12,800 YEN*.

*$128

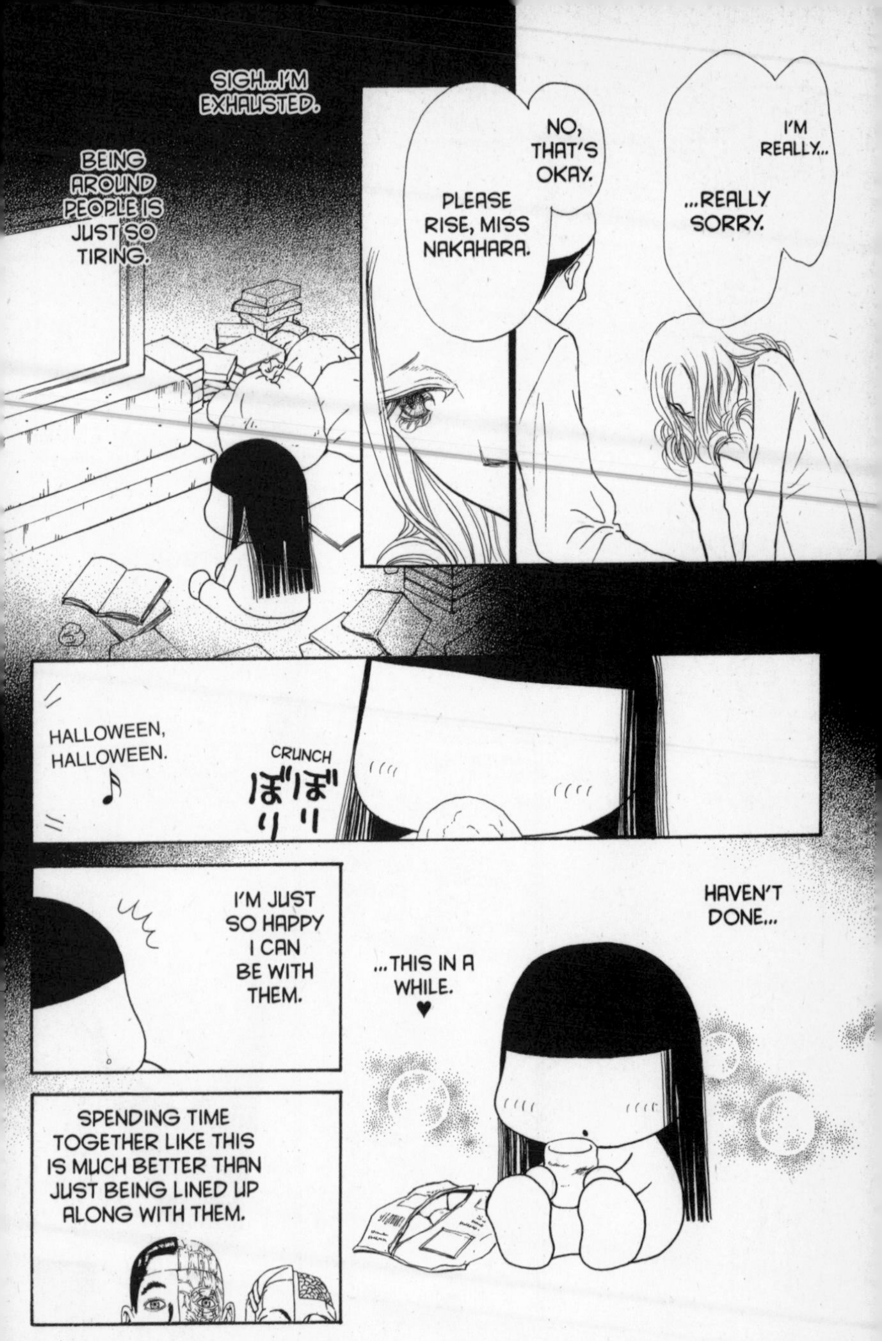
I'M REALLY...
...REALLY SORRY.
NO, THAT'S OKAY.
PLEASE RISE, MISS NAKAHARA.
SIGH...I'M EXHAUSTED.
BEING AROUND PEOPLE IS JUST SO TIRING.
CRUNCH
ぼりぼり
HALLOWEEN, HALLOWEEN. ♪
HAVEN'T DONE...
...THIS IN A WHILE. ♥
I'M JUST SO HAPPY I CAN BE WITH THEM.
SPENDING TIME TOGETHER LIKE THIS IS MUCH BETTER THAN JUST BEING LINED UP ALONG WITH THEM.

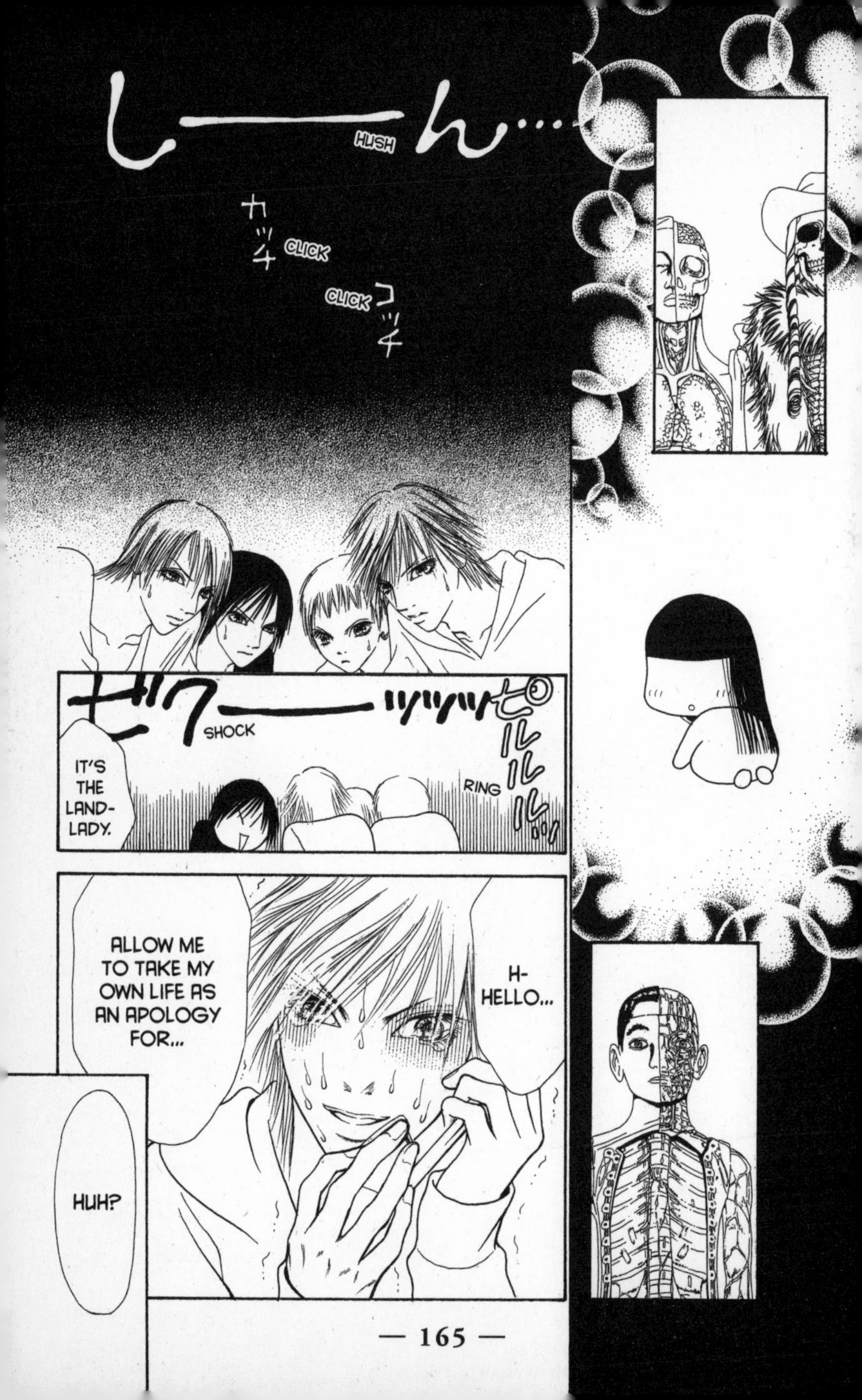
しーーん…
HUSH
カッチ
CLICK
CLICK
コッチ
ゾワーーッッッ
SHOCK
ピルルル
RING
IT'S THE LAND-LADY.
H-HELLO...
ALLOW ME TO TAKE MY OWN LIFE AS AN APOLOGY FOR...
HUH?

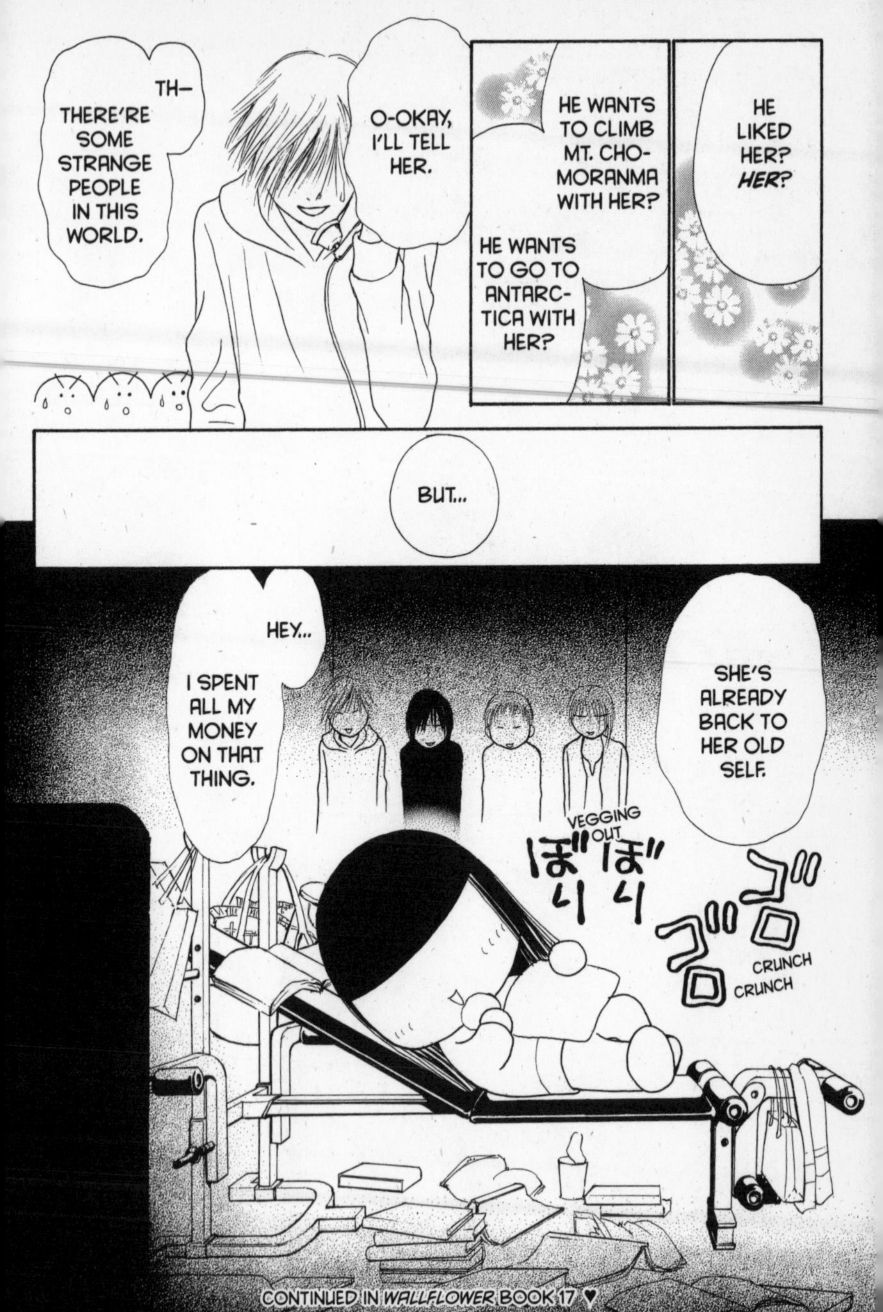
HE LIKED HER? *HER?*
HE WANTS TO CLIMB MT. CHO-MORANMA WITH HER?
HE WANTS TO GO TO ANTARCTICA WITH HER?
O-OKAY, I'LL TELL HER.
TH— THERE'RE SOME STRANGE PEOPLE IN THIS WORLD.
BUT...
SHE'S ALREADY BACK TO HER OLD SELF.
ゴロゴロ
CRUNCH CRUNCH
ぼりぼり
VEGGING OUT
HEY...
I SPENT ALL MY MONEY ON THAT THING.
CONTINUED IN *WALLFLOWER* BOOK 17 ♥

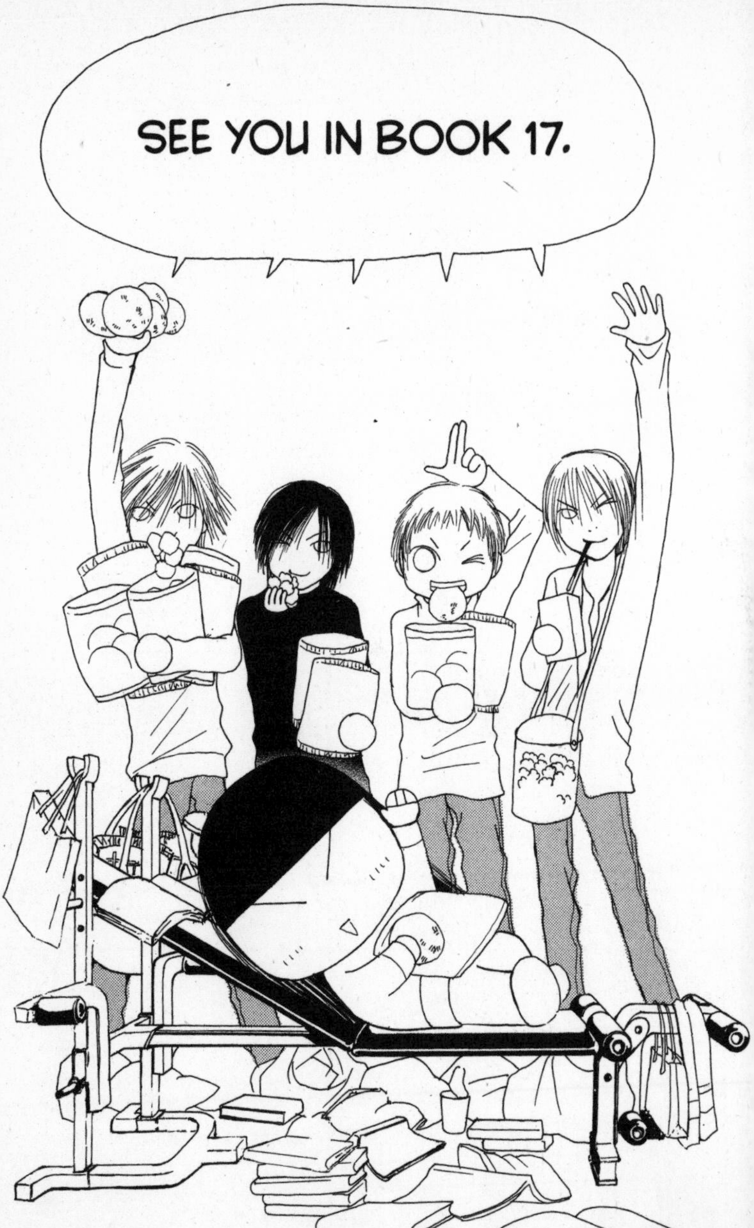
SEE YOU IN BOOK 17.

THIS IS *TEN.* ♥

HIS REAL NAME IS TENNOSUKE HAYAKAWA. ♥

I LOVE HIM LIKE HE'S MY LITTLE BABY. ♥

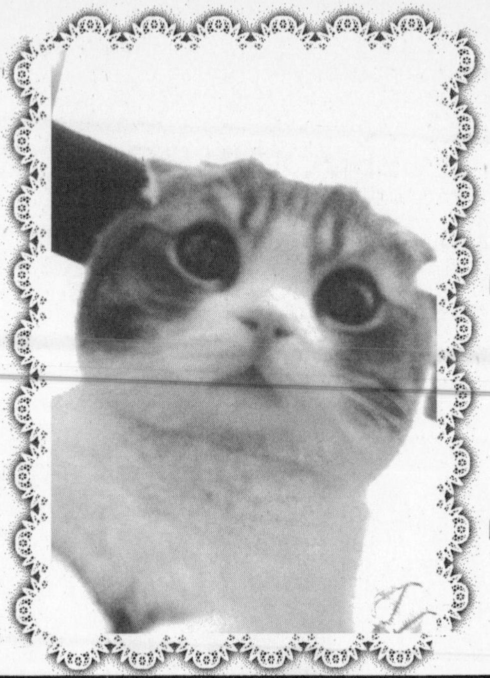

HE'S BEEN REALLY SWEET LATELY... AND HE'S CUTER THAN EVER. ♥

HE NEVER LEAVES MY SIDE.

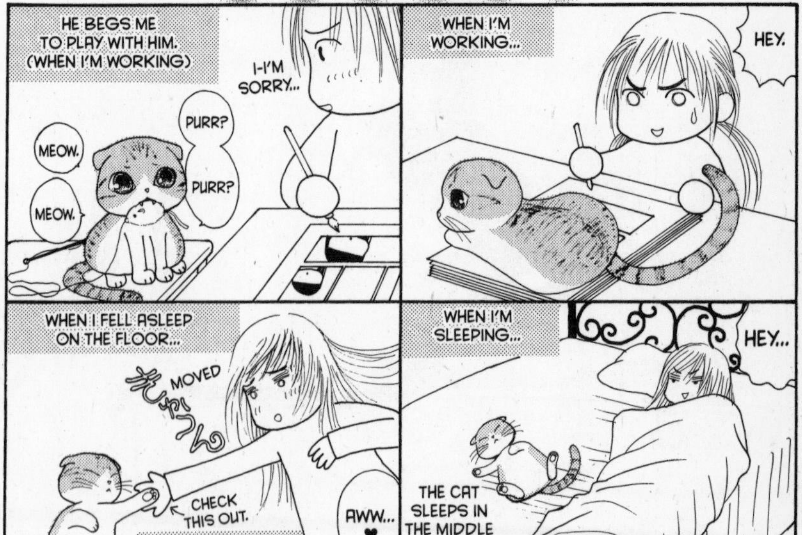

WHEN I'M WORKING...
HEY.
HE BEGS ME TO PLAY WITH HIM. (WHEN I'M WORKING)
I-I'M SORRY...
PURR?
MEOW.
PURR?
MEOW.
WHEN I'M SLEEPING...
HEY...
THE CAT SLEEPS IN THE MIDDLE
THE OWNER SLEEPS ON THE EDGE.
WHEN I FELL ASLEEP ON THE FLOOR...
MOVED
AWW... ♥
CHECK THIS OUT.
WE SLEPT IN EXACTLY THE SAME POSITION...♥

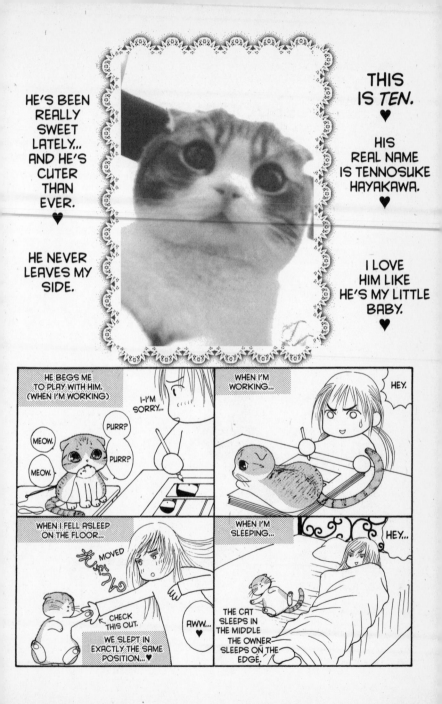

THANK'S FOR BUYING KODANSHA COMICS. ♥ ♥ ♥

I JUST CAME BACK FROM MICHII'S CONCERT, SO I'M ON A TOTAL NATURAL HIGH. ♥ MITSUHIRO OIKAWA-SAMA SURE WAS A *PRINCE*. ♥ HE WAS SO COOL. ♥ HIS SHOW WAS AWESOME. ♥ *RIE BABY* (ONE OF MICHII'S BACKUP SINGERS) TOTALLY KNOCKED ME OUT. SHE'S CUTE. ♥ NO, BEAUTIFUL. ♥ NO, COOL. ♥ AND SEXY. ♥ SHE'S SUCH A GREAT SINGER. ♥ SHE'S GOT AN AMAZING BODY. ♥ I SAW *NORIKO SHOUJI*-SAMA AT THE CONCERT. ♥ ♥ ♥ SHE WAS REALLY CUTE AND SWEET. ♥ ♥ ♥ WHAT A ROCKIN' MAMA. ♥ I WANNA THANK THE BEAUTIFUL WRITER N-SAMA FOR TAKING ME TO THE CONCERT. ♥ THANK YOU SO MUCH FOR TAKING CARE OF ME. ♥ ♥ ♥

LATELY, I'VE BEEN VISITING AN *AESTHETIC SALON*. IT'S THE FIRST TIME IN MY LIFE. IT'S SUCH A PERFECT PLACE FOR A PERSON LIKE ME. BECAUSE…↓

• I CAN'T LOSE WEIGHT ON MY OWN.
(I'M FORCING MY AGING BODY TO WORK REALLY HARD, AND I HAVE NO TIME TO DIET…)
WHAT AN EXCUSE.
• I LOVE CUTE GIRLS. ♥
(EVERY ONE WHO WORKS THERE IS REALLY CUTE. ♥)
• I'M UNDER SO MUCH STRESS, THAT I JUST NEED TO BE PAMPERED.
(I'M DYING…)

I REALLY HOPE I CAN REPORT SOME SUCCESS WITH MY WEIGHT LOSS IN BOOK 17.
WISH ME LUCK!

I'D LIKE TO THANK EVERYBODY WHO SENT ME LETTERS. ♥ ♥ ♥

YOU'RE THE SOURCE OF MY POWER! THANK'S SO MUCH. ♥
I'M HOPING TO HAVE ENOUGH BONUS PAGES SO THAT I CAN ANSWER ALL YOUR QUESTIONS IN BOOK 17. ♥
I REALLY HOPE IT'LL HAPPEN. I HOPE I GET MORE BONUS PAGES.

OKAY, I'LL SEE YOU GUYS IN BOOK 17. ♥ ♥ ♥

SPECIAL THANKS

CHOBI-SAN, TAEKO HABA-SAMA, TOMII, YOUICHIROU TOMITA-SAMA, NABEKO, EMI WATANABE-SAMA

MINE-SAMA, INNAN-SAMA, INO-SAMA, EVERYBODY AT THE EDITING DEPARTMENT

MIZUHO AIMOTO-SENSEI, MACHIKO SAKURAI, YUU YOSHII

EVERYBODY WHO'S READING THIS RIGHT NOW. ♥

About the Creator

Tomoko Hayakawa was born on March 4.

Since her debut as a manga creator, Tomoko Hayakawa has worked on many shojo titles with the theme of romantic love—only to realize that she could write about other subjects as well. She decided to pack her newest story with the things she likes most, which led to her current, enormously popular series, *The Wallflower*.

Her favorite things are: Tim Burton's *The Nightmare Before Christmas*, Jean Paul Gaultier, and samurai dramas on TV. Her hobbies are collecting items with skull designs and watching *bishonen* (beautiful boys). Her dream is to build a mansion like the one the Addams family lives in. Her favorite pastime is to lie around at home with her cat, Ten (whose full name is Tennosuke).

Her zodiac sign is Pisces, and her blood group is AB.

Translation Notes

Japanese is a tricky language for most Westerners, and translation is often more art than science. For your edification and reading pleasure, here are notes on some of the places where we could have gone in a different direction in our translation of the work, or where a Japanese cultural reference is used.

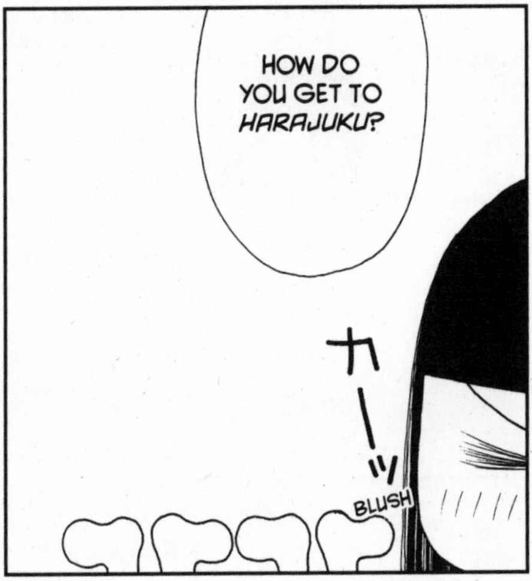
HOW DO
YOU GET TO
HARAJUKU?
カーッ
BLUSH

Harajuku, page 5

Harajuku is a district in Tokyo famous for its popularity among junior high and high school kids. Its main drag, Takeshita street, is full of boutiques, used clothing shops and knickknack stores. The Harajuku youth are also known for parading about in outrageous attire.

Yamanote-san, page 5

The Yamanote line is a train line that encircles the heart of Tokyo, passing through such famed areas as Shibuya, Shinjuku, Ikebukuro and Harajuku.

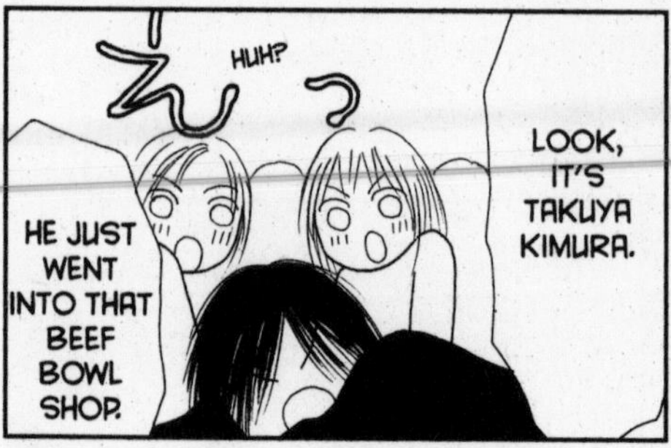
HUH?
LOOK, IT'S TAKUYA KIMURA.
HE JUST WENT INTO THAT BEEF BOWL SHOP.

Kimtaku, page 14

Takuya Kimura, also known as "Kimtaku," is a member of the band "Smap" and an actor in many J-dramas. He is one of Japan's most popular male celebs.

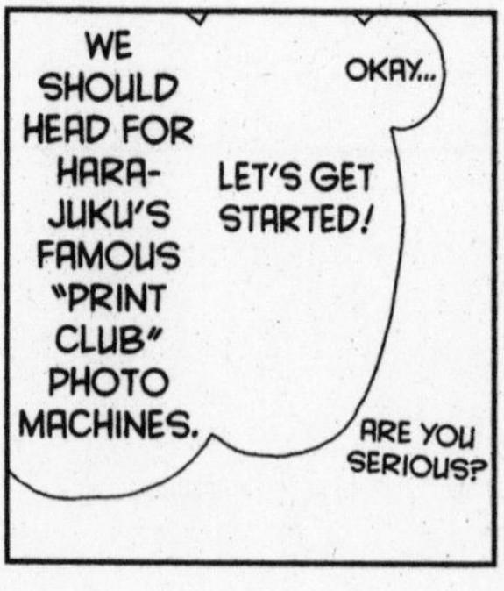
OKAY...
LET'S GET STARTED!
WE SHOULD HEAD FOR HARA-JUKU'S FAMOUS "PRINT CLUB" PHOTO MACHINES.
ARE YOU SERIOUS?

Print Club, page 18

Print Club, usually abbreviated to "Purikura" in Japanese, are photo booths that produce cute little photo stickers. You step inside the booth with your friends, take a few photos, and out pops a little sheet of photo stickers.

GRIN

NOW FOR MY SECRET WEAPON, MY PATENTED HEAD-BUTT TECHNIQUE!

Head-butt technique, page 74

Sunako is actually using the dated slang word *choopan* when she talks about head-butting Kyohei. The author explains the history of this word in the "Behind the Scenes" column on page 46. Unfortunately, there is no English equivalent for this old gangster slang term, so we had to go with plain ol' "head-butt."

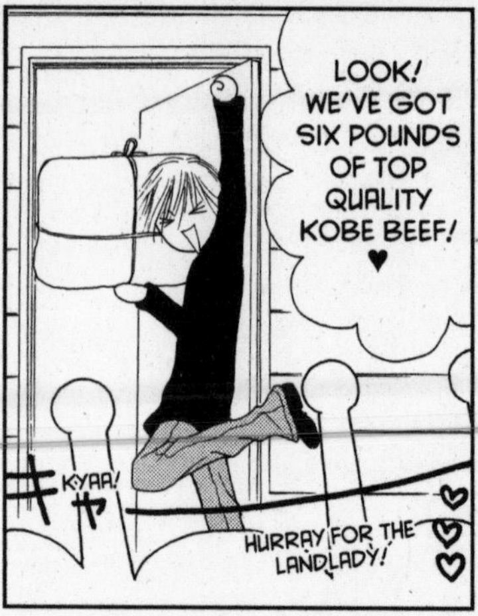
LOOK! WE'VE GOT SIX POUNDS OF TOP QUALITY KOBE BEEF! ♥
KYAA!
HURRAY FOR THE LANDLADY!

Kobe beef, page 90

Kobe beef is an extremely expensive type of gourmet beef. Six pounds of Kobe beef steaks would probably cost a minimum of $300. The beef comes from boutique farms which usually only raise a few, very pampered, cows at a time.

Mimura, page 96

Tomoko Hayakawa frequently references the Japanese comedy duo Summers. Summers is made up of Masakazu Mimura and Kazuki Ootake. Ootake plays the fool and Mimura plays the straight man, making clever quips in reply to Ootake's silly remarks. Here the author is suggesting that Kyohei is delivering the line "Jason isn't even real" in the style of Masakazu Mimura.

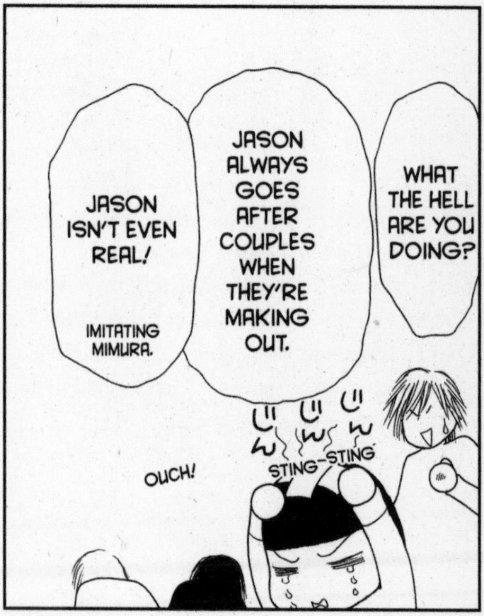
WHAT THE HELL ARE YOU DOING?
JASON ALWAYS GOES AFTER COUPLES WHEN THEY'RE MAKING OUT.
JASON ISN'T EVEN REAL!
IMITATING MIMURA.
STING-STING
OUCH!

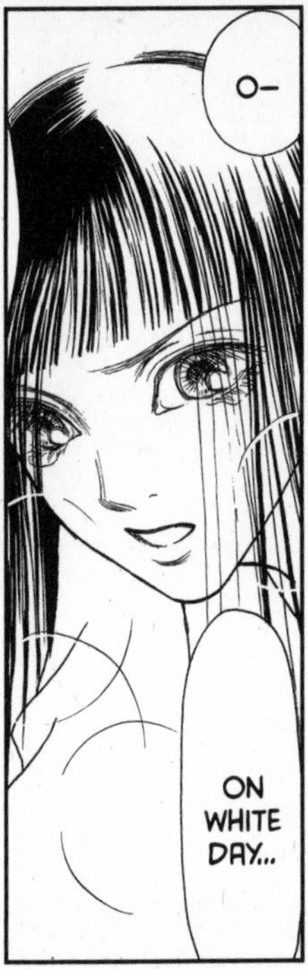
O-
ON WHITE DAY...

White Day, page 119

The Japanese version of Valentines Day is a bit different than the American tradition. In Japan, Valentines Day is a day when girls give presents to the boys they like (usually chocolate). This is followed by a holiday called White Day, when boys give presents in return to the girls.

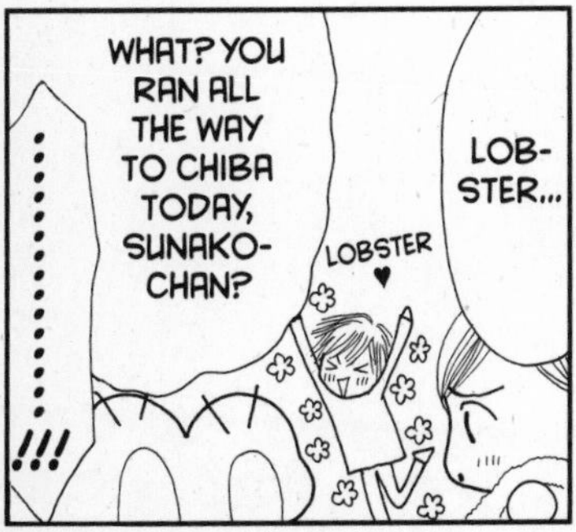
LOB-STER...
LOBSTER ♥
WHAT? YOU RAN ALL THE WAY TO CHIBA TODAY, SUNAKO-CHAN?
.............!!!

Chiba, page 141

Chiba is Tokyo's neighboring prefecture. It contains numerous suburbs and is also famous for being home to Tokyo Disneyland and the Tokyo/Narita airport.

Preview of volume 17

We're pleased to present you a preview from volume 17. Please check our website (www.delreymanga.com) to see when this volume will be available.

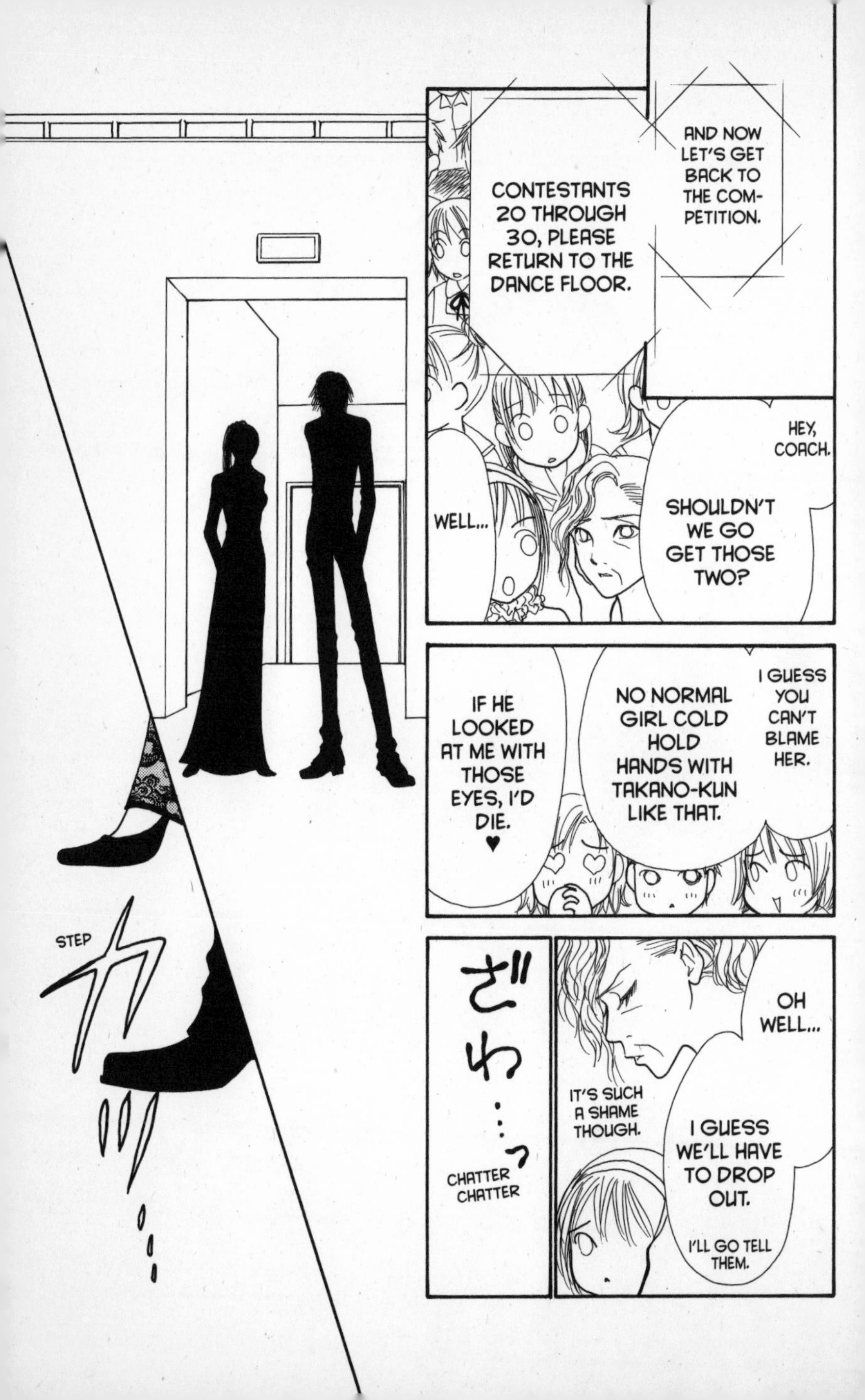
AND NOW LET'S GET BACK TO THE COM- PETITION.
CONTESTANTS 20 THROUGH 30, PLEASE RETURN TO THE DANCE FLOOR.
HEY, COACH.
SHOULDN'T WE GO GET THOSE TWO?
WELL...
I GUESS YOU CAN'T BLAME HER.
NO NORMAL GIRL COLD HOLD HANDS WITH TAKANO-KUN LIKE THAT.
IF HE LOOKED AT ME WITH THOSE EYES, I'D DIE. ♥
OH WELL...
I GUESS WE'LL HAVE TO DROP OUT.
I'LL GO TELL THEM.
IT'S SUCH A SHAME THOUGH.
ざわ…っ
CHATTER CHATTER
STEP

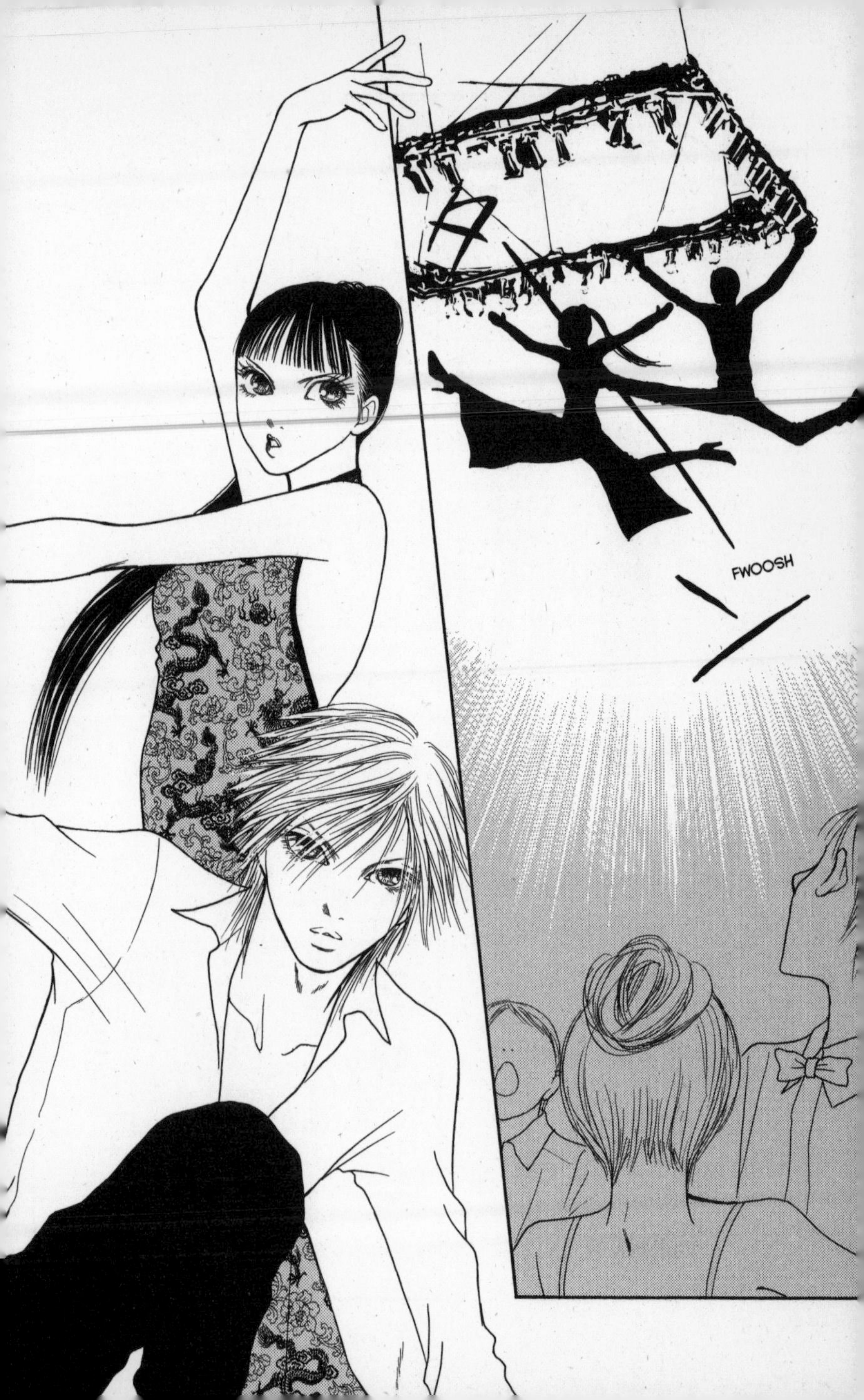
FWOOSH

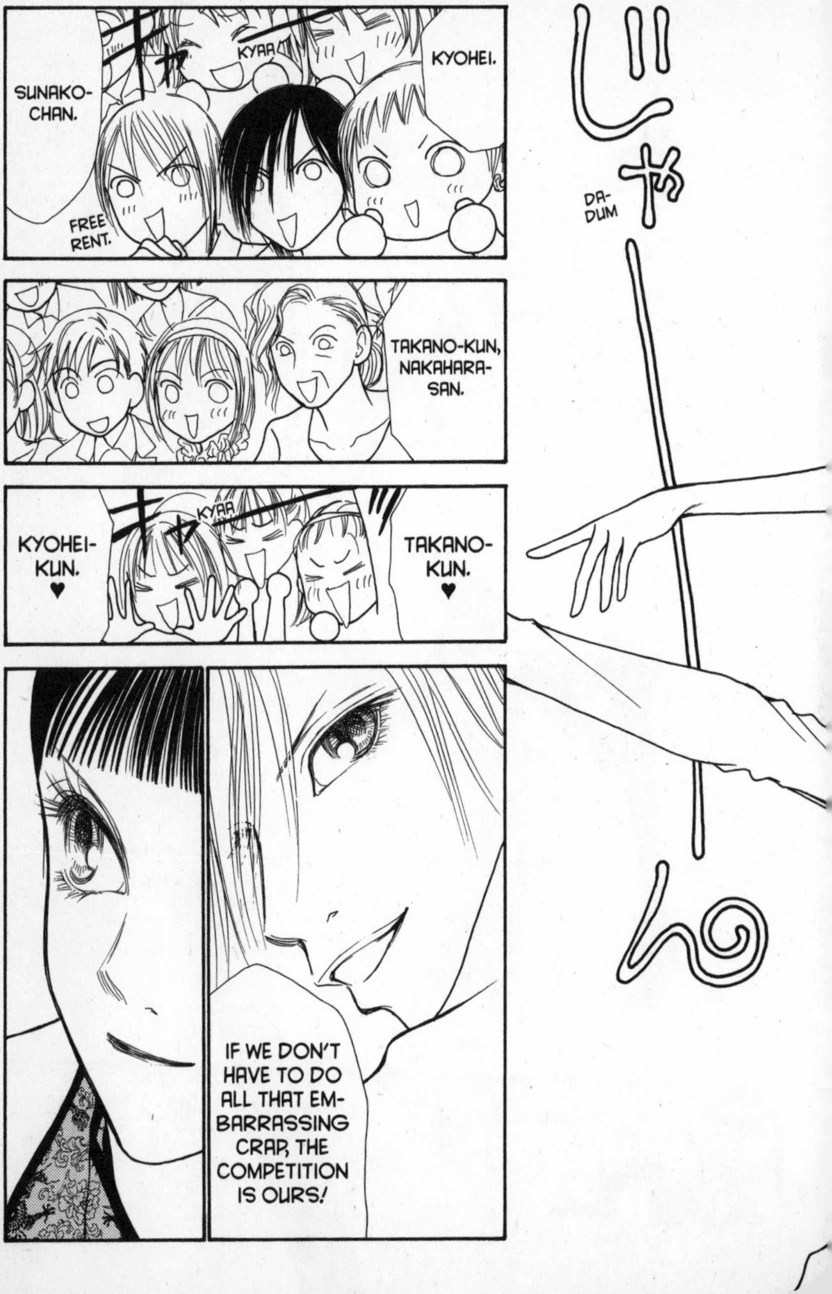
じゃーん
DA-DUM
KYOHEI.
KYAA
SUNAKO-CHAN.
FREE RENT.
TAKANO-KUN, NAKAHARA-SAN.
TAKANO-KUN. ♥
KYAA
KYOHEI-KUN. ♥
IF WE DON'T HAVE TO DO ALL THAT EM-BARRASSING CRAP, THE COMPETITION IS OURS!

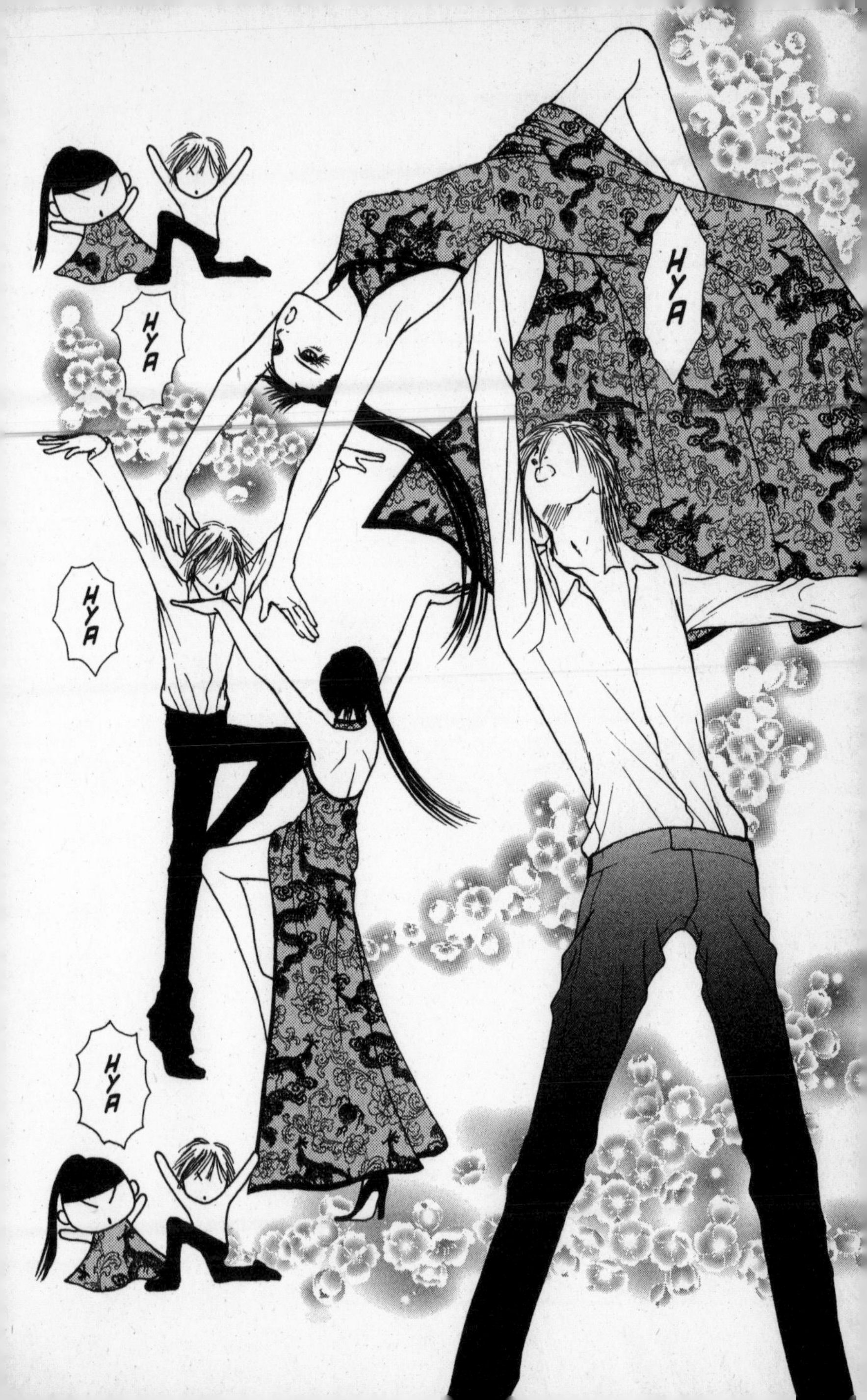

HYA
HYA
HYA
HYA

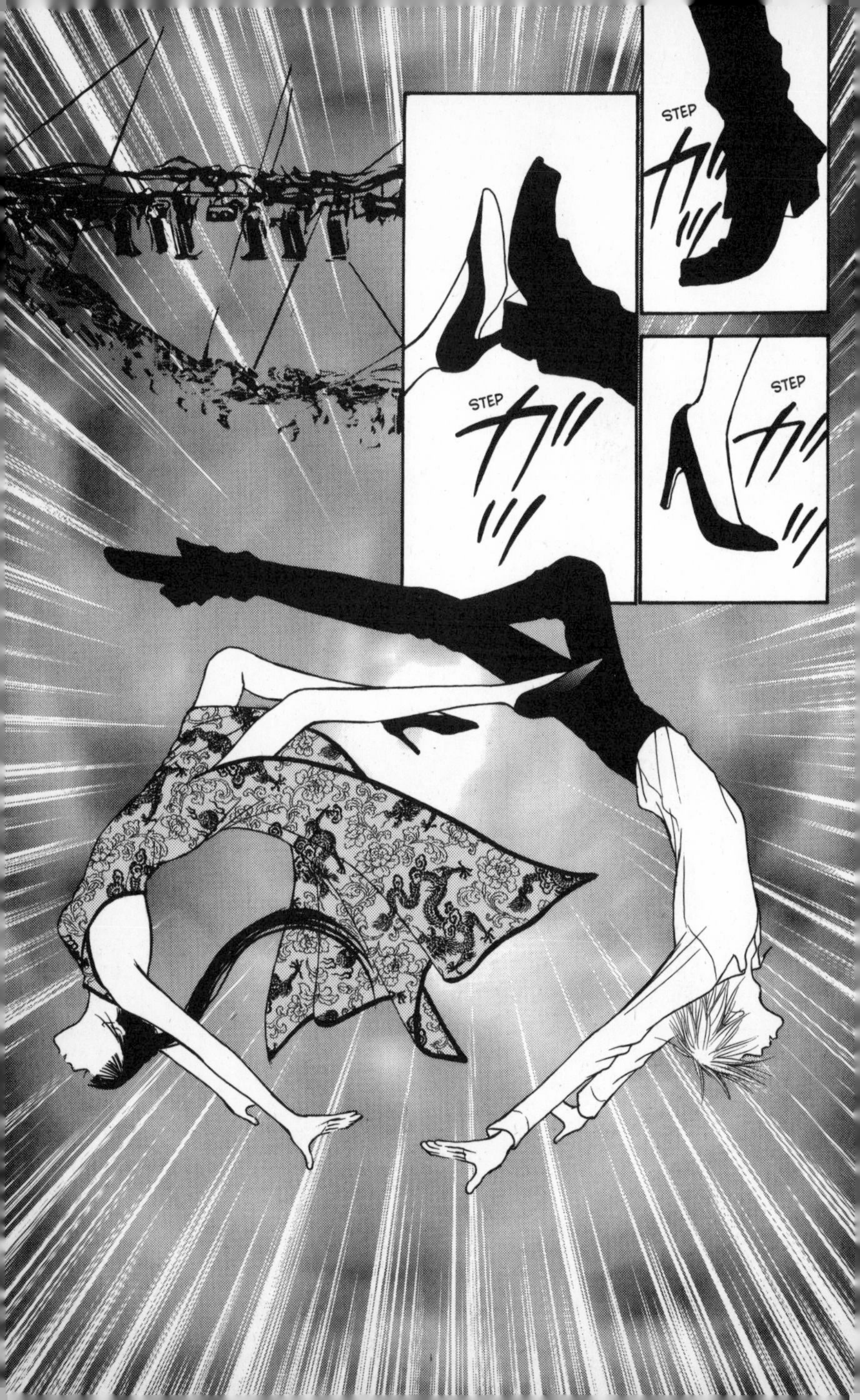
STEP
カツ
STEP
カツ
STEP
カツ

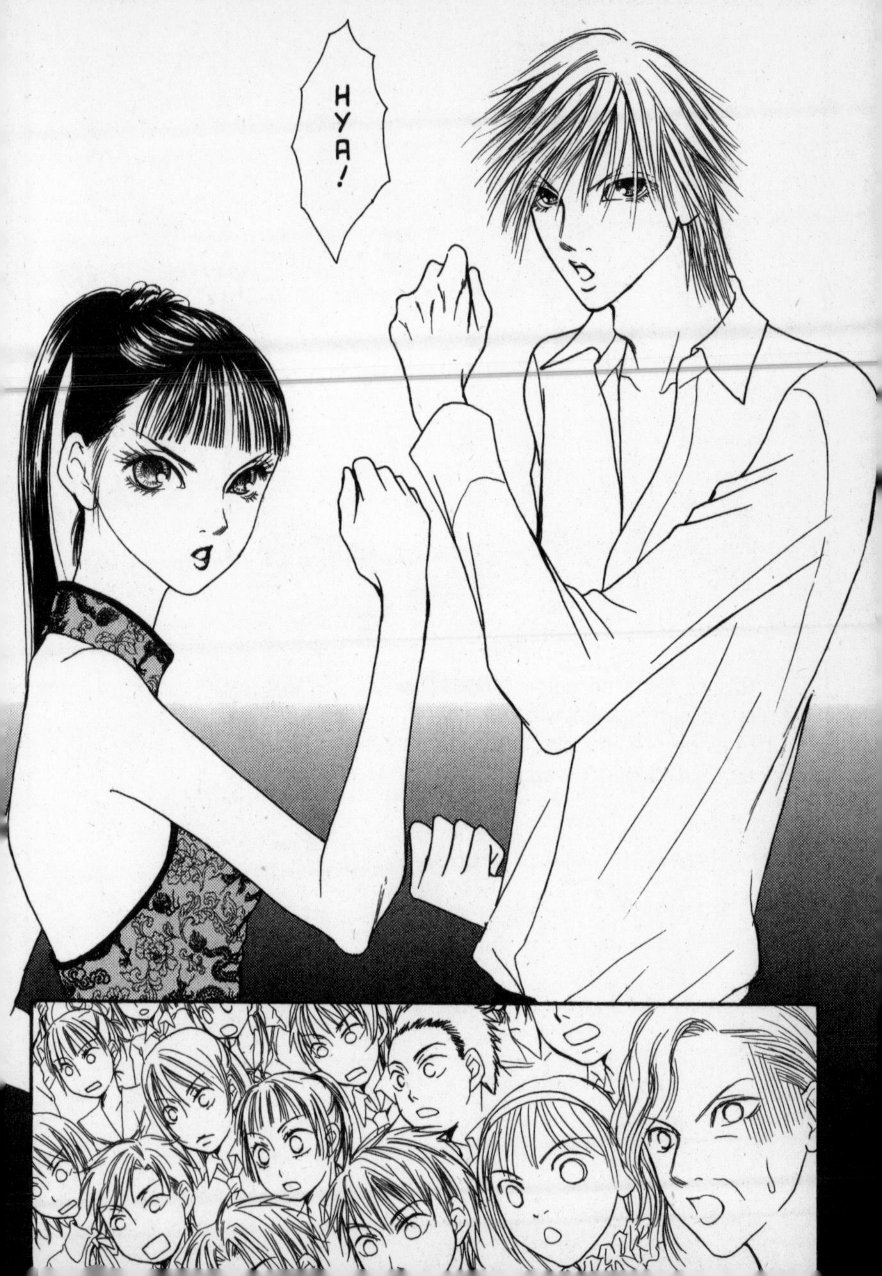
HYA!

MY HEAVENLY HOCKEY CLUB

BY AI MORINAGA

WHERE THE BOYS ARE!

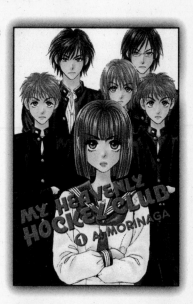

Hana Suzuki loves only two things in life: eating and sleeping. So when handsome classmate Izumi Oda asks Hana—his major crush—to join the school hockey club, convincing her proves to be a difficult task. True, the Grand Hockey Club is full of boys—and all the boys are super-cute—but, given a choice, Hana prefers a sizzling steak to a hot date. Then Izumi mentions the field trips to fancy resorts. Now Hana can't wait for the first away game, with its promise of delicious food and luxurious linens. Of course there's the getting up early, working hard, and playing well with others. How will Hana survive?

MY HEAVENLY HOCKEY CLUB
1 AI MORINAGA

Special extras in each volume! Read them all!

VISIT WWW.DELREYMANGA.COM TO:
- Read sample pages
- View release date calendars for upcoming volumes
- Sign up for Del Rey's free manga e-newsletter
- Find out the latest about new Del Rey Manga series

RATING AGES T 13+

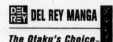

DEL REY MANGA

The Otaku's Choice™

Yozakura Quartet

BY SUZUHITO YASUDA

A DIFFERENT SET OF SUPERTEENS!

1
Yozakura Quartet
Suzuhito Yasuda

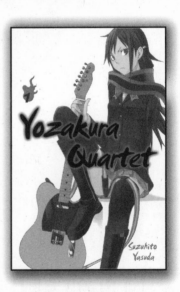

Hime is a superheroine. Ao can read minds. Kotoha can conjure up anything with the right word. And Akina . . . well, he's just a regular guy, surrounded by three girls with superpowers! Together, they are the Hizumi Everyday Life Consultation Office, dedicated to protect the town of Sakurashin. And with demon dogs and supernatural threats around every corner, there's plenty to keep them busy!

Special extras in each volume! Read them all!

VISIT WWW.DELREYMANGA.COM TO:

- Read sample pages
- View release date calendars for upcoming volumes
- Sign up for Del Rey's free manga e-newsletter
- Find out the latest about new Del Rey Manga series

RATING T AGES 13+

DEL REY MANGA デルレイ

The Otaku's Choice™

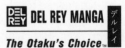

TOMARE!

止まれ

[STOP!]

You're going the wrong way!

Manga is a completely different type of reading experience.

To start at the *beginning*, go to the *end*!

That's right! Authentic manga is read the traditional Japanese way—from right to left. Exactly the *opposite* of how American books are read. It's easy to follow: Just go to the other end of the book, and read each page—and each panel—from right side to left side, starting at the top right. Now you're experiencing manga as it was meant to be!